ROSTER

OF

OHIO SOLDIERS

IN THE

WAR of 1812

Southern Historical Press, Inc.
Greenville, South Carolina

This volume was reproduced
from a personal copy located in
the Publishers private library

All rights reserved. No part of this publication may be reproduced,
stored in a retrieval system, transmitted in any form, posted
on the web in any form or by any means without the
prior written permission of the publisher.

Please direct all correspondence and book orders to:
SOUTHERN HISTORICAL PRESS, Inc.
1071 Park West Blvd.
Greenville, SC 29611

Published Columbus, OH. 1916
ISBN #978-1-63914-624-6
Printed in the United States of America

(House Bill No. 572.)

AN ACT

Authorizing the publication and distribution of a roster of Ohio soldiers in the war with Spain.

Be it enacted by the General Assembly of the State of Ohio:

Section 1. That the governor, secretary of state and adjutant general be, and they are, hereby authorized to secure the publication, in book form, of a complete roster of all Ohio soldiers who entered the volunteer service of the United States in the war with Spain and in the war of 1812; said publication to contain the main items of the record of each officer and soldier, as shown by the rolls in the adjutant general's office, and in the war department at Washington.

They shall begin such work as soon as practicable and continue the same until the roster is completed, the preparation, to be under the direction of the adjutant general, and the printing and binding to be under the direction of the supervisor of public printing.

For the preparation, printing and binding of such roster, of which not more than 10,000 copies shall be printed, there is hereby appropriated, out of any money in the state treasury to the credit of the general revenue fund, not otherwise appropriated, the sum of fifteen thousand dollars, or so much thereof as may be necessary for the purpose.

Section 2. The distribution of said volumes shall be under the direction of the adjutant general and shall be as follows:

To each member of the general assembly, ten copies.

To the adjutant general, for distribution to the adjutants general of each state and territory, and proper officials of the Ware Department at Washington, D. C., seventy copies.

To each state officer of Ohio (elective or appointive), to be kept as a part of the official records of his office, one copy.

To the state library, fifty copies for exchanges, and ten copies to be retained permanently therein.

To each incorporated public library of the state, one copy.

To each county recorder, to be by him kept in his office, and transferred to his successor as other public records, one copy.

The remainder of said copies after such distribution shall be placed on sale by the adjutant general, at a price not exceeding $1.00 per volume. He shall keep a record of such sales, and shall, at the end of each quarter of the fiscal year, pay into the state treasury the sum received, until all of said volumes are sold, unless otherwise directed by the general assembly; provided that he shall not sell more than one copy of each of said volumes to the same person.

CHARLES D. CONOVER,
Speaker of the House of Representatives.

C. J. HOWARD,
President pro tem. of the Senate.

Passed May 19, 1915.
Approved May 25, 1915.

FRANK B. WILLIS, Governor.

Press of The Edward T. Miller Co., Columbus, Ohio.

THE WAR of 1812

Because of war having been declared, President Madison issued instructions to Governor Return Jonathan Meigs of Ohio, on April 6, 1812, to assemble the Militia at Dayton, Ohio, to be drilled and prepared to march to Detroit.

By the end of the month more than the required number of men had been enrolled.

Early in May these troops were fairly equipped and had chosen their Field Officers. The President had commissioned Governor Hull of Michigan, as Brigadier General. General Hull arrived at Dayton, Ohio, on May 25, 1812, and left with his troops, June 1.

According to the records in The Adjutant General's Department at Columbus, Ohio furnished for this war 1759 Officers and 24,521 Enlisted men distributed as follows:

> First Regiment Infantry, 108 Companies.
> Second Regiment Infantry, 85 Companies.
> Third Regiment Infantry, 56 Companies.
> Unassigned Infantry, 185 Companies.
> Assigned to U. S. Infantry, 5 Companies.
> Mounted Infantry, 25 Companies.
> Cavalry, 13 Troops.
> Artillery, 1 Battery.

Page 142. Vol. I.
GENERAL AND FIELD OFFICERS WAR OF 1812-1813.
MAJOR GENERAL ELIJAH WADSWORTH. 4TH DIVISION. OHIO MILITIA.

Rank and Name of Soldier.	Rank and Name of Soldier.	Rank and Name of Soldier.
Maj. Gen. Elijah Wadsworth	Q. M. Gen. Nehemiah King.	Ass't Q. M. Gen. John Austin
Maj. Benjamin Fappeno	Maj. Elisha Whittlesey	Maj. and Insp. G. Pease
Surg. Elijah Coleman	Chaplain, Jonothan Leslie	A. A. G. Josiah M. Brown
P. F. M. Eliphalet Austin	P. W. M. James Hillman	Ass't. W. M. Fred K. Wadsworth
Ass't. F. M. James Kingsbury	Ass't W. M. Israel Robinson	Ass't. P. F. M. Robert Harper
Ass't Q. M. Gen. Lewis Hoyt.	Ass't. Dep. W. M. Jas. Quigley	Ass't. F. M. Wm. Ingersol
F. M. Eliphalet Austin, Jr.	Hosp. ——— Oristes K. Hawley	

Page 209 Vol. I.
BRIG. GEN. ROBERT LUCAS. SECOND BRIGADE. OHIO MILITIA.

Brig. Gen. Robert Lucas	Brig. Q. M. Ezra Osborn	Brig. Insp. Wm. Rutledge
Judge Ad. William K. Bond	Maj. P. D. Butler	Capt. Jason B. Curtis

Page 206 Vol. I.
PERSONAL PAYMENTS.

Brig. Gen. Edward W. Tupper	Brig. Gen. John Wingate	Lieut. Col. David Sutton
Maj. Robert Taylor	Maj. Isaiah Ferguson	Maj. Josiah Mott
Brig. Maj. Horace Nye	Maj. George Adams	Maj. Alexander C. Lanier
Maj. Henry Price	Maj. Charles Wolverton	Brig. Q. M. Robert Safford
Brig. Q. M. W. Marshall	Brig. Q. M. James Heaton	Brig. Insp. Horace Nye
Surg. James Wilson	Surg. Reuben Lamb	Q. M. Thomas Thompson
Q. M. Mathew Hewson	Chaplain, Elias Dickens	Capt. William Prince
Capt. R. Westfall	Adjt. E. Hutchinson	Adjt. Alexander Brown
Sergt. Maj. John McCabe	Surg. Mate, William B. Gould	Surg. Mate, Walter Buel
Surg. Mate, James Wilson	Surg. Mate, Able Slaybrook	Surg. Mate, Moses A. Ferris
Drum Maj. James Richardson	Fife Maj. Jacob Stewart	Q. M. Sergt. James Butler
Private, John McDonnell	William Lytle	

Page 207. Vol. I.

Brig. Gen. James Menary	Col. John Ferguson	Col. John McDonald
Col. William Keys	Col. Daniel Collier	Col. James Stewart
Col. Allen Trimble	Col. Jacob Noel	Col. Mills Stephenson
Maj. Benjamin Daniels	Maj. Geo. Edwards	Maj. John Lewis
Capt. Andrew Canell	Ensign Robert Stephens	

Page 208 Vol. I.

Brig. Gen. S. Perkins	Lieut. Col. Wm. W. Cotgreave	Lieut. Col. Thomas Kirkpatrick
Lieut. Col. Mills Stephenson	Maj. R. Beall	Maj. Anthony Pitzer
Maj. E. Whittlesay	Surg. Albron T. Crow	Brig. Q. M. Leyman Austin
Capt. William McConnell	Capt. William S. Drake	Capt. Robert McElwain
Capt. Joseph R. McClure	Capt. William Morrow	Capt. George Yoakin
Chaplain, Joseph Badger	Lieut. Thomas Ewing	Lieut. Jacob Wisecawere
Lieut. William Missner	Ensign John Brown	Surg. Mate, Samuel McKeehan
Surg. Mate, John McCullough	Private, William Morrow	

FIELD OFFICERS, STAFFS NOT GIVEN.

Page 118	Col. A. Butler		Page 193	Col. Campbell
" 87	Col. John T. Edwards		" 156	Col. Samuel Finley
" 16	Col. James McPherson		" 64	Col. A. Root
" 93	Maj. Andrew Byerly		" 78	Maj. William Ward
" 235	Maj. Womeldorf			

GENERAL AND FIELD OFFICERS.
Staffs Not Given.

Vol. 2.	Page 244	Maj. Gen. Wm. H. Harrison
		Brig. Gen. Edmund Munger
	Page 4	Brig. Gen. Simon Perkins
	" 363	Brig. Gen. John Wingate
	" 397	Brig. Gen. Robert Lucas
	" 244	Colonel Alexander Ewing
	" 132	Colonel John Furgeson, First Regiment.
	" 381	Colonel Samuel Findlay, First Regiment.
	" 97	Colonel Gano, First Regiment.
	" 105	Colonel William Key, First Regiment.
	" 119	Colonel James Mills, First Regiment.
	" 229	Colonel James Miller, First Regiment.
	" 95	Colonel John McDonald, First Regiment.
	" 174	Colonel Jacob Noel, First Regiment.
	" 111	Lieut. Col. John Riddle, First Regiment.
	" 239	Lieut. Col. Feron Holt, First Regiment.
	" 394	Lieut. Col. Robert Bay, First Cavalry.
	" 244	Major Paul F. Butler.
	" 244	Major William Beatty.
	" 244	Major James Colwell.
	" 244	Major Jerome Holt.
	" 244	Major Thomas Moore.
	" 211	Major George Adams, First Regiment.
	" 113	Major George Edwards, First Regiment.
	" 195	Major Jacob Myers, First Regiment.
	" 398	Major Samuel Connell, First Cavalry.
	" 395	Major Israel Dawson, First Cavalry.

ROSTER OF OHIO SOLDIERS IN WAR OF 1812

Pages 244-245 Vol. 2.

ROLL OF FIELD AND STAFF. WAR OF 1812-1813.
COL. DUNCAN McARTHUR. FIRST REGIMENT. OHIO MILITIA.

Rank and Name of Soldier.	Rank and Name of Soldier.	Rank and Name of Soldier.
Col. Duncan McArthur	Maj. James Denny	Maj. William A. Trimble
Adjt. Wm. H. Putthorf	Maj. Jeremiah Munson	Maj. Robert Morrison
Maj. Thomas A. Vanhorne	Q. M. Richard Douglas	Q. M. James Foster
Q. M. John McDonald	Q. M. Sergt. Avery Powers	Q. M. Sergt. John Fisher
Surg. Samuel Metadow	Surg. Mate, Lincoln Goodale	Pay Master, John McDonald
P. M's. Clk., Q. L. Pleissis	Drum Maj. Avery Buttles	Sergt. Maj. Thomas Lloyd
Sergt. Maj. Hugh Wood		Fife Maj. Solomon Fredericks
Fife Maj. Russell R. Chapman		

FIRST REGIMENT OHIO MILITIA. WAR OF 1812-1813.
ROLL OF CAPT. JAMES ALEXANDER'S COMPANY.
(Probably from Jefferson County.)

Page 3. Vol. 2.

Served from August 23 1812 until November 30, 1813.

Page 31.

Capt. James Alexander	Lieut. Henry Boyles	Ensign John Myers
Sergt. Samuel Andrews	Sergt. Alexander Barr	Sergt. Martin Saltzman
Sergt. James Tobin	Corp. David Williamson	Corp. Amos West
Corp. John Anderson	Corp. James Lyons	Corp. Hugh Adams

Privates.	Privates.	Privates.
Bay, Joseph	Alexander, William	Barr, James D.
Berry, James	Brooks, William	Barr, John
Bennet, William	Bennet, Griffith	Bawers, John
Call, David	Call, John	Crawford, Benedict
Casselman, David	Casselman, William	Culp, Jacob
Duke, William	France, John	Grover, Jacob
Groves, Peter	Gamble, Henry	Householder, George
Hytes, George	Hytes, John	Hartman, George
Johnston, John	Kinder, Peter	Lowery, Alexander
Lawrence, James	Laughlin, James	Laughlin, John
Laughlin, Nathaniel	Lawrence, William	Mathers, Levi
Peterson, Peter	Prichard, Ziphani	Painter, Jacob
Pittinger, Thomas	Peterson, William	Saltsman, Andrews
Saltsman, David.	Swickard, Daniel	Swickard, Daniel, Sr
Sapp, George	Stain, Michael	Wells, James
Wright, Jacob		

Page 80 Vol. I.

Privates.	Privates.	Privates.
Alexander, William	Bennett, Griffith	Bowers, John
Casselman, William	Duke, William	Hales, Joel
Johnson, John	Lawrence, William	Laughlin, John
Laughlin, Mathew	Lyons, James	Mathews, Levi
Peterson, Peter	Painter, Jacob	Pitteger, Thomas
Peterson, William	Starn, Michael	Saltman, Andrew
Saltman, Daniel	Swickard, Daniel, Jr.	Sapp, George
Wright, Jacob	Wells, James	

Page 4. Vol. 2.

LIEUT. COL. JOHN ANDREWS. FIRST REGIMENT. OHIO MILITIA.

Lieut. Col. John Andrews	Maj. Thomas Glenn	Maj. James Campbell
Maj. George Darrow	Maj. Jacob Frederick	Adjt. Mordecai Bartley
Q. M. Jacob Van Hoene	Q. M. Sergt. John Patterson	Surg. Thomas Campbell
Surg. Mate, Samuel McRickan	Sergt. Maj. John B. Lowden	Drum. Maj. John McClintock
Drum Maj. John Hytes	Fife Maj. John Neel	David Kinsey

Page 243. Vol. 2.

COLONEL JOHN DeLONG. FIRST REGIMENT. OHIO MILITIA.

Col. John DeLong	Maj. William Crooks	Maj. Wm. Henderson
Adjt. Anthony Weyer	Q. M. John Hanna	Q. M. Sergt. James Boy
Surg. Henry H. Evans	Surg. Mate, Thomas Host	Surg. Mate, John Harrison
Surg. Mate, Robert Young	Pay Master, Jonothan Carlton	

Page 242. Vol. 2.

COLONEL JOHN WILLIAMSON. FIRST REMIMENT. OHIO MILITIA.

Col. John Williamson	Surg. Timothy Burr	Q. M. Sergt. John H. Mifford

Page 243 Vol. 2.

MAJOR JOSEPH JENKINSON. FIRST REGIMENT. OHIO MILITIA.

Maj. Joseph Jenkinson	Adjt. John Pursel	Q. M. Joseph Warner
Q. M. Sergt. Coleman Avery	Surg. Stephen Woods	Drum Maj. Alvin Wheeler
Fife Maj. Samuel Bonnel		

Page 243 Vol. 2.
COLONEL DAVID SUTTON. FIRST REGIMENT. OHIO MILITIA.

Rank and Name of Soldier.	Rank and Name of Soldier.	Rank and Name of Soldier.
Col. David Sutton	Maj. James Galloway	Pay Master, John H. Smith
Lieut & Clk., John C. McMames.	Surg. Mate, Wm. Greenle	Sergt. Maj. James Reading.

Page 243 Vol. 2.
COLONEL JAMES DENNY. FRST REGIMENT. OHIO MILITIA.

Col. James Denny	Maj. Valentine Keffer	Maj. John Boggs
Adjt. Bartholomew Fryatt	Q. M. Ralph Osborn	Q. M. and Lieut. Joseph Yates
Q. M. Sergt. Samuel Pontius	Surg. Prentice Pork	Pay Master, Ralph Osborn
Sergt. Maj. Joseph Shelby	Sergt. Maj. Thomas Hair	Drum Maj. Charles Swangle

Page 243 Vol. 2.
LIEUT. COL. ALEXANDER ENOS. FIRST REGIMENT. OHIO MILITIA.

Lieut. Col. Alexander Enos	Maj. Samuel Watson	Adjt. Jacob Catterlin
Adjt. John Stilly	Q. M. Samuel Kratzer	Q. M. John Hawn

ROLL OF CAPT. AARON ALLEN'S COMPANY. (County Not Known.)
Pages 5-6-7-23-24-25. Vol. 2.

Served from September 15, 1812 until March 16, 1813.

Capt. Aaron Allen	Lieut. John Vantilburgh	Ensign, William Mills
Sergt. James Clare	Sergt. Richard Shaw	Sergt. John Farquer
Sergt. Thomas Henderson	Corp. Christopher Abel	Corp. Hugh Livingston
Corp. James Johnston	Corp. David Workman	

Privates.	Privates.	Privates.
Ault, Phillip	Avery, Samuel	Abel, Benjamin
Ayers, James	Asher, Anthony	Barr, John
Bay, Robert	Burchfield, Frederick	Beemer, Adam
Brown, Nehemiah	Burris, Emery	Brown, William
Barnes, Obediah	Corbit, Lewis	Carter, Ryan
Campbell, Alexander	Close, John	Cann, Alexander
Crofford, Alexander	Carson, John	Carson, Samuel
Caughey, Joseph	Davis, Henry	Degoin, John O.
Durall, Thomas	Doyell, Anthony	Ellison, James
Freet, David	Flecker, Abraham	Fishell, Frederick
Fisher, John	Fivecoat, Michael	George, John
Graden, Thomas	Grim, Martin	Gibson, Joseph
Glodman, Michael	Hardebrook, John	Hill, James
Hardebrook, Jerome	Hukell, James	Haller, Samuel
Haverfield, Joseph	Hill, William	Hoye, John
Haning, Jacob	Harriman, John	Hickory, John
Jinnings, Nathaniel	James, John	Jackman, Thomas
Kean, James	Kerr, Samuel	Logue, John
Lyons, John	Lees, Samuel	Lane, Samuel
Lisle, Jacob	Myers, Emanuel	Moody, John
Myers, Jacob	Mays, James	Malen, Joseph
Montgomery, William	Morehead, James	Myon, Jacob
Miller, Jacob	Main, Samuel	Milter, Jacob
McCloud, William	McNiles, Thomas	McCalley, William
McClintock, William	McClerg, Robert	McClelland, Felix
McCaskey, David	Hitchcock, John	Lyse, Robert
Pugh, Isaac	Palmer, George	Peterson, John
Packman, Thomas	Quin, John	Quillen, Adam
Rutledge, William	Ralston, Robert	Russell, Robert
Richardson, Mathew	Rickey, Daniel	Reynolds, Caleb
Roysell, Job	Ralston, Joseph	Ritter, Benjamin
Ray, James	Shaffer, Phillip	Shawber, Jacob
Stewart, James	Smith, Samuel	Smith, John
Stokes, John	Simmons, Adam	Steven, Daniel
Speed, Allen	Skelton, John	Skelton, William
Sissions, Benjamin	Taylor, John	Thompson, Moses
Shepherd, John	Welsh, Daniel	Willits, John
Wheeler, Nicholas		

ROLL OF CAPT. JACOB GILBERT'S COMPANY.
(Probably from Jefferson County.)
Pages 9-10-29-35-347-348. Vol. 2.

Served from August 25, 1812 until February 28, 1813.

Capt. Jacob Gilbert	Lieut. John Teeters	Ensign Abraham Fox
Ensign Conrad Myers	Sergt. David Shoemaker	Sergt. Samuel Eister
Sergt. Michael Coners	Sergt. Michael Shafer	Corp. Randall Smith
Corp. Peter Miller	Corp. John Eaton	Corp. John Lipley

Privates.	Privates.	Privates.
Alexander, Robert	Adams, William	Blackburn, William
Beacht, George	Barnes, Jacob	Bradfield, Benjamin
Brineman, Richard	Boatman, Henry	Bissilla, Betz
Condon, James	Cook, George	Catt, Phillip
Calihan, William	Clary, James M.	Cahammon, John M.
Estep, George	Engerstem, Henry	Fox, John

Vol. 2.
ROLL OF CAPT. JACOB GILBERT'S COMPANY. (Continued)

Rank and Name of Soldier.   Rank and Name of Soldier.   Rank and Name of Soldier.

Privates.

Frederick, John
Ford, William
Hohn, Adam
Hohn, Andrew
Haughman, Samuel
Harnish, John
Kley, John
Losure, David
Myers, Frederick
Mall, Henry
Musser, Michael
Meek, Samuel
Meek, John, Jr.
McElroy, John
Painter, James
Miller, Peter
Roller, Henry
Roller, Joseph
Rogers, Thomas
Speaker, Henry
Switzer, Jacob
Switzer, George
Thompson, John
Watkins, Benjamin
Wickersham, Joseph

Feler, Michael
Glass, Mathias
Hohn, John
Higgins, Samuel
Heemthorn, Peter
Kennel, Joseph
Kelley, Alexander
Lane, Samuel
Meeker, Michael
Metz, John
Johnston, David
Meek, Samuel, Jr.
Minton, John
McClelland, Felix
Palmer, Richard
Routzen, Nathaniel
Rainey, Charles
Roach, William
Richey, Isaac
Simons, George
Smith, Henry
Schultz, George
Trasey, James
Watkins, John
Yoobs, Austin

Fisher, Brice
Garringer, David
Helwick, Nicholas
Huffman, Jacob
Hevely, Christopher
Kerns, John
Lower, John
Lawrence, John
Machaman, John
Mowen, Jacob
Moore, Ezekiel
Meek, John
McClung, James
Preston, John
Pairs, Gainer
Randolph, John
Rudwill, John
Rock, Henry
Rough, William
Skidmore, William
Stewart, Hugh
Sanor, Michael
Wickert, John
Whiteleather, Christian

ROLL OF CAPTAIN JOSEPH HOLMES' COMPANY.
(Probably from Jefferson County.)

Pages 11-12-19-20.

Served from August 23, 1812 until February 28, 1813.

Capt. Joseph Holmes
Ensign David Mitchell
Sergt. Alexander Smith
Corp. John Pollock
Drummer John McClintick

Lieut. William Thorne
Sergt. Francis Popham
Sergt. John McCully
Corp. Thomas McBride
Drummer James Roff

Lieut. John Ramsey
Sergt. James Gilmore
Corp. Edward Vanhorn
Corp. Joseph Hagerman

Privates.

Arnold, Reason
Asher, Anthony
Brotell, John
Brown, James
Briggs, David
Chaffin, James
Edington, Isaac
Foster, Benjamin
Guttery, John A.
Hughes, Joseph
Kendall, Rhesa
Kyle, William
Leach, John
Madden, Patrick H.
Moore, James
McElroy, George
McDonald, Thomas
McClintock, John
Osler, Jacob
Potts, David
Robbins, Johnston
Roach, Jeremiah
Smith, Charles
Snider, Henry
Stevens, David
Tipton, Jonothan
West, Jonothan

Arnold, James
Barcus, William
Barks, William
Brookan, George
Carpenter, George
Elliott, Thomas
Ferguson, John
Glass, Thomas
Harper, William
Harriman, John
Kelley, Mathew
Laning, Jacob
Long, James
Miller, Charles M.
Meek, Jacob
McCullough, James
McClery, Benjamin
McFadden, Thomas
Parks, John
Robertson, Charles
Robertson, John
Roach, Ebenezer
Scholes, John
Strall, Joseph
Tipton, Luke
Van Bibben, Isaac
Yealdhall, Edwin

Arnold, Samuel
Brocaw, George
Belch, James
Birttel, John
Cahill, Phillip
Elliott, Finley
Ferguson, Thomas
Gilpin, Samuel
Henry, Isaac
Hawthorne, John
Kerr, Samuel
Logan, Richard
Minnis, James
Maxwell, Robert
McClay, Benjamin
McMillan, Charles
McClintock, William
Osborn, Jacob
Porter, Hugh
Ross, Richard
Ross, James
Reels, Isaac S.
Sankey, James
Sullivan, George
Tipton, William
White, Joseph

ROLL OF CAPT. WILLIAM FOULK'S COMPANY.
(Probably from Jefferson County.)

Pages 12-14-21-22-345-346.

Served from August 25, 1812 until February 28, 1813.

Capt. William Foulks
Ensign Jacob Crouse
Sergt. John Huston
Sergt. John Charing
Corp. Addison McKinnon
Corp. James Anderson

Lieut. John Burkdale
Sergt. John Hester
Sergt. John Chaney
Corp. Alexander Armstrong
Corp. Rudolph Brandaberry
Fifer Daniel McConkey

Ensign Robert Ramsey
Sergt. John Cannon
Sergt. Henry Fisher
Corp. James Swin
Corp. Andrew Armstrong

ROLL OF CAPT. WILLIAM FOULK'S COMPANY. (Continued)

Privates.

Bowman, Christian
Black, John
Cripps, John
Caughey, James
Crevan, John
Davis, William
Fisher, Henry
Grimm, George
Huston, Samuel
Hunter, George
Iddings, William
Lyon, Joseph
Melone, David
Marsh, Henry
Martin, Henry
McCready, William
McLaughlin, John
McMillen, James
McIntosh, Angus
McKee, Alexander
McConikey, Daniel
Phillips, William
Poe, Thomas
Randolph, James
Riley, Mathew
Rees, John
Saint, John
Swim, James
Smoot, William
Welch, Lewis
Zear, Anthony

Brandaberry, Jacob
Brady, William
Crowl, Henry
Credner, John
Cox, Thomas
Fish, Richard
Grou, Henry
Grace, Henry
Hartman, Solomon
Heddings, William
Jones, Abraham
Leslie, Joseph
Marshall, John
Maxwell, Robert
Miller, Henry
McCombs, Jacob
McMillen, Alexander
McKee, James
McCoy, Daniel
McKee, Daniel
Ogle, Hercules
Poe, William
Quinn, Daniel
Reed, Elias
Robinson, Aaron
Spacht, John
Sheehan, William
Spearth, John
Whitmore, John
Walker, Peter

Burback, Arthur
Cross, James
Cramer, John
Crouch, Henry
Davis, Abednego
Frederick, Samuel
Gribner, George
Gruner, George
Hull, Samuel
Henderson, James
Kees, John
Match, Henry
Muce, Jacob
March, Samuel
Moore, George
McLaughlin, Ephraim
McCoy, David
McKee, John
McKay, Daniel
McIntosh, Anguish
Perry, James
Perry, John
Randolph, William
Ritter, Jacob
Ritchie, Isaac
Smith, Jabez
Smith, Lewis
Smith, Jesse
Way, Eli
Year, Armstrong

Pages 15-16-41-42-17.

ROLL OF CAPT. THOMAS LATTA'S COMPANY.
(Probably from Jefferson County.)

Served from September 15, 1812 until March 21, 1813.

Capt. Thomas Latta
Ensign William Prichard
Sergt. Alexander Patterson
Sergt. John Haughey
Corp. Cornelius Peterson
Corp. Mathew Palmer

Lieut. John Buck
Sergt. George Browers
Sergt. Alexander Valters
Sergt. Isaac Wolms
Corp. William Betz

Lieut. Hugh Christy
Sergt. George Brown
Sergt. George Emaling
Sergt. Richard Brown
Corp. James Holes

Privates.

Argo, Jeremiah
Adams, Thomas
Bulger, Michael
Burk, Moses
Brown, John
Beamer, Adam
Bair, David
Brockar, John
Bamhill, William
Camp, Henry
Dick, John
Derry, William
Ellison, David
Ferguson, James
Gibson, William
Graham, Jesse
Glosson, John
Hanlon, Allen
Henry, George
Hayes, Richard
Holmes, Isaac
Johnston, Henry
Kyl, William
Lindreyd, Charles
Lemasten, Isaac
Meeks, Jacob
Murray, Patrick
Mills, Eli
McColley, Robert
McCullough, David
McClelland, William
McFall, Barnet
Patterson, Robert
Potts, Joshua
Pinckney, Adam
Revenaugh, Samuel

Agler, William
Adams, John
Bell, William
Browner, Samuel
Browern, Samuel
Boils, Richard
Beamer, Adam, Jr.
Brockar, William
Cook, James
Chase, Patrick
Dickey, James
Dickey, John
Ferguson, John
Franas, James
Gilliland, William
Green, Ebenezer
Gutshall, Henry
Henry, Henry
Hull, Joseph
Hunter, John
Heath, Solomon
Kelley, Jonothan
Lauthers, Alexander
Lisle, Robert
Miser, John
Montier, Robert
Morrison, James
Maxwell, William
McDonald, John
McFadden, Thomas
McCleary, John
Olbert, John
Potts, John
Prichard, John
Robb, William
Revenaugh, John

Allbaugh, Solomon
Allbaugh, George
Bell, Adam
Bailiss, William
Buckley, John
Baird, Andrew
Barnes, John
Bratell, John
Ceasson, John
Dick, Robert
Devore, James
Druchmiller, Frederick
Fisher, Thomas
Fulton, John
Greenlee, Alexander
Guttery, Samuel
Hanley, William
Hicks, James
Hirth, Holmes
Hanenan, David
Jelley, James
Kelley, William
Loury, John
Leather, Alexander
Marshall, Thomas
Messer, Boyd
Moore, William
McConnell, Joseph
McColin, James
McRankey, William
McGonigre, Thomas
Pool, Conrad
Palmer, Ephraim
Pipenger, Peter
Rippey, Joseph
Russell, Robert

ROLL OF CAPT. THOMAS LATTA'S COMPANY. (Continued)

Rank and Name of Soldier.   Rank and Name of Soldier.   Rank and Name of Soldier.

Privates.

Privates.	Privates.	Privates.
Right, Joseph	Rouse, Benjamin	Riddel, John
Rolleur, Johnston	Reed, John	Ragison, Jacob
Ruly, John	Sewlson, Benjamin	Spiken, Phillip
Swamby, Daniel	Swam, Hezekiah	Smith, Nathaniel
Snider, Adam	Saimmons, Cornelius	Scott, John
Scott, Thomas	Stevens, David	Sullivan, George
Simmons, Jacob	Spiker, Isaac	Strain, Robert
Sheebr, Nicholas	Smith, John	Stover, Samuel
Solomon, Samuel	Simmons, Adam	Smith, Andrew
Thompson, Isaac	Truckmiller, Frederick	Tharp, William
Thompson, John	Tipton, John	Turnipseed, John
Updegraft, James	Vaughn, John	Vubs, Isaac
Vaughn, Richard	Vaughn, Jonothan	Williby, Frederick
Willsby, Robert	Woistell, William	Welday, Jacob
Worley, Thomas	White, William	Wilkins, Archibold
Wallace, John		

Pages 27-28-51-52. Vol. 2.

ROLL OF CAPT. DAVID PECK'S COMPANY.
(From Either Harrison or Jefferson County.)

Served from August 25, 1812, until February 28, 1813.

Capt. David Peck	Lieut. Joseph Davis	Ensign Jacob Shaffer
Sergt. John Stoaks	Sergt. Daniel Higgins	Sergt. Dudley Smith
Sergt. Jesse Harnum	Corp. John Vaughn	Corp. James Davis
Corp. James Miller	Corp. Wm. McConkey	

Privates.	Privates.	Privates.
Albert, John	Armstrong, Archibald	Ayers, James
Barnes, Obediah	Bennet, Thomas	Beard, James
Burchfield, Charles	Busy, Joshua	Chambers, James
Christy, George	Chrys, George	Conn, Alexander
Crawford, Alexander	Dowden, John N.	Derry, William
Degar, Peter	Devore, Abraham	Devore, James
Dewall, Thomas N.	Dickey, William	Dickey, James
Fisher, Samuel	Fisher, Ephraim	Fisher, John
Gutshall, Henry	Gutshall, George	Gordon, George
Gibson, Joseph	Huffman, John	Hunter, John
Hosben, Michael	Johnston, Peter	Lyons, John
Lisle, Robert	Lisle, William	Morrison, Joseph
Morrison, William	Meach, Ephraim	Mann, Samuel
Miller, Isaac	Miller, Jacob	Montgomery, Abel
McCombs, John	McIntire, Archibold	McKinsea, Nathaniel
McKinner, Samuel	McCleary, Robert	McAdams, William
Quillen, Joshua	Quillen, Adam	Quillen, John
Pumphrey, Zachariah	Richards, Jacob	Ruley, John
Raynolds, Caleb	Rolston, Joseph	Ritter, Benjamin
Ross, William	Smith, Robert	Shepherd, John
Simmons, Adam	Spiker, Jacob	Scholes, John
Smith, Andrew	Smith, John	Spiker, Isaac
Taylor, Henry	Tipton, John	Tingley, Benjamin
Thompson, Robert	Tharp, William	Toppe, Abraham
Titus, Timothy	Woods, Josiah	

Pages 33-34. Vol. 2.

ROLL OF CAPT. WILLIAM STOAKES COMPANY.
(Probably from Harrison County.)

Served from August 21, 1812 until February 28, 1813.

Capt. William Stoakes	Lieut. Thomas Orr	Ensign John Cantwell
Sergt. John Elrod	Sergt. John Paramore	Sergt. David Hinzy or Kinzan
Sergt. William Bashford	Corp. Benjamin Dean	Corp. William Crothers
Corp. Isaac Bail	Corp. John Palmer	Fifer, Samuel Solomon
Drummer, Thomas Bay		

Privates.	Privates.	Privates.
Andrews, John	Archbod, Patrick	Benett, Benjamin
Bruce, Thomas	Baker, John	Barnett, George
Barnes, John	Beamer, Adam	Brokaw, William
Brokaw, John	Belknap, Horace	Clifford, James
Cowthers (or Carothers), Geo.	Cupp, John	Chambers, William
Conaway, John	Conaway, Michael	Davidson, Joshua
Emry, George	Eckley, George	Emery, Abraham
Fulton, John	Fletcher, Archibald	Guttery, Samuel
Hamilton, John	Hull, John	Hull, Jesse
Hartshorn, Spry	Hall, Andrew	Johnston, Daniel
Johnson, James	Joseph, Michael	Jack, Edward
Kizen, Jacob	Lutz, Henry	Moore, William
Martin, James	Moore, James	Muntier, Robert
McCatchen, Samuel	McEntire, Stephen	McGonegal, Thomas
McClary, John	Nixon, William	Peterson, Hugh

ROLL OF CAPT. WILLIAM STOAKES' COMPANY. (Continued)

Rank and Name of Soldier.	Rank and Name of Soldier.	Rank and Name of Soldier.
Privates.	Privates.	Privates.
Pittinger, Peter	Patterson, John	Porter, Samuel A.
Reed, John Sr.	Reed, John Jr.	Riley, James
Rider, Jacob	Rickey, John	Reed, Samuel
Spidel, Joseph	Spidy (or Speedy), William	Sanderlin, Thomas
Stuse (or Steer), Jacob	Simmons, Jacob	Skeels, Nicholas
Strain, Robert	Throckmorton, Thomas	Tranen, James
Updegraft, James	Updegraft, Jesse	Wallace, James
West, Robert	Wallace, John	Wingfield, Elijah
West, Joshua	Whitaker, Obed	Walker, John
White, William	Welch, John	Welkin, Archibald

Pages 35-36.

ROLL OF CAPT. ALLEN SCROGGS' COMPANY.
(Probably from Jefferson County.)

Served from September 21, 1812 until November 30, 1812.

Capt. Allen Scroggs	Lieut. John Ramsey	Ensign John Caldwell
Sergt. William Wilkin	Sergt. William Dunlap	Sergt. William Holson
Sergt. William Robertson	Corp. Samuel Avery	Corp. Joseph Haverfield
Corp. John Connaway	Corp. John Wallace	
Privates.	Privates.	Privates.
Abbott, Benjamin	Bebout, Peter	Brokan, John
Baricklow, Fanington	Beamer, Adam	Buris, Homeny
Brokan, William	Belknap, Horace	Connaway, Michael
Cann, James F.	Fletcher, Archibald	Francis, James
Foster, Benjamin	Fivecoats, Michael	Gladmore, Michael
Heinary, Abraham	Hitchcock, John	Holly, Samuel
Hill, William	Jack, Edward	Johnson, Henry
Gray, Ebenezer	Laurence, Duber	Dewalt, John
Findley, David	Lees, Samuel	Moffit, James
Mintier, Robert	Myers, Jacob	McClary, John
McCormack, John	McGonigle, Thomas	McFadden, Thomas
McKain, William	McCally, William	Parson, Charles
Pittinger, Peter	Porter, Samuel A.	Pessy, Stephen
Reed, John	Robertson, Charles	Reed, John Jr.
Reed, Samuel	Robb, Moses	Shale, Nicholas
Scholes, John	Smith, Samuel	Tenet, Charles
Thompson, Moses	Welch, John	Wilkins, Archibald
Yielhall, Edward		

Pages 43-44. Vol. 2

ROLL OF CAPT. DAVID LISTS' COMPANY. (From Franklin County.)

Served from July 28, 1813 until September 6, 1813.

Capt. David List	Lieut. Peter Bawsher	Ensign Daniel Puncher
Sergt. Henry Grim	Sergt. Henry Spiker	Sergt. Dunovan Reed
Sergt. David Hostetter	Corp. George List	Corp. Phillip, Sanfoss
Corp. Daniel Swaggert	Corp. John Clark	Musician, Jacob Grove
Privates.	Privates.	Privates.
Bowsher, Jacob	Bell, Joseph	Betser, Peter
Bawm, Jacob	Black, William	Bawsher, Anthony
Burney, Thomas	Bowsher, Henry	Bowsher, John
Clark, Alphus	Coons, John	Curtz, Hector
Dresbach, Samuel	Finck, Solomon	Grim, George
Greenoh, James	Greenoh, Jacob	Harman, Samuel
Hedges, Benjamin	Harmon, Jacob	Hossman, George
Harmon, George	Hiser, William	Harpster, Peter
Justice, Jesse	Johnston, Robert	Kile, William
Kintzel, Samuel	List, Phillip	Lloyd, John
Miller, Stephen	Martin, William	Neff, Adam
Overmieir, John	Row, Peter	Spelman, Thomas
Stover, Christopher	Smith, Elisha	Swigart, John
Smith, Phillip	Salarts, John	Puntius, Conrad
Till, John	Uartz, Christian	Vandorm, William
Walton, John	Weaver, Jacob	Winlin, William
Wize, Henry		

Pages 45-46-47.

ROLL OF CAPT. GEORGE GIBSON'S COMPANY. (County Unknown.)

Served from July 28, 1813 until September 6, 1813 and from August 23, 1814 until January 11, 1815.

Capt. George Gibson	Lieut. Archibald Campbell	Lieut. Mathew Littleton
Ensign David Coon	Ensign Henry Goetiery	Sergt. Mathew Mitchell
Sergt. John Stephens	Sergt. Andrew Reed	Sergt. Jacon Hawman
Sergt. John Armstrong	Sergt. James McCalister	Sergt. George Watson
Corp. Thomas Barton	Corp. John Hawthorn	Corp. Isaac Rinear
Corp. John Smith	Corp. Thomas Richardson	Corp. Richard Bradley
Corp. Leeds William	Drummer, Jacob Chion	Fifer, Thomas Littleton

ROLL OF CAPT. GEORGE GIBSON'S COMPANY. (Continued)

Rank and Name of Soldier.

Privates.

Adams, John
Brown, Samuel
Benjamin, William
Carpenter, George
Crumb, Thomas
Decker, Joseph
Davidson, John
Edwards, John
George, Henry
Huffhinds, William
Hoover, Jacob
Hetsel, Daniel
Heaston, Martin
Jones, Abel
Long, John
Muller, Benjamin
Morris, Richard
Menshall, Thomas
McCoy, John
Neadstay, John
Ritter, John
Ridenour, George
Ritchy, Andrew
Saul, John
Sweet, Stephen
Stutts, Jacob
Wolff, Mathias
Wood, Benjamin

Anderson, James
Bowen, William
Campbell, Hugh
Coon, George
Crossley, Henry
Decker, Luke
Ellis, Thomas
Fuller, Alexander
Groon, William
Huffhinds, Jacob
Hussetter, Jacob
Haverlow, William
Iggs, Daniel
King, Joshua
Leck, John
Martin, David
Mann, Reuben P.
McCartney, Duke
McArthur, Duncan
Purcell, John
Ridenour, David
Ridenour, John
Stephens, Ebenezer
Swaggart, Daniel
Smith, John
Teagarden, William
Waggoner, John
Wolf, Phillip

Argo, Abraham
Burton, Boswell
Cutler, James
Culbertson, Samuel
Culbertson, Robert
DeWitt, Robert
Elder, Thomas
Francisco, Joseph
Groom, Jobe
Huff, John
Harrison, James
Hamilton, James
Gerome, William
Kerr, James
Laverty, John
Machin, Thomas
Mason, James
McFadden, William
McCohn, Archibald
Rodes, Peter
Roberts, Thomas
Rogers, Philemon
Smith, Jacob
Scoomover, Abraham
Simpson, Richard
Tivel, John
Wood, Robert
Young, Phillip

Pages 53-54. Vol. 2.

ROLL OF CAPTAIN JOHN ALEXANDER'S COMPANY.
(Probably Harrison or Jefferson County.)

Served from Sept. 21, 1812, until Dec. 8, 1812, and from July 29, 1813, until Aug. 22, 1813.

Capt. John Alexander
Ensign David Jackson
Sergt. Robert Blackford
Sergt. Robert Stayton
Corp. William M. Coy
Corp. Charles Lunay
Fifer, John Neel

Lieut. Hugh Christy
Sergt. George Ermabringer
Sergt. Hugh McGee
Sergt. Robert Kennedy
Corp. Joseph Washburn
Corp. Thomas Mantial
Fifer, Rodman Gardner

Lieut. Angus McCoy
Sergt. John Linch
Sergt. Stephen Paugburn
Sergt. Robert Miller
Corp. Jeremiah Ango
Corp. William Ross

Privates.

Ayers, James
Burkis, Richard
Buckley, John
Brown, Samuel
Christ, George
Fisher, Darius
Frame, James
Greenlee, Alexander
Lisle, Robert Sr.
Mann, John
Meek, Jacob
Parker, Justus
Reynolds, Caleb
Russel, Robert
Scott, John
Shiveley, William
Smith, Nathaniel
Welday, James

Adams, Thomas
Barnes, Obadiah
Browner, Samuel
Boland, William
Deval, Thomas
Fisher, Ephraim
Ferguson, James
Harland, Michael
Lisle, Robert Jr.
Miller, James
McCollan, James
Quillin, Adam
Revenaugh, John
Riddle, John
Simpson, James
Scott, Thomas
Tipton, John
White, Joseph

Adams, John
Bailey, William
Brown, John
Crawford, Alexander
Ellison, David
Fisher, John
Gamble, William
Lowery, John
Lacock, Moses
Mansfield, Samuel
McCulloch, David
Reed, Mathew
Revenaugh, Samuel
Ross, Henry
Simmons, Cornelius
Smith, John
Worstell, William

Pages 55-56.

ROLL OF CAPTAIN MARTIN SHUEY'S COMPANY.
(Probably Montgomery County.)

Served from August 25, 1814, until February 26, 1815.

Capt. Martin Shuey
Sergt. Robert McKee
Sergt. Levi Williams
Corp. David Lamm
Drummer, John Lypcap

Lieut. Christopher Sranfe
Sergt. Lewis Sranfe
Corp. D. McCord
Corp. Robert Meper

Ensign George Sranfe
Sergt. John Confer
Corp. Jeremiah Bateman
Corp. Alvin Richison

Privates.

Antonides, Vincen
Boal, John
Baker, Bruget
Camler, David
Depriest, Charles
Frakes, Nathan
Grubb, Daniel

Basche, John
Barker, Joseph
Chivilier, Charles
Cavin, George N.
Ensey, Dennis
Gable, Daniel
Hurley, Connell

Bodder, John
Battrick, William
Curry, Josiah
Davidson, Abraham
Fields, Reuben
Glenn, Thomas
Heaton, Joseph

ROLL OF CAPT. MARTIN SHUEY'E COMPANY. (Continued)

Rank and Name of Soldier.	Rank and Name of Soldier.	Rank and Name of Soldier.
Privates.	**Privates.**	**Privates.**
Harshman, Jacob	Harshman, Henry	Harten, Frederick
Kelsey, Isaac	Martin, Moses	Murphey, John
Moorman, Pleastent	McLong, James	Nason, Daniel
Perry, Joseph	Peck, John	Ridler, Abraham
Ryan, Cornelius	Sanders, Arnsey	Smith, Spencer
Thomas, Alexander	Townsley, Samuel	Wilson, Francis
Wilson, John	Williams, James	Yazel, Jacob

Pages 57-58. Vol. 2.

ROLL OF CAPTAIN ASA HINCKLES' COMPANY.
(Probably Butler County.)

Served from Aug. 11, 1812, until Nov. 30, 1812, and from Jan. 1 until Feb. 15, 1813.

Capt. Asa Hinckle	Lieut. Benaiah Ayres	Ensign James Cummins
Sergt. Thomas Richey	Sergt. James Burns	Sergt. Calvan Tipman
Sergt. Joseph McNight	Corp. John Ferris	Corp. Garnit Swallow
Corp. Lewis Drake	Corp. Daniel Hunter	Musician, William H. Wilcox
Privates.	**Privates.**	**Privates.**
Brexcunt, David	Boys, Ezekial	Bonnel, Lewis
Brown, David	Beard, Samuel	Clark, John
Cosbey, Thomas	Chirington	Cosbey, Samuel
Danford, William	Denman, Nathaniel	Graham, Isaac
Haney, George	Hinckle, John	Hinckle, Ziba
Hinckle, Henry	Hinckle, John	Kennedy, David
Larne, Moses	Line, Joseph	Morse, John
Meland, James	Morris, Daniel	Murdock, John
Mathers, James	Murdock, William	McClelland
McClellan, William	Moncrief, Caleb	Nichols, Lenester
Nichols, Prosper	Pierson, Lewis	Redenbaugh, John
Redingban, Frederick	Riker, William	Rian, Martin
Redenbaugh, Jeremiah	Riker, Thomas	Redenbaugh, George
Runion, Isaac	Rickey, John	Redenbaugh, Adam
Rodenbaugh, Phillip	Riker, Jacob	Sipe, Charles
Stirlen, James	Sampson, John	Thompson, Joseph
Thornbill, William	White, Benjamin	

Page 59.

ROLL OF CAPTAIN MATTHIAS CORWIN'S COMPANY.
(Probably Butler County.)

Served from August 11 until November 30, 1812, and from January 5 until February 11, 1813.

Capt. Matthias Corwin	Lieut. Nathaniel McLean	Ensign John Ruser
Sergt. Jeremiah Smith		
Privates.	**Privates.**	**Privates.**
Adams, John	Bell, Simion	Bartleson, Andrew
Bishop, David W.	Birdrall, Henry	Cruters, Ezekial
Dunlary, Howard	Eddy, John	Jones, Henry C.
Lenawred, John	Maish, William	McWhorten, Tyler
Neville, David	Phillips, William	Rush, Abraham
Runion, Absalom	Ross, Joseph	Reeder, Micaiah
Richardson, Elijah	Reding, James	Skinner, David
Seward, John	Sinnard, Thoman	Timothy, Millard
Townsend, Benjamin	Voorhis, Jacob	Wiles, James
Wooters, Richard	Wolf, Michael	

Pages 61-62.

ROLL OF CAPTAIN JOSEPH W. ROSS' COMPANY.
(Probably Ross County.)

Served from September 1, 1813, until March 1, 1814.

Capt. Joseph Ross	Lieut. James Mullin	Ensign Zeptha Danes
Sergt. Elnathan Barlow	Sergt. James Robertson	Sergt. Frost Levi
Sergt. John Donnly	Sergt. James Brown	Corp. James Gohan
Corp. William Winnison	Corp. Calvin Danes	Corp. Samuel Firestone
Musician, Colemuel, Green	Musician, Benjamin Martin	
Privates.	**Privates.**	**Privates.**
Arbute, Abraham	Bolabob, Abraham	Bolabob, John
Brand, Adam	Brooks, Isaac	Burman, Frederick
Childers, Mosley	Collison, William	Cornett, Abraham
Cornett, John	Cremeens, Moses	Cremeens, Isaac
Crouch, Joseph	Crouse, Jacob	Denny, William
Dust, David	Eckert, John	Fisher, Benjamin
Fulton, Loammi	Ganer, Jacob	Gibson, James
Gibson, John	Gibson, George	Griffith, Abraham
Hall, Samuel	Hanna, John	Hertand, Joseph
Holden, John	Humphrey, James	Hunterock, Henry
Kikabiaugh, Reuben	Long, William Sr.	Long, William Jr.
Longbrake, Daniel	Mansfield, John	Martin, James

Vol. 2.
ROLL OF CAPTAIN JOSEPH W. ROSS' COMPANY. (Continued)

Rank and Name of Soldier.

Privates.

Mayse, Archibald
Morris, Elijah
McKee, Samuel
Parde, Richard
Prince, William
Purdy, William
Row, Phillip
Sumter, Richard
Waugh, Gory
Whitelock, James

Mathews, Nathan
Mayer, David
McKee, John
Phelps, Roswell
Price, John
Reeves, William
Royston, John
Thompson, Calvin
Webb, Hanley
Williams, Solomon

Miller, John
McDonald, David
Oversteel, John
Picket, Samuel
Price, Joseph
Rice, James
Stockwell, William
Vandemark, John
West, William
Wisely, John

Pages 63-64-65-66.

ROLL OF CAPTAIN JACOB SHINGLEDECKER'S COMPANY.
(From Greene County.)

Served August 24 until December 31, 1812.

Capt. Jacob Shingledecker
Sergt. John Todd
Sergt. Thomas Cottrell
Corp. Oliver Crawford
Corp. James Downey

Lieut. Samuel Butts
Sergt. Jacob Truby
Corp. John Wiland
Corp. John Davis
Trumpeter, William Burrows

Ensign William Yates
Sergt. Daniel Peterbaugh or Butterbaugh
Corp. Alexander Forbens

Privates.

Aley, John
Burres, William
Beal, Jonothan
Chambers, Adam
Cremwell, Samuel
Folck, George
Gray, Abraham
Hyers, Anthony
Keigler, Samuel
Kirkwood, William
Low, William
Miner, William
Messer, Henry
Nave, Jacob
Rue, Jacob
Shingledecker, Abraham
Stewart, Aaron
Tingley, John A.
Vogle, Peter
Wilson, William

Ankeney, Henry
Beal, George
Buker, Peter
Chambers, William
Coster, Henry
Fogle, Peter
Hoover, John
Holverstat, John
Kisor, Richard
Longstreth, Andrew
Livingston, Andrew
Minniear, William
McCormack, James
Ritter, Jacob
Rubart, Enos
Shingledecker, John
Steward, Moses
Trubee, John
Wilson, Michael
Westfall, Jonothan

Barkard, John
Beal, Aaron
Bochert, John
Crawford, Oliver
Eli, John
Gray, Henry
Haddix, Nimrod
Hollinger, Daniel
Kooglar, Samuel
Lee, John
Morningstar, George
May, George
Nelson, John
Ritter, John
Rethn, Jacob
Sipe, William
Smith, Jacob
Steward, Andrew
Wyland, John
Wilson, Jeremiah

Pages 67-68.

ROLL OF CAPTAIN WILLIAM STEPHENSON'S COMPANY.
(Probably Belmont County.)

Vol. 2.
Served from September 3, 1813, until March 20, 1814.

Capt. William Stephenson
Sergt. James Quigley
Sergt. Robert Yost
Corp. Thomas Holmes
Musician, James Tuttle

Lieut. Daniel Berry
Sergt. Hugh Brady
Corp. William McCormack
Corp. William McCraghill

Ensign John Bell
Sergt. John Hardesty
Corp. James Logan
Musician, James H. Ball

Privates.

Brem, Benjamin
Barton, William
Bright, Nicholas
Boneham, Aaron
Caruthers, Christopher
Engle, Michael
Floyd, Aaron
Grimes, John
Heske, Samuel
Harriman, David
Kinkead, Joseph
Mitchell, Peter
Maring, Phineas
McPherson, Daniel
McFadden, Charles
Price, Phineas
Parrish, Joseph
Payques, John
Rammage, William
Swark, John
Snelling, Aquilla
Stewart, Samuel
Taylor, James
Wagoner, John

Bun, George
Bramhall, William
Burney, John B.
Bundy, Joseph
Clifford, William
Elliott, Samuel
Farnon, Alpheus
Gilham, Thomas
Homdel, Richard
Irwin, John
Lyons, John
Mitchell, John
Murdock, Joseph
McConnell, James
Nichols, Eli
Parcels, Richard
Perry, William
Pitman, William
Robinson, Samuel
Stewart, Edie
Stilwell, Obediah
Stewart, John
Truex, Abraham
Yerian, John

Burk, Thomas
Brooke, Benjamin
Boy, John
Coss, George
Decker, Simon
Forrest, Gabriel
Findley, William
Henry, Joseph
Henry, Francis
Irwin, George
Lloyd, James
Maring, Peter
Murphy, William
McPherson, John
Naufossen, George
Park, William
Pyatt, Thomas
Reed, Jeremiah
Rush, James
Snidiker, Nicholas
Smith, Williams
Stypman, Stephen
Warren, Daniel
Zarbit, John

Pages 69-70.

ROLL OF CAPTAIN JOHN WILEY'S COMPANY.
(County Unknown.)

Served from August 30, 1813, until February 28, 1814.

Rank and Name of Soldier.	Rank and Name of Soldier.	Rank and Name of Soldier.
Capt. John Wiley	Lieut. David Hunter	Ensign Ephraim Bilderback
Sergt. William Rice	Sergt. John Barks	Sergt. John Wanwey
Sergt. James Hunter	Corp. John Westenbaegar	Corp. Elijah Atha
Corp. William Ingmand	Corp. Jacob Barler	Corp. William Wolf
Privates.	**Privates.**	**Privates.**
Allen, Whiting	Allspaugh, John	Allen, Judiah
Allspaugh, Henry	Bay, James	Bailes, James
Brukebill, Peter	Bailer, Samuel	Bernhart, Peter
Bernhart, Jacob	Beary, Abraham	Clarton, John
Cox, John	Curtis, Jonothan	Caves, Nath
Cline, Andrew	Deafenbaugh, Adam	England, William
Gessell, William	Greer, William	Hutton, Isaac
Hedges, Joseph	Huffman, Julius	Hedges, Peter
Horne, Christian	Hedges, Josiah	Howard, Joseph
Ingman, Henry	Kigar, George	Kinnard, James
Kigar, Peter	Kraniac, James	Kamele, Michael
Kinser, Peter	Kirk, George	Lockhart, William M.
Linzee, William	Lane, Dutton	Murray, William
Miller, Abraham	Mackrell, Samuel	Miller, Emanuel
Miller, Phillip	McCormack, Moses	McFerston, Alexander
Newman, Henry	Ponenmyer, Samuel	Potter, Nathaniel
Peterson, John	Pinkstath, Frederick	Peaugh, George
Radon, George	Rogers, James	Reynolds, Caleb
Shope, William	Shoemaker, William	Striper, Warner
Shode, James	Smith, John, Sr.	Smith, John, Jr.
Swiles, John	Sheaffer, Peter	Thompson, Andrew
Tolbert, John	Trout, Jacob	Vandermart, John
Walters, Christopher	White, Jeremiah	Young, William
Young, Robert		

Pages 71-72 Vol. 2.

ROLL OF CAPT. JACOB CATTERLINE'S COMPANY. (County Unknown)

Served from Sept. 1, 1813 until March 1, 1814.

Capt. Jacob Catterline	Lieut. James Hooper	Ensign Jared Bonn
Sergt. Henry Smith	Sergt. Thomas Warner	Sergt. Edwin Croose
Sergt. Daniel Ponce	Corp. George Norris	Corp. Henry Hannah
Corp. William Mast	Corp. Jesse Cloud	Fifer, George Hallinger
Drummer, Nathan Bonn		
Privates.	**Privates.**	**Privates.**
Boyle, James	Baker, Christian	Browning, Leonard
Bury, Elijah	Black, George	Clayton, John
Cooley, Edward	Copeland, Caleb	Copeland, William
Clayton, Joseph	Fulk, Nicholas	Found, William
Fate, George	Foster, George	Huffman, Henry
Helser, John	Hall, William	Johnston, John
Johnston, Luke	Kirkland, John	Lamb, Jacob
Lewis, John	Murphy, Benjamin	Mannon, Jacob
Miksell, Adam	Primmer, Adam	Phillips, John
Pelly, Moses	Ridenhour, John	Ridenhour, Jacob
Ridenhour, Luderick	Reed, John	Roberts, Jonothan
Ruffner, Jacob	Rightley, Coonrod	Stally, George
Smith, Christian	Smith, Joseph	Smith, Andrew
Stephenson, Edward	Sartman, Henry	Torbet, William
Vanalla, John	Wagoner, John	Wallard, Henry

Pages 75-76

ROLL OF CAPT. JOHN THORNLEY'S COMPANY.
(Probably from Washington County.)

Served from January 6, until March 6, 1814.

Capt. John Thornley or Thornliey	Lieut. David Merchant or Meredith	Ensign, Elisha Chapman
Sergt. St. Clear Kelley	Sergt. Lemanuel Cooper	Sergt. Thomas Ady
Sergt. Daniel McClain	Corp. William Henkins	Corp. Solomon Tise
Corp. William Smith	Fifer, David Cox	Corp. David Alpha
Drummer, William Magee		
Privates.	**Privates.**	**Privates.**
Archer, John	Andrews, Jerid	Batchet, Jonah
Bell, John	Borth, Daniel	Banthan, Perry G.
Bird, William	Beamer, Henry	Barkey, Samuel
Brown, Jesse	Bennett, Joel	Corbet, Robert
Clark, William	Cline, George	Crouch, Samuel
Chapman, Simeon	Creig, John	Chapman, Hezekiah
Connet, John	Connet, Abraham	Darling, Jonothan
Davidson, Mathew	Edward, David	Emerson, Luke

ROLL OF CAPT. JOHN THORNLEY'S CO.—(Continued)

Rank and Name of Soldier. Rank and Name of Soldier. Rank and Name of Soldier.

Privates.

Privates.	Privates.	Privates.
Fugate, Jeremiah	Ferguson, Abner	Fost, Ephraim
Grose, John	Hill, Thomas	Hartley, Thomas
Harris, George	Hepsen, Benjamin	Jolley, William
Keiser, John	Kidd, William	Lynn, John
Lamb, Benjamin	Marshall, Thomas	Millford, Joseph
McCleain, Andrew	Newel, Thomas	Oglesby, James
Petty, Pressley	Ramsey, William	Ramsey, John
Ramsey, Samuel	Row, Nicholas	Riley, James
Skipton, John	Saltingstall, John	Smith, John
Sills, Jonothan	Stanley, Francis	Tison, Zephamiah
Tipton, Solomon	Vulgenoit, Jacob	Vaughan, Alexander
Willis, Richard	Walker, William	

Pages 77-78

ROLL OF CAPT. WILLIAM WILSON'S COMPANY. (County Unknown.)

Served from August 1, until September 9, 1812.

Capt. William Wilson	Lieut. John Robinson	Ensign, John Philbey
Sergt. Jacob Marris	Sergt. William Forgason	Sergt. George Ritchey
Sergt. John Day		

Privates.	Privates.	Privates.
Ashiraft, Jonothan	Binter, Jacob	Baughman, Henry
Chambers, Joseph	Chambers, Mathew	Conn, Thomas
Davis, William	Ewing, Edmond	Fletcher, Spinier
Fox, John	Graves, Benjamin	Greenfield, John
Haldesty, Samuel	Hawkins, William	Hadesty, Urich
Hawker, Christian	Hensley, John	Hayman, Abijah
Helms, Daniel	Latimore, Jesse	Lane, Samuel
Mariaty, John	Mathews, Noah	Mathews, Thomas
Moore, Henry	Moore, David	Pryer, Frederick
Rowell, Moses	Ripe, John	Rodwick, Lewis
Richey, Gideon	Slaughter, Elias	Stoner, John
Sebring, Rudolph	Stradley, Ayers	Starkey, John
Smith, Silas	Taylor, William	Thompson, William
Tharp, William	Tharp, John	Vanwikle, Paul
Winters, James	Wagoner, Daniel	Wagoner, Joseph
Wilson, George	Welch, James	Welch, John
Wheeler, John	Wells, John	Young, Ephraim
Zane, Joel		

Pages 79-80

ROLL OF CAPT. ABNER BARRETT'S COMPANY.
(Probably from Champaign County.)

Served from August 21, until October 21, 1812 and from January 1, until February 21, 1813.

Capt. Abner Barrett	Lieut. William Chenoweth	Ensign, John Owen
Sergt. Wanet Owen	Sergt. Thomas Green	Sergt. Jesse Frankelberger
Sergt. Daniel Weal	Corp. Daniel Helmick	Corp. James Walker
Corp. Stephen Runyon	Corp. William Runyon	Drummer, John Rupe
Fifer, John Swisher		

Privates.	Privates.	Privates.
Brousman, Nicodemus	Bay, Robert	Beatty, William
Blue, William	Bouseman, John	Bishop, Aquilla
Blue, William	Bay, Hugh	Coon, Barnabus
Carbert, Thomas	Clark, Abraham	Cowan, Miles
Coterel, Hiram	Cosan, Thomas	Conkel, Michal
Curl, Jeremiah	Dawson, William	Frerwode, John
Flood, Francis	Frerwods, John	Gilpin, Elias
Graften, James	Gilmore, John	Green, William
Gran, William	Hendrix, John	Hoge, James
Huffman, Abraham	Hashparger, Christian	Hobson, John
Helmick, Daniel	Kelley, John	Kizer, Joseph
Leeper, James	Littell, David	Lonsdale, Thomas
Mayfield, Emanuel	Morris, John	Mathews, George
Merchant, Joseph	Moody, David	Monmar, William
Menice, John	McKinney, Edward	Neville, James
Nicles, Ninion	Nunengan, William	Pettiend, Horatio
Peno, Jacob	Reed, James	Rector, William
Rodes, William	Russell, James	Rees, Jeremiah
Rodes, Conway	Shepard, William	Sweet, Joshua
Sargent, Enock	Stanley, Thomas	Stanley, William
Sprey, Lodman	Swisher, Jacob	Sibart, George
Stanford, E.	Storm, Henry	Scribner, Aaron
Standford, Elijah	Templin, James	Waltz, Edward
Weever, Aaron	West, Stake	Wells, Joseph
Yutsler, Jacob		

Pages 81-82   Vol. 2.

ROLL OF CAPT. MARTIN ARMSTRONG'S COMPANY. (County Unknown)

Served from August 22, 1812 until February 22, 1813.

Rank and Name of Soldier.	Rank and Name of Soldier.	Rank and Name of Soldier.
Capt. Martin Armstrong	Lieut. James Bryan	Ensign, Andrew McKew
Sergt. Hartley Melone	Sergt. Adam Cell	Sergt. Robert Brown
Sergt. Andrew Kelley	Corp. George Boots	Corp. Phillip Waldren
Corp. William Odle	Corp. Caleb Odle	Drummer, Jesse Howe

Privates.

Alexander, Joseph	Brown, Nimrod	Bell, John
Boots, Martin	Bagby, Thomas	Cating, Edward
Carpenter, Jesse	Camble, Jonothan	Doll, Daniel
Fryar, Benjamin	Doll, Abraham	Gilmore, Andrew
Garrison, Asbe	Hanks, John	Hanks, Joseph
Kelley, James	Kelley, John, Sr.	Kelley, John, Jr.
Kelley, William	Kelley, Andrew	Kelley, Alexander
Jacobs, Samuel	Linton, Lawson	Linton, Zecharia
Loury, Samuel	Lockard, James	Lockard, Joseph
Malone, Richard	Miller, Isaac	Miller, Robert
McClintock, Alexander	McClintock, Joseph	McClintock, John
Pearce, James	Queen, John	Reynolds, Anthony
Ross, John	Smith, James	Smith, Samuel
Seymore, Solomon	Smith, David	Salts, John
Van Embaugh, Abraham	Williams, John	Windpan, Frederick
Zeigler, George		

Pages 83-84

ROLL OF CAPT. JOHN SPENCER'S COMPANY.
(Probably from Ross County.)

Served from June 1, 1812 until May 31, 1813.

Capt. John Spencer	Lieut. Robert Davidson	Ensign, Andrew Ellison
Sergt. James Gibson	Sergt. Samuel Smith	Sergt. James Seymour
Sergt. Joseph Statelu	Corp. Thomas Hughs	Corp. Joseph Cunningham
Corp. Samuel Murphy	Corp. Elias Hughs	

Privates.

Barrack, John	Bernard, Jacob	Bernard, Mathew
Bevard, Jacob	Cunningham, William	Casey, Archibald
Casey, Jonothan	Chadwick, James	Cadwick, David
Drum, John	Devour, Enos	Drum, Thomas
Davis, Moses	Davis, Thomas	Evans, John
Evans, Joshua	Farn, John	Furry, John
Harris, John	Hall, John	Harris, Joshua
Jones, Thomas	Johnston, John	Kimannon, ————
Little, Jacob	Myers, Henry	Mutherbaugh, John
Mepenger, David	Marfoot, Samuel	McCawn, Robert
Pickering, Jacob	Parr, William	Paris, John
Roe, William	Steward, Andrew	Scott, James
Smith, Archibald	Spelman, Spencer	Smith, James
Shaddock, John	Walker, William	Wright, Joseph
Young, William		

Pages 85-86

ROLL OF CAPT. DANIEL CONNER'S COMPANY.
(Probably from Belmont County.)

Served from January 13, until March 17, 1814.

Capt. Daniel Conner	Lieut. Thomas Dunn	Ensign, Alfred Weeden
Sergt. Thomas Henry	Sergt. Absalom Waddell	Sergt. James Edwards
Sergt. Henry Van Fossen	Sergt. Eli Nichols	Corp. William Clifford
Corp. William West	Corp. David Milar	Corp. Samuel Perkins
Fifer, Isaac Midkiff	Drummer, Peter Hanson	

Privates.

Boyd, John	Bonehan, Aaron	Bundy, Joseph
Clark, James	Conklin, David	DeWitt, John
Decker, Simion	Findley, William	Ferrier, John
Grove, Barnet	Gassway, Robert	Harrington, Charles
Hart, John	Harper, Francis	Holmes, Samuel
Howel, Daniel	Honnel, Richard	Hupp, Phillip
Heaney, John	Joyques, John	Lanham, Elisha
Lloyd, James	Lonner, Thomas	Murphy, Westley
Murphey, William	Medley, Joseph	McFadden, Charles
Perkins, John	Pitman, Elias	Pitman, William
Pyatte, Thomas	Read, Jeremiah	Simmons, Thomas
Stellar, Mathias	Stella, Henry	Smith, Nichols
Stewart, John	Silvis, John	Scott, James
Shipman, Stephen	Truax, Abraham	Vanfossen, George
Waddle, James	Ware, Robert	Wagoner, John
West Enos	Yerian, George	

Pages 87-88 Vol. 2.

ROLL OF CAPT. JOEL COLLIN'S COMPANY.
(Probably from Butler County.)
Served from August 11, 1812 until February, 1813.

Rank and Name of Soldier.	Rank and Name of Soldier.	Rank and Name of Soldier.
Capt. Joel Collins	Lieut. Ephraim Gard	Ensign, John Hall
Sergt. Jeremiah Gard	Sergt. David Sutton	Sergt. Joseph Haines
Sergt. John Price	Corp. Zechariah Parish	Corp. Joseph Douglas
Corp. George Sutton	Corp. Jacob Gard	Fifer, Hays Taylor
Drummer, Henry Thompson		

Privates.

Anderson, James	Bone, John	Broadbury, Simeon
Broadbury, James	Brown, John	Beeler, George
Boys, George	Casker, James	Carr, James
Carper, John	Crane, William	Dencen, John
DeCamp, William	Dillcoe, Vincent	Dickard, Jacob
Gray, Robert	Gower, Jacob	Gates, Jacob
Garver, Peter	Gard, Moses	Heath, William
Howard, Thomas	Hyder, John	Isaacs, John
Jones, Henry	Kirkpatrick, George	Kerr, Jacob
Lintner, Andrew	Malone, John	Mosteller, Christopher
Martin, James	Malone, Samuel	Megongle, Phillip
Mansfield, John	McManus, William	McKinstry, John
McMaken, Joseph	McNeal, James	Newkirk, Robinson
Owens, Silas	Pine, Benjamin	Price, Joseph
Pilson, Robert	Rainy, William	Rinehart, Jacob
Rutledge, Isaac	Scott, John E.	Stell, Alexander
Scott, Richard	Sinnors, John	Stark, Archibald
Stephen, Thomas	Smith, William	Smith, David
Smiley, John	Smiley, James	Shields, John
Smith, Andrew	Salmon, Jacob	Stephens, Samuel
Sackett, John	Sullivan, William	Sullivan, Patrick
Steele, Samuel	Simpson, Samuel	Sutton, William
Stonebrake, John	Tigard, George	Tigard, William
Thompson, Samuel	Taylor, Robert	Watson, Eber
Wilson, Thomas	Watson, Isaac	Woodfin, Nicholas
Wickart, Joseph	Wilever, Joseph	Woods, Andrew

Pages 89-90

ROLL OF CAPT. GEORGE RICHARDSON'S COMPANY. (County Unknown.)
Served from August 31, until December 1, 1813.

Capt. George Richardson	Lieut. John Ward	Ensign, John Kline
Sergt. Edward Jackson	Sergt. Samuel Bay	Sergt. Samuel Linton
Sergt. Samuel Waters	Corp. Thomas Jackson	Corp. Joseph Steins
Corp. John Huchinson	Corp. Abraham Cherryhohney	Drummer, George Rummel

Privates.

Ashton, William	Allen, Jacob M.	Burges, Samuel
Baker, John	Biddinger, Henry	Bates, John
Bay, James	Bryan, William	Burris, John
Bumtrager, John	Casebear, Samuel	Clumm, John
Collins, Elijah	Cherry, William	Collis, David
Croy, Mathew	DeLong, James	DuWitt, Paul
Everhart, Frederick	Fuller, Joseph	Frederick, Peter
Garnet, Francis	Gibson, George	Hall, Joseph
Hall, Hamilton	Hall, Samuel	Hughs, Jacob
Hosack, William	Hedges, Aaron	Hedges, Israel
Hoy, Samuel	Harper, William	Howe, Jacob
Jennings, Bailess	Koon, George	Krutzer, Henry
Kellar, Martin	Lidman, John	Mizer, George
Miller, John	Miller, Henry	Moorehead, James
Marling, John	Milslagel, Andrew	Moorehead, William
McMullin, Joseph	Neal, Joseph	Oldham, James
Price, Christopher	Phillips, Enoch	Roop, Jacob
Robb, Joshua	Reeves, Joshua	Reamer, John
Reamer, Adam	Shaneman, Henry	Seward, William
Smith, Thomas	Shepard, William	Smith, Jacob
Seaton, Robert	Sherick, Everett	Thompson, Michael
Trumble, John	Waller, Lewis	Waller, John
Zeiglar, Phillip.		

Pages 91-92-93-94.

ROLL OF CAPT. JOHN JONES' COMPANY.
(Probably from Highland County.)
Served from May 1, 1812 until May 1, 1813.

Capt. John Jones	Lieut. James Patterson	Ensign, Thomas Rogers
Sergt. John Fisher	Sergt. James McConnel	Sergt. Jacob Baker
Sergt. Elijah C. Wilkerson	Sergt. Thomas Smith	Corp. Chalfin Robert
Corp. John Campbell	Corp. James Strain	Corp. James Stanbury
Corp. Walker Baldwin	Corp. Robert Strain	Drummer, William Bunten
Fifer, Samuel Stephenson		

ROLL OF CAPT. JOHN JONES' COMPANY. (Continued)

Privates.

- Belser, Micajah
- Braidy, Harrison
- Baldwin, Walton
- Countryman, Henry
- Gall, George
- Hastings, Henry
- Harper, Alexander
- Jonikin, Noah
- Lynch, John
- Miller, Peter
- Newman, Howard
- Plott, William
- Roads, George
- Reed, Rezin
- Stanberry, James
- Slaughter, Moses
- Swisher, Abraham
- Ward, Samuel

Privates.

- Baker, Jacob
- Bell, George
- Coons, William R.
- Earls, David
- Hathaway, David
- Hart, Silas
- Harvey, Beacher
- Leaverton, John
- Little, Alexander
- McConnel, James
- Nicely, David
- Reader, Charles
- Roades, Phillip
- Ramsey, John L.
- Strain, Robert
- Swadley, Jacob
- Therman, John
- Williams, Mathew

Privates.

- Bunten, William
- Bell, John
- Childers, Joseph
- Earls, Isaac
- Hastings, George
- Hartman, Jacob
- Jonikin, Eli
- Leaverton, James
- Leaverton, Thomas
- Nelson, Charles
- Patchel, John
- Rosebrough, John
- Rees, Owen
- Rubb or Ruble, Owen
- Shoemaker, Simeon
- Still, Samuel
- Thornton, Samuel

Page 95.

ROLL OF CAPT. HENRY MALLON'S COMPANY.
(Probably from Ross County.)

Served from July 28, until August 16, 1813.

- Capt. Henry Mallon
- Sergt. Christopher Popejoy
- Sergt. Edward Briant
- Corp. John Briant

- Lieut. Solomon Bonner
- Sergt. Martin Patterson
- Corp. Aaron Orahood
- Corp. William McCartney

- Ensign, Charles Wells
- Sergt. William Popejoy
- Corp. John Hoddy

Privates.

- Briggs, Samuel
- Briant, Jonothan
- Christian, Leathlin
- Crowley, Joseph
- Criminie, Jacob
- Day, Overton
- Huffman, Leonard
- McCartney, Duke
- Stookey, Daniel
- Stookey, Jacob
- Toohinder, Thomas
- Woolf, Jonothan

Privates.

- Boyd, Francis
- Bowers, Michael
- Christie, Joel
- Clark, James
- Carr, Martin
- Fennemore, John
- Huffman, Joseph
- McCoy, John
- Strader, Christopher
- Stingley, Leonard
- Wells, Squire
- Whetstone, Abraham

Privates.

- Boots, Jacob
- Bennet, Isaac
- Clouser, John
- Clark, Robert
- Day, Martin
- Gregg, William
- Monroe, Lemule
- McCartney, John
- Strader, Michael
- Shaw, Giddeon
- Wonsoy, Daniel

Pages 97-98.

ROLL OF CAPT. WILLIAM HUMPHREY'S COMPANY. (County Unknown.)

Served from April, 1812 until ———————.

- Capt. William Humphrey
- Sergt. Andrew Robbe
- Sergt. Mathias Dean
- Corp. Josiah Bradway

- Lieut. Peter Deardorf
- Sergt. Wright Ellott
- Corp. Hezekiah Cartwright
- Corp. John Flemming

- Ensign Robert Sweeney
- Sergt. James Thirby
- Corp. John Young

Privates.

- Anderson, John
- Cummins, John
- Fisher, David
- Garrison, John
- Garrison, David
- Hight, Abraham
- Hamilton, Elias
- Kindespeker, Jacob
- Lee, John
- Mullen, John
- Nicholson, Andrew
- Rees, Boon
- Thomas, David
- Venard, John

Privates.

- Blake, Nathan
- Fitzgerel, Asen
- Garwood, William
- Garrison, Jeremiah
- Garrison, Hezekiah
- Hand, Benjamin
- Hyde, Samuel
- Long, William D.
- Murphy, Benjamin
- Martin, John
- Patten, William
- Spencer, James
- Stanbrough, Nehemiah
- Warts, John

Privates.

- Branstetter, Andrew
- Fisher, Jacob
- Garrison, Benjamin
- Garrison, Persons
- Harris, James
- Hesbr, Jacob
- Holcombe, Asen
- Lasey, John
- Monroe, Charles
- Marley, William
- Reaglen, Wright
- Seward, John
- Treland, William
- Wright, George

Page 99.

ROLL OF CAPT. WILLIAM SUMNER'S COMPANY.
(Probably from Fairfield County.)

Served from July 31, until September 6, 1813.

- Capt. William Sumner
- Sergt. John Bly
- Sergt. Archibald Carnian
- Corp. Asa Hubble

- Lieut. William Martin
- Sergt. Isaac Painter
- Corp. Mathew Wolford
- Corp. Ira Bing

- Lieut. Sostehenese McCabe
- Sergt. Daniel Brumback
- Corp. George Lafery
- Musician, Richard Thompson

Vol. 2.
ROLL OF CAPT. WILLIAM SUMMER'S COMPANY. (Continued)

Rank and Name of Soldier.
Privates.
Arendt, Peter
Bretz, Conrad
Cagy, Jacob
Giger, Martin
Hutchinson, James
Little, George
McCabe, Ezra
Polly, Jacob
Sechrist, Peter
Thompson, William
Weaver, Christian
Watson, Richard

Rank and Name of Soldier.
Privates.
Bryan, William
Bretz, John
Frieze, Peter
Hershberger, David
Hammond, Michael
Musser, Muly
Oiler, George
Reed, John
Senior, Jacob
Tricker, John
Wolf, Henry

Rank and Name of Soldier.
Privates.
Bush, Martin
Brown, Joseph
Goss, Jacob
Harod, James
Lamb, William
Myers, Jacob
Phelps, Hezekiah
Swartz, Frederick
Spitler, Warner
Winter, Abraham
Watson, James

Pages 101-102.

ROLL OF CAPT. WILLIAM McMAIN'S (or McMean's) COMPANY.
(From Clermont or Butler Counties.)
Served from August 11, 1812 until February 11, 1813.

Capt. William McMain (or Mc-Mean)
Sergt. Archibald Clinton
Sergt. John Coteral
Corp. Enoch McMaines

Lieut. Paul Rush
Sergt. Joseph Cotteral
Sergt. Isaac Elston
Corp. Edwin Hughs

Ensign Robert Orn
Sergt. Henry Stroman
Corp. Joseph Hutchinson
Corp. James Mullin

Privates.
Abat, Jeremiah
Barber, Daniel
Clark, William
Crawford, Charles
Davison, William
Durham, Silas
Easton, William
Farden, Christopher
Fisher, Samuel
Hughes, Isaac
Hutchinson, Joseph
Long, Frank
Lenning, David
Megrue, Charles
Malot, Peter
McCollum, James
Price, Jeremiah
Pobst, Frederick
Sinnard, Abraham
Shields, David
Wakeland, Charles

Privates.
Brown, John
Cotrell, William
Cummins, John
Crawford, Clark
Daniels, William
Eastwood, Joseph
Elston, William
Flagle, Valentine
Gilmon, Daniel
Hughes, James
Jones, James
Long, Jacob
Lenet, Adam
Megrue, Paul
Motsiner, Felix
McDonnough, Samuel
Parks, James
Reeves, Alexander
Stewart, Hall
Webster, John
Wableton, John

Privates.
Briding, Thomas
Cramer, David
Cambo, Thomas
Dougherty, David
Davis, Thomas
Eacret, William
Frazer, David
Finlong, Lewis
Gost, Jacob
Huddleston, James
Jones, Thomas
Lenning, Nicholas
Lining, Gabriel
Merrit, Isaac
McMains, Benjamin
Notruge, Felix
Porter, Victor
Ramsey, George
Stronie, Collen
Wikkel, James

Pages 103-104.

ROLL OF CAPT. ROBERT HAYES' COMPANY. (County Unknown.)
Served from April 27, 1812 until ―――――――.

Capt. Robert Hayes
Sergt. Bryan Williams
Sergt. Samuel S. Jack
Corp. John Robinson

Lieut. Samuel Pope
Sergt. Michael Brown
Corp. Joseph McEdwards
Corp. Seth St. John

Ensign John Sheet
Sergt. John Ross
Corp. Isaac Heaton

Privates.
Brenney, John
Baker, Clark
Camron, John
Estel, William L.
Graham, Levi
Huthoe, John
Hutchinson, James
Hoole, James
Jester, Eli
Leoman, Christopher
Manning, Daniel
McDaniel, William
McCristy, Jesse
Rochefiter, Samuel
Stiles, Henry
Snooke, Martin
Smoot, Dixon
Thatcher, Elijah
Tuttle, Isaiah
Trump, Andrew
Voorhis, Jeremiah
Weain, Adam

Privates.
Bowers, David
Caslet, Alexander
Disberry, James
Farmer, Michael
Goodpasture, Jesse
Hayes, John
Hercules, William
Jack, James
Jennings, David
Martin, William
Mosbry, John
McCollister, Hugh
Powell, Jacob
Roberts, Aaron
Snuff, Jacob
Sharohan, John
Stearns, Jabez
Trimble, Moses
Trimble, James
Turman, John
Wear, Robert
Waters, Richard

Privates.
Bowen, John
Cairil, Alexander
Dill, John
Frourdale, Samuel
Hamilton, Jacob
Hardy, James
Hoges, William
Jeffries, George
Kitchel, James L.
Miller, John
Macy, Seth
McCullister, John
Rhynearson, Miller
Shaw, Archibald
Sutton, John
Stiles, John A.
Samson, Jehiel
Tutler, John
Trudle, George
Vanskike, David
Wallace, William
Wear, Elisha

Pages 105-106. Vol. 2.

ROLL OF CAPT. JAMES ODELL'S COMPANY. (County Unknown.)

Served from July 29, until September 8, 1813.

Rank and Name of Soldier.	Rank and Name of Soldier.	Rank and Name of Soldier.
Capt. James Odell	Lieut. David Johnson	Ensign James Rogers
Sergt. John McCombs	Sergt. Thomas Grover	Sergt. James B. Strain
Sergt. Joseph Smalley	Corp. Thomas McStrain	Corp. James McCollon
Corp. William Johnson	Corp. John Bereman	

Privates.

Brown, Nathan	Bigley, Peter	Brower, David
Barngroover, David	Barngroover, John	Brown, Charles
Bell, Andrew	Bonar, Joseph	Chapman, John
Collins, Isaac	Chapman, David	Chapman, Aschel
Galaspy, Thomas	His, James	Henderson, Joseph
Hough, Ashford	Hamilton, Alexander	McGee, Thomas
McGee, John	McNeeley, George	Nays, Thomas
Prather, Thomas	Pettijohn, Abraham	Ross, John
Roberts, James	Smith, Archibald	Smally, Thomas
Smally, Isaac	Strain, John H.	Small, Jacob
Strain, John C.	Strain, John	Therman, Talbot
Thermon, James	Thermon, David	White, William
Wilkin, John	Walker, Elijah	Whitley, John
Whitley, Thomas	White, Joseph	

Pages 107-108.

ROLL OF CAPT. ROBERT MORRISON'S COMPANY.
(Probably from Belmont County.)

Served from July 29, until September 8, 1813.

Capt. Robert Morrison	Lieut. Thomas Wason	Ensign David Young
Sergt. Robert Findlay	Sergt. Robert Young	Sergt. Abraham Thomas
Sergt. Alexander Baldridge	Corp. James Winter	Corp. John McClure
Corp. William Smith	Corp. Alexander Liget	Drummer, William Hamilton
Fifer, David Smith		

Privates.

Alexander, Benjamin	Alexander, Gabriel	Alexander, James
Burnett, Lewis	Bair, George	Bovel, John
Bisship, Peter	Brown, John	Bilbee, John
Bailey, James	Caskey, James	Craig, Robert
Clark, John	Coppel, Daniel	Crust, Henry
Cross, William	Cross, Richard	Edginton, George
Eyler, Joseph	Eginton, Joseph	Findley, William
Findley, Samuel	Foster, John	Gleze, Nathan
Gordon, James	Kruzen, Thomas	Liget, William
Mailatt, George	Mehafey, John	Mintire, George
Mehafey, Andrew	McNeal, James	McNeal, Joseph
McNeal, John	McColpen, Robert	McColgan, William
Morris, John	Nelson, James	Odell, Thomas
Parker, Silvenes	Patton, William	Patton, Nathaniel
Ramsey, William	Rodgers, William	Reed, Nathaniel
Smith, John	Sargent, James	Smittel, David
Thompson, Robert	Wilson, Robert	Wilkes, John
Washburn, ————	Wright, Joseph	Wright, William
Wright, Stephen	Williamson, James	Young, James
Young, Thomas		

Pages 109-110-111-112.

ROLL OF CAPT. LUTHER LEONARD'S COMPANY.
(Probably from Butler County.)

Served from August 11, until November 30, 1812, and from July 5, until July 23, 1814.

Capt. Luther Leonard	Lieut. Clarkson Price	Lieut. Nathaniel Terwillegar
Ensign William Mitchell	Sergt. William Cochran	Sergt. John Terwillegar
Sergt. Jonothan Harris	Sergt. John Mellen	Sergt. Henry Miller
Sergt. Burgan Miller	Sergt. Samuel McKee	Corp. James Mitchell
Corp. William Robinson	Corp. John Moore	Corp. John Hetzer
Corp. Mathias Roosa	Corp. Benjamin Danford	

Privates.

Bolser, John H.	Bolner, John	Bolser, Henry
Boraff, Michael	Bolsel, John C.	Boran, Jesse
Broadwell, Elliott	Black, Mathias	Burns, John
Bowman, John	Bradwell, David	Bowerly, Tapin
Bowman, George W.	Byfield, Horatio	Cochran, John
Cochran Joseph	Cochran, Richard	Cochran, Samuel
Christ, Abraham	Cummings, William	Cummings, Peter W.
Cummings, John D.	Canter, Shaffield	Christ, Joseph
Card, Abraham	Cochran, Thomas	Cochran, Nathaniel
Doughty, John	Dunlap, Josiah	Elliott, Simon
Everhart, Frederick	Edwards, Noah	Evans, Jeremiah
Edwards, Thomas	Edwards, John	Flinn, Jacob
Finney, Thomas	Frazer, John	Fitzwater, Samuel

Vol. 2.
ROLL OF CAPT. LUTHER LEONARD'S COMPANY. (Continued)

Rank and Name of Soldier. Rank and Name of Soldier. Rank and Name of Soldier.

Privates.

Gomly, Thomas
Ganard, Will
Husler, or Hustin, George
Jones, Evan
Kitchel, Moses
Kerns, Joseph
Landon, William
Mulin, Mathew
Madaris, William
McCown, John
Nash, John
Price, Peter
Roosa, Jacob
Ramsey, John
Slaughter, Jeremiah
Snyder, William
Smith, Abraham
Thompson, Aaron
Tunttiger, Mathew
Willer, John
Whiteman, Robert
Ward, Silas

Privates.

Griffin, Wilson
Harris, Amos
Haggerty, John H.
Jones, Oliver
Kerns, Daniel
Jones, William
Lions, Henry
Morrison, William
Mathews, Abraham
McGee, Joseph
Porter, Thomas
Perry, William
Rude, James
Reeder, Reuben
Snyder, John
Skinner, Joseph M.
Smith, James
Thompson, Caleb
Voorhees, Jacob N.
Whitside, William
Whitcomb, John
Wortman, John

Privates.

Gambriel, Travis
Harris, William
Hoover, Michael
James, William
Kerns, Jacob
Little, David
Landon, John
Mondor, Jacob
McCain, Robert
McCohn, Thomas
Patterson, Moses
Price, Clarkson
Roosa, Abraham
Ramsey, Robert
Shaffer, Joseph
Seaman, Abraham
Taselman, John
Thompson, Joshua
Waggoner, Joseph
Whiteride, James
Ward, Squier
Whitsell, William

Pages 113-114.
ROLL OF CAPT. ABRAHAM SHEPHERD'S COMPANY.
(Probably from Ross County.)

Served from September 2, until October 2, 1812 and from July 29, until August 22, 1813.

Capt. Abraham Shepherd
Sergt. Silas Thomas
Sergt. Samuel Mathers
Sergt. Joseph Bratten
Corp. William McCelgin
Fifer, George Reynolds

Lieut. Robert Wright
Sergt. Robert Moore
Sergt. Terry Womacks
Corp. David Reynolds
Corp. Huston Martin
Drummer, William Reynolds

Ensign Samuel Evans
Sergt. Samuel Buth
Sergt. William Reynolds
Corp. James Blaze
Corp. William Colgan

Privates.

Cary, Isaac
Graham, David
Hatfield, John
Jorden, Samuel
Kirkpatrick, Charles
Kinnett, Thomas
Myers, William
McKilkrick, William
Newland, James
Reynolds, Stephen
Snedakerger, Warren
Snedaker, Ganett
Wilson, Josiah

Privates.

Carter, Thomas
Grant, William
Howland, John
Kinkaid, Samuel
Kanet, Samuel
Letters, Jacob
Martin, Hutson
Nilson, or Wilson, James
Pettijohn, Isaac
Robbins, Vinien
Seller, Michael
Wright, Samuel

Privates.

Edwards, John
Glendaning, William
Hewitt, Jacob
Kratzer, Jacob
Kinnett, James
Morrow, Robert
Mathers, Samuel
Nilson or Wilson, John
Reynolds, Oliver
Sillman, John
Shaw, Anthony
Wyckoff, Asher

Page 115.
ROLL OF CAPT. ROBERT WEST'S COMPANY.
(Probably from Ross County.)

Served from July 30, until August 23, 1813.

Capt. Robert West
Sergt. William Reid
Fifer, Samuel Wilson

Lieut. Joseph Daniel
Sergt. William Baggeass
Drummer, Benjamin Perry

Sergt. Samuel Jacobs
Sergt. John McNown

Privates.

Anderson, William
Griffith, Benjamin
Hayman, Wilson
Laney, Samuel

Corn, Joseph
Housh, John, Jr.
Lang, John
Scott, Robert J.

Privates.

Gilbert, William
Hodges, Nathaniel
Lowill, James

Page 117.
ROLL OF LIEUT. DANIEL COE'S COMPANY.
(Probably from Adams County.)

Served from July 30, until August 29, 1813.

Lieut. Daniel Coe
Ensign, Robert Stevers

Sergt. William Newell
Corp. Jorn Purdon

Sergt. Mathew Gentree

Privates.

Ballard, Lyman
Kingan, William
Sames, Stephen

Privates.

Crusan, Israel
Moore, William
Woods, James

Privates.

Fisher, John
Newell, Thomas

Pages 119-120-121-122. Vol. 2.

ROLL OF CAPT. ELIJAH MARTIN'S COMPANY.
(Probably from Brown County.)

Served from February 1, until August 12, 1813.

Rank and Name of Soldier.	Rank and Name of Soldier.	Rank and Name of Soldier.
Capt. Elijah Martin	Lieut. Jacob Jacobs	Lieut. Zechariah Riggs
Ensign, Joseph Stewart	Sergt. David Flaugher	Sergt. Henry Hawk
Sergt. William Yates	Sergt. Archibald Parker	Sergt. William Dixon
Sergt. James Higgins	Corp. Richard Brown	Corp. John Hawk
Corp. Henry Haidesty	Musician, Jeremiah Martin	

Privates.

Brown, William	Cochran, Jacob	Cooper, John
Creed, Mathew	Churin, Thomas R.	Dixon, William
Dixon, David	Dixon, John	Davis, Henson
Douglas, Samuel	Dougherty, Samuel	Flauglar, David
Flaugher, Henry	Flaugher, Jacob	Fisher, George
Forbus, William	Findley, James	Gibson, Thomas
Godfrey, James	Gotliffe, John S.	Higgins, James
Hawk, Phillip	Hughes, William	Jones, William
Leachman, Thomas	Linn, John	Lathen, James
Middlesworth, James	Middletown, Thomas	McFerron, David
Newell, Robert	Parker, Archibald	Panmire, Ellis
Panner, James	Panner, William	Page, David
Riley, Benjamin	Stewart, Joseph	Savage, John
Staton, Hill	Stephens, Samuel D.	Sharp, Isaac
	Wallace, William	

Page 123.

ROLL OF LIEUT. BARNET RISTEIN'S COMPANY.
(Probably from Ross County.)

Served from July 29, until August 22, 1813.

Ensign John Coppel	Sergt. Icabod Howland	Sergt. Elijah Hendrickson

Privates.

Acton, Phillip	Askrin, David	Brooks, Mason
Bayn, Samuel	Cox, Thomas	Howland, Isatis
Husband, John	Harbaugh, Phillip	Huey, Samuel
Hughs, Joseph	Johnston, Robert	Liginbotham, John
Montgomery, David	Mahaffey, John	Moore, Samuel
Moore, Thomas	Mahaffey, William	Rittenger, William
Sparkes, James	Shaw, Samuel	Shilton, William
Sargent, James	Wilson, Samuel	

Page 125.

ROLL OF LIEUT. FRANCIS CUNNINGHAM'S COMPANY. (County Unknown.)

Served from July 5, until July 23, 1814.

Lieut. Francis Cunningham	Ensign, Titus Everhart	Sergt. Martin Robinson
Sergt. Thomas Biggs	Sergt. Abner Hibber	Corp. James Buckles
Corp. Samuel Pearson	Corp. Thomas Baning	Drummer, Howell, Campbell
Fifer, Daniel Crane		

Privates.

Buckles, William	Brewer, Charles	Carman, Joshua
Case, John	Cochran, Robert	Day, Peter
Ensby, Christopher	Freed, John	Gullifer, Stephen
Goode, Burwell	Jones, Joshua	Lucas, Francis
Moore, Hugh	McKinsey, Nehemiah	McKewn, John
Pierson, Barton	Reagan, Wright	Wilson, David
Wilson, George	Whickear, Luke	Wilson, Isaiah
Waldorf, Isaac	Wilson, Gabriel	Williams, William
Whickear, Asa	Wright, Stephen	

Page 127.

ROLL OF CAPT. NICHOLAS MURRAY'S COMPANY.
(From Jefferson County.)

Served from August 25, until December 25, 1812.

Capt. Nicholas Murray	Lieut. Nathaniel Windryer, or Wintringer	Ensign, John Camell
Sergt. Phillip Fulton	Sergt. George Beatty	Sergt. Joseph Batchlor
Sergt. James Kernahan		Corp. James Patten
Corp. Kames Hakill		

Privates.

Anderson, David	Ashby, Abel	Bayley, Joshua
Brown, George	Blackburn, John	Bow, Curtis
Collins, John	Carrel, James	Carlisle, James
Cummins, Robert	Carter, Bryan	Evans, Richard
Erwin, Robert	Fowler, James	Gillis, James B.
Henderson, James	Hunt, George	Murray, Charles
McPake, Thomas	McClelland, William	Niblack, John
Parker, John	Reder, George	Richards, Samuel
Steel, Josiah	Snyder, Jacob	Thompson, Lewis
Williams, Samuel	Worstell, Joseph	

Pages 129-130. Vol. 2.

ROLL OF CAPTAIN WILLIAM DUNLAP'S COMPANY.
(Probably from Highland County.)
Served from July 29, until September 8, 1913.

Rank and Name of Soldier.	Rank and Name of Soldier.	Rank and Name of Soldier.
Capt. William Dunlap	Lieut. Daniel Coe	Ensign Henry Bayne
Sergt. Stephen Parker	Sergt. Thomas Bayne	Sergt. Ebenezer David
Sergt. Timothy Shirely	Sergt. Benjamin Cutler	Sergt. Arthur O'Hara
Corp. James Henland	Corp. Abraham McDaniel	Corp. John Meyars
Corp. George Davidson	Corp. John Readman	
Privates.	**Privates.**	**Privates.**
Austain, Nelson	Beard, John	Bayne, William
Beasley, Jepther	Bayne, John	Cummings, Anthony
Carr, John	Carter, John	Cumberland, Thomas
Carr, James	Cavet, James	Canady, James
Cartmill, John	Dickins, Thomas	Dryden, Thomas
Finley, Reisten	Fetters, Daniel	Fisher, Jacob
Games, John W.	Hopkins, Robert	Hopkins, John
Hock, John	Hathaway, Aaron	Hall, Joseph
Hineman, John	Hanover, Isaac	Highes, William
Howard, Abner	Henany, James	Jacoby, William
Jacobs, William	King, James	Little, Thomas
Lewis, George	Lang, Elijah	Long, Benjamin
Masters, Vaschel	Mather, William	Moore, Levi
Martin, John	McKinney, Hezekiah	McClean, John
McCoy, John	Neal, Samuel	Potter, Barnabus
Parker, Christopher	Race, Moses	Rewes, Daniel
Snyder, Daniel	Sutherland, Ebenezer	Smith, Isaac
Shelton, John	Shepherd, John	Salisbury, Thomas
Strain, Thomas	Woods, James	Wallace, Edward
	Wright, Samuel	

Pages 131-132.

ROLL OF CAPT. JOHN H. LINDSEY'S COMPANY.
(Probably from Scioto County.)
Served from July 28, until August 28, 1813.

Capt. John H. Lindsey	Lieut. Jesse Marshall	Ensign, William Rollins
Sergt. Robert B. Scott	Sergt. John Higgins	Sergt. William Plumb
Sergt. James Thompson	Corp. Allen Moore	Corp. David Crull
Corp. John Bennet	Corp. William Moore	
Privates.	**Privates.**	**Privates.**
Bachus, Michael	Biber, John Van	Biber, Jacob Van
Benson, Joseph	Bowen, John	Bowen, William
Bennet, Benjamin	Barkelov, Edward	Collins, Martin
Culp, Cornelius	Craig, William	Day, Ezekial
Dilawter, Isaac	Dilawter, Lawrence	Holland, Francis
Keys, John	Kneff, George	Lindsey, William
Lindsey, Peter	Marshall, Samuel	McDowell, William
McKenney, Theodore	McDowell, James	Nelson, Ralph
Nelson, Jonothan R.	Perry, Samuel	Pyles, Absalom
Priest, Richard	Snyder, Andrew	Shunkweiler, Simon
Shunkweiler, Daniel	Shope, John	Snedecor, John
Shope, William	Sikes, Levi	Stroufver, John
Sikes, Edwin	Shoupe, John	Traxler, William
Thompson, Robert	Utt, John	Utt, Jacob
Utt, Henry	Wilson, Alexander	

Pages 133-134.

ROLL OF CAPT. ISAAC MONNETT'S COMPANY. (From Ross County.)
Served from July 28, until September 6, 1813.

Capt. Isaac Monnett	Lieut. Samuel Jones	Ensign, Thomas Armstrong
Sergt. Thomas Reid	Sergt. Adam Bawhan	Sergt. Ellis Minshal
Sergt. Jacob Plummer	Corp. Jonas Markel	Corp. Samuel Federolph
Corp. Humphrey Mounts	Corp. John Wilson	
Privates.	**Privates.**	**Privates.**
Andersin, Griffith	Biaccus, Joseph	Bowsher, William
Brown, Henry	Caldwell, William	Cade, Robert
Caldwell, Alexander	Clayton, William	Campbell, Hiram
Dresbach, Benjamin	Depbach, Henry	Dunn, Christian
Davis, Albar C.	Dunn, Peter	Dyser, Stephen
Dunn, Henry	Doty, John M.	Exline, Edward
Ferrin, Daniel	Frye, George	Glover, William
Goodenough, Solomon	Hinton, Thomas	Hedington, John
Higgins, Lemuel	Haynes, Frederick	Heinly, Jacob
Holverstott, Jacob	Henry, James	Harper, John
Ingham, Isaiah	Jones, Henry	Jones, Davis
Justine, Jesse	Knife, Peter	Moss, Joseph
Mullott, John	Moses, Jacob	Myers, Jacob
Miller, John	Morris, Jeremiah	Niece, Andrew
Patten, Thomas	Ross, Solomon	Reedy, Michael
Reedy, John	Strosser, Peter	Straw, Solomon
Spong, John	Stutterbach, John	Signer, George
Strosser, Henry	Throgmorton, John	Throgmorton, Peter
Van Blarecon, Samuel	Weider, Henry	White, Jeremiah
	Warline, Samuel	

Page 135. Vol. 2.

ROLL OF CAPT. JOHN A. COLLINS' COMPANY. (County Unknown.)

Served from July 31, until August 14, 1813.

Rank and Name of Soldier.	Rank and Name of Soldier.	Rank and Name of Soldier.
Capt. John A. Collins	Lieut. Ellison Martin	Ensign, John McClung
Sergt. John McCrorg	Sergt. John Trusner	Sergt. John Shaw
Sergt. Abraham Hiestand	Corp. John Cook	Corp. Christian Hiestand
Corp. William Kennard	Corp. Moses Thompson	Drummer, David Thompson
Privates.	**Privates.**	**Privates.**
Arendt, Peter	Brown, David	Bretz, Conrad
Bretz, John	Collins, John	Frieze, Peter
Hufford, Daniel	Hunsbach, Conrad	Herod, James
Hutchinson, James	Lariner, John	Martin, James
Mawyers, Jacob	Phelph, Hezekiah	Shaw, Andrew
Smith, William	Stephenson, Elijah	Shisler, John
Swarts, Frederick	Thompson, William	Wills, Samuel
Wolf, Henry		

Page 136.

ROLL OF CAPT. JONOTHAN BABB'S COMPANY. (County Unknown.)

Served from July 31, until August 14, 1813.

Capt. Jonothan Babb	Lieut. Thomas Hammond	Ensign, George Frunk
Sergt. Jacob Maines	Sergt. Jacob Collins	Sergt. Jacob Trout
Corp. Isaiah Buck	Corp. John Smith	Drummer, John Finke
Fifer, William Lashly		
Privates.	**Privates.**	**Privates.**
Alexander, James	Breome, George	Brandt, John
Hardin, James	Jackson, George	Jarvis, William
McGehron, John	Reynolds, Levi	Reed, William
Staimates, Peter	Shiner, Daniel	Trout, John

Page 137.

ROLL OF CAPT. JOHN DAVIDSON'S COMPANY.
(Probably from Adams County.)

Served from July 28, until September 8, 1813.

Capt. John Davidson	Lieut. Andrew McIntire	Ensign, Robert Glasgon
Ensign, Absalom Kirkpatrick	Ensign, James McIntire	Ensign, Edward Scott
Ensign, James Campbell	Corp. James Stockwell	Corp. Hugh Montgomery
Corp. Jacob Sebret	Corp. John Wallis	Drummer, Jacob Storms
Fifer, Andrew Burns	Wagoner, John Hayes	
Privates.	**Privates.**	**Privates.**
Beard, Samuel	Campbell, George	Cain, Jesse
Campbell, William	Cain, Stephen	Dryden, William
Drenan, David	Elliott, Andrew	Elliott, Robert Jr.
Featherkille, Andrew	Fenton, Samuel	Goody, John
Izzard, Eli	Kemp, Richard	Kirkpatrick, George
Kirkpatrick, Samuel	Kirkpatrick, James	Lockart, Moses
Montgomery, Adam	Murphy, Robert	Marshall, David
Moore, Michael	McIntire, William	McCheney, Alexander
Pelson, Francis	Paris, William	Penniwit, Mark
Pyke, William	Robbins, John	Redman, William
Robbins, Thomas	Smith, John	Simons, Jacob
Tucker, Levin	Vanpelt, John	Williamson, Timothy, Jr.
Williamson, Timothy, Sr.	White, John	Whaley, John

Page 139.

ROLL OF CAPT. ROBERT RUSSELL'S COMPANY. (County Unknown.)

Served from July 28, until September 8, 1813.

Capt. Robert Russell	Lieut. Samuel Davidson	Ensign, John Harris
Sergt. Joseph Westbrook	Sergt. Simion Smith	Sergt. James Hayslip
Sergt. William Riggs	Corp. Daniel Cline	Corp. Joseph McGlone
Corp. Robert Conn	Corp. Mathew Kincaid	
Privates.	**Privates.**	**Privates.**
Adams, Henry H.	Akins, William	Anderson, John
Black, James	Brikan, Absalom	Cannon, John
Colvin, George	Eaton, Thomas R.	Foster, Samuel
Fethers, Charles	Fetters, Michael	Hutson, William
Henderson, Thomas	Hughes, Samuel	Keyon, Daniel
Kilpatrick, John	Leech, James	Leech, John
McClaren, James	Nixon, William	Oldrid, John
Nash, Thomas	Pennewit, Tavender	Pollard, Robert
Russell, Alexander	Riggs, James	Scott, Moses
Stickler, John	Stout, Josiah	Stethern, William
Smith, William	Storer, William	Tucker, Kelley
Thompson, Hugh	Thatcher, Joseph	Wood, Joseph
Washborn, Abraham	Young, George	

ROLL OF CAPT. WATSON DOUGLAS' COMPANY.
(Probably from Ross County.)
Served from July 29, until August 26, 1813.

Rank and Name of Soldier.
Capt. Watson Douglas
Corp. Robert Morrow
Privates.
Bell, Joseph
Coffey, John
Duval, Samuel
Elwood, William
Elwood, George
Hickson, Joseph
Leverton, Daniel
McVilan, Thomas
Patten, William
Strain, John R.
Thurman, Daniel

Rank and Name of Soldier.
Sergt. Gavin Mitchell
Privates.
Bell, Josiah D.
Clevenger, Titus
Eray, Nathan
Elwood, Henry
Garret, William
Johnston, Andrew
Lloyd, Charles
Minor, Rufus
Strain, Thomas
Thornton, John
Wright, William
West, Herman K.

Rank and Name of Soldier.
Sergt. Alexander Morrow
Corp. Edward Bian
Privates.
Ballard, Thomas
Combs, Joeb
Eisley, Aaron
Elwood, Robert
Hughey, William
Johnston, James
Morrow, William
Patten, James
Strain, David
Thurman, Thomas
Wright, James

ROLL OF LIEUT. JOSEPH DRYDEN'S COMPANY.
(Probably from Ross County.)
Served from July 29, until August 26, 1813.

Lieut. Joseph Dryden
Corp. Robert Patterson
Privates.
Adair, Hugh
Chaney, Nathan
Creek, James
Jolly, William
Nelson, Charles
Tomlin, Terry

Sergt. John Worson
Privates.
Benjamin, John
Creed, D. C.
Creek, Jacob
Joslin, William
Robbins, Thomas
Troupe, Jacob

Sergt. Newton Doggett
Privates.
Beason, Benjamin
Creed, James
Gamer, Reuben
Murfin, William
Shinn, George
Vanzant, James

ROLL OF CAPT. ROBERT KERR'S COMPANY.
(Probably from Adams County.)
Served from July 28, until September 8, 1813.

Capt. Robert Kerr
Sergt. Samuel Burkett
Sergt. Mathew Williams
Corp. William Newman
Privates.
Allen, Liman
Copas, Thomas
Dilworth, William
Ellison, George
Freeland, Isaac
Helmer, George
Jones, Mathew
Moore, Henry
Mitchell, George
McDermit, David
Peterson, Thomas
Roebuck, Aaron
Storey, William

Lieut. William Wickoff
Sergt. Benjamin Kennels
Corp. Samuel McClure
Corp. Nathaniel Newman
Privates.
Brewer, Charles
Cane, Cornelius
DeCamps, David
Fry, Henry
Grooms, John
Jack, Andrew
King, Patrick
Moore, Aaron
McCoy, James
McCall, James
Pile, Henry
Stuce, Henry
Waggoner, Adam
Young, William

Ensign James Davis
Sergt. Turmin Moore
Corp. Jacob Hempleman
Fifer, John Copas
Privates.
Buzzard, Henry
Collier, Daniel
Engle, Thomas
Freeland, Aaron
Helterbrand, Solomon
Jack, James
Kerr, Samuel
Murphy, Asa
McColum, Isaac
Osman, Jabus
Rodgers, John
Shewmaker, Solomon
Williams, Joseph

ROLL OF CAPT. WILLIAM KEY'S COMPANY.
(Probably from Ross County.)
Served from April 27, until June 30, 1812.

Capt. William Keys
Sergt. James Foster
Sergt. John Irwin
Corp. Richard Cavett
Privates.
Bachan, John
Chonay, Ralph
Dolsen, Peter
England, Titus
Fry, Jacob
Graytes, Nathaniel
Hutchinson, Robert
Harrison, Elisha
Jones, Thomas
Layton, William
Maron, Thomas
McCrady, William
Otter, Robert
Smith, Peter
Winder, James

Lieut. Andrew Lindsay
Sergt. Adam R. Keys
Corp. Henry Doyle
Corp. Moses Morgan
Privates.
Byers, Isaac
Cavett, Richard
Davidson, Thomas
England, Joseph
Grant, John H.
Garrett, Edward
Housmond, George
Hoover, Henry
Jordan, Isaac
Lloyd, Thomas
Minshall, Edward
McArthur, Duncan
Sands, Joseph
Sinn, Jacob
Wilson, Robert

Ensign Isaac N. Riley
Sergt. Obed Harrison
Corp. Henry Wistbay
Musician, George Grover
Privates.
Blane, William
Connor, John
Dexan, Caleb
Emberry, Abner Van
Greenman, Jeremiah
Gallbraith, William
Hurd, Samuel
Heath, William
Kerns, Felix
Lake, Jonothan
Moffett, Nath
McCollister, Clement
Sponge, Henry
White, Robert
Wall, Jeptha

ROSTER OF OHIO SOLDIERS IN WAR OF 1812

Pages 149-150. Vol. 2.
ROLL OF CAPT. HENRY ULNEY'S COMPANY. (County Unknown.)
Served From April 27, until June 30, 1812.

Rank and Name of Soldier.	Rank and Name of Soldier.	Rank and Name of Soldier.
Capt. Henry Ulney	Lieut. Peter Frederick	Ensign Henry Frederick
Sergt. John G. Caldwell	Sergt. John Roberts	Sergt. John Crouch
Sergt. William Evans	Corp. Henry Coza	Corp. Henry Roberts
Corp. Henry Bun	Corp. Jacob Gray	
Privates.	**Privates.**	**Privates.**
Bitzer, Jacob	Brown, John	Bawn, John
Bush, Joseph	Bitzer, William	Bunn, David
Cox, James	Cozad, Joe	Cozad, Daniel
Caldwell, William	Clark, Thomas	Campbell, Thomas
Claypool, Jacob	Cannor, Aaron	DeHaven, John
DeHaven, Abraham	DeHaven, Harman	Dysart, Joseph
Dillon, William	Elder, Thomas	Exline, Edward
Elder, James	Ferguson, John	Finnemore, John
Frederick, Solomon	Fugate, Samuel	Gump, William
Hurt, Clement	Hays, John	Jenkins, James
James, Samuel	Johnston, William	Kempt, John
King, Garret	Lynes, William	Miller, Jesse
Maden, Alfred	McKanna, Hugh	McCall, Samuel
Nelson, John	Ritten, Henry	Ruse, Jeremiah
Richardson, Jonothan	Simes, William	Shruh Garnett
Steel, Samuel	Tidd, Moses	Teets, Lawrence
Vanhoot, Thomas	Wolf, Henry	Waggoner, John
	Webster, John	

Pages 151-152.
ROLL OF CAPT. DAVID RUPE'S (or Roop) COMPANY. (Probably from Scioto County.)
Served from April 27, until September 30, 1812.

Capt. David Rupe or Roop	Lieut. Thomas Arnold	Ensign Richard McDugal
Sergt. Benjamin Rankins	Sergt. James Cochran	Sergt. William Coberly
Sergt. Meshach Plowman	Corp. Beasan Faily	Corp. John Carey
Corp. Thomas Bevins	Corp. Daniel Rardin	Drummer, Enos Mustard
Privates.	**Privates.**	**Privates.**
Brewer, Richard	Collins, Thomas	Clark, John
Carey, William	Darlington, Abisha	Dover, James
Deve, William	Feuit, Gabriel	Glaze, John
Glaze, Pachart	Glaze, Andrew	Groninger, John
Groninger, Abraham	Hollan, James Mill	Harris, William
Leforgah, John	Moore, John	Mustard, Joseph
Moholen, Charles	McDougal, George	McDougal, Joseph
Noel, John Sr.	Noel, John Jr.	Noel, Daniel
Noel, Peter Sr.	Noel, Peter Jr.	Noel, Abraham
Noel, Jacob	Noel, Phillip	Nicols, Joseph
Nicholas, Noel	Rinely, Henry	Randan, John
Randan, James	Smith, John	Shelpman, Spicer
Smith, Isaac	Steward, Paul	Smith, John
Stewart, Paul	Willcoxen, Walta	Wilcoxen, Levin
Williamson Francis	Wright, William	Wilcoxen, George
	Wilcoxen, Thomas	

Pages 153-154.
ROLL OF CAPT. JOSIAH LOCKHART'S COMPANY. (County Unknown.)
Served from May 4 until July 4, 1812.

Capt. Josiah Lockhart	Lieut. Edward Wade	Lieut. John Woods
Ensign William Robbins	Sergt. William Adams	Sergt. James Bradfield
Sergt. John Bryan	Sergt. John Higgenbotham	Corp. Jacob Copple
Corp. James Peaseley	Corp. Fountain Pemberton	Corp. John Downing
Corp. Enoch Laycock	Fifer, John Grimmings	
Privates.	**Privates.**	**Privates.**
Aldrid, John	Adams, David	Bonner, Reuben
Booncutter, Martin	Borcin, John	Berry, Joseph
Bergls, James	Baughman, John	Burcaw, Peter
Cartmile, John	Conn, Joshua	Crawford, George
Collier, Thomas	Cameron, Augus	Earley, George
Greenley, William	Groomer, Abraham	Horsberry, John
Hemphill, John	Hayes, John	Highbans, William
Jones, Benjamin	Jennings, John	Kultz, John
Lucas, James	Laycock, William	Lane, Elias, Jr.
Lockhart, Robert	Laycock, Moses	Losh, Charles
Laycock, Levi	Moore, Samuel	Murphy, William
Miller, James	Murphy, Asa	Malory, Lamon
Moore, Corp. Samuel	McElroy, James	McKinney, George
McCollester, Samuel	McCollester, John	Osman, Zodoc
Odell, John W.	Parker, Hiram	Page, David
Pitty, John	Pucket, Redmond	Robinson, Richard
Redmond, William	Reed, John	Robinson, William
Soms, Nehemiah	Segert, Thomas	Stephenson, James
Stivers, Samuel H.	Sharp, Hugh	Stephenson, William
Stanbury, John	Spiers, William	Thomas, William
Underwood, Benjamin	Washburn, John	Williams, Benjamin
Wright, John	Ellis, Samuel, Drummer	

Pages 155-156. Vol. 2.

ROLL OF CAPT. SAMUEL SPANGLER'S COMPANY. (County Unknown.)

Served from July 31, 1813, until January 1, 1815.

Rank and Name of Soldier.	Rank and Name of Soldier.	Rank and Name of Soldier.
Capt. Samuel Spangler	Ensign Samuel Nigh	Lieut. Daniel Lethers
Sergt. George Nigh	Sergt. Daniel Peters	Sergt. Jacob Hoke
Sergt. David Campbell	Corp. Jacob Peters	Corp. Zephamah Dixon
Corp. James Decker	Corp. John Henry	Corp. Henry Christy
Corp. Peter Good	Sergt. George Delshaver	Sergt. John Christie
Musician, Adam Nigh	Musician, Michael Kisner	

Privates.

Allen, Aaron	Allen, Moses	Antricks, Frederick
Barr, Thomas	Bloo, Frederick	Bruner, Jacob
Beul, Joseph	Baumgardner, John	Brine, George
Baumgardner, Henry	Bruner, Jacob	Bresslee, Jacob
Brian, Caleb	Bobbenmyer, John	Conrad, John
Clayton, Henry	Detzler, Daniel	Ditto, John
DeLong, Isaac	Dilshaver, Henry	Duke, Joseph
Decker, James	Everman, John	Farrell, Noah
Fassnaught, Jacob	Hialt, Hezekiah	Hyett, William
Hoffman, Frederick	Heighey, Nathan	Harnel, George
Huffer, Isaac	Huffer, Henry	Hunter, Thomas
Hiland, Edward	Kunp, Jacob	Miller, Bush
Mooney, Jacob	Neff, Jacob	Neff, John
Neff, George	Nigh, John	Owen, James
Pimcions, Peter	Peters, Daniel	Riggan, John
Road, Daniel	Ridenour, George	Ridenour, Michael
Ridenour, John	Stall, Alexander	Sholenberger, Jonas
Shaw, Alexander	Stall, Isaac	Shoop, John
Vandey, Jacob	Wheeler, Thomas	Wiand, Frederick
Waibt, George	Weshamer, Frederick	

Pages 157-158.

ROLL OF CAPT. JAMES CRITTEN'S COMPANY.
(Probably from Licking County.)

Served from July 30 until August 16, 1813.

Capt. James Critten	Lieut. Jeremiah Johnson	Ensign William Evans
Sergt. Jacob Stult	Sergt. John Levenston	Sergt. James Cunningham
Sergt. James Ward	Corp. Jacob Hahn	Corp. Samuel Murfoot
Corp. Adam Stultz	Corp. James Cauel	

Privates.

Baker, Ephraim	Boucher, John	Baker, Joseph
Bawick, William	Carlisle, John	Cocclon, Jeremiah
Channel, Joseph	Cool, Isaac	Denman, William
Denman, Hathaway	Dunn, Benjamin	DeWeese, Get
Doty, William	Duke, Levi	Elliott, Alexander
Gladman, Thomas	Gilmore, John	Green, William
Gibson, James	Harding, Abraham	Harris, Isaac
Hoover, Eli	Hoover, Sam	Harris, Joshua
Livingston, Tobias	Little, Shubel	Moody, John
Montgomery, William	Nicholas, Joseph	Nicholas, John
Robe, William	Simpson, Isaac	Suthard, Francis
Shadwick, James	Shepard, James	Simpson, William
Silers, William	Wells, Osmond	Whealer, Samuel
Wilson, Benjamin		

Pages 159-160.

ROLL OF CAPT. PETER LAMB'S COMPANY. (County Unknown.)

Served from July 31 until August 4, 1813, and from August 31, 1813, until March 4, 1814.

Capt. Peter Lamb	Lieut. Thomas McMachten	Lieut. William Wagner
Ensign William Hill	Sergt. Jobe Baker	Sergt. David Geiger
Sergt. Abraham Miller	Sergt. Henry Baker	Sergt. Hugh Mills
Sergt. Abraham Rean	Sergt. Lemuel Steel	Sergt. Frederick Stonebring
Corp. Daniel Baker	Corp. Samuel Trovinger	Corp. Samuel Baker
Corp. George McNames	Corp. Henry Bratz	Corp. Michael Spiedle
Corp. William M. Moore	Corp. Benjamin William	Drummer, John Beaver
Fifer, Isaac Becker		

Privates.

Brombach, Daniel	Ashbaugh, John	Ashbaugh, Frederick
Bryan, William	Brown, Joseph	Baldin, James
Brookhart, Henry	Borrow, Joseph	Bellaire, John
Cugy, Jacob	Croffad, Robert	Conner, Abraham
Disherty, Joseph	Dupret, John B.	Duplete, Lanis
Farmer, William	Fouler, Miles	Fitzgerald, Henry
Funk, Daniel	Geiger, Jacob	Geiger, Martin
Gaster, John	Hite, Samuel	Hite, Joseph
Hill, Jonothan	Hoover, Joseph	Hashbarger, David
Hamnon, Michael	Hall, Daniel	Lamb, William
Lemmon, Adam	Lampher, Hynser	Lambright, John

Vol. 2.

ROLL OF CAPT. PETER LAMB'S COMPANY. (Continued)

Rank and Name of Soldier.

Privates.
- Mires, Jacob
- Murphy, David
- Mackeral, John
- Nolen, Samuel
- Reed, John
- Roods, Benjamin
- Reynolds, Ephraim
- Siple, Frederick
- Stupe, William
- Troovinger, Samuel
- Watson, Richard

Rank and Name of Soldier.

Privates.
- Morehart, Christian
- Mason, Thomas
- McNaghten, James
- Poling, Samuel
- Rely, Jacob
- Reynolds, Thomas
- Rudloph, Henry
- Sturgeon, Robert
- Signar, George
- Wagg, Phillip
- Winters, Abraham

Rank and Name of Soldier.

Privates.
- Mock, Daniel
- Murray, John
- McCrary, Solomon
- Reed, Stephen
- Roods, William
- Reynolds, Dickerson
- Raredon, Smith, John C.
- Springer, Henry
- Soledy, Frederick
- Watson, James
- Young, John

Page 161.

ROLL OF CAPT. ABRAHAM MYERS' COMPANY. (County Unknown.)

Served from July 31, until August 15, 1813.

- Capt. Abraham Myers
- Sergt. John Ridenour
- Sergt. Thomas Shelby
- Corp. William Hunter

- Lieut. John List
- Sergt. Eli Barker
- Corp. John Roberts
- Corp. Joseph England

- Ensign Jacon Gardner
- Sergt. John Tarrance
- Corp. Thomas Smith

Privates.
- Benhelmer, John
- Bressler, Jacob
- Bressler, Valentine
- Ehuman, John
- Hufferd, Isaac
- Kessler, Samuel
- Ridenour, George

Privates.
- Bobenmoyer, George
- Bobenmoyer, John
- Barr, John
- Hunter, Robert
- Hufferd, Henry
- Morris, James
- Weaver, Jacob

Privates.
- Bryan, Caleb
- Brandhever, Adam
- Bobenmoyer, Samuel
- Hyland, Edward
- Hunter, Thomas
- Ridenour, Michael

Page 162.

ROLL OF LIEUT. JOHN HAMBERGER'S COMPANY. (County Unknown.)

Served from July 31, until August 31, 1813.

- Lieut. John Hamberger
- Sergt. Jacob Wetmer
- Corp. John Boyer
- Corp. Benjamin Ausbach

- Ensign John Spohn
- Sergt. Christian Ausbauch
- Corp. Jacob Christ
- Drummer, John Ausbauch

- Sergt. John Crull
- Sergt. Leonard Hartz
- Corp. James Anderson
- Fifer, Jonothan Zootman

Privates.
- Becker, John
- Fisher, John
- Huffman, Henry
- King, David
- Parr, Richard

Privates.
- Dorenhour, John
- Fisher, Michael
- Johnston, John
- Lessler, George
- Spohn, Jacob

Privates.
- Fisher, Adam
- Hullenberger, Peter
- King, Christian
- Miller, Lewis
- Zignen, George

Pages 163-164.

ROLL OF CAPT. DANIEL LIDEY'S COMPANY. (County Unknown.)

Served from July 31, until September 6, 1813.

- Capt. Daniel Lidey
- Sergt. George Overmire
- Sergt. Jacob Pence
- Corp. John Heck
- Drummer, Michael Dittoe

- Lieut. John Humberger
- Sergt. John Harris
- Corp. John Miller
- Corp. Adam Householder

- Ensign Jacob Rankle
- Sergt. Henry Strong
- Corp. James Vanatta
- Fifer, Peter Dittoe

Privates.
- Alexander, James
- Auspach, Michaael
- Brent, John
- Blatner, Conrad
- Clines, Moses
- Fisher, John
- Haritz, John
- Huffman, Henry
- Jackson, George
- King, Christian
- McCormick, James
- Petty, John
- Runkle, John
- Sauft, Henry
- Spies, Philip
- Voland, William

Privates.
- Alsback, Bastion
- Auspach, Benjamin
- Brame, George
- Beard, Bennet
- Denny, George
- Hairact, Jacob
- Huistar, John
- Heintz, Leonard
- Kemft, Jacob
- Loefler, George
- McCormick, John
- Parr, Richard
- Spohn, Daniel
- Strobe, John N.
- Stoltz, Samuel
- Vanderman, George
- Wilson, Joseph

Privates.
- Auspach, Adam
- Bowman, Henry
- Boyer, John
- Beard, Samuel
- Fisher, Adam
- Hardin, Thomas
- Horden, James
- Henderson, James
- Kitzmiller, William
- Miller, Henry
- Petty, Moses
- Plumer, George
- Steir, Jacob
- Stoltz, Henry
- Shirer, Daniel
- Vanattate, Aaron

Page 165.

ROLL OF CAPT. GEORGE HOSIER'S COMPANY. (County Unknown.)

Served from July 31, until August 14, 1813.

- Capt. George Hosier
- Sergt. John Miller
- Corp. John Claus

- Lieut. Jacob Overmier
- Sergt. John Fisher
- Corp. James Baley

- Ensign, Aaron Vansatta
- Sergt. George Blatner
- Drummer, William Boen

Vol. 2.
ROLL OF CAPT. GEORGE HOSIER'S COMPANY. (Continued)

Rank and Name of Soldier.   Rank and Name of Soldier.   Rank and Name of Soldier.

Privates.

Alspach, Daniel
Baugher, John
Fuller, Henry
Nicason, John
Thrash, Michael

Privates.

Antrink, Jacob
Black, John
Knoyer, Samuel
Orwig, Henry

Privates.

Bonslater, William
Edging, Asa
Miller, Conrad
Rader, Jacob

Page 166.
ROLL OF CAPT. JOHN HARRISON'S COMPANY. (County Unknown.)
Served from July 31, until August 14, 1813.

Capt. John Harrison
Sergt. Robinson Fletcher
Sergt. Benjamin Allen
Corp. James Harrison
Drummer, Christian Graybill

Lieut. Dathan Lane
Sergt. Thomas Ashy
Corp. Joshua Cole
Corp. Thomas Burrows

Ensign Peter Huber
Sergt. Reuben Williams
Corp. Christian Morehart
Fifer, Rudolph Death

Privates.

Brooks, Joseph
Bear, George
Falkner, Martin
Huber, Philip
Long, Thomas
Myers, John
McFarland, Walter
Whitehouse, Jacob

Privates.

Brooks, James
Davis, Nathan
Growel, George
Holder, Daniel
Long, John
Menser, John
Russle, Jacob
Wotring, Abraham

Privates.

Burman, Henry
Dibert, John
Hood, Robert
Keizer, Jacob
Morehart, Jacob
Miller, Daniel
Vandemark, Daniel

Pages 167-168.
ROLL OF CAPT. SAMUEL DUNNAVAN'S COMPANY. (County Unknown.)
Served from July 31, until September 5, 1813.

Capt. Samuel Dunnavan
Sergt. Samuel Stewart
Sergt. Hiram P. Rose
Corp. James McGinley

Lieut. Josiah Graves
Sergt. Wothy Pratt
Corp. Stephen Hinthorn
Drummer, James Olive

Ensign Noble Root
Sergt. Joseph Linnet
Corp. Amos Carpenter
Fifer, Jesse Larne

Privates.

Abraham, James
Benner, Daniel
Barlow, Abraham
Cornell, Abraham
Crouch, Reason
Campbell, James
Drake, David
Evans, Robert
Farmer, Elias
Gray, William
Haydon, William
Hunter, Samuel
James, Henry
Kelley, Leonard
Mallory, Ira
Payn, John
Pugh, Samuel
Riley, Jacob
Stephenson, Asa
Scott, Robert
Winchit, Silas
Willias, David

Privates.

Abbot, Elisha
Benner, Peter
Bort, E. Jesse
Carpenter, Samuel
Cramer, John
Donnelly, Felix
Davis, Samuel
Elliott, Cornelius
Ginnings, Benjamin
Garrit, Markus A.
Harris, Jonah
Inscho, John
Jones, Erasmus
Moore, Lucius
McLain, John
Pratt, John
Robinson, Martin
Rigely, Bazeled
Scott, James
Thomas, John
Wright, Abraham
Wesh, William

Privates.

Bowman, Jacob
Baumont, Isaiah
Cooley, Hosea
Cargey, John
Critchet, Mathew N.
Davis, John
Evans, George
Frye, Jacob
Goodrich, Stephen
Harris, Samuel
Hayes, William
Johnston, David
Jamison, Joseph
Moats, David
McKitterick, James
Pugh, Cran
Robinson, Joel
Stephens, Justus
Smith, Charles
Twig, Charles
Williamson, John

Pages 169-170.
ROLL OF CAPT. JOHN BARTHOLOMEW'S COMPANY. (County Unknown.)
Served from July 31, until September 5, 1813.

Capt. John Bartholomew
Lieut. George Hull
Sergt. James Cunningham
Sergt. George Gregar
Corp. Samuel Morphey
Corp. Joshua Brown

Lieut. Jeremiah Johnson
Sergt. Abraham Bennet
Sergt. James Ward
Corp. William Sain
Corp. Levi Duke

Ensign Samuel Hull
Sergt. Peter Card
Sergt. Hannah Fory
Corp. George Hull
Corp. Henry Trout

Privates.

Allberry, Thomas
Burn, Daniel
Brown, James
Critten, James
Coffman, Peter
Clark, William
Elliott, Samuel
Farmer, Samuel
Green, William
Green, Michael

Privates.

Baker, Joseph
Beam, Benjamin
Brown, Jacob
Cool, Isaac
Chapman, William
Debott, William
Elliott, Alexander
Fiddler, John
Green, John
Galor, Jacob

Privates.

Baker, Ephraim
Beam, John
Courssen, John
Coklo, Jeremiah
Claybough, William
Dixon, John
Evans, John H.
Farmer, Isaac
Gilmore, John
Haines, Isaac

Vol. 2.
ROLL OF CAPT. JOHN BARTHOLOMEW'S COMPANY. (Continued)

Rank and Name of Soldier. Rank and Name of Soldier. Rank and Name of Soldier.

Privates.

Hunter, John
Harris, Isaac
Harris, William
Haniel, James
Hamil, Thomas
Johnston, William
Livingston, Peter
Lipengelt, Ephraim
Parr, John
Pogne, Samuel
Stotts, Daniel
Sellers, William
Wayman, James
Wilkins, Samuel

Hull, Uriah
Hoover, Eli
Howel, David
Herbeit, James
Hunter, Adam
Johnston, Henry
Luke, Redmond
Marbed, John
Parr, Thomas
Roads, John
Simpson, William
Sprag, David
Wheeler, Samuel
Young, John

Harris, John
Hoover, Samuel
Haines, Joseph
Horn, William
Iler, John
Kneff, George
Lake, Willis
Orr, Robert
Pickering, Jacob
Sutton, John
Shepher, James
Siglar, Peter
Winegaide, Adam

Pages 171-172.

ROLL OF CAPT. JOHN CHONNER'S COMPANY. (County Unknown.)
Served from July 31, until August 14, 1813.

Capt. John Chonner
Sergt. George Willis
Sergt. Joseph Wells
Corp. John Mays
Musician, James Olive

Lieut. James Holmes
Sergt. Samuel Jameson
Corp. John Moone
Corp. Ben Farmer

Ensign Aaron Brown
Sergt. William Holmes
Corp. Cornelius Lane
Musician, Jesse Larne

Privates.

Bush, George
Camble, James
Dickson, William
Engliss, John
Forsyth, Thomas
Gavit, Markus A.
Huston, Andrew
Hunter, Robert
Jones, Arasmus
McKitrick, James
Page, Jeremiah
Smith, Charles
Thompson, John
Williamson, John

Black, John
Critten, Gabriel
Elliott, Cornelius
Frye, Jacob
Forsyth, William
Green, John
Hunter, Samuel
Helphrey, John
Jamison, Joseph
McCown, John
Ridgle,y Razaleel
Scott, Robert
Trump, Jacob
Welch, William

Barlow, Abraham
Dickson, Samuel
Evans, Joseph
Farmer, Elias
Green, Ezekial
Hase, William
Hunter, George
Iles, Frederick
Jones, Lemuel
Pew, Samuel
Scott, James
Sully, Leonard
Williams, David
Young, William

Pages 173-174.

ROLL OF CAPT. BARTHOLOMEW FRYATT'S COMPANY. (County Unknown.)
Served from April 27, until June 30, 1812.

Capt. Bartholomew Fryatt
Sergt. Thomas Spillman
Sergt. James Burns
Corp. James Salsbury

Lieut. R. Douglas
Sergt. Hugh Woods
Corp. Enos Strawn
Corp. James Lindsey

Ensign David Killey
Sergt. Mark Cook
Corp. William Black

Privates.

Buck, John
Bleekman, Nathan
Denny, William
Ellas, Jonothan
Hopkins, Robert
Hostleton, Joseph
Johnston, John
Knight, William
Mouser, Thomas
Nevel, Robert
Shenfelt, William
Sliger, David
Sullavan, William

Bouse, Michael
Cooder, Jonothan
Downing, Timothy
Edwards, William
Hillary, Joseph
Harvey, Golwell
Jones, William
Milton, Rendal
McFardin, William
Perry, Ebenezer
Strese, Phillip
Salyard, John
Trimble, Abner
Wilson, Daniel

Brown, Henry
Cook, Thomas
Denam, John
Gold, William
Hobaugh, Andrew
Hunt, George
James, John
Marbel, David
McChine, David
Reed, Joshua
Strauss, Joseph
Shaverdecker, Jacob
Wildbahn, George

Page 174.

ROLL OF LIEUT. DAVID STORER'S COMPANY.
(Probably from Scioto County.)
Served from July 28, until August 28, 1813.

Lieut. David Storer
Sergt. Adam Logen
Corp. Isaac Wooley

Ensign James Hutton
Sergt. James Smith

Sergt. Peter Lewis
Corp. William Hower

Privates.

Andrews, James
Cooper, Samuel
Grimes, Consider
Hamilton, Reuben
Salsbury, William
Wright, Isaac

Bondle, Enoch
Dean, William
Grubb, Joseph
McLaughlin, Bonman
Smith, John

Cowper, John
Green, Bun
Hutton, Charles P.
Nichols, David
Wood, Daniel

ROSTER OF OHIO SOLDIERS IN WAR OF 1812

Page 175. Vol. 2.

ROLL OF CAPT. HUGH ROGERS' COMPANY.
(Probably from Highland County.)
Served from July 28, until August 26, 1813.

Rank and Name of Soldier.	Rank and Name of Soldier.	Rank and Name of Soldier.
Capt. Hugh Rogers	Lieut. John Evans	Ensign Eli Blunt
Sergt. Roland Rogers	Sergt. Hugh Hill	Sergt. Pearce Evans
Sergt. M. D. Swearengen	Corp. Joseph Chaney	Corp. Isaac Evans

Privates.

Blount, Andrew	Calvin, Thomas	Davidson, Joseph
Davidson, Thomas	Evans, Dan	Evans, Amos
Ferguson, John	Frederick, George	Hinton, Evan
Hinton, William	Hinton, Benjamin	Headman, John
Houghman, Isaac	Houghman, Moses	Hare, William
Hunter, Thomas	Rouse, Henry	Stillman, William
Stafford, James	Savage, James	Shaver, Andrew
Swartz, Sebastian	Wright, William	Wilkinson, William
Wilken, Philip	Wilkin, Benjamin	Walter, John

Pages 177-178.

ROLL OF CAPT. JAMES PATTERSON'S COMPANY.
(Probably from Highland County.)
Served from July 28, until September 8, 1813.

Capt. James Patterson	Lieut. Oliver Harris	Ensign Jacob Moury
Sergt. Samuel Boyd	Sergt. John Shefer	Sergt. George Caley
Sergt. William Thompson	Corp. David McConnel	Corp. John Gosselt
Corp. Jacob Shafer	Corp. Ozwell Ayers	

Privates.

Berryman, Thomas	Blunt, Solomon	Boyd, James
Barr, Thomas	Barnes, John	Chailes, Andrew
Calvin, James	Davidson, David	Dill, Thomas
Eakins, John	Emry, John	Flinn, Joshua
Flinn, John	Gasset, Moses	Harvey, Samuel
Giblen, John	Hatter, Andrew	Gribby, Frederick
Hicks, Nathan	Hair, Stephenson	Hiltebrand, Philip
Hair, William	Houghan, John	Kingery, David
Layman, David	Lear, Andrew	Malcolm, Joseph
Midsker, David	Midsker, Isaac	Mathews, Peter
Murrey, John	McNeal, Archibald	McLaughlin, John
Pittenger, Isaac	Patten, Robert	Patterson, Joseph
Ray, William	Roush, George	Rush, James
Richards, Augustus	Richards, William	Swartz, Henry
Smithson, George	Smith, George Jr.	Sanderson, George
Vanmater, Pierce	Walter, Gaudin	

Page 179.

ROLL OF CAPT. SAMUEL LYBRAND'S COMPANY.
(Probably from Franklin County.)
Served from July 28, until September 6, 1813.

Capt. Samuel Lybrand	Lieut. Cornelius Casey	Ensign Philip Wheitzell
Sergt. Jacob O. Lutz	Sergt. Jacob H. Lutz	Sergt. Noble Roberts
Sergt. Isaiah Willetts	Corp. Robert Field	Corp. Jesse Willets
Corp. Jacob Whitesell		

Privates.

Busbey, John	Culp, Sebastian	Culp, Peter
Dunkel, John	Fogler, John	Fogler, Henry
Grundy, Abraham	Heller, George	Judey, Simon
Justice, Griffith	Kline, Henry	Koons, Peter
Myers, John	Marts, Peter	Markel, Abraham
Palmer, Jesse	Richeldaifer, Henry	Shisler, John
Stump, Joel	Whitzell, George	Willits, Isaac
Willits, James	Willits, William	Wildban, George
Zearing, Peter		

Pages 181-182.

ROLL OF CAPT. HUGH CRAIGHTON'S COMPANY. (County Unknown.)
Served from July 28, until September 6, 1813, and part served until 1816.

Capt. Hugh Craighton	Lieut. Edward Larkin	Ensign George Deal
Sergt. George Louther	Sergt. George A. Gordon	Sergt. Amos Barr
Sergt. Charles McDonald	Corp. John Laverty	Corp. Felix Miller
Corp. Jacob L. Levi	Corp. Charles Winims	

Privates.

Altman, Adam	Brown, Joshua	Brown, Elisha
Brown, Bryan	Barnhart, Simon	Baker, Philip
Bartley, Jacob	Bennet, John	Broton, James
Cloar, John	Clark, Elias	Clark, Robert
Cherry, Burris	Coonrad, John C.	Coonrad, John, Jr.

Vol. 2.

ROLL OF CAPT. HUGH CRAIGHTON'S COMPANY. (Continued.)

Rank and Name of Soldier.	Rank and Name of Soldier.	Rank and Name of Soldier.
Privates.	**Privates.**	**Privates.**
Cherry, John	Cramer, William	Cherry, Jesse
Collins, William K.	Donelson, Moses	Davies, Samuel
Early, William	Ellis, John	French, John
Gordon, George A.	Hall, Joshua	Hott, Jacob
Hott, Adam	Hoover, Thomas	Hoover, Christian
Holmes, James	Hudson, Thomas	Heifkin, George
Hor, Jacob	Kile, William	Kile, Enoch
Kimble, Jacob	Kimble, Jonothan	Kinsel, John
Louther, George	Laverty, James	Miller, Felix
Menterly, Amos	McDaniel, Charles	McCandless, John
Palmer, Purmeal	Rolston, Benjamin	Rowl, William
Rinkin, William	Searfas, John	Smith, John
Stimmel, Daniel	Thompson, Thomas	Thomas, John
VanVickel, Daniel	Williamson, Abraham	Wilson, John
Wilson, James	Winis, Charley	

Pages 183-184.

ROLL OF CAPT. ADAM BERRY'S COMPANY. (County Unknown.)

Served from July 28, until September 6, 1813.

Capt. Adam Berry	Lieut. John Pain	Ensign John Harnan
Sergt. Parker Lee	Sergt. Adam Zering	Sergt. Jacob Mathias
Sergt. Absalom Adams	Corp. Jacob Smith	Corp. Jacob Repner
Corp. Richard Holbs	Corp. Jacob Zering	Drummer, Jacob Spangler
Fifer, George Spangler		

Privates.	**Privates.**	**Privates.**
Allison, Jesse	Boyer, Stephen	Boyer, George
Bear, Peter	Black, Charles	Beventon, Charles
Cashner, Martin	Cashner, George	Deal, Adam
Diam, Henry	Fowler, Samuel	Filson, Reuben
Fields, Jonothan	Grimm, John	Hillary, John
Hinton, Michael	Hollory, Jeremiah	Johnston, Henry
Lonbach, Henry	Lim, James	Lois, William
Moore, James	Marts, Abraham	Monnett, Osborn
Miller, George	Mathews, John	Mosh, Peter
Mounts, Ormphrey	Myers, John	Mandy, John
March, George	Moon, James	McBroom, Robert
North, James	Odle, Stephen	Pontius, George
Penty, George	Provatt, Thomas	Peters, Jacob
Raybourn, Hugh	Reickeldarfer, John	Saylor, Michael
Simmons, Erterling	Stall, Hugh	Throgmorton, Elijah
Veail, John	Veail, Thomas	Veliogall, Jacob
Veoge, Abraham	Volns, William	Witmoer, John
Willetts, James	Whetsel, Abraham	Whetsel, John
Worline, Jacob	Whisler, John	Wescot, Isaac
Weiser, Frederick		

Pages 185-186.

ROLL OF CAPT. LEVI PINNEY'S COMPANY. (County Unknown.)

Served from May 1, until December 12, 1812.

Capt. Levi Pinney	Lieut. John Moore	Ensign John Gwinne
Sergt. Peter Barker	Sergt. David Douglas	Sergt. William Elliott
Sergt. William Noteman	Corp. Henry Skeels	Corp. John McNutt
Corp. William Johnson	Corp. Henry W. Judy	Fifer, Roswell Chapman
Drummer, Charles Crosby		

Privates.	**Privates.**	**Privates.**
Adair, Samuel	Bennet, Elijah	Bennet, Henry
Blair, John	Bradley, William	Bradley, Hiram
Beardsley, Hyman	Ballard, James	Brown, James
Boyard, Joseph	Brading, James	Champ, Nathaniel
Douglas, George	Downing, Josiah	Davies, William
Downing, John	Denny, John	Denny, David
Edson, Luther	Ewing, Samuel	Frye, Jacob
Frazer, Alexander	Gatewood, Philip	Hughey, James
Hoskins, Jeremiah	Harriman, David	Hedges, Davis
Hedges, Obed	Ice, George	Jelland, David
Lane, Samuel	Love, Henry	Lewin, John
Lyne, Lewis	McNutt, Samuel	McConnell, William
McHenry, Alexander	McLane, Jacob	McCanless, John
Marckel, Ezra	Marckel, Samuel	Noiswenter, Fred
Osterhout, William	Osterhout, Gideon	Pierce, Asahel
Russell, Thomas	Strain, William	Simkins, Thomas
Ragan, William	Springer, Shadrach	Stevenson, Zechariah
Tucker, Frederick	Todd, Robert	Whitford, John B.
Tullis, Jonothan	White, James	Wolf, Charles
Zimmerman, Henry		

ROSTER OF OHIO SOLDIERS IN WAR OF 1812

ROLL OF CAPT. CHRISTIAN BROTHERLAN'S COMPANY. (County Unknown.)
Served from July 28, until September 6, 1813.

Rank and Name of Soldier.
Capt. Christian Brotherlan
Sergt. Thomas Ing
Sergt. Titus Hubbert
Corp. William Bilsland
Musician, George Rager

Privates.
Badkin, George
Coberley, James
Cutright, Samuel
Davis, Robert
Evans, John
Hopkins, Archibald
Hoss, Jacob
Hobough, Solomon
Kingery, Stephen
Loofbarrow, Ebenezer
Morris, Benjamin
Pollard, John
Reed, James
Verdon, Alinson
Warner, John
Watson, David

Rank and Name of Soldier.
Lieut. Jacob Willenmeyer
Sergt. John Fultz
Corp. Samuel Watkins
Corp. Jacob Hasleton

Privates.
Cline, Jacob
Coberley, William
Carr, Richard
Davis, William H.
Fortner, John
Hopkins, James
Hill, William
Johnson, David
Loofbarrow, Benjamin
Messick, George
Morris, Isaac
Richter, George
Trey, Jacob
Will, David
Warner, Robert
Watson, Abraham

Rank and Name of Soldier.
Ensign, William Clune
Sergt. John Tryback
Corp. William Black
Musician, Andrew Fultz

Privates.
Cutrite, William
Coberley, Jobe
Dickson, George N.
Evans, Jonah
Graham, James
Hoss, John
Harris, David
Kingery, David
Loofbarrow, Nathan
Messer, Joseph
McFarland, John
Richardson, John
Thompson, John
Wright, John
Wingett, William
Waggoner, Daniel

ROLL OF CAPT. ROBERT REID'S COMPANY.
(Probably from Delaware County.)
Served from July 28, until Sept. 6, 1813.

Capt. Robert Reid
Lieut. George Teagarden
Sergt. James Tollman
Sergt. Isaac Hoffhines
Corp. John Reid
Sergt. ———— Missamore

Privates.
Anderson, John
Butlinger, George
Brinker, George
Bishop, William
Bennet, Henry
Cuttler, Enos
Coonrad, Henry
Champ, John
Edwards, William
Gibson, James
Hardesty, Richard
Hatten, Charles
Kuikendall, John
Lofer, John
Miller, Joseph
Meet, Bazel
Nigh, Jacob
Punches, George
Swisher, Abraham
Shoup, Jacob
Turner, Daniel

Lieut. John Hedges
Sergt. Joshua Hedges
Corp. John Childs
Corp. Isaiah Bell
Sergt. James Reid

Privates.
Bell, Abner
Butlinger, John
Briner, John
Brown, William
Cole, Joshua
Clark, William
Cup, Phillip
Columber, Richard
Fridley, Lewis
Hagerman, Thomas
Hughes, Jesse
King, Trueman
Henry, Enoch
Lape, John
Moore, Elijah
McLane, Zechariah
Nigh, George
Paul, Zechariah
Smith, Henry
Sockrider, John
Writter, Henry

Ensign, John Cole
Sergt. Henry Bennet
Corp. Benjamin Smith
Sergt. James Lallern
Sergt. John Winterstein

Privates.
Burton, Bazel
Bell, James
Burgett, Jacob
Brown, Samuel
Champ, William
Cock, David
Cuttler, Jonothan
Cupt, Conrad
Gothrop, Richard
Hayes, Luther
Hiland, John
Kilwell, James
Kuikendall, George
Miller, Peter
Morris, Jacob
Noys, John
Punches, Peter
Swisher, John
Stultz, Henry
Teagarden, Jacob

ROLL OF CAPT. JOHN LUCAS' COMPANY.
(Scioto County.)
Served from April 27, until September 30, 1812.

Capt. John Lucas
Sergt. William Baird
Sergt. Richard Hammell
Corp. Robert Givens

Privates.
Andrews, James
Bennet, James
Bonser, Joseph
Cadow, Claudious
Davis, Levi
Gee, Joseph
Hotzenbecklar, Henry
Johnson, John
Love, William
Miller, James
Offner, John
Runnelds, William
Sampson, Violet
Vaser, Peter
Williams, Nathan

Lieut. Dennis Murphy
Sergt. Jeremiah Downing
Sergt. William Clerk
Corp. Richard McAuley

Privates.
Benson, Joseph.
Barber, Samuel
Brient, Isaac
Cochrain, James
Emmins, William
George, John
Houset, Samuel
Lawson, John
Lucas, Robert
Magill, James
Powell, Charles
Stanely, James
Tomlinson, Jesse
Vanrinort, ————

Ensign, Joseph Barber
Sergt. Robert Darlington
Corp. William Nice
Corp. Noah Davis

Privates.
Burk, John
Bennet, Joshua
Clark, William
Downing, John
Emmet, Johnston
Gilleland, Samuel
Johnson, William
Lamkins, Prosper
Moore, Thomas
Moore, John
Rook, John
Samples, David
Travis, Abraham
Vontorer, George

Page 193. Vol. 2.

ROLL OF ENSIGN WILLIAM CLOSSON'S COMPANY.
(Probably from Ross County.)

Served from July 28, until August 16, 1813.

Rank and Name of Soldier.	Rank and Name of Soldier.	Rank and Name of Soldier.
Ensign, William Closson	Sergt. Richard Hoddy	Sergt. William Stachel
Sergt. George Mark	Sergt. Curtis Jones	

Privates.

Crabb, Daniel	Clifton, George	Crabb, Roswell
Cory, Stephen	Camun, John	Cochran, William
Evans, James	Fluharty, William	Haggert, William
Moses, Thomas	McNeal, John	McIna, James
Morris, John	Roseboom, Andrew	Roseboom, Garret
Russell, Pire	Shepherd, John	Shepherd, David
Sisk, John	Vanderwolt, Samuel	

Page 194.

ROLL OF CAPT. JOHN GRAY'S COMPANY.
(Probably from Ross County.)

Served from August 30, until October 9, 1812.

Capt. John Gray	Lieut. Michael Ginsel	Ensign, Warford Bonhan
Sergt. William Stockton	Sergt. John Patterson	Sergt. Joseph Reader
Sergt. Amos Reader	Corp. John Edmiston	Corp. David Taylor
Corp. John Santee	Corp. William Black	

Privates.

Bragg, John	Berry, Stephen	Crawford, Alexander
Caldwell, John	Dunlap, John	Dunlap, Robert
Ewing, Samuel	Gardner, Samuel	Gaul, Jacob
Hartley, Joseph	Hartley, Thomas	Hartley, John
Irwin, William	King, John	Kent, Peter
Murphy, William	Maloney, Isaac	McKenzie, John
McClure, William	Prickett, John	Taylor, John
Truber, Joseph	Tuthill, James	Turrell, John
Warnoch, William	Wilson, Nathaniel	

Pages 195-196.

ROLL OF CAPT. GEORGE BRIANT'S COMPANY.
(Probably from Ross County.)

Served from July 28, until August 21, 1813.

Capt. George O. Briant	Lieut. Joseph O. Briant	Ensign, John Stouten
Sergt. James Davis	Sergt. Lawrence Grove	Sergt. John Bartan
Sergt. John Hendershot	Corp. Providence Williams	Corp. John Leeth
Corp. Charles O. Briant	Corp. Benjamin Bromley	Drummer, James Latin

Privates.

Boviker, John	Briant, Enoch O.	Briant, Peter O.
Beckman, William	Beckman, Abraham	Briant, Elijah O.
Briant, James O.	Beckman, Christian	Beckman, Aaron
Clay, William	Elliott, Burgess	Foster, Lawrence
Fernan, Philip	Groves, Michael	Gardiner, Thomas
Groves, George	Grover, Frederick	Irons, James
Irons, Thomas	Johnston, John	Kincaid, William
Lowman, Joseph	Long, John	Lane, James
Lowman, Michael	Layton, Asher	Layton, Elias
Mustard, George	Marquis, Isaac	McCoy, James
McFarland, Garrison	McBride, William	Powelson, Cornelius
Pillers, Josiah	Price, Robert	Parkerson, William
Parker, William	Strattan, Charles	Skouten, Samuel
Wheaton, Humphrey	Wyckoff, Isaac	Williams, George

Pages 197-198.

ROLL OF CAPT. NICHOLAS CUNNINGHAM'S COMPANY. (County Unknown.)

Served from April 27, until October 27, 1812.

Capt. Nicholas Cunningham	Lieut. John Harness	Ensign, Henry Flesher
Sergt. Eccleston Smith	Sergt. William McDonald	Sergt. William Loveless
Sergt. Thomas Chill	Corp. William McCarrol	Corp. Andrew Hayes
Corp. John Bailey	Corp. Benjamin Rogers	Musician, Ebenezer Mattox
Fifer, Alston Phillips		

Privates.

Berkolur, Tiberius	Becket, Bider	Black, Charles
Clover, Joshua	Clifford, George	Corwin, Oliver
Clevenger, William	Carsey, Randolph	Cisna, Stephen
Clifton, Philip	Donemire, Daniel	Davis, James
Everts, Ebenezer	Familiar, John	Fanata, Samuel
Layton, George	Miller, Adam	Martin, John
Martin, Tubman	Mablise, Joshua	McCallister, James
McCall, Montgomery	Neley, Nicholas	Powers, Jacob
Powers, Joseph	Pain, Adam	Roof, Samuel
Rankin, John M.	Stuthard, John	Saunders, Benjamin
Thomas, Jeremiah	Thompson, David	Thompson, John
Vanveal, Aaron	Venson, Thomas	Wilson, James
William Bazel	Williams, Samuel	White, William
Williams, Joseph	Williams, John	Wats, Henkson
Wilcock, David	Webb, William	Willcocks, Jonothan
Young, Solomon	Young, Jacob	

Page 199. Vol. 2.

ROLL OF CAPT. DAVID ELLIOTT'S COMPANY.
(Probably from Ross County.)
Served from July 28, until August 17, 1813.

Rank and Name of Soldier.	Rank and Name of Soldier.	Rank and Name of Soldier.
Capt. David Elliott	Lieut. John Allemang	Ensign, Jacob Hare
Sergt. William Ross	Sergt. Phillip Hare	Sergt. Henry Long
Sergt. John Williams	Sergt. John Lewis	Sergt. Jacob Myers
Corp. Charles Mahan	Corp. Nathan Rotan	Corp. William Johnson
Corp. Solomon Clover	Drummer, Daniel Johnstown	Fifer, Frederick Recob
Privates.	**Privates.**	**Privates.**
Bishop, David	Bishop, Frederick	Cochran, Hugh
Cochran, Andrew	Cover, Christian	Cove, Henry
Files, Robert	Grub, Jacob	Grub, Daniel
Hopkins, William	Hoskinson, John	Kerr, George
Lewis, John	Long, John	Michel, Frederick
Myers, John	Moots, Charles	Myers, Jacob
McCracken, Isaac	Newland, Jacob	Platter, Henry
Powell, Emery	Rambo, Michael	Stagner, Peter
Sadler, William	Shoemaker, David	Strwy, Peter
Teeter, George	Turner, James	Williams, John

Page 200.

ROLL OF LIEUT. JORDAN MANNING'S COMPANY.
(Probably from Clinton County.)
Served from November 28, 1814, until April 10, 1815.

Lieut. Jordan Manning	Ensign, John Hill	Sergt. Benjamin Harber
Sergt. Thomas Jett	Corp. Richard Dowler	Corp. William Cook
Musician, John Pickens		
Privates.	**Privates.**	**Privates.**
Allison, Charles	Brandeberry, Frederick	Brooks, William
Brooks, Thomas	Butler, James	Chaplin, Francis R.
Conner, Adam	Davidson, Murray	Gardner, Daniel
Howe, Balzille	Hewitt, Aaron	Kidd, Isaac
McMahan, William	Phillips, Jesse	Signer, George
Seward, Samuel	Phelps, Hiram	Terry, Samuel
Tate, George	Wallace, John	Weese, John

Page 201.

ROLL OF ENSIGN AMAZIAH MORGAN'S COMPANY.
(Ross County.)
Served from July 28, until August 9, 1813.

Ensign, Amaziah Morgan	Sergt. David Campbell	Sergt. Robert Darling
Sergt. Levi Wells	Sergt. Righ Ford	Corp. James Irwin
Corp. Adam Gilfillan	Corp. Peter Clover	Corp. Valentine Knight
Privates.	**Privates.**	**Privates.**
Black, Abraham	Baigle, Henry	Devorss, John
Dill, Robert	Devorss, Daniel	Devorss, Joseph
Freshour, Abraham	Farley, Joseph	Ladd, Elison
Slater, James	Slater, Jeremiah	Slater, John
Woolcut, Johnson		

Pages 203-204.

ROLL OF CAPT. JAMES JEFFRIES' COMPANY. (County Unknown.)
Served from August 29, until September 9, 1812.

Capt. James Jeffries	Capt. Samuel Baird	Ensign, John Day
Privates.	**Privates.**	**Privates.**
Armstrong, James	Bateson, Samuel	Bonny, Nathaniel
Beard, Benjamin	Burgess, Joseph	Brown, Joshua
Baird, James	Ball, James	Betchman, Joseph
Bush, Jacob	Carroll, Thomas	Carroll, David
Croy, Benjamin	Curick, John	Cowden, John
Crooks, Jacob	Clayhold, Joseph H.	Chandler, Daniel
Cussack, Andrew	Dusinberry, John	Decaver, Levi
Dile, Burton	Dile, John P.	Edgell, Asa
Edgell, Moses	Evans, John	Embrick, John
Ellison, Thomas	Ferson, Robert	Foreacre, John
Flowers, Joseph	Gooden, Moses	Good, Jacob
Graper, George	Gibson, Thomas	German, Moses
Gooden, Samuel	Howler, John	Hull, John
Hanner, George	Harrington, John	Hamilton, Samuel
Hammell, Charles	Hammell, Mathias	Hartsell, John
Hendrick, John	Kreizer, George	Knox, Tillman
Longwell, James	Mills, Joseph	Martin, Joseph
Mills, Samuel	Phillips, John	Parker, Benyan
Petite, Thomas	Petite, Samuel	Pierce, Nicholas
Ryder, Adam	Robarm, Charles	Russell, Richard
Richmond, Joseph	Rum, John	Rees, Michael
Skinner, George	Stakeley, David	Sniff, Martin
Shaw, John	Stapers, William	Sample, Benjamin
Smith, Jesse	Turner, William	Throert, James
Tonner, David	Tool, Benjamin	Walls, Eli
Wallace, James C.		

Pages 205-206. Vol. 2.

ROLL OF CAPT. AMMI MALTBIE'S COMPANY. (County Unknown.)

Served from August 25, until September 29, 1812.

Rank and Name of Soldier.	Rank and Name of Soldier.	Rank and Name of Soldier.
Capt. Ammi Maltbie	Lieut. Benjamin Haines	Ensign, John Buckles
Sergt. John Gowdy	Sergt. Samuel Larne	Sergt. Joshua Carraman
Sergt. John B. Burrel	Corp. Henry Bist	Corp. Robert McConnell
Corp. James Webb	Corp. Henry Buckles	Fifer, John Nocks
Bugler, Thomas Morgan		

Privates.

Anderson, James	Anderson, John	Anderson, Mason
Barrett, Phillip	Bird, Andrew	Bell, David
Beakes, William	Burney, James	Bane, James
Bussel, Samuel	Buckles, David	Carprass, Adam
Clark, William	Elam, John	Gillian, Jesse
Hale, John	Honk, John	Innman, John
Jolly, John	Kennedy, James	King, William
Lawrence, William	Lamme, William	Lamme, David
Marshall, John	Morgan, George	Miller, Augustus
Mock, Daniel	Martin, Ezekial	Murphy, John
Morgan, Jonothan	Owens, Jonothan	Owens, George
Owens, James	Porter, James	Snodgrass, James
Sanders, Faris	Starett, Robert	Sutton, Robert
Starett, Joseph	Stips, Isaac	Stephens, John
Torrence, William	Towell, John	Vance, John
Vance, Joseph	Williams, John	Williams, Garrett
Whicker, Mathew	Williams, Remembrance	Wolcott, John H.
	Gillian, Andrew	

Page 207.

ROLL OF CAPT. WILLIAM McCONNELL'S COMPANY. (County Unknown.)

Served from August 29, until Sept. 9, 1812.

Capt. William McConnell	Lieut. Jacob Wisecarver	Ensign, John Brown
Sergt. John Handle	Sergt. Samuel Walters or Wat-	Sergt. Robert Willson
Sergt. Phillip Baker	tens.	

Privates.

Ayers, William	Bower, Jacob	Boggs, Robert
Bower, John	Border, George	Bell, John
Boggs, James	Banit, Hauson	Culbertson, Robert
Cooksey, Josiah	Caphart, Anthony	Durogen, Wanen
Echbury, John	Darmer, Daniel	Darmer, Jacob
Hart, David	Hover, Jacob	Hocks, Robert
Hunter, David	Harden, William	Jardem, John
Kinney, William	Kinney, Thomas	Moon, Robert
Moon, John	Mann, Daniel	Muchlin, Henry
McConnell, Joseph	Paton, Robert	Robinson, David
Starker, Jacob	Starker, George	Stout, Jacob
Spurgin, William	Vernam, Joseph	Vernam, Samuel
Vainum, John	Walters, Jacob	Walters, John
Walters, Benjamin		

Pages 209-210.

ROLL OF CAPT. LLEWELLYN PIERCE'S COMPANY. (County Unknown.)

Served from Aug. 29, until September 9, 181

Capt. Llewellyn Pierce	Lieut. Stephen Reeves	Ensign, George Crandalls
Sergt. Samuel Scott	Sergt. John Messer	Sergt. Solomon Devedaugh
Sergt. Sanford Ramsey		

Privates.

Ayers, Lewis	Armstrong, James	Allen, Thomas
Briggs, James	Bell, William	Bliss, Samuel
Culver, Levi	Christ, Daniel	Collins, Samuel
Culbertson, Samuel W.	Culver, Phillip	Chambers, Manlove
Campbell, Archibald	Crane, Evan	Celix, David
Deckle, Moses	Devalt, Isaac	Dickson, Thomas
Dickson, Joseph	Ecleberry, William	Forrest, James
Green, Samuel	Gardner, Robert	Green, Isaac
Green, John	Graham, George	Geer, John
Gardner, William	Granger, Ebenezer	Gibbon, George
Hover, Jacob	Herron, David	Harris, John
Hamilton, Alexander	Hardesty, Abraham	Hoover, William
Herron, Nathaniel	James, David	Joseph, William
Jett, Daniel	Lehugh, Spencer	Linn, James
Murphy, William	Mitchell, Mathew	Merwin, Simion
Moore, James	Monroe, Robert	McDonald, John
McDonald, Joseph	McLean, Alexander	McCutcheon, James
Narman, Isaac	Norris, Moses	Newman, George
Norris, William	Phillis, John	Risoner, Solomon
Raney, Jacob	Roof, Peter	Ruck, John
Spangler, Henry	Sawyer, Porter	Spangler, Jacob
Shilling, Amos	Smeltzer, Valentine	Stover, Henry
Tomtiz, Frederick	Tucker, Alexander	Taylor, John
Tulk, James	Watson, James	Woodward, Willis
William, Joseph	Yoder, Henry	

Page 211. Vol. 2.

ROLL OF CAPT. MICHAEL GUNCKEL'S COMPANY. (County Unknown.)

Served from August 23, 1812 until February 22, 1813.

Rank and Name of Soldier.	Rank and Name of Soldier.	Rank and Name of Soldier.
Capt. Michael Gunckel	Lieut. John Protzman	Ensign, Jacob Suzart
Sergt. Felix Gunckel	Sergt. Peter Shefer	Sergt. Henry Smith
Sergt. John Shideler	Corp. Phillip Hartzel	Corp. Jacob Mullenowe
Corp. William Wirick	Corp. George Wolf	Fifer, George Boyer
Drummer, Henry Zeller		

Privates.

Brewer, John	Chest, Jacob	Emerick, Christopher
Foust, Phillip	Foust, Andrew	Gunckel, Daniel
Gushwa, Peter	Gephart, Philip	Gephart, John
Gephart, George	Gebhart, Philip	Istry, Conrad
Istry, Daniel	Katterman, Michael	Kester, George
Kirker, Jacob	Karn, George	Kaug, Phillip
Loye, Jacob	Leslie, Daniel	Moyer, John
Micksell, David	Miller, Moses	Meyers, David
Nutts, George	Pickle, George	Reagel, John
Stump, John	Sonab, John	Trion, Peter
Ungren, Daniel	Wirick, David	Zeller, John

Pages 213-214.

ROLL OF CAPT. WILLIAM S. DRAKE'S COMPANY. (County Unknown.)

Served from February 14, until August 14, 1813.

Capt. William S. Drake	Lieut. Robert McGowan	Ensign, John Mark
Sergt. William Blane	Sergt. Nicholas McCally	Sergt. Lansing Lewis
Sergt. John Martin	Corp. Jacob Cline	Corp. Newman Mitchel
Corp. Jacob B. Tucker	Corp. Samuel Monohan	

Privates.

Anderson, Ezekial	Adams, Johnson	Berry, Conrad
Blaugher, Jacob	Bowman, William	Bishop, William
Cherry, Abraham	Carrel, Samuel	DeWitt, Barnet
Ewing, William	Francis, Rezin	Grant, William
Groves, Thomas	Gard, Job	Hays, Raymond
Hurst, Henry	Johon, Thomas	Isahart, Jacob
Kensor, Adam	Lampheir, Pierce	Moss, John
Martin, Joseph	Mathew, C. Joseph	Mitchel, Robert
Meeker, Aaron	Parmester, Erastus	Parish, Ira
Plummer, Banach	Rose, Cornelius	Rush, Francis
Simmons, John	Simpson, Richard	Shaw, John
Stagle, Jacob J.	Shoat, Story	Simmons, Thomas
Sherwood, Lewis	Thompson, John	Totten, John
Williams, Lewis	Weeks, Daniel	William Richard
Winsed, Joseph	Young, Samuel	

Pages 215-216.

ROLL OF CAPT. DANIEL HEATON'S COMPANY. (County Unknown.)

Served from March 27, until September 26, 1813.

Capt. Daniel Heaton	Lieut. James Sherard	Ensign Lewis Moore
Sergt. John Davis	Sergt. John Andrew	Sergt. Samuel Schenck
Sergt. Edward Hokmer	Corp. Solomon Symonds	Corp. John Clark
Corp. William Payn	Corp. Phillip Ray	Drummer, John Flower
Fifer, John Johnson		

Privates.

Andrews, Adam	Ashby, Milton	Athel, Furgeson
Allen, Jacob	Ble, John	Baker, William
Burnes, Thomas	Comhwast, John	Cornelison, John
Cornelison, Marsh	Digby, John	Davis, Daniel
Flowers, James	Flowers, Aaron	Flowers, Andrew
Fitsort, Abraham	Gilkey, Robert	Gee, William
Huffman, Jacob	Hougham, Jonothan	Hardisty, Daniel
Johnson, Gideon	Kepshart, John	Long, Stephen
Moyer, Jacob	Moore, Phillip	Morris, John
Mills, Joseph	Morris, William	Mires, Jacob
Patten, Isaac	Patten, Isaac, Jr.	Reson, Bailey
Russell, Jesse	Ray, Andrew	Symonds, John
Smith, Jacob	Sherard, Samuel	Smith, William
Shaffer, Abraham	Southard, George	Sunderland, Cornelius
Timmards, George	Thompson, William	Templar, James
Wesling, Jacob	Welch, Benjamin	Woodruff, Israel
	Whitacre, John	

Pages 217-218.

ROLL OF CAPT. NATHAN HATFIELD'S COMPANY. (County Unknown.)

Served from March 20, until September 19, 1813.

Capt. Nathan Hatfield	Lieut. Charles Johnson	Ensign, Andrew McMahon
Sergt. Stephen Cobley	Sergt. Benjamin Sutton	Sergt. James Gordon
Sergt. Alonzo Applegate	Corp. Henry Riggs	Corp. Robert Hawkins
Corp. Robert Welsh	Corp. Abraham Miley	

ROLL OF CAPT. NATHAN HATFIELD'S COMPANY. (Continued)

Rank and Name of Soldier.	Rank and Name of Soldier.	Rank and Name of Soldier.
Privates.	**Privates.**	**Privates.**
Askin, Thomas	Abbott, Elisha	Birtsill, Josiah
Burnett, Abel	Brown, Joshua	Brude, Daniel
Bridger, Benjamin	Bennett, Samuel	Black, David W.
Clark, Joseph	Clark, Daniel	Coleman, James
Coleman, Charles	Cailey, James S.	Coon, Levi
Dunseth, Samuel	Denike, Samuel	Gray, George
Ganard, John	Griffin, Joseph	Herrin, William
Hunsiker, Waite	Henley, Cornelius	Hahan, Samuel
Hawkins, Rexin	Hawkins, Cardil	Hathorn, John
Hawkins, William	Hawkins, Joseph	Heron, Daniel
Ketchum, Richard	Lindsey, Elijah	Miley, Abraham
Morrison, Alexander	Mathews, Joseph	Martin, William
McMahon, Hugh	McLaughlin, William	McAdams, Thomas
Reed, Martin	Scamehorn, Amos	Silvers, Enoch
Spencer, Ezra	Vail, Isaac	Wells, William
Welch, Thomas	Woodruff, Hezekiah	Wilson, James

Pages 219-220.

ROLL OF CAPT. THOMAS SETON'S COMPANY. (County Unknown.)
Served from February 5, until Aug. 12, 1813.

Capt. Thomas Seton	Lieut. William Ogden	Ensign, John Tweed
Sergt. Lewis Keyt	Sergt. Thomas Scott	Sergt. Joshua Gordan
Sergt. Phillip P. Byron	Corp. Samuel Tatman	Corp. Rezin Tevis
Corp. William Taylor	Corp. William Holmes	Musician Jeremiah Smith
Privates.	**Privates.**	**Privates.**
Abraham, Joseph	Blue, David	Bruse, Frederick
Byrn, Lawrence	Cookns, Jacob	Conley, Rhiza
Debrubar, Jacob	Debruber, John	Foncher, William
Flora, James	Fisher, David	Graham, John
Goodin, James	Holmes, William, Sr.	Jones, George
Knight, James	Kenton, Simon	Lippencock, Morgan
Moore, William	Martin, Edmund	Morris, Randolph
Mahala, John	McCoy, Duncan	McConnel, John
McEvain, David	Perry, William	Ray, Isaac
Riley, Alexsis	Swim, Jacob	Skidmore, Ralph
Shenkle, Jacob	Smith, Benton	Simmerman, Frederick
Smith, Jeremiah	Woodruff, William	Watson, Jacob
Wharton, Henry	Wilson, John	Wright, George
	Younger, William	

Page 221.

ROLL OF CAPT. THEOPHILUS SIMONTON'S COMPANY. (County Unknown.)
Served from March 23, until October 1, 1813.

Capt. Theophilus Simonton	Lieut. William Hopkins	Ensign, William Spence
Sergt. Abraham Hany	Sergt. Thomas Clark	Sergt. James Johnson
Sergt. Samuel Coburn	Corp. Hugh McCullough	Corp. James Kelley
Corp. Samuel B. Walker	Corp. William Burton	
Privates.	**Privates.**	**Privates.**
Anderson, Samuel	Bannon, Michael	Bigam, John
Bigam, Alexander	Briant, John	Briant, William
Brown, Stacey	Coburn, William	Crawford, Thomas
Entel, Valentine	Fargner, Charles	Gillis, John
Hill, James	Hart, James	Livingston, David
McCollister, Alexander	McCollister, James	Orr, William
Patten, William	Riggs, Amos	Snyder, Arnold
Shields, Robert	Swank, Daniel	Snell, Henry
Simonton, Alexander	Thompson, Roden	Vanderwort, Jonah
Vanderwort, Paul	Vanderwort, John	Vernon, Joseph
Wilson, Sylvester	Wilkinson, Moses	Work, Alexander
	Wasson, Theophilus	

Page 222.

ROLL OF CAPT. DAVID E. HENDRICK'S COMPANY. (County Unknown.)
Served from May 1, until Nov. 18, 1813.

Capt. David E. Hendricks	Capt. Richard L. Leason	Ensign, Mathew Harbison
Sergt. Conrad Bonbrake	Sergt. Samuel Truax	Sergt. Samuel Parker
Sergt. John Truax	Corp. Whitesel Dan	Corp. Jonothan Harris
Corp. John Larsh	Drummer, Absalom Starr	Fifer, Adam Whitesell
Privates.	**Privates.**	**Privates.**
Bonebrake, Adam	Bristow, Henry	Bristow, Payton
Bonebrake, Peter	Carr, Samuel	Dooley, Silas
Duggin, Henry	Hand, Chas.	Harbison, John
Kincaid, John	Llewellan, Thomas	Larsh, Lewis
Moon, James	Moore, John	Marks, John
McDonald, Hugh	McClung, James	McCalla, James C.
McCormick, William	McClung, Mathew	Patterson, John
Potterf, Jacob	Potterf, John	Potterf, Joseph
Rimion, Robert	Singer, Thomas	Sarsh, John
Starr, John	Strader, Daniel	Stuart, Chas.
Truax, Nathan	Wolf, Andrew	Wirgent, Chas.
Worshen, Daniel	White, James	Wade, John

Pages 223-224. Vol. 2.

ROLL OF CAPT. DANIEL HOSBROOK'S COMPANY. (County Unknown.)

Served from February 5, until August 12, 1813.

Capt. Daniel Hosbrook
Sergt. David R. VanWinkle
Sergt. Lawrence Swing
Corp. William Johnson
Fifer, Robert Ross

Lieut. Joseph Davis
Sergt. Baxter Broadwell
Corp. Robert Lewis
Corp. William Patterson

Ensign, William Shilling
Sergt. Jacob Bradbury
Corp. Isaac Covalt
Drummer, Lewis Bailey

Privates.

Abbott, Joseph
Barton, Joseph
Bowman, George
Curry, John
Couch, Isaiah
Dowden, Thomas
Fleek, John
Goldalhy, William
Hamilton, John
Ketchum, Jeremiah
Landor, John
Landon, John
Mathews, G. W.
Neely, John
Plicard, Henry
Shederly, Henry
South, Peter
Thompson, James
Wooley, Joseph
Wright, Zephamiah
Winner, John

Privates.

Bailey, James
Bridges, Elisha
Campbell, James
Crank, John G.
Daniel, Isaac
Edinger, Boyd
Flora, Thomas
Gillman, Ichabod W.
Irwin, John
Job, Archibald R.
Linning, Joseph
Lovel, John
McNeilly, Robert
Neville, William
Patterson, Thomas
Strickland, Mark
Shinn, Joab
Tibelghein, Leo
Weir, James
White, Forman
Woodworth, Daniel

Privates.

Burris, John
Bennett, Leonard
Clark, Jonothan
Carter, John
Dougherty, James
Farmer, Fred
Gaston, William
Grey, Runey
Jenkins, Henry
Knott, John
Laird, David
Muney, Charles
McMullin, Loe
Pine, William
Sedgwick, George
Skinner, Caleb
Trukle, Henry
Tomley, Amos
Westerfield, Peter
Warbington, James

Pages 225-226.

ROLL OF CAPT. MATTHIAS ENGLE'S COMPANY. (County Unknown.)

Served from February 6, until August 5, 1813.

Capt. Matthias Engle
Sergt. Elisha Harrison
Sergt. Noah Clark
Corp. Anderson Hunter
Musician, George Painter

Lieut. Henry Henson
Sergt. Henry Hathaw
Corp. William Betts
Corp. Robert Cladwell

Ensign, Jacob Culp
Sergt. Jacob Sin
Corp. Charles Cook
Musician Zechariah Hart.

Privates.

Applegate, Charles
Blocksom, Moses
Bryant, Isaac
Bradshaw, Robert
Casey, John
Dolby, John
Enlit, Thomas
Gilbreath, William
Gaston, Thomas
Hitchins, George
Johnson, John
Moore, William
Norlam, James
Reynolds, John
Shewald, Isaiah
Shingler, John
Stewart, James
Willis, John

Privates.

Bennett, George
Brown, Henry
Basculoe, Isaac
Beach, John
Callthan, Samuel
Daily, John
Frederick, Henry
Gay, George
Huws, William
Harr, David
Keller, Jacob
Melone, John
Poffinberger, John
Ragger, John
Stotts, Jacob
Sewill, John
Thomas, Jesse
Widner, David

Privates.

Burtle, John
Byers, Isaac
Butler, John
Bouron, Alexander
Cane, Charles
Dollerhide, John
Free, Adam
Goodin, Thomas
Humes, John
Jacobs, Jacob
Morrison, Samuel
Moore, William I.
Power, William
Robinson, William G.
Swegart, Daniel
Smith, Archibald
Wolf, Thomas

Pages 227-228.

ROLL OF CAPT. VAN M. HENRY'S COMPANY. (County Unknown.)

Served from February 5, until August 4, 1813.

Capt. Van M. Henry
Ensign ———, Goodwin
Sergt. Conrad Plow
Corp. Chas. Stephens

Lieut. William Thomas
Sergt. Thomas D. Wheelan
Sergt. Gad Waggonner
Corp. Richard L. Campbell

Ensign Jonothan Markland
Sergt. Justice Gibbs
Corp. James Armstrong
Corp. Samuel Dodson

Privates.

Arnold, William
Boyer, Sweden
Campbell, William F.
Ford, William
Frasier, David
Harcourt, Enoch
Ingersol, Joseph
Longfellow, Thomas
Miller, Frederick
DuMont, Peter
Mizner, Jacob
Olendorf, Frederick

Privates.

Davis, James
Chaisman, Henry
Davis, Thomas
Fenton, Jacob
Frost, John
Howard, Phillip
Ireland, Moses
Lancaster, John F.
Mitchel, William
Marshall, William
Norris, Caleb
Plow, Phillip

Privates.

Burnett, Daniel
Cox, Benjamin B.
Freedly, John
Frazer, Samuel
Herrin, Beverly
Hartman, Joseph
Jacobs, John
Marshall, James
Millholland, William
Menel, Adam
Nugin, Thomas
Posy, Armsted

Pages 227-228.   Vol. 2.
ROLL OF CAPT. VAN M. HENRY'S COMPANY. (Continued.)

Rank and Name of Soldier.	Rank and Name of Soldier.	Rank and Name of Soldier.
Privates.	**Privates.**	**Privates.**
Richardson, Jacob	Risner, John	Stout, Andrew S.
Sargent, John	Stout, Thomas T.	Smith, William
Shupe, Daniel	Stewart, Charles	Sherwin, William
Scogin, Eli	Tollar, Asa	Teaboult, Uriah
Torrence, John C.	Taylor, Cornelius	Taylor, Henry
Veach, John	Willey, George	Wilkinson, Joel T.
	Wallis, Aaron	Walden, James

Pages 229-230.
ROLL OF CAPT. JOHN HAMILTON'S COMPANY.
(From Ross or Butler County.)

Served from February 6, until August 6, 1813. Part of company served until 1816.

Capt. John Hamilton	Lieut. William Sheafor	Ensign James Harper
Sergt. John Haynes	Sergt. Adam Stonebaker	Sergt. Benjamin Barry
Sergt. Eli Davis	Corp. Nicholas Bailey	Corp. John Miller
Corp. John Cain	Corp. John Porter	Drummer, Mark Briny
Privates.	**Privates.**	**Privates.**
Anthony, Mark	Abbott, Joseph	Baker, Daniel
Bailey, John	Brosure, Peter	Briam, Joshua
Craig, John	Clark, Daniel	Chambers, Samuel
Cain, Robert	Colby, Samuel	Carlisle, James
Dickey, James	Denney, Joseph	Emerson, Winthrop
Fraser, Joseph	Feaster, John	Flemming, Alexander
Flemming, Samuel	Gregory, Thomas	Galloway, Enoch
Hunter, John	Heaton, James	Huffman, Abraham
Immick, John	Jordon, Robert	Johnson, Thomas
Kiger, Christopher	Linder, Stephen	Martin, John
Miller, Jacob	McCloskey, John	Price, William
Potts, William	Park, Arthur	Pierce, John
Russell, Geo.	Squire, David	Stine, Christian
Stone, Benjamin	Shuckman, John	Spencer, Thomas
Scuder, Stephen	Thomas, Henry	Thompson, John
Vansickle, Robert	Vansickle, Evert	Vansickle, Robert, Sr.
Vinage, David	Winn, Benjamin	Winn, James
Weir, Thomas	Wells, John	Winn, Warner

Pages 231-232.
ROLL OF CAPT. PATRICK SHAW'S COMPANY. (County Unknown.)

Served from February 8, until August 6, 1813.

Capt. Patrick Shaw	Lieut. Jacob Vance	Ensign William Dill
Sergt. Byrim William	Sergt. Richard Camplin	Sergt. Peter Keenin
Sergt. Joseph Dill	Corp. James Kitchel	Corp. John Wiley
Corp. James Kennedy	Corp. William Laren	Musician, Daniel Fister
Musician, John Tuttle		
Privates.	**Privates.**	**Privates.**
Abbott, James	Briney, Frederick	Bailey, Thomas Z.
Burns, Thomas	Cummin, James	Cowan, William
Coleman, Philip	Cartwright, Levan W.	Drake, Joseph
Dunham, Edward	Drake, Peter	Fordice, James
Harris, Samuel	Hibbs, Ezer	Hunter, Nicholas
Irwin, James	Jester, Eli	Little, William
King, Alexander	Murphy, Nathaniel	Moore, William
Moore, Irvin	Martin, William	McCain, William
McCristey, John	Newport, Train	Osborn, Barzels
Perro, George	Rynearson, John	Robertson, David
Stanton, John	Sutton, James	Snook, Jacob
Stearnes, Jabez	Spirling, Jesse	Sutton, John
Spencer, Thomas W.	Tapin, John	Tullis, Michael
Terry, Daniel	Thompson, Thomas	Weer, Elisha
White, Robert	Wallace, Thomas	Weeks, James

Page 233.
ROLL OF CAPT. WILLIAM B. FORDYCE'S COMPANY. (County Unknown.)

Served from September 4, 1812, until March 15, 1814.

Capt. William B. Fordyce	Ensign Jonas Baldwin	Sergt. Larkins Reynolds
Sergt. David Bennet	Sergt. David Newport	Sergt. James Shepler
Corp. Ausbourn Cooper	Corp. William Cummins	Corp. Thomas Moorhead
Corp. Cornelius Voorhins	Corp. Um Stranbaugh	Musician, Aaron Brown
Musician, Samuel Shannon	Musician, John York	
Privates.	**Privates.**	**Privates.**
Archer, Chas. or Jack	Ballard, Isaac	Bates, William
Biggs, William	Burr, Peter	Bush, Abraham
Bone or Bowen, Thomas	Claspell, Joseph	Cast, Ezekial
Coughlin, Jacob	Clebinger, David	Deane, Uriah
Deane, Aaron	Danhan, David	Garrison, Emanuel
Gard, Joab	Gard, Daniel	Hathaway, Daniel
Hardin, Samuel	Person, Enoch	Rogan, Elijah
Sampson, John	Wilson, Joseph	Wright, Samuel

Pages 235-236. Vol. 2.
ROLL OF CAPT. THOMAS SHANNON'S COMPANY. (County Unknown.)
Served from January 13, until March 17, 1814.

Rank and Name of Soldier.	Rank and Name of Soldier.	Rank and Name of Soldier.
Capt. Thomas Shannon	Lieut. Thomas Henderson	Ensign Robert Grier
Sergt. Thomas Grier	Sergt. Thomas Dougher	Sergt. Samuel Marlow
Sergt. James Boler	Corp. John Douglas	Corp. Robert Stewart
Corp. John Dillon	Corp. Christopher Craten	
Privates.	**Privates.**	**Privates.**
Ager, William	Adindel, Cornelius	Blaylock, Richard
Barton, Benjamin	Barrett, John	Bates, Humphrey
Brevard, Charles	Brevard, William	Barnes, Ebenezer
Brill, George	Brill, Henry	Coffield, James
Craton, Andrew	Doherty, Andrew	Douglas, William
Devore, John	Devore, Henry	Erwin, James
Ford Hugh	Floyd, Aaron	Forest, Archibald
Gilliland, John	Grier, Thomas, Sr.	Harris, George
Hall, James	Holmes, Henry	Henry, Francis
Hutchinson, James	Hager, Jacob	Jenkins, Jacob
Kinkead, Joseph	Linly, William	Muizel, John
Masters, Robert	Moore, James	McMillen, Joseph
Newben, Abraham	Pully, Samuel	Roof, Daniel
Rogers, Joseph	Stewart, Samuel	Scoggans, John
Smith, James	Thorp, Job	Thompson, William
Vance, James	Vamoy, Joseph	Wherry, James
Wilson, William	Wilson, Samuel	Watkins, Thomas
	Williams, William	

Pages 237-238.
ROLL OF CAPT. JOHN HOWELL'S COMPANY.
(From Belmont County.)
Served from September 3, 1813, until January 3 and March 16, 1814.

Capt. John Howell	Lieut. Jacob Moore	Ensign Mathew Howell
James Brown	Sergt. Gilbert McCoy	Sergt. James Westlake
Sergt. Robert Millawy	Sergt. Robert Hathaway	Sergt. Isaiah Shepherd
Corp. Richard McElhiney	Corp. John Arick	Corp. John Shepard
Corp. Moses DeLong	Drummer, Phines Shephard	Fifer, Joseph Reed
Privates.	**Privates.**	**Privates.**
Ault, Johann	Ault, Jacob, Sr.	Alban, Geo.
Aurs, Reuben	Brown, James	Bonor James
Belville, James	Boker, Jacob	Carpenter, David
Carpenter, Joseph	Carpenter, John	Cobman, Samuel
Crow, John	Dinford, William	Dunfield, Joseph
Devall, John	Ferler, John	Grimes, Arthir
Hubbs, Isaac	Hartley, David	Joy, John
King, Robert	Henthorn, Adam	Kitz, Joseph
Kitz, Henry	Limley, George	Latimore, Thomas
Lashley, Caleb	Miller, Francis	Miers, George
Moore, Samuel	Miller, Frederick	Moose, John
McGaughey, William	McElhiny, Richard	Noble, Alexander
Petman, Elias	Pound, Joseph	Price, Nathan
Ross, Enoch	Ruble, Isaac	Ross, Robinson
Rutter, Peter	Rutter, Jonothan	Reed, John
Smith, John	Shipman, Mathias	Sprags, John
Shepherd, John	Sutton, William	Walters, David
Silvers, John	Ward, Moses	Vaneter, Mordicai
Workman, Abraham	Wiley, Joseph	Yoke, Samuel

Pages 239-240.
ROLL OF CAPT. WILLIAM VAN CLEVE'S COMPANY. (County Unknown.)
Served from May 21, until July 24, 1812.

Capt. William Van Cleve	Lieut. James Barnett	Ensign David Steele
Sergt. James Wilson	Sergt. Joseph Kemp	Sergt. Isaac Westfall
Sergt. Nicholas Stephens	Corp. William McCleary	Corp. William Westfall
Corp. William Burnes	Corp. Lewis Davis	Corp. Henry King
Fifer, Peter Musselman		
Privates.	**Privates.**	**Privates.**
Archer, Zechariah	Alten, Jeremiah	Brown, Joseph
Butt, Henry	Butler, Thomas	Baltimore, Philip
Berryhill, James	Barlon, William A.	Cox, Abraham
Carney, Lott	Cline, Abraham	Consolver, Jacob
Codington, Isaac	Dean, Adam	Enoch, John
Ellzroth, John	Harvey, Abraham	Harmon, Solomon
Harrit, Robert	Hamon, William	Ingenon, Benjamin
Isenogel, Abraham	John, Thomas	Johnston, Elisha
Kyle, John	Leachman, John	Law, William
Miller, Conkling	Miller, Charles	Miller, Jacob
Miller, Isaac	McLain, James	McCun, John
McGrew, Archibald	McCune, Alexander	McClane, John
Neff, Lewis	Neff, Abraham	Poncott, Edward
Patterson, Samuel R.	Reed, John	Rose, Benjamin
Richardson, Abram	Sathren, John	Scott, Benjamin

Vol. 2.
ROLL OF CAPT. WILLIAM VAN CLEVE'S COMPANY (Continued).

Rank and Name of Soldier.	Rank and Name of Soldier.	Rank and Name of Soldier.
Privates.	**Privates.**	**Privates.**
Slagle, John	Swartwood, Abraham	Snodgrass, William
Speare, Peter	Shepherd, Thomas	Tennet, Alexander
Vanasdol, William	Witters, Jacob	Wolf, John
Woodman, John	Wolf, Conrad	Westfall, John

Pages 241-242.

ROLL OF CAPT. JACOB BOERSTLER'S COMPANY.
(From Clermont County.)

Served from April 24, until May 23, 1812.

Capt. Jacob Boerstler	Lieut. Thomas Kain	Ensign Thomas Foster
Sergt. Daniel Campbell	Sergt. Edward Brown	Sergt. Hally Raper
Sergt. Chas. Waites	Corp. John Conroy	Corp. Samuel Raper
Corp. John Hankins	Corp. Jaspar Shopwell	
Privates.	**Privates.**	**Privates.**
Arthurs, Abner	Brunk, Joseph	Buchaman, John
Berry, Michael E.	Chambers, James	Compton, William
Colthard, James	Colthard, Isaac	Denham, James
Davis, William	Davis, Lewis	Dennis, Richard
Davis, John	Digbee, William	Fite, John
Fite, John W.	Frazer, John	Gibson, Arch
Gould, Daniel	Hunt, Thomas	Hunt, Geo.
Harris, Hiram	Kenton, Simon	Little, Joel
Last, John	Little, Jonothan	Martin, Joseph
Maloot, Sam R.	McCollun, Daniel	McHarm, James
McMillan, Geo.	Neff, Geo.	Naylor, John
Oakman, John	Reed, James	Smalwood, Richard
Smith, Peter	Stephens, Walker	Tollia, Farro Jones
Tuble, Cornelius	Wood, Joseph	Waits, Peter
Waidlaw, Hugh	Waidlaw, William	Waits, Reuben
Williams, Thomas	Walker, John D.	

Page 389. Vol. 2.
ROLL OF FIELD AND STAFF, WAR OF 1812-1813.
COLONEL JAMES FINDLAY, SECOND REGIMENT, OHIO MILITIA.

Rank and Name of Soldier.	Rank and Name of Soldier.	Rank and Name of Soldier.
Col. James Findlay	Maj. Thomas B. Vanhorn	Pay Master & Q. M. Thos. Dugan
Pay Master & Q. M. Clk., P.Q. M. Sergt. Math. S. Spencer		
T. Schenck	Musician, Enoch Jackman	Sergt. Maj. Allison C. Looker
Surg. Mate, Edward Y. Kemper		

Page 389. Vol. 2.
COLONEL JAMES RENICK, SECOND REGIMENT, OHIO MILITIA.

Col. James Renick	Maj. Aaron Strong	Maj. Joseph Campbell
Adjt. James R. Hulse	Q. M. Daniel Hoofman	Q. M. William Gibson
Q. M. Sergt. Jonothan Renick	Surg. Mate, Thomas Shieves	Sergt. Maj. John Stephenson
Fife Maj. Moses Abderson		

Page 239. Vol. 2.
COLONEL WILLIAM W. COTGREAVE, SECOND REGIMENT, OHIO MILITIA.

Col. William Cotgreave	Maj. Jacob Roller	Adjt. David Bell
Q. M., E. J. Hoover	Q. M. Sergt. John Frank	Surg. J. B. Harmon
Surg. Mate, Sylvanus Suly	Pay Master, W. Morrow	Sergt. Maj. L. F. Leavitt

Page 389. Vol. 2.
COLONEL ROBERT SAFFORD, SECOND REGIMENT, OHIO MILITIA.

Col. Robert Safford	Maj. Nehemiah Beasley	Maj. Jeheil Linsey
Adjt. Hugh Rogers	Q. M. John Roadamour	Q. M. Sergt. Caleb McDaniel
Surg. Leonard Jewitt	Surg. Mate William Beebe	Pay Master Horace Nye
Sergt. Maj. Stephen Reynolds	Drum Maj. Benjamin Mills	Fife Maj. Jacob Walters

Page 390. Vol. 2.
MAJOR STEPHEN MASON, SECOND REGIMENT, OHIO MILITIA.

Maj. Stephen Mason	Maj. Thaddeus Andrews	Adjt. Erastus Skinner
Q. M. Rufus Edwards	Q. M. Charles Curtis	Q. M. Sergt. William Kennedy
Surg. Joseph DeWolf	Pay Master Hiram Roundy	Sergt. Maj. Arthur Anderson
Fife Maj. Philo Hall		

Page 390. Vol. 2.
COLONEL JOHN HINDMAN, SECOND REGIMENT, OHIO MILITIA.

Rank and Name of Soldier.	Rank and Name of Soldier.	Rank and Name of Soldier.
Col. John Hindman	Maj. Peter Musser	Maj. Jacob Frederick
Adjt. Jacob Musser	Adjt. John Care	Q. M. John Taggart
Q. M. James Alexander	Q. M. Sergt. James Alexander	Q. M. Sergt. Robert Alexander
Pay Master David Clendenin	Surg. John Menary	Surg. Mate John McKeehan
Sergt. Maj. James Blackburn	Sergt. Maj. Stephen Miller	Drum Maj. Sylvanus Burk
Fife Maj. Stephen Palmer		

Page 390. Vol. 2.
MAJOR GEORGE DARROW, ODD BATTALION, OHIO MILITIA.

Maj. George Darrow	Adjt. Benjamin Whedom	Q. M. Ebenezer Sheldon, Jr.
Q. M. Sergt. John Cochran	Q. M. Pt. George Pense	Surg. Moses Thompson
Surg. Mate Jonothan Metcalf	Pay Master Samuel King	Clerk Joseph Darrow
For. M. Stephen Butler	Drum Maj. Josiah Starr	Fife Maj. James Darrow
Sergt. Maj. James Robinson		

FIELD OFFICERS, STAFFS NOT GIVEN.

Page 259. Col. Daniel Collins, 2nd Regt.	Page 1. Lt. Col. Henry Zumalt, 2nd Regt.
Page 73. Col. John Dougherty, 2nd Regt.	Page 367. Maj. Anthony Pitzer, 2nd Regt.
Page 312. Col. John Mann, 2nd Regt.	Page 361. Maj. Henry Price, 2nd Regt.
Page 382. Col. Allen Trimble, 2nd Regt.	Page 287. Maj. John Willetts, 2nd Regt.

SECOND REGIMENT, OHIO MILITIA, WAR OF 1812-1813.
ROLL OF CAPT. JOSEPH CARPENTER'S COMPANY
(Probably from Hamilton Co.)
Pages 1, 2, 375, 376, 377, 378. Vol. 2.

Served from January 4, until March 17, 1814.

Capt. John Carpenter	Lieut. William L. Stake	Ensign Benjamin Loder
Sergt. William Preston	Sergt. Jacob Fomble	Sergt. John Swain
Sergt. William F. Smith	Corp. Ashur Uloolley	Corp. James McAulley
Corp. William Johnson	Corp. David Seisco	Musician, Nimrod Troutwine

Privates.

Auter, Thomas	Arthurs, Samuel	Brown, Titus
Babbet, Calvin	Bowman, John	Batchelder, Jonothan
Collard, Isaac	Cole, Robert	Clark, Robert
Cogswell, William	Collard, Nathaniel	Cormac, Lewis
Dove, John	Edwin, John	Edwards, Thomas
Gillis, William	Gamble, James	Green, Moses
Gatton, Jeremiah	Hamill, Christopher	Hill, John
Hinckley, Abner	Hathaway, Abner	Johnson, William
Johnson, William	Johnson, Caleb	Johnson, James
Laughlin, Brownson	Lord, Joseph	Love, William
Lyon, Moses	Millholland, William	Miller, Moses
Miller, David H.	May, James	McIntof, Emanuel
McVay, William	McNeall, James	Morton, John
Nichols, William	Neavis, Daniel	Pixley, William
Patterson, Martin	Reagin, Rezin	Russell, Rowley
Rodgers, Seever	Somen, Thomas	Smith, Ebenezer
Sutton, Amos	Smith, Joel	Spooner, Reed
Simmins, Richard	Thornly, Enoch	Tucker, James
Wood, David	Woodruff, David	Wilson, William
White, Alexander	Wright, John Sr.	Wright, John Jr.
Williams, Joshua	Wykoff, Jacob	Wilson, James
Warden, Jesse	Williams, Nathaniel	

Pages 73, 257.
ROLL OF CAPT. ARTHUR LAYTON'S CO. (Probaably from Champaign Co.)

Served from December 11, 1812, until January 11, 1813.

Capt. Arthur Layton	Lieut. Nathaniel Williams	Ensign Elias Baker
Sergt. John Layton	Sergt. John John	Sergt. Aaron Werner
Sergt. Adam Howel	Corp. William Layton	Corp. Philip Mower
Fifer. John Husted		

Privates.

Albin, Gabriel	Albin, Samuel	Crites, Conrad
Gregory, Joshua	Hicks, William	Hughel, Richard
Husted, Moses	Husted, Solomon	Husted, Isaac
Husted, Samuel	Hulbert, Isaac	Jones, Gabriel
Kelley, John	Lawman, Joseph	Minich, Michael
McKinley, James	McDonough, Edward	Ray, Lewis
Reed, Benjamin	Reifer, Joseph	Rankin, James
Smith, Henry	Tunderburg, Jacob	Williams, Thomas
Wood, Thomas	Wallace, Reuben	Wood, James

Pages 251-252. Vol. 2.

ROLL OF CAPT. JOHN JONES' COMPANY.
(Probably from Ross and Highland Counties.)

Served from July 29, until September 8, 1813.

Rank and Name of Soldier.	Rank and Name of Soldier.	Rank and Name of Soldier.
Capt. John Jones	Lieut. Alexander Morrow	Ensign Samuel Kilgore
Sergt. John Robbins	Sergt. Robert Duncan	Sergt. John King
Sergt. Henry Anderson	Corp. Richard P. Johnson	Corp. Jeremiah Lane
Corp. Frederick Dueknall	Corp. Thomas Coffey	
Privates.	**Privates.**	**Privates.**
Anderson, Balaam	Adams, David	Bell, Charles
Brackney, Eli	Bronce, Frederick	Benton, Moses
Baldwin, Richard	Byles, Thomas	Cupps, William
Charweater, Thomas	Currey, Nathaniel	Caw, Nathaniel
Collins, James	Caps, James	Chaney, Gabriel
Garret, Charles	Grad, James	Hutsenpeller, John
Hunt, Ira	Hicks, Moses	Hoten, James
Johnson, Simeon	Jones, Thomas	Johnson, Larkin
Johnson, James	Leaverton, Wilson	Kingery, Benjamin
Milligan, James	Miller, Isaac	Mathews, Ira
Moore, Elijah	Morris, John	McMillen, William N.
Perkins, Andrew	Potter, George	Reece, Hiram
Richardson, Samuel	Stewart, William	Spence, Robert
Shukey, Christian	Sharp, Henry	Trop, Henry
Thornberry, Abel	Wilson, Benjamin	Wright, James
Wright, John, Sr.	Wright, John Jr.	Wright, Samuel
Wever, Stephen		

Pages 253-254.

ROLL OF CAPT. NEHEMIAH GREGORY'S COMPANY (County Unknown.)

Served from January 1, until February 21, 1813.

Capt. Nehemiah Gregory	Lieut. James Crippen	Ensign William McKinstry
Sergt. David Vaughan	Sergt. Israel Wood	Sergt. William Starr
Sergt. David Walt	Corp. Barnet Brice	Corp. David Shideles
Corp. Thaddius Crippen	Corp. William Williams	
Privates.	**Privates.**	**Privates.**
Boils, John	Beeb, Peter	Boils, Martin
Bowers, William	Bowman, Jabez	Cullison, Thomas
Cross, Israel	Chadwick, Thomas	Coe, John
Caplin, Cyrus	Davis, Bial	Dains, Calvin
Driggs, George	Field, Simons	Feltch, Joel
Fulton, Samuel	Foster, Ira	Gibbs, Almond
Hoskenson, Joshua	Gibbs, James	Hanning, Moses
Hecox, Jeptha	Hewitt, John	Hanning, Aaron
Hilliard, James	Haney, David	Hatch, Ebenezer
Haney, James	Husey, Jarvis	Jones, Jared
Kimes, Abraham	McKinstry, John	Paull, Ebenezer
Polk, Alpheus	Rowell, Daniel	Reeves, Reuben
Reynolds, Samuel H.	Ross, Henry	Rice, Jonas
Stroud, Joel	Still, William	Stewart, Andrew
Stewart, Charles	Sloan, John	Sage, Joel
Smith, Jonas	Stanby, John	Varner, John
Wood, Joshua, Jr.	Weckham, John	Weir, James
Waterman, Asher		

Page 256.

ROLL OF CAPT. THOMAS WISBEY'S CO. (Probably from Highland Co.)

Served from July 29, until August 19, 1813.

Capt. Thomas Wisbey	Lieut. Nathaniel Campbell	Ensign Jacob Moury
Sergt. Isaac Collins	Sergt. Thomas McCoy	Corp. Samuel W. Finley
Corp. Andrew Badgley		
Privates.	**Privates.**	**Privates.**
Boatman, George	Bell, Andrew	Coffman, Phillip
Chapman, Isaac	Chapman, Asabel	Duncan, Amos
Gibler, Daniel	Gossett, John	Lantz, Henry
Lantz, John	Ross, St. Clair	Ross, Isaiah
Sloan, James	Super, Henry	Stoot, Jacob

Page 255.

ROLL OF CAPT. JEHIEL GREGORY, JR.'S CO. (County Unknown).

Served from August 9, until February 19, 1812.

Capt. Jehiel Gregory	Lieut. Nehemiah Gregory	Ensign William McKintry
Sergt. James Crippen	Sergt. Isaac Wood	Sergt. Abel Stedman
Sergt. William Starr	Corp. Barnet Bour	Corp. David Shidler
Corp. Peter Beeb	Corp. William Williams	Fifer, Jacob Waters
Drummer Jarvis Haley		

Vol. 2.
ROLL OF CAPT. JEHIEL GREGORY, JR.'S CO. (Continued)

Rank and Name of Soldier.   Rank and Name of Soldier.   Rank and Name of Soldier.

Privates.

Bechs, William
Coe, John
Frost, Joseph
Griffin, Thaddeus
Hatch, Ebenezer
Haney, Moses
Jones, Jerret
Polk, Eber
Reivs, Reuben
Slane, John
Stewart, Charles
Varner, John
Watt, David
Wire, James

Boyles, Martin
Davies, Bial
Fulton, Samuel
Hilliard, James
Haney, James
Hiacon, Jeptha
Muney, Daniel
Roso, Henry
Rice, Jonas
Stilt, William
Taylor, John
Wood, John Jr.
Wickham, John

Catlin, Cyrus
Foster, Hiram
Gibbs, Abraham
Haney, David
Haney, Aaron
Hines, Abraham
McKintry, John
Reynolds, Samuel H.
Strand, Joel
Stewart, Andrew
Vaughn, David
Wood, John, Sr.
Watkins, George

Page 258.
ROLL OF ENSIGN WILLIAM LAMMA'S COMPANY (Probably from Clark Co.)
Served from September 18, until October 18, 1813.

Ensign William Lamma
Sergt. Thomas Stafford
Corp. Moses Fuller

Sergt. Daniel Hubbell
Corp. James Black

Sergt. Samuel McKinney
Corp. James Henderson

Privates.

Batcher, Joseph
Cruca, John
Foagey, Stewart
Lamma, James
McPorson, Samuel
Stafford, George
Verdiar, Adam
Conner, Jacob

Privates.

Brandeburg, Henry
Chestnut, Joseph
Howell, Joab
Long, Brumfield
Nail, William
Simes, William
Wallace, John

Privates.

Black, Andrew
Fongy, John
Kelley, Solomon
Mitchell, Archibald
Reyburn, James
Stapleton, William
Wallace, Moses

Page 259.
ROLL OF LIEUT. ANDREW McINTIRE'S COMPANY (County Unknown).
Served from July 28, until August 22, 1813.

Lieut. Andrew McIntire

Privates.

Auburn, James
Burnes, Mathew
Dryden, Samuel
Glasgow, Joseph
Montgomery, Andrew
McCormick, William
McWright, William
Patton, Thomas
Spurgeon, James

Privates.

Bayles, Jemiel
Gavin, John
Fethercile, Andrew
Milligen, William
Mattox, Michael
McClelland, Thomas
McWright, James
Smiley, James
Shepherd, John

Privates.

Burnes, James
Clay, Mathew
Glasgow, William
Montgomery, John
McWright, David
McCulloch, Alexander
Noland, James
Scott, Moses
Van Pelt, John

Page 260.
ROLL OF CAPT. CHARLES CHESTNUT'S CO. (Probably from Ross County).
Served from July 20, until August 10, 1813.

Capt. Charles Chestnut
Sergt. John Lee
Corp. James Trego

Lieut. David Ogden
Sergt. William Worley

Ensign Peter Clark
Corp. Samuel Vinson

Privates.

Bird, James
Groves, John
Heth, David
Parks, John
Rithard, Samuel
Tuttle, Isaiah

Privates.

Baker, Peter
Hyde, Nathan
Lloyd, Morris
Park, Daniel
Stinson, Hugh
Wade, Thomas

Privates.

Gansoy, Samuel
Gilmore, Robert
McFarland, John
Ross, Armstrong
Summerset, John
Yokey, John

Pages 261-262.
ROLL OF CAPT. DAVID LYON'S CO. (Probably from Ross County).
Served from July 28, until September 4, 1813.

Capt. David Lyon
Ensign William How
Sergt. George Beshong
Corp. Joseph Loke
Drummer, Peter Fisher

Lieut. Levi Hodges
Sergt. John Berry
Sergt. William Rhea
Corp. Peter Provott
Fifer, Henry Rout

Lieut. Abraham Bennet
Sergt. John Loke
Corp. James Tewell
Corp. James Morrison

Privates.

Albright, Henry
Brown, John
Chinworth, William
Davis, Remembrance W.

Privates.

Blake, William
Burk, Robert
Clemans, Joseph
Downing, William

Privates.

Bailey, Stephen
Burk, William
Drake, Jordan
Dougherty, James

ROLL OF CAPT. DAVID LYON'S CO. (Continued)

Rank and Name of Soldier.	Rank and Name of Soldier.	Rank and Name of Soldier.
Privates.	**Privates.**	**Privates.**
Foster, Joseph Jr.	Foster, William	Foster, Isaac
Guthrie, George	Higginbotham, James	Hampton, Francis
Hellenbach, William	Howard, Ephraim	House, John
Higginbotham, William	Johnston, John	Johnston, George
Kellenger, Jacob	Kellison, John	Loney, James
Lewis, Samuel	Lewis, Joseph	Lewis, John
Mathews, Joseph	Mathews, John	Moore, Edward
Mounts, Asa	Miller, David	McCray, Alexander
McCray, Nathan	Nolland, William	Nixon, Allen
Ogg, John	Ottwell, John	Pry, Jacob
Peters, Thomas	Phillips, Benjamin	Provott, Thomas
Parsons, Ezekial	Pittenger, James	Summers, Benjamin
Sewell, Joseph	Sergeant, James	Switzer, Abraham
Thorp, Thomas	Wright, James	Williams, John

Pages 263-264-265-266.

ROLL OF CAPT. THOMAS MORGAN'S CO. (From Ross and Scioto Counties).

Served from July 28, until September 9, 1813, and from February 13, until March 18, 1814.

Capt. Thomas Morgan	Lieut. James Emerson	Ensign James McLain
Ensign John Clemens	Sergt. Nathaniel Barber	Sergt. John Barber
Sergt. Samuel Wilson	Sergt. George Weider	Sergt. Job Goslee
Sergt. Isaac Johnston	Corp. James Dawson	Corp. Jesse Martin
Corp. William Sullivan	Corp. Thomas Lasborough	Corp. James Furnace
Corp. John Thebus	Fifer, John Funk	Drummer, Isaac Wheeler
Privates.	**Privates.**	**Privates.**
Armstrong, Jeremiah	Baccus, James	Black, James
Bell, Benjamin	Baty, Alexander	Bramble, James
Brown, William	Beyely, R.	Ballard, Fountain
Bilsley, William	Baker, Henry	Berer, Peter
Colegrove, William	Crull, John	Cutright, William
Colwell, Thomas	Coon, Jacob	Cline, Jacob
Cochran, Benjamin	Dawson, John	Duncan, John
Daniels, Samuel	Denny, John	Dealle, Adam
Elza, Nicholas	Eakin, William	Essex, Isaac
Ferguson, Eli	Ferguson, John	Fisher, Frederick
Greene, Bunn	Grafton, Ambrose	Gilliland, John
Grins, James	Hall, John	Hard, James
Hatticks, Phillip	Hively, Jacob	Harper, John
Hewitt, William	Howard, Martin	Hook, Jacob
Hobbs, Richard	Hughs, James	Hughs, Nathan
Kirkendall, Daniel	Knight, William	Julin, John
Justice, Jesse	Lutz, John D.	Lawson, Enoch
Louderbach, John	Louderbach, Peter	Louderbach, Conrad
Moore, William	Melvin, Jonothan	Mathews, James
Miller, John, Sr.	Miller, John, Jr.	Monroe, Aaron
Morris, Richard	Murray, George	Moore, Douglas
McCann, Daniel	McCann, John	McCanly, John
McCoy, William	McCullough, John	McFarland, John
McAlister, John	McDonald, Thomas	Niece, George
Niece, Andrew	Peters, Jacob	Ridnour, Frederick
Runcle, George	Retter, Frederick	Starkham, Aaron
Salada, David	Stuckman, Aaron	Sallady, David
Wheeler, Isaac	Watt, James	Wolford, Frederick

Pages 267-268.

ROLL OF CAPT. JOHN RUSSELL'S COMPANY (Probably from Ross County).

Served from July 28, until September 9, 1813.

Capt. John Russell	Lieut. David McMullin	Ensign William Carpenter
Sergt. William Hadley	Sergt. Christian Yingling	Sergt. David Jamison
Sergt. John McCall	Corp. John Salisbury	Corp. Presley Gilliland
Corp. Walter Meal	Corp. John Liston	Drummer, John Smith
Fifer, John Brooks		
Privates.	**Privates.**	**Privates.**
Aldwick, Luke	Abbot, Jeremiah	Brown, Aaron
Bell, Isaac	Bump, Ignatius	Broner, John
Cross, John	Cohall, Edward	Curtis, William
Clark, Cornelius	Curry, William	Chemith, Richard
Conard, John	Cattim, Samuel	Didmerty, William
Fisher, John	Gilruth, James	Grubb, William
Green, Clark	Hepler, Jacob	Haley, Andrew
Jones, Isaac	Kimmel, Andrew	Link, Jacob
Lewbarger, Peter	Lewis, William	Lee, Daniel
Moore, David	Miller, Abraham	Nottingham, Thomas
Nichlass, William	Powell, William	Reeves, Thomas
Russell, James	Slaughter, Ezekial	Stover, John
Spary, Francis	Shute, Richard	Suiter, Hiram
Tawey, George	Vantine, Samuel	West, Samuel
West, William		

Pages 269-270.   Vol. 2.

ROLL OF CAPT. JOHN ENTREKIN'S COMPANY (Probably from Ross Co.)

Served from July 28, until September 7, 1813.

Rank and Name of Soldier.	Rank and Name of Soldier.	Rank and Name of Soldier.
Capt. John Entrikin	Lieut. Levi Willoby	Lieut. Jacob Eckleberne
Ensign James McLean	Sergt. John Downs	Sergt. George Ramsey
Sergt. Jacob Cryder	Sergt. David Downs	Sergt. Edward Oldham
Corp. Finney Collumber	Corp. Peter Fortner	Corp. George Linkswiler
Corp. William Ramer	Corp. Samuel McRoberts	

Privates.

Andrew, Ager	Abonather, James	Boakley, Samuel
Barber, Edward	Baker, Peter	Cryder, David
Crooks, Alexander	Chad, George	Downs, James
Dunlap, William	Denson, Samuel	Evans, William
Echelberger, Stephen	Edmonds, Edmond	Edmonds, Robert
Fulton, William	Gant, John	Gilmore, Robert
Himes, John	Hines, Jacob	Hines, Phillip
Hines, Adam	Hadix, Samuel	Hagley, Isaac
Huse, John	Huston, James	Hutts, Richard
Hyde, Nathan	Immel, Jacob	Immel, Israel
Justice, James	Johnston, Isaac	Little, James
Little, Hugh	Musselman, Benjamin	Mitchell, James
McFarland, Archibald	Overly, Jacob	Overly, David
Painter, Daniel	Parks, Daniel	Rasey, George
Rudesell, Jonas	Severell, William	Sturgeon, Robert
Sidenbender, Henry	Senff, Michael	Spong, Henry
Stinson, Daniel	Summerset, John	Thompson, Wheeler
Tuttle, Isaiah	Walling, John	Wead, Thomas
Wheeland, George	Wheeland, Peter	Wolloughby, Job
Welder, Michael	Winters, John	Yeaky, John

Pages 271-272.

ROLL OF CAPT. JAMES WALLACE'S COMPANY (Probably from Ross Co.)

Served from July 28, until September 7, 1813.

Capt. James Wallace	Lieut. William J. Lee	Ensign, Geo. Stanhope
Sergt. Abraham Miller	Sergt. Edward Caling	Sergt. Andrew Thompson
Sergt. John Kelley	Corp. Frederick Winfaugh	Corp. Hollis Hanson
Corp. Charles Medeira	Corp. Samuel Hanson	Sergt. John Cutright.

Privates.

Argebute, Frederick	Aid, Jacob	Andrew, Thomas
Aters, Thomas	Bunn, Hannan	Baker, John
Bulgar, Elijah	Bour, Adam	Baker, John
Boblits, John	Boots, John	Conner, James, Jr.
Conner, Jesse	Conner, John	Carpenter, Elisha
Clark, Thomas	Conner, James, Sr.	Cutright, Andrew
Cutright, Henry	Cox, Thomas	Dolahan, Hugh
Dunn, Silas	Dixon, Caleb	Eseny, Thomas
Evans, Robert	Ferguson, Isaac	Franklin, Samuel
Francis, Oliver	Gaits, John	Greene, Joseph
Gundey, Cornelius	Gundey, John	Gundey, Benjamin
Graves, Lewis	Hanson, Benjamin	Hendricks, James
Hushaw, Benjamin	Ricson, Elijah	Hushaw, John
Irwin, James	Jones, Henry	Jones, Zechariah
Kelley, Samuel	Morrison, John	Morrison, James
Morrison, James, Sr.	Mooney, George	Meakre, Aaron
Morrison, John	McClure, James	Nichols, Samuel
Neff, George	Neff, Cornelius	Olcott, Josiah
Ortman, John	Odle, William	Pierce, Burget
Pemberton, William	Rowles, James	Ray, James
Regan, Richard	Russel John	Rolbuck, Abner
Salts, Edward	Shriekengust, George	Smeed, Jesse
Tomlinson, William	Ulm, John	Wolf, William
Wallace, James	Wilkinson, Robert	Wilfong, Charles
Wilfong, Christopher	Wallace, Richard	Woolsey, James
Yeakey, Peter		

Pages 273-274.

ROLL OF CAPT. CALEB ODLE'S COMPANY (Probably from Ross County).

Served from Oct. 26, until Nov. 12, 1813. Part of company served from July 28, until Aug. 18, 1813.

Capt. Caleb Odle	Lieut. Arthur McKee	Ensign, Benjamin Brown
Ensign, John Ulm	Sergt. James Stephens	Sergt. Henry Wisber
Sergt. James Trego	Sergt. Richard Reagon	Sergt. Marmaduke Earlick
Sergt. Elijah Bulger	Sergt. Benjamin Drummond	Corp. James Alexander
Corp. Thomas Andrews	Corp. Henry Hoover	Corp. John Collumber

Privates.

Alexander, John	Alexander, Joseph	Borrer, Abraham
Borrer, Adam	Barker, Joseph	Bennet, Peter
Brown, William	Bowers, Daniel	Cox, Thomas
Connel, Hiram	Castner, John	Carpenter, Elisha
Downs, David	Denson, Samuel	Dye, Alexander

ROLL OF CAPT. CALEB ODLE'S COMPANY. (Continued)

Rank and Name of Soldier.

Privates.

Cullember, Phenhes
Davis, George
Franklin, John
Gates, John
Graves, William
Hopson, Charles
Harshall, Samuel
Jurdon, William
Lish, Henry
Mackelheny, Robert
McClintock, Adam
Neff, Cornelius
Pealman, Jacob
Ruddick, Jesse
Rains, Isaac
Shagley, Jacob
Smith, Christopher
Tanquary, William
Vangembey, John
Wold, William
Wilson, Benjamin
Webster, Thomas

Elm, Edward
Elsey, Nicholas
Francis, Jonothan
Gender, Samuel V.
Hotticks, Samuel
Hobough, Andrew
Huston, James
Johnston, Joseph
Jones, Henry
Miller, Jacob
McFarland, John
Morris, Benjamin
Roads, John
Read, Enoch
Roules, James
Sidenbender, Henry
Thompson, Wheeler
Tuttle, Isaiah
Welsh, Jacob
Weetard, Peter
Wilkins, Thomas
Yeakey, Peter

Ferguson, Eli
Foy, Jacob
Grove, John
Hines, Phillip
Hatton, James
Johnson, James
Jones, Zechariah
Mussleman, Benjamin
McClintock, John
Neff, George
Orr, Zebulon
Rains, John
Ross, William
Ratcliff, Jesse
Starr, John
Smith, David
Timons, Samuel
Ulm, Daniel
Wolf, Isaac
Wilkisson, Solomon
Widner, James

Pages 275-276.

ROLL OF CAPT. SAMUEL JONES' COMPANY (Probably from Ross County).

Served from July 20, until September 7, 1813.

Capt. Samuel L. Jones
Sergt. Daniel Bonner
Sergt. Ebenezer F. Scaman
Sergt. James Johnson
Corp. Samuel McCormick
Corp. James Boyd

Lieut. Jacob Eikelbern
Sergt. Michael Ott
Sergt. Richard Armstrong
Corp. George Horn
Corp. Robert Long

Ensign, William Wallace
Sergt. Frederick Fisher
Sergt. John Mitchell
Corp. Daniel McColister
Corp. John H. Swain

Privates.

Arington, David
Bond, William K.
Cissna, Robert
Dowley, George
Footney, Peter
Flemming, W. W.
Gray, Francis
Hammut, John
Howard, Martin
Lunback, Henry
Looless, Benjamin
Miller, William
McKean, Hugh
Ott, Jacob
Smith, George H.
Scott, James A. P.
Thompson, William
Watson, David

Bell, George
Bowman, Robert
Copes, William
Evans, Job
Fultz, Conrad
Feoru, Jacob
Garret, Joseph
Hoover, Henry
Hunter, John
Lunback, William
Linninger, Fred
Moore, James
Nuner, William
Pickens, John
Shriver, Andrew
Stall, Frederick
Williams, William
Warden, John

Bowers, Price
Bateman, Clement
Douglas, John
England, Joseph
Fimmore, John
Gilmore, William
Higgins, A. N.
Hall, John
Hidrick, Nicholas
Layman, Barnet
Miller, Joseph
McElheny, Robert
Ott, Adam
Pollard, William
Shaver, James
Snyder, Richard
Ward, Elever

Page 277.

ROLL OF CAPT. ANDREW CORRELL'S COMPANY (Probably from Ross Co.)

Served from July 28, until August 20, 1813.

Capt. Andrew Correll
Sergt. Frank Winsough
Corp. George Shagley

Ensign, Benjamin Brown
Sergt. Richard Rogan

Sergt. Thomas McNeal
Corp. James Doren

Privates.

Andrew, Thomas
Baker, Christopher
Cardre, Jacob
Franklin, James
Franklin, Samuel
Hanson, John
Harrison, John
Meakre, Wheeler
Mooney, George
Miller, Alexander
Robinson, William
Tonlinson, William
Vanskoy, Timothy
Wolf, William

Aid, Jacob
Boren, Abraham
Clark, Thomas
Franklin, John
Green, Joseph
Heath, John
Longshore, Mahlon
Miller, Robert
Meakre, Aaron
Odle, Lott
Redfern, John
Tweet, Jesse
Wolf, Samuel
Wood, Joab

Bour, Adam
Boren, Peter
Duncan, Zechariah
France, Oliver
Hickson, Elijah
Harris, Daniel
Lewis, Thomas
Mooney, John
Madary, Charles
Rease, Thomas
Smith, John
Vanskoy, Jonothan
Wolf, Isaac

Page 278. Vol. 2.
ROLL OF CAPT. DANIEL McCREERY'S COMPANY (Probably from Ross Co.)
Served from July 29, until September 6, 1813.

Rank and Name of Soldier.
Capt. Daniel McCreery
Sergt. William Hulit
Sergt. Isaac Roads
Corp. Wells Jones
Privates.
Ault, Christian
Brown, Orlando
Bayles, William
Dutton, James
Housman, David
Lucas, Charles
Marshawn, Daniel
Niseley, Samuel
Polland, William
Rhodes, Phillip
Stultz, John
Shaw, Joseph
Swane, Samuel
Troth, Isaac

Rank and Name of Soldier.
Lieut. Isaac Hortman
Sergt. Adam Razier
Corp. John Darby
Corp. Peter Housman
Privates.
Ankerman, John
Baldwin, Daniel
Darby, Stephen
Hatter, Leonard
Jonsojin, Eli
Janiken, Drury
McVay, William
Ninemyor, Jacob
Rhodes, Jacob
Rhodes, John
Smith, Benjamin
Stephens, John
Shields, John
Williams, Thomas

Rank and Name of Soldier.
Ensign, Barton Lucas
Sergt. Thomas Davis
Corp. Christian Housman
Privates.
Bilzer, John
Beason, Jonothan
Darby, Samuel
Housman, George
Lamings, Samuel
Linten, William
McGraw, Hugh
Pudle, Gabriel
Reed, Leonard
Reed, George
Stultz, Peter
Shewmaker, Daniel
Trivet, Joseph
Washburn, James

Page 279.
ROLL OF CAPT. MARTIN ARMSTRONG'S COMPANY
(Probably from Ross Co.)
Served from July 28, until August 18, 1813.

Capt. Martin Armstrong
Sergt. Hartley Malone
Corp. William Odle
Corp. Phillip Waldrer
Privates.
Alexander, Joseph
Boots, Martin
Doll, Daniel
Gilmore, Andrew
Kelley, William
Howe, Jesse
Kelley, John, Sr.
Lockhart, Joseph
Malone, Richard
Pierce, Samuel
Reyphole, Anthony
Rhidenour, John
Sell, Adam
Seymour, Solomon

Lieut. James Bryan
Sergt. Edward Caling
Corp. Caleb Odle
Privates.
Bell, John
Boots, John
Doll, Abraham
Hanks, Joseph
Kelley, John, Jr.
Hanks, John
Linton, Lawson
Lockhart, James
McClintock, Joseph
Pierce, Bingett
Ross, John
Smith, James
Sigler, George
Williams, John

Ensign, Andrew McKee
Sergt. Robert Brown
Corp. George Boots
Privates.
Brown, Nimrod
Cogill, Alexander
Fryar, Benjamin
Hendricks, James
Kelley, James
Kelley, Andrew
Linton, Zechariah
Miller, Robert
McClintock, Alexander
Queen, John
Rhidenour, Jacob
Smith, Samuel
Salts, John

Page 280.
ROLL OF CAPT. ISAAC TAYLOR'S COMPANY (Probably from Ross Co.)
Served from July 29, until August 26, 1813.

Capt. Isaac Taylor
Sergt. David Rees
Privates.
Ams, Samuel D.
Beckwer, James
Beason, Benjamin
Cowger, George
Dunham, Samuel
Haller, Jacob
Janegan, Isaac
Kirkpatrick, John
Mannon, Isaac
Powermaster, Henry
Rockhold, John
Stroup, Michael
Tompson, Amos
Wisecoop, Jonas

Lieut John Palmer
Sergt. Edward Hughes
Privates.
Boyd, Jonothan
Burris, Brewster
Countryman, Henry
Coms, John
Davis, Elihu
Hatter, Peter
Kelse, Michael
Lucas, Hugh
Meir, Hugh
Reslinger, John
Rodgers, Aaron
Stewart, Isaac
Troth, Isaac
Wedmore, John
Yorger, Joseph

Ensign, Thomas Wilson
Sergt. Jacob Meyer
Privates.
Burris, Miles
Bates, Hezekiah
Coplinger, William
Cooper, John
Falk, John
Jessup, John
Kellough, George
Lucas, Joshua
Cricket, John
Roads, Jacob
Smith, Zechariah
Troth, William
White, William
Wilson, John

Page 282.
ROLL OF CAPT. EZEKIAL BUNN'S COMPANY (Probably from Ross Co.)
Served from————————.

Capt. Ezekial Bunn
Sergt. John Roberts
Privates.
Bitzer, Anthony
Dozzard, Stephen
James, Samuel
Ritter, Richard
James, Samuel

Lieut. George Frederick
Corp. John Kirk
Privates.
Bunn, James
Dehaven, Abraham
Mitchel, James
Snyder, John

Ensign, John Brown
Privates.
Crouch, James
Hayes, James
Mathias, John
Straw, Solomon

Pages 281-282. Vol. 2.

ROLL OF CAPT. JOHN SPENCER'S COMPANY (County Unknown).

Served from May 5, until May 20, 1813.

Rank and Name of Soldier.	Rank and Name of Soldier.	Rank and Name of Soldier.
Capt. John Spencer	Lieut. James Gibson	Lieut. Elias Hughes
Ensign, John I. Tullass	Sergt. Morris A. Newman	Sergt. James Seymore
Sergt. Thomas Cannon	Sergt. Timothy Spellman	Corp. William Blackburn
Corp. John Chonner	Corp. George McMilles	Corp. Joseph Statelar

Privates.

Abraham, John	Arnold, Anthony	Baker, Ephraim
Baker, Daniel	Brown, Aaron	Beard, Andrew
Boucher, John	Coffey, Amos	Curtis, Hairsmore
Cunningham, John	Cunningham, William	Channel, John
Coulter, James	Doughman, James	Dewees, Jethre
Denman, Hathaway	Davis, Christopher	Fulton, Thomas
Gavit, Asa B.	Green, Michael	Gavit, Benjamin
Gilmore, John	Henderson, Titan	Hoover, Samuel
Helphrey, John	Hunter, Robert	Hook, John
Hughes, Elias	Johnston, John, Sr.	Johnston, John Jr.
Insco, John	Insco, Moses	Kirkpatrick, Nathan
Kissinger, George	Kite, Adam	Klever, Mathew
Moody, John	Mathews, Benjamin	McKinley, John
Powell, Samuel	Parks, George	Pegg, Benjamin C.
Pence, Isaac	Rowe, William	Robinson, James
Robinson, Martin	Ridgley, Basil	Rodgers, Elijah
Shedmick, James	Scott, Robert	Stanberry, Job
Sutton, Jehiel	Thrall, James	Vance, Christian
Vance, Joseph	Ward, James	Wheeler, Thomas
Wilson, Archibald	Ward, Jonas	

Pages 283-284.

ROLL OF CAPT. ISAAC BUTLER'S COMPANY (County Unknown).

Served from August 9, until October 9, 1812.

Capt. Isaac Butler	Lieut. John Raydor	Ensign, Nathan Burrow
Sergt. Caleb McDaniel	Sergt. James Jardin	Sergt. John K. Holmes
Sergt. Jehiel McDaniel	Corp. William Peth John	Corp. William Smith
Corp. Leonard Hendrick	Corp. Adam Padse	Fifer, Francis Buell
Drummer, Benjamin Mills		

Privates.

Allison, Jesse	Burel, Francis	Blaze, Peter
Berthe, Lewis	Crow, Abraham	Callison, Robert
Callison, John	Crow, William	Corden, Burgess
Childers, John	Dickeson, John	Brennen, Charles
Ellison, Samuel	Ellison, John	Farmer, Thomas
Frasy, Andrew	Haney, George	Harris, William
Hoislit, John	Jones, William	Kizer, Henry
Knox, Nehemiah	Long, Elisha	Little, George
Long, Benjamin	Lemons, Jacob	Miller, Brison
McDaniel, James	McLoud, Collin	Poor, Alexander
Poor, Marton	Pettijohn, John	Pruse, Daniel
Rickabaugh, John	Rice, James	Rickabaugh, Adam
Rarger, John Moss	Ross, William	Rickabaugh, John
Russell, Reuben	Sturgeon, Robert	Scott, Andrew
Umphreys, Robert	Waugh, Francis	Waugh, Solomon
Whitten, Louis	Ward, Charles	Williams, John
Yates, Samuel		

Page 285.

ROLL OF CAPT. EBENEZER BENEDICT'S COMPANY (County Unknown.)

Served from August 24, until September 20, 1812.

Capt. Ebenezer Benedict	Lieut. Benjamin White	Ensign, Sheldon Osborn
Sergt. Jesse Alderman	Sergt. Oliver R. Guild	Sergt. Caleb Holcomb, Jr.
Sergt. Nathaniel Cook	Corp. Urial Loomis	Corp. Isaac Huff
Corp. Linus Tracey	Corp. Whitney Smith	Fifer, Elijah Daniels
Drummer, Zerah Cook		

Privates.

Adgate, John	Benedict, Billy	Bell, David
Boyer, John	Cook, Christopher	Clark, Isaac
Cloe, Samuel	Clark, James H.	Fish, Abner
Guild, Jarius	Harsh, Jacob	Johnson, Anson
Kline, Philip	Lyons, John	Mansfield, Mancen
Maxwell, Robert	North, Samuel	Penny, Levi
Smith, Daniel	Scofield, Edward	Stow, Harvey
Taylor, Simon	Toft, Aaron	Bartholomew, Charley
Winter, Alpheus		

Page 286. Vol. 2.
ROLL OF CAPT. JOHN CLARK'S COMPANY (Probably from Ross County).
Served from July 28, until August 13, 1813.

Rank and Name of Soldier.	Rank and Name of Soldier.	Rank and Name of Soldier.
Capt. John Clark	Lieut. Armel Holloway	Ensign, Robert Brady
Sergt. John Hill	Sergt. Leonard Timons	Sergt. Stephen Clark
Sergt. Isachai Pepper	Corp. Samuel Clark	Corp. Robert Bennis
Corp. David Dormin	Corp. Asther Lewis	
Privates.	**Privates.**	**Privates.**
Breddy, James	Brown, Zechariah	Brady, Benjamin
Coxwell, Leven	Collins, Joseph	Dennis, Mathias
Dennis, Putnell	Dennis, Jonothan	Godden, Levi
Hamilton, William	Hardy, David	Hart, Brinkley
Jones, Samuel	King, James	Lackey, John
Listersen, William	Lewis, Jesse	Larrence, Elisha
Mickens, John	Parker, Charles	Ridley, James
Simms, Jesse	Smith, Thomas	Timmons, John W.
Timmons, Perry	Williams, Gamage	

Page 290.
ROLL OF CAPT. CLEMENT BROWN'S COMPANY (From Ross County).
Served from July 28, until August 20, 1813.

Capt. Clement Brown	Lieut. Lemuel Darcuth	Ensign, Arthur McArthur
Sergt. Thomas Watson	Sergt. John Brown	Sergt. Isaac Timplin
Sergt. James Timplin	Corp. Charles Rollins	Corp. George Severs
Corp. Nicholas Divault	Corp. George Hudson	Musician, Noah Downs
Privates.	**Privates.**	**Privates.**
Anderson, William	Arnold, Samuel	Betts, John
Brittenham, Aaron	Brittenham, Mathias	Brown, Phillip
Boyd, Robert	Betts, Thomas	Clarkson, Major
Cochran, James	Goldsberry, Thomas	Hardey, Thomas
Hoddy, Robert	Hewitt, William	McAfferty, John
Porter, William	Timmons, Amarias	Timmons, George
Timplin, John	Wroten, Henry	Watson, Alexander

Page 287.
ROLL OF CAPT. WILLIAM STOCKTON'S COMPANY (Probably from Ross Co.)
Served from July 28, until August 20, 1813.

Capt. William Stockton	Lieut. Mathias Littleton	Ensign, William Littleton
Sergt. John Armstrong	Sergt. John Kirkbridge	Sergt. Clement Carroll
Sergt. Stanley Cook	Corp. William Miskimins	Corp. James McCalister
Corp. John Williams	Fifer, Joseph Cox	Drummer, James Baltimore
Privates.	**Privates.**	**Privates.**
Bradley, Arthur	Blissard, John	Brown, James
Baden, Rosel	Cox, John	Corbet, David
Cook, James	Carroll, Samuel	Calhoun, John
Dimes, James	Dunlap, James	Earl, James
Fisher, John	Hennis, William	Junk, John
Logue, John	Mace, John	Mathias, Samuel
Minear, Phillip	Minear, Stephen	Mitchel, John
McCollister, Thomas	McCoy, Dixon	McCoy, Alexander
McAllister, Robert	Ogden, John	Phelps, William
Richardson, Peter	Rodgers, John	Richards, William
Robinson, Henry	Stockton, William	Short, George
Shoemaker, Peter	Thorn, Jacob	Walker, Charles

Page 288.
ROLL OF LIEUT. ROBERT HARVEY'S COMPANY (Probably from Ross Co.)
Served from July 13, until August 17, 1813.

Lieut. Robert Harvey	Ensign, William Holloway	Sergt. Tighlman Willis
Sergt. Richard Berry	Sergt. James Kirkpatrick	Sergt. Lewis Roughton
Corp. William Dixson	Corp. Alexander Bowman	Corp. Edward Graham
Privates.	**Privates.**	**Privates.**
Adams, Thomas	Adams, John	Brown, Edward
Cummings, Joseph	Clifton, John	Corbet, Joseph
Chappell, George	Crispin, Francis	Dulgain, William
Furrow, Adam	Furrow, Solomon	Green, Moses
Gibson, Jacob	Hood, Edward	Holloway, Isaiah
Holloway, Thomas	Jones, Amos	Long, George
Maughmen, Jacob	Miller, John	Ramsey, David
Ramsey, Joseph	Romine, Amos	Smith, White
Strotherd Sephnius	Thompson, William	Tootle, Thomas
Tootle, Egleston	Walker, John	

Page 289. Vol. 2.
ROLL OF CAPT. JOHN JACKSON'S COMPANY (From Ross County).
Served from July 28, until August 15, 1813.

Rank and Name of Soldier.	Rank and Name of Soldier.	Rank and Name of Soldier.
Capt. John Jackson	Lieut. Jonothan Crabill	Ensign, Andrew White
Sergt. David T. Hull	Sergt. William Peters	Sergt. Willis Grant
Corp. William Graham	Corp. Joseph James	Drummer, Daniel Jones
Privates.	**Privates.**	**Privates.**
Arnesworth, Abraham	Ater, Abraham	Ater, Thomas
Brown, Joseph	Brown, Thomas	Briggs, Walter
Bowdle, Joseph	Baker, Josiah	Champ, John
Dolbee, Peter	Fisher, William	Flemming, Isaac
Gillaspie, Zach.	Gillaspie, Alexander	King, George
Kindall, Abraham	Keikenedall, Isaac	Mercer, Robert
Mizzick, Nathan	Martin, Benjamin	Nolin, Edward
Ross, Levin	Shanton, Abraham	Shanton, Charles
Tanganary, Abe	Wyer, Obed	Zoops, Adam

Pages 291-292.
ROLL OF CAPT. ALEXANDER ROBINSON'S COMPANY (From Ross County).
Served from July 28, until August 16, 1813.

Capt. Alexander Robinson	Lieut. Enos Pursel	Ensign, Jesse Wiley
Sergt. Thomas Sheilds	Sergt. James B. Johnston	Sergt. Christian Hill
Sergt. James Porter	Corp. Robert Lindsay	Corp. James Ross
Corp. Ephraim Worthington	Corp. Jacob Gooley	
Privates.	**Privates.**	**Privates.**
Brownfield, Robert	Blue, Daniel	Breedlove, David
Clark, Joseph	Davis, James	Dysert, John
Gadberry, James A.	Howard, Nicholas	Haynes, Henry, Sr.
Haynes, Henry, Jr.	Hubbert, Thornton	Hosselton, John
Logue, Samuel	Montgomery, James	McArthur Duncan
McDill, Robert	Nye, Jared	Norris, William
Porter, Peter	Pleasant, Enos	Summerset, Henry
Shepard, Philip	Worthington, John	Wiley, William

Following men were from Pickaway county:
Served from August 30, until October 9, 1812.

Lieut. Asa L. Heath	Ensign, Thomas Hunt	Sergt. Henry Cook
Sergt. Henry Smith	Sergt. Thomas Holloway	Sergt. William Good
Corp. Philip Shentaffer	Corp. Charles Hunt	Corp. Thomas Bootle
Corp. Samuel Atcheson	Corp. Samuel Ater	
Privates.	**Privates.**	**Privates.**
Brown, Edward	Crabb, Thomas	Clark, James
Cooper, Joel	Corkwell, Henry	Clarkson, Major
Dayton, Spencer	Heater, David	Holloway, Abisha
Herstater, Henry	Hust, James	High, Jonothan
Hager, William	King, Isaac	King, James
Kiddy, William	Loury, John	Lynch, Balitha
Lister, William	Laury, John	Linart, Thomas
Manly, Samuel	McArthur, Samuel	McAfferty, William
Norris, Otho	Phebus, Henry	Phebus, George
Renick, Asahel	Renick, Abel	Rickey, Thomas
Radcliffe, Isaac	Freyhart, Henry	Russell, Perry
Salters, John	Toots, Adam	Tumman, William
Ward, Abraham	Young, Hugh	Zeister, Peter

Page 293.
ROLL OF CAPT. GEORGE WOLF'S COMPANY (From Pickaway County).
Served from July 28, until August 26, 1813.

Capt. George Wolf	Lieut. George Steely	Ensign, Jesse Cook
Sergt. John Scott	Sergt. Jonas Baum	Sergt. Wesley Rush
Sergt. William Cook	Corp. Moses Rush	Corp. Joseph Cravistone
Corp. David Vale	Corp. Josiah Rush	
Privates.	**Privates.**	**Privates.**
Brougher, Conrad	Burnes, Joseph	Baum, Peter
Creigh, Samuel	Chedd, Daniel	Denny, William
Earnest, Michael	Fressman, Hugh	Graham, Robert
Gordon, Alexander	Headley, George	Hiser, William
Julian, John	Lutz, John D.	Lutz, Samuel
Leonard, Abraham	Michael, John	Morehous, Augustine
May, John	Mevgult, John	McClintock, Jeheil
McClintock, William	Nebb, Christian	Neace, George
Rush, Peter	Ross, Jacob B.	Scott, Moses
Shoemake, John	Shoemaker, Jacob	Sharp, George
Torbet, James	Vance, Elisha	Wolf, John

Page. 294. Vol. 2.

ROLL OF CAPT. JACOB RITCHHART'S COMPANY (From Ross County).
Served from July 28, until August 18, 1813.

Capt. Jacob Ritchhart
Sergt. Elisha Emons
Sergt. William Taylor
Corp. Thomas Noland

Lieut. James Hall
Sergt. Henry Wishart
Corp. George Holloway
Corp. David Lilley

Ensign, Andrew Nichols
Sergt. George Clevinger
Corp. William Jewett
Drummer, John Huffman

Privates.
Armon, George
Crossley, John
Ferguson, David
Henderson, Nathaniel
Morris, Samuel
Ritchhart Henry
Shouts, Jacob
Thompson, Oswell

Privates.
Bevers, Michael
Davenport, Abraham
Fulton, Alexander
Loyear, Jacob
Morlana, William
Smith, Aaron
Shirley, Nathan
Thompson, Ignatius

Privates.
Cooper, Joel
Fulton, William
Glascock, Stephen
Lendsey, Abraham
Ritchhart, Abraham
Simpson, John
Thompson, William
Vistel, John

Pages 295-296.

ROLL OF CAPT. ALEXANDER MENARY'S COMPANY (From Ross County).
Served from August 30, until October 12, 1812. Part of Company served from July 28, until September 5, 1813.

Capt. Alexander Menary
Sergt. Ebenezer Petty
Lieut. Enos Pursel

Lieut. Samuel Jenkins,
Sergt. William Wilcox

Ensign, Reuben Pursel
Lieut. William Cochran

Privates.
Acton, William
Bradley, Richard
Earls, Mathew
Johnston, Bazil
Lawyer, Jacob
McElvey, John
Pool, Thomas
Row, James M.
Welch, Joseph

Brown, Joseph, Sr.
Baker, Josiah
Dolly, Peter
Fuller, William
Ferguson, David
Hull, David D.
Swanny, John
Simpson, John
Tompson, Abraham

Privates.
Acton, Richard
Brown, Thomas
Funston, Thomas
Jenkins, Alexander
McQuea, Daniel
McDonald, David
Robinson, John
Strain, John M.
Yates, Morris

Brown, Joseph, Jr.
Crossley, John
Earls, Mathew, Jr.
Flemin, Isaac
Hill, Christian
Lawyer, Jacob, Jr.
Sherley, Nathan
Smith, Aaron
Tangnary, Abraham

Privates.
Ashley, Daniel
Coon, Samuel
Goodwin, Levi
Junk, John
McClintock, Alexander
Noble, Thomas
Robinson, Samuel
Severs, George

Following men under Col John McDonald:
Beavers, Michael
Champ, John
Finnemore, William
Gilaspie, Alexander
Hutson, David
Pursel, Zodock
Shouts, Jacob
Shrokley, Archibald
Teral, John

Page 297.

ROLL OF CAPT. GEORGE YOCUM'S COMPANY (County Unknown).
Served from August 30, until October 9, 1812.

Capt. George Yocum
Sergt. Robert Harley
Sergt. Cornelius Michael
Corp. John Lewis

Lieut. John McArthur
Sergt. Mires
Corp. Francis Tully
Corp. John Ofnear

Ensign, William Arboe
Sergt. James G. Gray
Corp. Jonothan Jones

Privates.
Bishop, Robert
Baigle, Henry
Clover, Solomon
Darlin, Robert
Day, Addison
Harrington, James
Ladd, Ellison
Lloyd, Shadrach
Mustard, George
McElroy, Daniel
O'Brien, Charles
Steen, Moses
Toots, Daniel
Wilson, Thomas
Watts, James

Privates.
Baker, John
Crumhien, James
Campbell, David
Durmp, James
Finley, Joseph
Jefferson, Thomas
Lowman, Joseph
Mayhan, William
Moore, Elisha
McNeal, Archibald
Saddler, William
St. Clair, John
Terret, Daniel
William, Providence
Watts, Leven

Privates.
Baker, James
Clover, Jacob
Copsey, Hezekiah
Devoss, Joseph
Flemming, Robert
Johnston, William
Lank, Elisha
Mark, Michael
McIntire, Samuel
Nowland, John
Slaughter, John
Thirman, Robert
Verdin, Isaac
Wiley, William

Page 298.

ROLL OF CAPT. JOB. RADCLIFF'S COMPANY (County Unknown).
Served from July 26, until August 26, 1813.

Capt. Job Radcliff
Sergt. John Shepard
Sergt. Benjamin Radcliff

Lieut. Jacob Foster
Sergt. Richard Seamore

Ensign, Aaron Seamore
Sergt. John Polsten

Privates.
Argo, John
Coon, George
Jones, James
Morris, Joseph
Messer, Isaac
Pierce, James, Sr.
Rawlings, Nathan
West, Frederick

Privates.
Beckett, Benjamin
Dawitt, Barnett
Johnston, James
Morris, Thomas
McMins, Robert
Polstin, Cornelius
Tipton, Thomas
Williams, Henry, Jr.

Privates.
Clark, Daniel
Galbrith, John
Laverty, James
Miller, James
O'Niel, Johnston
Rawlings, Moses
Vannieter, Abraham

Pages 299-300. Vol. 2.

ROLL OF CAPT. JOHN WILSON'S COMPANY (County Unknown).

Served from May 8, until May 29, 1813, and from July 26, until August 26, 1813.

Rank and Name of Soldier.	Rank and Name of Soldier.	Rank and Name of Soldier.
Capt. John Wilson	Ensign, Elias Brock	Sergt. William Gibson
Sergt. David Groves	Sergt. Michael Bash	Sergt. Levi Cantrell
Cor. John Phebus	Corp. Solomon Crose	Corp. John C. Davis
Corp. Joseph Downing	Corp. John Scott	Corp. Henry Warner
Musician, Alexander Ross	Musician, Isaac Hutchison	
Privates.	**Privates.**	**Privates.**
Adder, John	Anderson, Joel	Alkue, Samuel
Blair, Michael	Buck, James	Brock, William
Clemons, John	Cherry, Moses	Cartright, Samuel
Carpenter, Ira	Cubberly, Job	Crath, James
Cartwal, Samuel	Cubberly, William	Cochran, Thomas
Craft, James	Cochern, Cornelius	Crawford, George
Casto, Abel	Carder, George	Downing, Francis
Dawson, James	Dickison, Charles	Dennison, James
Dawson, Isaac	Downing, Robert	Foster, Joshua
Graham, James	Gregg, William	Gates, Nehemiah
Hanis, David	Hubbard, Titus	Hobough, Samuel
Hand, George	Harriman, Charles	Hosey, Anderson
Harris, Jonothan	Harris, John	Johnston, Abraham
Jimmison, William	Kingsey, Stephen	King, John
Kerr, Samuel	Kingsey, Michael	Knox, Ralph
Lafford, Joseph	Legg, Elijah	Moore, Nicholas
Morris, Samuel	Mann, William	Montgomery, Hugh
Martin, John	Potter, John	Powers, Joseph
Oxford, Abel	Patton, John	Rowan, William
Pancake, Joseph	Shields, John	Spencer, Thomas
Roseberry, John	Stone, Marshall	Springer, Thomas
Saward, Robert	Scott, Robert	Stockton, David
Stewart, Robert	Troxell, Isaac	Watson, Abraham
Thompson, John	Warner, Robert	Watson, David
Vance, Daniel	Wright, James	Wright, Ira
	Warner, John	

Page 301.

ROLL OF CAPT. ROBERT BRADSHAW'S COMPANY (From Ross County).

Served from July 26, until August 26, 1813.

Capt. Robert Bradshaw	Lieut. William Burbridge	Ensign, Simon Hornbeck
Sergt. John Mitts	Sergt. George Phebus	Sergt. John Phebus
Sergt. Sam. R. Davidson	Corp. John M. Alkire	Corp. John Young
Corp. Adam Metts	Corp. Platt, Hull	
Privates.	**Privates.**	**Privates.**
Abbott, Thomas	Burbridge, Benjamin	Baker, Martin
Burbridge, James	Boggs, Caleb	Baker, William
Baker, Joseph	Beer, William	Blue, John
Caide, Abraham	Crable, John	Colstin, Henry
Dart, David	Dixon, William	Freeman, Benjamin
Gowinge, Joseph	Hayes, Jesse	Harrison, George
Hayes, Maurice H.	Hayes, Charles	Hayes, Samuel
Hornback, Isaac	Knoles, Ephraim	Knowls, William
Lewis, Solomon	Maddox, Lazarus	McAlister, John
Powell, Abel	Phebis, Samuel	Reeves, Owen T.
Reeves, Samuel	Scott, William	Treheran, George
Timmons, John	Timmons, Peter	Watson, Levin
Webb, Robert	Wilson, James	Woodsworth, Ezra
	Yates, David	

Page 302.

ROLL OF LIEUT. CHARLES GILBERT'S COMPANY
(Probably from Portage County).

Served from August 24, until September 4, 1812.

Lieut. Charles Gilbert	Sergt. Hugh McDaniel	Sergt. Lyman T. Gilbert
Sergt. Truman Gilbert	Corp. Gains Smith	Corp. Zebulon Walker
Privates.	**Privates.**	**Privates.**
Amasa, Preston	Boswick, Abnah	Baldwin, John F.,
Fisher, John	Gilbert, Marvin	Gano, David
Hazzard, James	Jewell, William	Kane, Gabriel
Loury, Chauncey	Lewis, Joseph	McKelvey, John
Smith, Roswell	Shank, Nicholas	Shaw, John
Tuttle, James	Trowbridge, Dayton	

Page 302.

ROLL OF CAPT. ASA BERRAUGH'S COMPANY
(Probably from Portage County).

Served from August 28 until September 24, 1812.

Capt. Asa K. Berraugh	Lieut. Hezekiah Hime	Ensign, Richard E. Gay
Sergt. Samuel Menson	Drummer, Horace Berraugh	Fifer, Greawhood Berraugh
Privates.	**Privates.**	**Privates.**
Baker, Joel	Brown, Ephraim	Bradley, Benjamin
Hine, Abel	Hine, Lyman	

Page 303. Vol. 2.
ROLL OF CAPT. GEORGE SKIDMORE'S CO. (From Franklin County).

Served from August 26, until October 10, 1812.

Rank and Name of Soldier.	Rank and Name of Soldier.	Rank and Name of Soldier.
Capt. George Skidmore	Lieut. John Skidmore	Ensign, William Marshall
Sergt. Robert Riley	Sergt. Thomas Jones	Sergt. John Hickman
Sergt. Joseph Skidmore	Corp. William Stiarwolt	Corp. Chester P. Cole
Corp. John Skinner	Corp. Charles Sells	Fifer, Frederick Stirwolt
Drummer, Ashbaugh		

Privates.	Privates.	Privates.
Brickle, John	Beer, Conrad	Cooper, Alexander
Droddy, John	Droddy, Aaron	Flemmin, William
Fuller, William	Ford, Frederick	Hickman, Townsend
Harrington, Daniel	Hamilton, John	Hess, Bolser
Hearsoff, John	Justice, David	Johnston, John
Jones, John	Keasnor, Michael	Kinser, Adam
Marsh, Thomas	Manning, Elisha	Manning, William
Morehead, Thomas	Postler, Job	Postler, Solomon
Rodgers, John	Shipman, Samuel	Skinner, James
Step, John	Sells, William	Thomas, Elijah
Thomas, Wesley	Thomas, James	Vana, Alexander
Winset, Joseph	Williams, Lewis	Waite, George

Page 304.
ROLL OF CAPT. GEORGE WILLIAM'S COMPANY
(Probably from Franklin Co.)

Served from August 26, until October 10, 1812.

Capt.- George Williams	Lieut. Jacob Foster	Ensign, Robert Breckenridge
Sergt. William Duff	Sergt. John Goldsmith	Sergt. John Carnohan
Sergt. Mathew Brown	Corp. William White	Corp. Charles O'Neil
Corp. John Hoover	Corp. John Stephenson	Fifer, Thomas Shreves
Drummer, William McKibben		

Privates.	Privates.	Privates.
Bennet, Joseph	Balenger, Joseph	Chinowith, Thomas
Clark, Richard	Carter, Joseph	Clark, Daniel
DeWitt, Martin	England, Jacob	Hoffman, Henry
Hoover, Abraham	Johnston, James	Jones, James
Kelsel, Nicholas	Knis, John	Morris, Joseph
Martin, John	Messer, Isaac	Mathews, Hiram
McLaughlin, Hiram	O'Neil, Johnston	Parish, Reuben
Potston, Cornelius	Radcliffe, Job	Romine, Elias
Seymour, Richard	Seeds, John	Tanner, Peter
Weatherington, John	Williams, John	

Page 305
ROLL OF CAPT. TIMOTHY CULVER'S COMPANY
(Probably from Portage Co.)

Served from August 24, until September 4, 1812.

Capt. Timothy Culver	Lieut. Isaac Merriman	Sergt. Walter Dickinson
Sergt. William Rogers	Corp. Ephraim Sabin	Corp. Oliver C. Dickenson
Corp. Abel Sabine	Drummer, Daniel Ward	

Privates.	Privates.	Privates.
Cross, Theophilus	Goss, John	Harris, Joseph
Mosher, Henry P.	Savage, Jehiel	Sears, Elisha
Sears, Nathan, Jr.	Sears, Elias	Upson, Arad
Upson, Freeman	Ward, Joshua	

Page 305.
ROLL OF CAPT. JOSHUA WOODWARD'S COMPANY
(Probably from Portage County).

Served from August 24, until September 4, 1812.

Capt. Joshua Woodward	Lieut. Linus Curtis	Ensign Anson Beeman
Sergt. Almon Babcock	Sergt. Elijah Smith	

Privates.	Privates.	Privates.
Alancon, Baldwin	Barnes, George	Broadway, Ebenezer
Crosby, David	Cook, James	Forsburg, Abel
King, John	Knowlton, James	Loomis, Babzemon
Noble, Quarter	Miller, Jesse	Owen, Silas N.
Smith, John B.	Thompson, Abel	Walfort, Peter

ROSTER OF OHIO SOLDIERS IN WAR OF 1812

Page 306. Vol. 2.

ROLL OF CAPT. IRA MORSE'S COMPANY (Probably from Portage County.)

Served from August 24, until September 4, 1812.

Rank and Name of Soldier.	Rank and Name of Soldier.	Rank and Name of Soldier.
Lieut. Ira Morse	Sergt. Hamlet Coe	Sergt. Alexander K. Hubbard
Sergt. Jeremiah Jones	Corp. Caleb Mattoon	
Privates.	**Privates.**	**Privates.**
Baldwin, Moses	Bucksley, Asabel	Baldwin, Allen E.
Baldwin, Ami	Carter, James	Chittendon, Almon
Day, Oratio	Granger, Ralph	Hartzell, William
Hubbard, Ephraim B.	Hartsell, John	Hartsell, Peter
Hartsell, Abraham	Laughlin, James	Mott, Elijah
Mott, Ezekial	Mason, Peter	Morse, Amos
Quier, John	Strong, William A.	Sutliff, Jesse
Taylor, Robert	Whittlessey, John H.	

Page 307.

ROLL OF CAPT. FREDERICK CARIS' COMPANY.
(Probably from Portage County.)

Served from August 22, until September 4, 1812.

Capt. Frederick Caris	Sergt. David Collins	Sergt. Titus Belding
Sergt. Samuel Coe	Sergt. Graham Norris	Corp. Samuel B. Spellman
Corp. Ariel Case	Corp. Lemuel Chapman, Jr.	Drummer, Alpheus Andrews
Fifer, Ashur Guerley		
Privates.	**Privates.**	**Privates.**
Bostwick, Charles H.	Bostwick, Joseph R.	Chapman, Ephraim
Chapman, Chester	Elsworth, Colvin	Heroff, John
Chapman, Beman	Collins, Daniel L.	Newberry, William
McKnight, Robert	Reed, Abraham	Reed, Timothy
Richardson, Mason	Willyard, John	

Page 308.

ROLL OF CAPT. HEZEKIAH NOONEY'S COMPANY.
(Probably from Portage County.)

Served from August 24, until September 4, 1812.

Capt. Hezekiah Nooney	Lieut. Oliver Snow	Ensign Ella Wilmot
Sergt. Seth Harmon	Sergt. Gershom Judson	Sergt. Horace Ladd
Sergt. Ariel Walden	Corp. Henry Blair	Corp. Phinas Pond
Corp. Moses McIntosh	Corp. Basil Windsor	Drummer Virgil Moore
Fifer, Joseph Skinner		
Privates.	**Privates.**	**Privates.**
Atwater, Jonothan	Bright, Thomas	Carlton, Peter
Gardner, John	Judson, Samuel	Ladd, Eleazar
Ladd, Ezekial	Leeland, Lyman	Moore, Samuel, Jr.
Pond, Moses	Pond, David	Ray, Patrick
Russell, William	Snow, Franklin	Terris, Henry B.

Pages 309-371-310.

ROLL OF CAPT. DELANNE MILLS' COMPANY (Probably from Portage Co.)

Served from September 28, until October 12, 1812. From March 7, until September 6, 1814. From August 24, until September 4, 1812. From February 24, until March 14, 1815.

Capt. Delanne Mills	Lieut. John Caris	Lieut. David Barret
Lieut. John Redden	Lieut. Thomas Robison	Ensign Asa Trusedale
Ensign John Brooks	Sergt. Titus Belding	Sergt. Gershon Norris
Sergt. Chester Adams	Sergt. Samuel Coe	Sergt. Oliver Mills
Sergt. George Young	Sergt. Benjamin Higley	Sergt. John Streator
Sergt. John Randall	Sergt. John Smith	Sergt. John M. Baldwin
Sergt. George G. Redden	Sergt. Daniel Sawtell	Sergt. Griswold Gillet
Corp. David A. Ramsey	Corp. Caleb Stow	Corp. Moses McIntosh
Corp. Elisha Hutchinson	Corp. Hiram Messenger	Corp. Lorenzo Holly
Corp. John Spooner	Fifer, Freeman Conet	Fifer, Oliver Wheeler
Drummer, Warren Squires		
Privates.	**Privates.**	**Privates.**
Alfred, Oliver	Alferd, Levi	Artemar, Baker
Achison, Benjamin	Bostwick, Joseph R.	Bancroft, Randolphus
Blair, Asahel	Babcock, Simon	Bundy, Caleb L.
Bell, John	Bell, Samuel	Cahoon, Joel B.
Castor, John	Cole, Lemuel	Carpenter, Lewis
Dyton, Abraham	Donaldson, James	Duck, Samuel
Devens, James	Dixon, James	Dundey, John
Evans, George	Ferris, Henry R.	Fanch, Joseph
Fish, Moses	Finlay, John	Guvoner, John
Gershon, Judson	Gate, Mathew	Granger, Benjamin
Higley, Hezekiah	Hacket, Ephraim	Hitchcock, David
Huston, David	Haley, Ezra	Hill, John
Hill, Jacob	Hanks, John	Hendrickson, George
Johnson, Thomas	Jackson, Edward	Kempton, William
Lindsey, Richard	Mackey, John	Manly, Martin
Mott, Elijah	Morkier, Thomas	Macombo, John
McCloud, Francis	McKinney, James	Noble, Quarter
Olds, Kingsley	Pitkin, Orin	Perry, Hesea
Parker, Elihu	Redden, John	Reed, Jeremiah
Shaylor, John	Skinner, Joseph	Southworth, Joseph
Seley, Ephraim H.	Stratton, John	Stanley, Marshall
Taylor, Oratio	Thorp, Baralleel	Terrel, Elijah L.
Turner, Samuel	Willyard, John	Windsor, Basil, Jr.
Ward, Daniel	Wilcox, David	Ward, Elisha
Warner, Chauncey	Wilmott, Elisha	

Page 311. Vol. 2.
ROLL OF CAPT. JOSEPH VANCE'S COMPANY (County Unknown).
Served from August 19, until August 29, 1812.

Rank and Name of Soldier.	Rank and Name of Soldier.	Rank and Name of Soldier.
Capt. Joseph Vance	Lieut. William Ward	Ensign Isaac Mynes
Sergt. Charles Harrison	Sergt. Zebulon G. Cantrell	Sergt. William H. Tyffe
Sergt. David Henry	Corp. John Taylor	Corp. William McRoberts
Corp. Frederick Ambrose	Corp. John Dawson	
Privates.	**Privates.**	**Privates.**
Custer, Abraham	Custer, Isaac	Coffen, Henry
Clifton, Moses	Dowden, Archibald	Duncan, Joseph
Egnon, Jesse	Gillaspie, Mathew M.	Lewis, Britain
McGrew, William	McGrew, Archibald	Newcomb, Daniel
Petty, Solomon	Richards, Andrew	Richards, Elijah
Rigdon, Lewis	Rigdon, John	Sargent, William
Stephens, William	Taber, Bennet, Jr.	Tharp, Andrew
Thomas, Joel	Thomas, Ward	Turner, Isaac
Vance, William	Wiley, John	

Page 312.
ROLL OF CAPT. JACOB MANN'S COMPANY (County Unknown).
Served from November 14, 1812, until May 13, 1813.

Capt. Jacob Mann	Ensign John Knight	Sergt. Vincent Dye
Corp. John Dye		
Privates.	**Privates.**	**Privates.**
Blue, Uriah	Brown, Abraham	Cox, Absolom
Fallman, Henry	Gregg, Noah	Goble, Joseph
Gissarion, William	Harter, Benjamin	Haines, John
Harter, Peter	Kiser, Thomas	Levan, John
Scudder, James	Woodburn, Robert	Winnings, Richard
Weaver, Peter	Weaver, John	Williams, Lewis
Young, Thomas		

Page 313.
ROLL OF CAPT. THOMAS RENICK'S COMPANY (From Pickaway County).
Served from July 26, until August 26, 1813.

Capt. Thomas Renick	Lieut. Asahel Heath	Ensign James Halle
Sergt. Johnston Hemphill	Sergt. Michael Phillip	Sergt. Edward Conroy
Sergt. David Marsh		
Privates.	**Privates.**	**Privates.**
Baley, William	Baley, Robert	Barnes, William
Campbell, James	Cole, John	Caster, James
Cuppin, Joseph	Dixson, William	Dixson, Alexander
Davis, George	Davis, John	Fulson, Joshua
Gleeze, Adam	Gaster, Jacob	Heath, William
Kearns, Abner	Linton, William	Martin, John
Madden, John	Marquis, Abraham	Madden, Rowzewed
McKinney, Henry	Pierce, John	Pense, John
Renick, William	Stiveson, David	Swank, William
Shreeves, Thomas	Swank, Richard	Short, Stephen
Shawbrad, William	Shoat, Stoy	Thomas, David
Ward, Abraham	Williams, John	Williams, Henry
Williams, Joseph		

Pages 315-316.
ROLL OF CAPT. JOHN ROBINSON'S COMPANY (Probably from Butler Co.)
Served from July 1, 1812, until April 26, 1813.

Capt. John Robinson	Lieut. John Nelson	Ensign Edward Roby
Sergt. Stephen Ball	Sergt. Nicholas Yeager	Sergt. Thomas Virgin
Sergt. Joseph Nichol	Corp. Benjamin Virgin	Corp. David Hayes
Corp. Robert Reid	Corp. William Loury	Musician, Ezekial Powers
Musician, Jonas Smalley		
Privates.	**Privates.**	**Privates.**
Austin, Joseph	Arthur, John	Boggs, James
Brees, John	Brackney, John	Barber, Henry
Bracken, Joseph	Carson, John	Cullen, Allen
Clark, Barzilla	Clark, David	Carnihan, William
Davis, Robert	Finney, John	Freeman, George
Goble, William	Gregory, William	Gregory, James
Graham, James	Garryson, Jacob	Graham, Samuel
Heaton, John	Harlin, Ishmael	Hudgall, John
Hall, Thomas	Hahn, Joseph	Kountz, Phillip
Loury, Samuel	Loury, Fleming	Landon, David
Lytle, William	Miller, Samuel	Murphy, James
Misner, Charles D.	McGouggal, Daniel	McAdams, Thomas
McIntyre, James	Peak, Samuel	Potts, Jacob
Powers, Jonothan	Powers, John	Place, Philip
Priddy, Daniel	Popejoy, Edward	Popejoy, Nathan
Reed, William	Robby, Isaac	Roby, Abraham
Reed, Charles	S'sersan, Robert	Sproot, David
Thomas, Lewis	Thompson, William	Virgin, William
Vanscoyoe, Jacob	Waggamon, Asher	Willis, Joseph
Whittlesey, Duran	Westfall, Jacob	Wade, George

Pages 317-318-319. Vol. 2.
ROLL OF CAPT. ROBERT GILCHRIST'S COMPANY (County Unknown).
Served from April 25, until October 26, 1812.

Rank and Name of Soldier.	Rank and Name of Soldier.	Rank and Name of Soldier.
Capt. Robert Gilchrist	Lieut. George Minnick	Ensign Daniel Shearer
Ensign Samuel Broogher	Ensign Samuel Booker	Sergt. Thomas Ray
Sergt. John Shaffer	Sergt. Jesse Johnson	Sergt. Thomas Patterson
Sergt. John Bradford	Corp. Peter Coblentz	Corp. Austin Webb
Corp. Archibald Meekle	Corp. Thomas Nicholson	Corp. Solomon Cross
Privates.	**Privates.**	**Privates.**
Bayler, John	Baker, Japtha	Beer, John
Broomershine, Jacob	Bell, John	Boyd, Samuel
Crider, John	Carney, Shem	Cresswell, James S.
Coffey, John	Cross, Israel	Crowel, Henry
Cless, John	Dever, Benjamin	Emerson, W.
Fitap, George	Grimes, Jacob	Houser, Henry
Haines, Thomas	Hozler, Robert	Hack, Jacob
Holler, Jacob	Ifert, Jacob	Jackson, James
Key, Caleb	Kiser, Aaron	Kuhn, Jacob
Kirkpatrick, George	Koue, Jacob	Lemen, James L.
Low, John	Looks, John	Laty, John
Murphy, Aquila	Murphy, James	Meek, Jacob
Milier, Jacob	Miller, George	Mikesel, Peter
Maxwell, Peter	Minnich, Leonard	McKeel, Daniel
McNeal, Thomas	McNeal, Daniel	McClary, Thomas
Nicholson, William	Phillips, George	Petticrew, Samuel
Roof, P.	Rider, James	Ryan, Joseph
Robbe, John	Ray, Thomas	Ream, John
Smith, Gregg	Sayre, John	Sheaniks, C.
Shaw, Daniel	Scott, Dunphy	Shaw, Ludwic
Scott, William	Stoker, Jacob	Smith, Nathan
Tolbert, Oliver	Taylor, Joseph	Tinkeys, George
Tigle, George	VanNott, Joseph	Vail, Samuel
Whitersell, John	Westfall, Joel	Weaver, Henry
Waggoner, Michael	Whitersell, George	Waggoner, George
Winthrop, Emerson	Wagamen, Jacob	Wagner, George
Wagner, Michael	Withersell, George	Withersell, John
Wright, John	Zwerner, Christopher	

Pages 320-326.
ROLL OF CAPT. JOHN SHEETS' COMPANY (County Unknown).
Served from April 27, 1812, for one year.

Capt. John Sheets	Lieut. Samuel Pope	Lieut. Samuel Miller
Sergt. Bryan Williams	Sergt. Michael Bowser	Sergt. John Ross
Sergt. Samuel S. Jack	Corp. Joseph M. Edwards	Corp. Isaac Heaton
Corp. Seth St. John	Corp. John Hole	Musician, John Tuttle
Privates.	**Privates.**	**Privates.**
Able, John	Clyne, Ezekial	Caslet, Alexander
Crichor, Henry	Estil, William L.	Grimes, Levi
Hardy, James	Hayes, John	Hart, David
Heaton, Samuel	Hutchinson, John	Hamilton, Elias
Hamilton, Jacob	Jennings, David	Munroe, Charles
Masey, Seth	McDaniel, William	McCulloch, John
Nicholson, Andrew	Spencer, Dennis	Sterns, Jabez
Stiles, Henry	Shaw, Archibald	Thatcher, Elijah
Trimble, Moses	Tuttle, Isaiah	Tearman, John
Weare, Elijah	Weare, Robert	Wortz, John
	Vanchorck, David	

Pages 321-322.
ROLL OF CAPT. EPHRAIM BROWN'S COMPANY (County Unknown).
Served from July 2, 1812, until April 24, 1813.

Capt. Ephraim Brown	Lieut. Robert Guthrie	Ensign John W. Jones
Sergt. Lyman Crary	Sergt. Joseph Cady	Sergt. William Gard
Sergt. John Slaybock	Corp. James Risk	Corp. Nathaniel French
Corp. Roswell Hazeltine	Corp. Daniel Jessup	
Privates.	**Privates.**	**Privates.**
Auter, Thomas	Beard, David	Brocaw, Henry
Babbit, Calvin	Baxter, Thomas	Culbages, George
Cox, Asa	Cooper, Hiram	Carle, Stephen
Dunseth, David Jr.	Danford, Benjamin	Doty, Zachariah
Furbush, Ephraim	Fulton, Abraham T.	Gamble, Samuel
Guthrie, William	Guthrie, John	Handcock, Daniel
Heckweller, Daniel	Johnston, James	Johnston, Thomas
Jenkinson, John G.	Laurance, Azel	Ledoi, John
Love, John	Martin, Henry	Morton, Washington
Mattox, David A.	Matts, Christopher	Milton, George
Master, David	Miller, John	McLee, William
McCammon, Isaac	Newkirk, John	Nichols, John
Patterson, Martin	Preston, John	Pasmore, Henry
Preston, Abijah	Preston, Joseph	Pain, Daniel
Rall, Isaac	Redenbaugh, James	Riley, Joshua
Sawyer, Stephen	Shadley, James	Steele, John
Swin, Ezer S.	Sisco, John	Tucker, Samuel
Twaddle, James	Updegraff, Andrew	Wilkinson, John

Pages 323-324. Vol. 2.
ROLL OF CAPT. JOHN FERRIS' COMPANY (County Unknown).
Served from April 25, until October 25, 1812.

Rank and Name of Soldier.	Rank and Name of Soldier.	Rank and Name of Soldier.
Capt. John Ferris	Lieut. Israel Joslen	Ensign Richard Shourd
Sergt. Samuel Starns	Sergt. Adam Weaver	Sergt. Benjamin Watkins
Sergt. James Mundel	Corp. Theophilus Case	Corp. William Scudder
Corp. David McLaughlin	Drummer, John S. Burt	
Privates.	**Privates.**	**Privates.**
Andrew, Samuel	Bruner, William	Bannett, Isaiah
Butler, Benjamin	Cunningham, George	Clark, Jonothan
Clark, Caleb	Clark, Dennis	Deens, Thomas
Edwards, James	Erwin, James	Fleak, Joseph
Fitzgirl, Zadoc	Gentle, John	Gobin, James L.
Grayham, George	Hughes, William	Hill, Ezra
Humphrey, Robert	Hoover, Daniel	Hauet, Thomas
Heizer, Lewis	Israel, William	Jones, Isaac
Jones, Philip	Jennings, Elijah	Jones, John
Kerr, H.	Langley, John	Long, Stephen
Manpeny, Thomas	Mullin, Robert	Miller, Alexander
McNeely, Robert	McKee, Alenxander	Orr, Samuel
Rettinhouse, E.	Redding, Elijah	Rich, Jacob
Sackwood, William	Seaman, Jaconiah	Sproul, Hugh
Smith, Benjamin	Sellwood, Henry	Sheets, Adam
Sanburn, John	Taylor, William	Thompson, John
Whetstone, Reuben	Ware, Thomas	Wilson, Benjamin
Wilson, Henry	Willis, Samuel	Williamson, S.
	Zimmerman, John	

Page 325.
ROLL OF CAPT. SAMUEL B. KYLE'S COMPANY. (County Unknown.)
Served from December 1, 1812, until April, 24, 1813.

Capt. Samuel B. Kyle	Lieut. Joseph Silley	Ensign David Kelly
Sergt. James Fox	Sergt. Joseph Gosset	Sergt. Stephen Ridlen
Corp. Samuel Ridlen	Corp. Richard Benham	Corp. John Fisher
Privates.	**Privates.**	**Privates.**
Ashbrook, James	Arthur, Joseph	Bingaman, George
Bates, Amos	Barkdoll, Abraham	Carvin, Sylvester
Dufer, George	Dumford, John	Garrison, Jacob
Gardner, William	Grey, Amney	Green, Martin
Gilman, John	Grey, Nathaniel	Hamblen, Benjamin
Hixson, James	Horner, William	Harrison, John
Humphrey, William	Hazlett, Robert	Jackman, Bernard
Kelley, John	Lovel, Timothy	Mallott, David
Marsh, Solomon	Mack, Dudley	Meyer, Frederick
McCall, John	McGill, Stewart	Nice, David
Pollock, Aaron	Polsen, Philip	Peek, Jacob
Smith, Joshua	Roman, Jonothan	Steel, William
Shick, Peter	Shick, Lewis	Thompson, John
Templeton, James	VanCurin, John	Williamson, Jacob
White, George	Wilkinson, Thomas B.	Wilkinson, Samuel
	Wilson, William	

Pages 327-328-329-330.
ROLL OF CAPT. DAVID SUTTON'S COMPANY.
(Probably from Butler County.)
Served from April 27, until October 27, 1812

Capt. David Sutton	Lieut. Robert Sweeney	Ensign John Vowen
Sergt. Andrew Robb	Sergt. Wright Elliott	Sergt. D. Bowers
Sergt. William Hercules	Corp. John Shawhan	Corp. William DeLong
Corp. John Young	Corp. John Flaming	Fifer. Benjamin Murphy
Drummer, John Thompson	Corp. Josiah Bradway	
Privates.	**Privates.**	**Privates.**
Anderson, John	Blake, Nathan	Bunnel, William
Bowers, Reese	Cunningham, Nathaniel	Cahill, Alexander
Collister, Hugh W.	Cahill, Abraham	Cummin, J. N.
Dill, John	Fisher, David	Fisher, Jacob
Garrison, Benjamin	Garrison, John	Garrison, Person
Garrison, David	Garrison, Ezekial	Goodposter, Isaac
Hutchinson, James	Hyde, Samuel	Hester, Jacob
Jeffries, George	Kitchell, James L.	Kindelspeaker, Jacob
Mullin, John	Martin, John	Manly, William
Moore, William	Martin, William	Miller, John
McCollister, Michael	Powell, Jacob	Patton, William
Rinedson, N.	Stets, John	Snoox, Jacob
Snook, Mart	Smoot, Dixon	Suten, James
Seward, John	Thomas, David	Trimble, James
Trump, Andrew	Tindles, J.	Vorhes, John
Vingard, John	Weeks, Job	Wallach, William
Warren, Zachariah	Wright, George	
Bannon, John	Fitzgerald, Eson	Fisher, James
Garrison, Jeremiah	Holcomb, Asa	Hand, Benjamin
Jester, Eli	Long, William D.	Lee, John
McCollister, Hugh	Nearson, Minary	Ress, Bown
Snuff, Jacob	Stiles, John	Tingel, George
Thompson, John	Vorhis, Jeremiah	Wright, Ragen

Pages 331-332. Vol. 2.
ROLL OF CAPT. SAMUEL STEWART'S COMPANY. (County Unknown.)
Served from April, until October 20, 1812.

Rank and Name of Soldier.
Capt. Samuel Stewart
Sergt. John Reed
Sergt. Jacob Koogler
Sergt. Evan Stephens
Corp. George Slukin
Corp. James Barnes

Privates.
Albon, George
Brown, William
Beasley, Isaac
Curtis, William
Cartree, Hiram
Davis, Noah
Ennis, Jeremiah
Hardman, Henry
Hughes, John
Gutridge, William
Jefferson, James
Looker, Allison C.
Millpolland, Hugh
Moore, John
McDonald, Daniel
Polen, John
Perry, Allen
Shackly, Clement
Sherry, John
Stevens, James
Tarbutton, Edward
Watson, Joshua
Williams, Reed

Rank and Name of Soldier.
Lieut. Jacob Pentz
Sergt. Samuel Pollack
Sergt. Elijah Weaver
Sergt. William Pringle
Corp. Abner S. Millard
Drummer, M. Gibson

Privates.
Busby, John
Boyce, Samuel
Bacon, George
Childers, Henry
Dill, George
Daugherty, Thomas
Hathaway, Wesley
Hall, Moses
Hindman, William
Gard, Daniel
Kerr, Jesse
Long, Daniel
Miller, Adam
Myers, William
Oliver, John
Paxton, James
Rhoades, William
Seward, Malen
Smith, Solomon
Tarrbutton, Eli
Thornton, John
Wolff, John
Wilson, Valentine

Rank and Name of Soldier.
Ensign Daniel Jones
Sergt. Samuel Smith
Sergt. Mathew S. Spencer
Corp. James Barnes
Corp. Elijah Ross
Fifer, Robert Pringle

Privates.
Botkin, C.
Butcher, David
Cummins, Joseph
Curl, Jeremiah
Davis, Daniel
Ennis, Thompson
Hixon, Joel
Hughey, William
Hutchinson, John
Jackson, John
Kizer, William
Lufton, John
Morrison, Michell
McBery, Duncan
Perry, Ebenezer
Porter, Thomas
Seward, Samuel
Smith, Ballard
Sutton, Jeremiah
Talor, Peter
Thornton, William
Williams, William

Pages 333-334.
ROLL OF CAPT. WILLIAM RAYNOLD'S COMPANY. (County Unknown.)
Served from April 12, 1812, until April 13, 1813.

Capt. William Raynolds
Sergt. Henry Foore
Corp. James M. Wood
Corp. Samuel Johnstone

Privates.
Anser, Lloyd
Blake, John
Bland, Thomas
Barron, William
Cass, Eyre
Craig, William
Dowell, John
Eddington, Robert
Frye, Isaac
Groves, Solomon
Howey, Peter
Hardesty, George
Johnstone, James
Lane, Walter
Lackey, Andrew
Moore, Thomas
McFadden, Neal
McKinley, Thomas
Pigman, John G.
Petitt, Joseph
Smith, Alexander
Shenard, David
Shadley, Henry
Virden, Lacy S.
Wassin, James

Lieut. Joseph Cairns
Sergt. James Nixon
Corp. William Smith

Privates.
Anser, John
Bland, William
Blake, Nehemiah
Cairns, Richard
Cordray, James
Coats, John
Dennis, Samuel
Fickle, Michael
Furthy, Isaac
Hare, Josiah
Hartley, Thomas
Jones, William
Keerns, John
Lawson, Septimus
Marshall, Thomas
Moore, Robert
McNeal, Alexander
Pratt, Robert
Pevise, William
Parker, Benjamin
Sutton, Joseph
Seybring, Robert
Upp, Upp
Welsh, Moses
Winner, John

Ensign Isaac Van Horne
Sergt. John Eagin
Corp. Mathias Hollandback

Privates.
Armstrong, James
Blunt, James
Blake, Henry
Colly, Benjamin
Carhart, William
Cantwell, James
Dorrel, Thomas B.
Fickle, George M.
Gilkinson, Jonothan
Harris, George
Hare, Joseph
Jeffers, Jonas
Lackey, Hugh
Loar, John
Moore, Peter
Mums, John
McDonald, Stephen
Peatt, Peter
Peatt, Stephen
Richards, Jacob
Smith, Benjamin
Smith, Nathaniel B.
Van Sickle, James
Watson, James C.
Williams, Littleton

Pages 337-338.
ROLL OF CAPT. THOMAS McCONNELL'S COMPANY. (County Unknown.)
Served from September 4, until December 31, 1813.

Capt. Thomas McConnell
Sergt. George Scott
Sergt. Isaac Sutton
Corp. William C. Goff

Privates.
Brundon, Andrew
Bradley, William

Lieut. Alexander Hill
Sergt. Enoch Buchanon
Corp. Joseph Aldridge
Corp. John McCarter
Fifer, William Martin

Privates.
Bush, Isaac
Butler, John

Ensign William Fee
Sergt. Pennel Davis
Corp. George Fisher
Drummer, John W. Tyler

Privates.
Brush, Israel
Cook, Rudolph

Vol. 2.
ROLL OF CAPT. THOMAS McCONNELL'S COMPANY. (Continued)

Rank and Name of Soldier.

Privates.

Cochran, John
Cochran, James
Dyal, John
Foor, Adam
Gano, Joseph
Hanna, James, Jr.
Haynes, Nathan
Johnson, John
Kyte, Joel
Kirkpatrick, Alexander
Lorel, Joseph
Murray, Daniel
Martin, John
McKee, James
Ogden, John
Richardson, John
Sargent, Elijah
Shaw, Hugh
Shumanion, Samuel R.
Steirs, Andrew
Tyler, Morris
White, Amos
Young, Roger

Rank and Name of Soldier.

Privates.

Conner, Florence
Danforth, Eli
Dye, William
Foor, John
Hill, Daniel
Henderson, James
Higon, Wesley
Jones, Tarpley
Kilpatrick, David
Lanham, William
Lindsey, John
McKinney, Cain
McCarter, William
Masters, John
Pinnel, Edward
Richardson, Lemuel
Stewart, William
Simen, Peter
Shurran, David
Scott, Trummel
Welsh, Thomas
Woodruff, David

Rank and Name of Soldier.

Privates.

Cook, William
Davison, James
Day, Thomas
Griggs, Caleb
Hanna, James Sr.
Henderson, William
Hill, William
Kindle, Joseph
Kindle, David
Leusey, Enoch
Lemmont, James
Manahan, Samuel
Moore, Augustus
Neever, James C.
Ralston, James
Sullivan, William
Shepherd, Solomon
Springer, John
Schooley, Jonothan
Tyler, Joseph
Waterfield, Jacob
Washburn, Cornelius

Pages 339-340.

ROLL OF CAPT. THOMAS FREEMAN'S COMPANY. (County Unknown.)

Served from September 5, 1813, until January 21, 1814.

Capt. Thomas Freeman
Ensign Peter Sey
Sergt. Paul Michael
Corp. Joseph Abbott
Corp. Samuel Burns

Lieut. Joseph Stephens
Sergt. James Mills
Sergt. Thomas Monloyne
Corp. William Street
Drummer, Ralph Vorhees

Sergt. Michael Murray
Sergt. Phillip Place
Corp. Joseph Willis
Corp. George Reprogle
Fifer, Jonothan Potter

Privates.

Buchanan, James
Breece, Valentine
Broderick, Nehemiah
Badene, Clemens
Coldwell, Joseph
Cox, Andrew
Davis, George
Fields, Foster
Foster, Isaac
Grubbs, George
Hudgill, John
Lewman, William
Missner, Richard
Meredith, Absolom
McEown, James
McKee, Robert
Place, Philip
Reynolds, Jeremiah
Robison, John
Stine, Daniel
Taylor, Hayse
VanLeer, Daniel
Wilson, John Sr.

Privates.

Bensley, William
Ball, Isaiah
Boyland, Nicholas
Coalby, Joseph
Clark, Alexander
Dickey, Samuel
Deckey, John H.
Fleming, David
Fields, James
Hall, James
Kiger, John
LaClear, Peter
Masterson, William
Morton, James
McNeal, Lazarus
Newcum, Emanuel
Parsons, David
Riprogle, Jacob
Shappell, Jacob
Sutton, Daniel
Taylor, William
Watson, Joseph
Wilson, John Jr.
Ward, Daniel

Privates.

Bridge, Ebenezer
Bant, Silas
Bala, Amma
Caterlin, Joseph
Coon, George
Davis, Robert
Doty, William
Fergesson, Samuel

Hunter, Andrew
Keller, Jonothan
Logan, Joseph
Maxwell, Samuel
Miller, Jacob
McDowell, Joshua
Orson, Joseph
Reed, John
Reece, William
Spencer, John
Spinning, Jonothan
VanLeer, Cornelius
Wallace, James
Weaver, George

Pages 341-342.

ROLL OF CAPT. JAMES DOWNING'S COMPANY.
(Probably from Jefferson County.)

Served from August 23, until November 30, 1812.

Capt. James Downing
Sergt. John Forsythe
Sergt. Samuel Richards
Corp. John Warden

Lieut. Peter Johnson
Sergt. John Barber
Corp. Abraham Bair
Corp. Joseph Balsfore
Drummer, Daniel Smith

Ensign Thomas Smith
Sergt. Michael McGowen
Corp. Benjamin A. Kinson
Fifer, Jesse Ellis

Privates.

Adam, John
Baird, John
Barden, Henry
Crites, William
Funk, Samuel
Holts, John
Hoster, Jacob
King, Peter

Privates.

Baindan, Jacob
Bawn, Henry
Baird, John
Chapman, Thomas
Fouls, George
Hawman, Isaac
Hefner, David
Knap, Caleb

Privates.

Buck, John
Bair, David
Baired, Andrew
Forsythe, Andrew
Grubb, John
Henning, Jacob
Hartman, David
Kepler, Andrew

Vol. 2.
ROLL OF CAPT. THOMAS FREEMAN'S COMPANY. (Continued.)

Rank and Name of Soldier.

Privates.
Kinny, Peter
Mettz, Abraham
McKintorpe, John
Patten, Mathew
Price, Benjamin
Rogers, Levi
Stoner, John

Page 343.

Rank and Name of Soldier.

Privates.
Leatherman, Peter
Miles, Eli
Nelson, William
Powell, John
Price, John
Leed, Adam
Shook, David
Stover, Samuel

Rank and Name of Soldier.

Privates.
Mirur, Boyd
McCaughey, Joseph
Neighdick, Samuel
Perkins, James
Richards, Daniel
Strickland, Edward
Smith, Jacob

ROLL OF CAPT. GEORGE STIDGER'S COMPANY.
(Probably from Stark County.)

Served from August 23, 1812, until January 19, 1813.

Capt. George Stidger
Sergt. Daniel McClure
Sergt. William B. Chamberlain
Corp. Jacob Essig

Privates.
Alexander, Ezekial
Black, James
Chisimore, George
Croninger, Benjamin
DeWalt, George
Forber, Daniel
Kroft, John
Livingston, Henry
Moore, James
Rogers, John
Rowland, John
Swigart, Jacob
Stephens, Daniel

Page 344.

Lieut. Robert Cameron
Sergt. John Miller
Sergt. Christian Flickenger
Corp. Moses Andrews

Privates.
Andrews, James
Brouse, Philip
Clinger, John
Cresson, Gamett
Elder, John
Gaff, John
Kuntz, John
Monroe, George
McClelland, Samuel
Roose, Abraham
Rice, John
Shisson, John
Short, John

Ensign Daniel McClure
Sergt. John Shorb
Corp. George Cribs
Bugleman, Thomas Neely

Privates.
Brown, William
Cutthall, John
Carper, John
Duck, Samuel
Essig, Adam
Gaff, Robert
Kirkpatrick, George
Myers, Jacob
Potts, John
Riddle, James
Smith, William
Shields, Thomas
Sheinbarger, John

ROLL OF CAPT. JOSEPH ZIMMERMAN'S COMPANY.
(Probably from Jefferson County.)

Served from August 25, until November 30, 1812.

Capt. Joseph Zimmerman
Sergt. George Estep
Sergt. Christian Krepps
Corp. Ezekiel Moore

Privates.
Augustine, Henry
Blackburn, William
Cook, George
Ford, William
Gilson, John
Hahan, Andrew
Kelly, Alexander
Meek, Samuel, Jr.
Minton, John
McClary, John
Rogers, Thomas
Shultz, George
Thompson, John

Lieut. James Kerr
Sergt. George Schultz
Corp. George Switzer
Corp. Samuel Meek

Privates.
Becht, George
Crecy, James
Catt, Philip
Fairr, Michael
Hoffman, Jacob
Heckinthorn, Peter
Kemp, Jonothan
Meek, John
Miett, Frederick
Palmer, Richard
Richy, Isaac
Smith, John
Wickersham, Joseph

Ensign Conrad Monzer or Myers
Sergt. William Rough or Pouch
Corp. John Lawrence
Drummer, Byneal Moore

Privates.
Barnett, Jacob
Callahan, William
Fisher, Brice
Garringer, David
Higgins, Samuel
Kalep, John
Myers, Silas
Meek, John Sr.
McClellan, Felix
Ruck, Henry
Saner, Michael
Thomas, Robert

Page 349.

ROLL OF CAPT. WILLIAM BLACKBURN'S COMPANY.
(Probably from Columbiana County.)

Served from August 22, until November 30, 1812.

Capt. William Blackburn
Sergt. Stephen Miller
Sergt. Benjamin Hohne
Corp. Daniel Cross

Privates.
Brown, Joseph
Betz, Frederick
Booker, Isaiah
Curls, Charles
Harwood, Eaton
Jump, Henry
Miller, Stephen
Patterson, Joseph
Sheets, George
Twimpseed, John
Woolf, George

Lieut. Samuel Ferguson
Sergt. William Milnor
Sergt. William Kerr
Corp. Joseph Earle

Privates.
Britz, George
Bidenger, Joseph
Burnes, George
Grimes, John
Hahn, Caleb
Kutz, Emanuel
Miller, Conrad
Rudinan, Jacob
Soey, Benjamin
Woolf, John
Webb, Richard

Ensign George Grimes
Sergt. George Wiseman
Corp. Andrew Gibson

Privates.
Branderberry, Conrad
Blake, Price B.
Caughey, Joseph
Gaskill, David
Jumper, Joseph
Moody, Joseph
Palmer, Jesse
Rogers, George
Soey, Samuel
Wolf, Philip

Page 350. Vol. 2.

ROLL OF CAPT. DANIEL HARBAUGH'S COMPANY.
(Probably from Columbiana County.)
Served from August 25, 1812, until February —, 1813.

Rank and Name of Soldier.

Capt. Daniel Harbaugh
Cornet, Michael Wirtz
Sergt. Mordecai Moore

Privates.

Allison, Abner
Campbell, John
Graham, David
Mathews, Jacob
Moore, William
Sheehan, Cornelius
Willibey, John
Zeaner, Jacob

Rank and Name of Soldier.

Lieut. David Scott
Sergt. James Sharp
Sergt. Henry Hepner
Trumpeter, Daniel L. Smith

Privates.

Blackburn, Samuel
Fifer, David
Humbel, James
Morris, Morris E.
McKinsey, John
Swearinigen Elimeleeh
Willibey, Andrew

Rank and Name of Soldier.

Lieut. George Clark
Sergt. Jonothan Whitacre
Farrier, John Kuntz

Privates.

Blackburn, John
Goble, John
Hunt, John
Meese, Philip
Redick, John
Wilson, George
Watson, James

Pages 351-352.

ROLL OF CAPT. SAMUEL MARTIN'S COMPANY.
(Probably from Greene County.)
Served from August 24, 1813, until February 24, 1814.

Capt. Samuel Martin
Sergt. John Jackson
Sergt. William Phelps
Corp. Phillip Branaberry

Privates.

Anderson, Andrew
Bradfield, Joseph
Bell, William
Brinker, Peter
Dougherty, Samuel
Fulks, Charles
Gilson, David
Helmick, Adam
Knight, Robert
Lamboon, Josiah
Myers, John
Robinson, John
Stephens, Jacob
Smaley, John
Wollam, Henry
Willits, John

Lieut. David Hannah
Sergt. Noah Frederick
Corp. Thomas Armstrong
Corp. Benjamin Stephens
Drummer, Frederick Blaker

Privates.

Anderson, James
Bittenger, John
Bishop, Joseph
Brown, William
Frederick, Thomas
Fiskel, Fred
Gibson, John
Harrison, Daniel
Kilton, John S.
Manning, William
Quin, Samuel
Rossel, Jacob
Smith, Sampson
Tagart, William
Wollam, Jacob

Ensign Jacob Crouse
Sergt. Robert Corning
Corp. James Bennet
Fifer, David M. Casky

Privates.

Armstrong, Thomas
Britton, Archibald
Basham, Ezekial
Bowlin, Eli
Farmer, Thomas
Geddes, James
Hickman, Nicholas
Jones, Nicholas
Kurtz, John
Mann, Philip
Quin, John
Robins, John
Shaw, Jacob
Trippy, George
Welker, William

Pages 353-354.

ROLL OF CAPT. JOHN RAMSEY'S COMPANY.
(Probably from Columbiana County.)
Served from August 24, until November 30, 1812.

Capt. John Ramsey
Sergt. Thomas Rosebaugh
Corp. John Hunter
Fifer, Jacob Grin

Privates.

Augustine, Henry
Cannon, Thomas
Craig, William
Daugherty, James
Fife, James
Frank, Adam
Forney, Adam
Goss, Mathias
Graham, John
Hamilton, William
Heek, Jacob
Kees, Russell
Meek, William
McLilly, Samuel
McLaughlin, William
Pollock, Andrew
Paul, William
Robinson, Jonah
Sheets, John
Shivers, Samuel
Vanfresson, Arnold
Wall, Richard

Lieut. James Andrews
Sergt. James Craighead
Corp. Philip Foult
Drummer, Peter Shirts

Privates.

Beer, James
Craig, Robert
Craig, John
Early, James
Fife, Samuel
Forney, John
Fibe, William
Gardner, Jacob
Hamilton, Jonothan
Hayes, David M.
Hamilton, Joseph
Meek, Samuel
McLaughlin, Robert
McCullough, James
McCalle, Thomas
Paul, Benjamin
Pollock, Thomas
Rippord, Jonah
Sancock, Michael
Thompson, John L.
Watson, James
Whitmore, John

Ensign Lindsay Cannon
Sergt. James Ramsey
Corp. Joseph Fife

Privates.

Brown, Joseph
Carnes, George
Cambel, John
Early, David
Fergens, Samuel
Forney, Peter
Fegley, Joseph
Guthrie, William
Hunter, Samuel
Hoffman, John
Jolley, Samuel
Meek, Robert
McDonald, Duncan
McCredy, William
Opdyche, Albert
Paul, Henry
Pierce, William
Sheets, Jacob
Shook, George
Ton, Alexander
Wright, Gilbert
Yeanin, Mathias

ROLL OF CAPT. THOMAS ROWLAND'S COMPANY.
(Probably from Columbiana County.)

Served from July, 1812, until January, 1813.

Capt. Thomas Rowland
Ensign Charles Hoy
Sergt. Samuel Ravers
Corp. Aaron Reese

Lieut. Nathaniel McCracken
Sergt. Thomas R. McKnight
Sergt. James Dyers
Corp. Andre Wesley

Lieut. David Hostetter
Sergt. John Millinger
Corp. Jacob Watson
Corp. Thomas McCracken

Privates.
Byel, James
Buchanan, James
Dull, Aaron
Glenn, William
Haley, William
Krupp, Samuel
Mansion, George
McAlister, John
McCann, Peter
Poe, John
Reed, James
Shang, William
Updegraff, John
Willington, Thomas

Privates.
Bates, David
Creighton, John
Fishall, George
Hull, Abner
Hill, Jonothan
Kamp, Samuel
McCulloch, James
McBride, Jeff
McAllister, Walter
Petticord, Oratio
Spidle, John
Thompson, Robert
Wilson, Thomas
Wiley, William
Yarnell, Abraham

Privates.
Boots, Willis
Crane, John
Graham, Daniel
Hunter, John
Keisinger, George
Murray, James
McAlister, James
McLaughlin, Robert
Nool, John
Ritten, Benjamin
Stoner, George
Toppen, Archibald
Wright, Ruel
Yarnell, Alexander

ROLL OF CAPT. JOSEPH CHEWS' COMPANY.
(Probably from Ross County.)

Served from May 8, until May 16, and from July 28, until August 18, 1813.

Capt. Joseph Chews
Sergt. Peter Nichols

Lieut. Hiram Hurdin
Sergt. William Heath

Ensign Abraham Thomas

Privates.
Burnett, William
Barker, Joshua
Groves, William
Johnson, Isaac
Kirkpatrick, Joseph
Rollston, Benjamin
Stinson, Daniel
Smith, Samuel

Privates.
Bennett, John
Clark, William
Grimm, Jacob
Jordon, Isaac
McKinley, John
Richie, David
Stinson, John
Smith, Green N.

Privates.
Brown, Samuel
Grimm, Jonothan
Harrison, Mirajah
Johnston, John
Phillips, James
Richie, William
Shirley, Laurence
Spong, Henry

ROLL OF CAPT. JOSIAH KILBOURN'S COMPANY.
(Probably from Ross County.)

Served from July 28, until August 20, 1813.

Capt. Josiah Kilbourn
Sergt. Phillip Ayubright

Lieut. Jeremiah Cox
Sergt. Joshua Speakman
Corp. Edward McCann

Sergt. James Carter
Corp. Samuel Richardson

Privates.
Barby, Hasel
Dixon, Simon
Huddle, George
Looker, William
Ray, William
Williams, William

Privates.
Barby, Daniel
Day, Thomas
Jordon, William
Pay, John
Ratcliff, John
Wyckoff, William

Privates.
Dixon, Jacob
Francis, Jonothan
Kelly, William
Ruddick, Jesse
Slossen, William
Willfong, David

ROLL OF LIEUT. THOMAS LLOYD'S COMPANY. (County Unknown.)

Served from July 28, until August 10, 1813.

Lieut. Thomas Lloyd
Corp. John Householder

Ensign Robert Robison
Corp. Joseph McKee

Sergt. Samuel Davison

Privates.
Anderson, John
Bramble, James
Delano, Ira
Gibbs, James
Leister, Peter
Riddle, William
Whitecale, Hiram

Privates.
Brown, Edward
Crumpton, John
Daly, E.
Johnson, John
McAllister, Daniel
Romine, Elias
White, Thorley Lee
Gallager, David

Privates.
Brown, Peter
Cook, Samuel
Greenwood, John
Kelley, Jonothan
McKensey, Eli
Witheutt, John
Robison, John H.

ROLL OF CAPT. JAMES TAYLOR'S COMPANY.
(From Ross County.)

Served from August 21, until October 10, 1812.

Capt. James Taylor
Sergt. Henry Cahoon
Sergt. Thomas Wood
Drummer, Abel Houson

Lieut. Abiatha Taylor
Sergt. Amos Cox
Corp. James Kile

Ensign John Gufey
Sergt. Robert Wilson
Fifer, David Taylor

Vol. 2.

ROLL OF CAPT. JAMES TAYLOR'S COMPANY. (Continued)

Rank and Name of Soldier.

Privates.

Bright, John
Clymer, John
Cramer, George
Hires, Walter
Johnson, Barnabus
Long, John
Pursell, Samuel
Ross, Alexander
Suddick, James
Taylor, John A.
Vencamp, William

Rank and Name of Soldier.

Privates.

Casey, Thomas
Chevergar, William
Creamer, John
Hires, James
King, Phillip
Medford, Charles
Pursell, Jacob
Steveson, George
Swihser, John
Taylor, James A.
Wood, Charles

Rank and Name of Soldier.

Privates.

Chaney, John
Crawford, David
Flemming, Joseph
Hooper, Phillip
Long, Edward
Needles, Cubage
Ross, James
Swaring, William
Taylor, Robert
Vencamp, John
Whitnell, Henry

Page 360.

ROLL OF CAPT. JOSEPH GORTON'S COMPANY.
(Probably from Franklin County.)

Served from August 25, until October 10, 1812.

Capt. Joseph Gorton
Sergt. Mathew Mathews
Drummer, Andrew Corpus

Privates.

Breckenrige, James
Benton, Nathan
Hopper, Robert
Moody, James
Primrose, William
Simmons, John

Privates.

Badger, William
Grubb, Jacob
Instice, John
McNutt, William
Penix, Edward
Webb, Thomas

Privates.

Baille, Stewart
Gordon, John
John, John
Overdeer, Jacob
Robertson, Francis

Pages 361-362

ROLL OF CAPT. CHARLES HILLIARD'S COMPANY.
(Probably from Miami County.)

Served from February 22, until August 21, 1813.

Capt. Charles Hilliard
Sergt. James Frost
Sergt. Samuel Clark
Corp. Lewis Winans
Musician, John Manning

Lieut. John Hill
Sergt. Thomas Ross
Sergt. Benjamin Nogle
Corp. William Ramsey
Corp. William Brown

Ensign John Kiser
Sergt. Thomas Gilbert
Corp. Benjamin B. Winans
Musician, Samuel Haney

Privates.

Anderson, Samuel
Brown, Abraham
Battroll, John
Cary, David
Crawford, James
Foster, Elijah
Hance, Benjamin
Jowles, George
Julin, Isaac
Landry, Simon
Manning, Edward
McReynolds, Robert
Reyonlds, Robert
Weatherhead, John
Whiten, Stephen
Webb, John

Privates.

Blue, Barnabus
Bedler, Calvin
Cox, John
Castle, Ralph
Dunn, Terwin
Favorite, Abraham
Harter, Jacob
Jackson, John
Kimble, Edward
Langley, Benett W.
Miller, David
Pierson, Jacob
Ross, Job
Wilson, Alexander
Wyatt, Andrew
Whitney, Stephen

Privates.

Browning, Abraham
Bayman, Thomas
Cary, Thomas
Castle, Ralph, Sr.
Eller, Adam
Green, James
Ingle, Michael
James, Levi
Krise, Daniel
Livingood, George
Miller, Jacob
Ross, Martin
Studilaker, David
Webb, Joseph B.
Wyatt, John G.
Yontes, George

Pages 363-364.

ROLL OF CAPT. RICHARD SUNDERLAND'S COMPANY. (County Unknown.)

Served from February 16, until August 15, 1813.

Capt. Richard Sunderland
Sergt. William Guy
Corp. William Fryback

Lieut. Asa John
Sergt. John Murphy
Corp. James Wead
Corp. Ephraim Haines

Ensign, John C. Negley
Sergt. Robert Kendall
Corp. James German

Privates.

Ainsworth, John
Buxton, Charles
Coffman, Henry
Cline, Christian
Dawson, John
Ewing, William G.
Guess, Joseph
Harding, Daniel
Holderman, John
Kazee, Randall
Linen, James L.
Littell, Absalom
Middogh, John G.

Privates.

Alhed, Isaac
Barlow, William A.
Codington, Isaac
Croy, David
Duncan, Peter
Greer, Joshua
Hossier, Isaac
Houser, Martin
Isenogle, Abraham
Keggins, Robert
Loveless, Sileness
Loury, James
Martin, William

Privates.

Burgh, William Denning
Bowghman, George
Campbell, John
Dille, Samuel
Elliott, Groseberry
Goode, John
Harding, Richard
Hatfield, Moses
Knee, Philip
Kiser, John
Lumphian, Charles
Michael, Jacob
Miller, John

ROLL OF CAPT. RICHARD SUNDERLAND'S COMPANY. (Continued)

Privates.

McDonald, Daniel
Perkey, Frederick
Ramsey, Samuel
Swartwood, Abraham
Tennant, Alexander
Vanscoyk, Joseph
Weaver, Peter

Neff, Daniel
Robbins, Thomas
Smith, Adam
Stoner, Jacob
Tolbit, William
Ward, George
Waggner, Michael

Peck, Jacob
Rose, Benjamin
Shantz, Peter
Sproul, Hugh
Vanscoyk, John
Wood, Elijah

Pages 365-366.

ROLL OF CAPT. DANIEL REX'S COMPANY. (County Unknown.)

Served from April 3, until October 3, 1813.

Capt. Daniel Rex
Sergt. David Hendershot
Sergt. Thomas Shiers
Corp. Frederick Michael

Lieut. James Medill
Sergt. William Rash
Corp. John McClarkin
Corp. Benjamin Morphew

Ensign, William Campbell
Sergt. William Ross
Corp. Elijah Allen

Privates.

Allen, John
Alexander, James
Bayne, Samuel
Black, Joseph
Christman, David
Cloyde, James
Easlinger, John
Flick, William
Huffman, Allen
Kelough, William
Knear, Henry
Michael, John
Morphey, Nathan
Owens, Samuel
Price, Daniel
Reed, William
Steel, John K.
Show, John
Sproul, Samuel
Utt, Muchael
Worle, Samuel Jr.

Achmand, Alexander
Butler, James
Biggs, Aaron
Bishop, Levin
Caldwell, Jonothan
Dervees, Ezekial
Flemming, James
Heuston, Samuel
Hamilton, Samuel
Kirk, Thomas
Lambert, Courtland
Moore, Alexander
McLarkin, James
Pearson, Thomas
Reid, John
Rooker, William
Stone, William
Smith, Philip
Shull, Philip
Warrell, Attwell
Worle, James, Sr.

Adkins, George
Black, Daniel
Boyd, William
Caldwell, Manlove
Crawfort, Jacob
Day, William
Flashman, Peter
Holliday, Samuel
Ireland, James
Knoddle, Jacob
Landers, Samuel
Manlove, George
Nickum, Peter
Payne, Isaac
Russell, Charles
Simonton, John
Shidler, Jacob
Strou, Michael
Tibbs, John
Wickle, Frederick
Williams, Jonothan

Page 367.

ROLL OF CAPT. ROBERT IRWIN'S COMPANY.
(Probably from Belmont County.)

Served from June 1, until August 12, 1813.

Capt. Robert Irwin
Sergt. David Kirkland
Sergt. William Reneson
Corp. John Richardson

Lieut. Thomas Pribble
Sergt. Absalom Dilly
Corp. Solomon James
Corp. William Crothers

Ensign, Thomas McNight
Sergt. Francis Smith
Corp. Samuel Coonts
Drummer, Jacob Castle

Privates.

Barker, Amos
Bruver, John
Boyles, Thomas
Devall, John
Forest, John
Hall, John
Heness, John
Jones, Thomas
Keller, John
Miller, James
Neally, John
Richards, George

Bates, Jesse
Billman, Henry
Campbell, James
Ferguson, George
Goomon, William
Hammond, David
Jenkins, John
King, Cornelius
Lattimore, William
McMullen, Samuel
Proudfoot, Alexander
Richards, Daniel

Boggs, James
Bryan, Richard
Coss, Daniel
Fleshaman, Jesse
Higgins, William
Hillhouse, John
Johnston, William
King, Samuel
Lormmy, William
McCoy, Rallston
Richards, James
Stout, Joseph

Page 368.

ROLL OF CAPT. ADAM BINCKLEY'S COMPANY.
(From Perry and Fairfield Counties.)

Served from June 1, until August 12, 1813.

Capt. Adam Binckley
Sergt. William B. Davis
Sergt. Henry M. Davis
Corp. John Henry

Lieut. John Middaugh
Sergt. John Overmire
Corp. Peter King
Corp. John Winner

Ensign, Richard Grabb
Sergt. John Fowler
Corp. John Leidy

Privates.

Amspach, Adam
Acker, George
Bowland, Hugh
Bucket, William
Cock, Jacob

Ammach, Abraham
Baker, Henry
Breson, George
Bonesteel, Henry
Deal, David

Acklin, Alexander
Bouler, Alexander
Buckson, Thomas
Crosby, Edward
Downhouer, Jacob

ROLL OF CAPT. ADAM BINCKLEY'S COMPANY. (Continued)

Privates.

Dubler, Philip
Grelle, Philip
Hutsman, Jesse
Lancaster, William
Miller, Philip
Rannels, Thomas
Stener, Jacob
Smith, Daniel

Dubler, John
Houty, Christian
Hall, Benjamin
Landfer, Benjamin
Moyer, John
Richard, Samuel
Swinehart, John
Spohn, Adam

Fogt, Michael
Hawk, Solomon
Kinnon, William
Lane, Peter
Notestine, John
Sain, David
Shunk, Henry

Page 369.

ROLL OF CAPT. STEPHEN AIVATT'S COMPANY. (County Unknown.)

Served from March 7, until September 7, 1814.

Capt. Stephen Aivatt
Sergt. Almarin Brooks
Sergt. Oliver Lewis
Corp. Andrew C. Nuerker

Lieut. Asa L. Banning
Sergt. Fillington Moary
Corp. Henry Dennison
Corp. Isaac R. Allen

Ensign, Robert Short
Sergt. Calvin Smith
Corp. Jacob Winas

Privates.

Burnan, Nathaniel
Croft, Jacob
Crooks, Thomas
Dixon, Walter
Goncher, John
Hood, Simon
Johnson, William
King, Samuel
Mackey, John
McCullough, Thomas
Nicholas, William
Rutan, John
Sprague, William
Tamer, Samuel
Weber, Peter

Buchanan, Abraham
Chalfint, David
Crawford, Gurron
Elliott, William
Gates, Mathias
Hannah, Isaac
Kincaid, Alexander
Lord, Mathew
McConnel, Elias
McMiller, John
Rolston, Nathaniel
Riche, John
Tend, Roswell
Snider, William

Broadwell, Jacob
Crooks, John
Dixon, James
Fannah, Isaac
Gates, John
Johnson, Nathan
Kidd, John
Lightburn, Joseph
McConnel, Mathew
McLinly, William
Robbins, Bowman
Sullivan, William
Thompson, Patrick
Wood, Jonah

Page 370.

ROLL OF CAPT. BARUCH DICKERSON'S COMPANY.
(Probably from Harrison County.)

Served from March 12, until September 12, 1814.

Capt. Baruch Dickerson
Sergt. William Hagerfield
Musician, James Roff

Lieut. John Jamison
Sergt. Charles Holmes
Musician, David Young

Ensign, Samuel Gilmore
Sergt. Laken Wells

Privates.

Browning, Samuel
Carson, John
Foster, Moses
Haverfield, James
Holmes, Samuel
McConkey, James
Parrish, Joseph
Scott, David
Wrist, Nathaniel
Young, George

Chambers, Ezekial
Craig, Joseph
Fivecoats, Michael
Hovey, John
Holmes, Elsy
McConkey, Samuel
Richison, John
Steel, Bazallel
Walraven, John

Carson, Samuel
Foster, Andrew
Hitchcock, Isaac
Hurless, John
Mechan, Aaron
Nelson, Benjamin
Smith, Francis
Warpenbay, Francis
Welday, Henry

Page 372.

ROLL OF CAPT. ISAAC WARNER'S COMPANY.
(Probably from Columbiana County.)

Served from March 11, until September 11, 1814.

Capt. Isaac Warner
Corp. Michael Musser

Lieut. George Akins
Corp. John Wilkins
Musician, William Altman

Sergt. Reuben Taylor
Corp. Joseph Gastin

Privates.

Bradfield, Benjamin
Cormick, George
Harper, Jacob
McCollister, Jacob
Powell, Michael
Rock, George
Snyder, Stephen
Widick, John
Welker, William

Butz, Samuel
Fulk, Johnston
Motinger, George
Piper, Henry
Rogers, John
Switzer, Jacob
Sheets, Christian
Walter, Henry
Wilson, William

Babb, Peter
Hahn, Andrew
Morbet, Charles
Pense, Gainer
Ramsey, Charles
Stephens, Peter
Thomas, Michael
Welker, George
Willington, Morgan

Pages 373-374. Vol. 2.

ROLL OF CAPT. WILLIAM ALBAN'S COMPANY. (County Unknown.)

Served from March 12, until September 12, 1814.

Rank and Name of Soldier.	Rank and Name of Soldier.	Rank and Name of Soldier.
Capt. William Alban	Lieut. William Withrow	Ensign, Solomon Gladden
Sergt. Thomas Bolin	Sergt. Thomas B. Roe	Sergt. Joseph Brown
Sergt. William Reed	Corp. George Betz	Corp. John Glenn
Corp. George Shultz	Corp. James Morrison	
Privates.	**Privates.**	**Privates.**
Andrews, Daniel	Anspaugh, Leonard	Brown, William
Bell, Adam	Barr, Samuel	Bruk, Moses
Burgess, Joseph	Barnhill, Samuel	Cole, Ezekial
Cole, Elijah	Caruthers, James	Duke, William
Doman, Jacob	Erick, George	Elliott, Thomas
Fisher, Brice	Frank, John	Freet, George
Farbar, Philip	Gibson, George	Gooden, Abedneyo
Galbraith, James	Groog, John	Hardenbrooks, Samuel
Hoft, Jacob	Jolly, William	Kyle, Samuel
Miller, John	Metcalf, Mepon	Miller, Phillip
Minay, Patrick	Marshall, William	Martin, James
McCullough, Daniel	Newstetler, Henry	Otis, Ezekial
Patterson, Richard	Patterson, William	Riddle, Samuel
Spangley, Michael	Spielle, John	Shoop, David
Smith, Michael	Stone, Jesse	Swigar, John
Smallwood, Richard	Smith, John	Sullivan, Henry
Taylor, Valentine	Tipton, Luke	Van Horn, Peter
White, Joseph	Wright, Richard	Zimmerman, David

Page 379.

ROLL OF CAPT. THOMAS LEWIS' COMPANY.
(Probably from Adams County.)

Served from July 28, until September 1, 1813.

Capt. Thomas Lewis	Lieut. Samuel Bradford	Ensign, George Sample
Cornet, Isaac Foster	Sergt. Nathan Rogers	Sergt. William Stout
	Sergt. Jacob Shults	
Privates.	**Privates.**	**Privates.**
Baigs, Thomas	Badridge, Samuel	Brigintine, John
Bratton, Jacob	Collins, Elijah	Carr, Daniel
Hanna, William	Little, Thomas	Lockhart, Samuel
Moore, John	Milligin, James	Moore, Aaron
Markland, Jesse	McDermott, John	McHenry, Alexander
McMilligan, J. D.	Paull, James	Pennington, Obediah
Raulston, Robert	Rowland, William	Russell, John, Sr.
Stockard, Thomas	Sanders, Francis	Warner, Peter
	Williamson, Samuel	

Page 380.

ROLL OF LIEUT. JAMES BLACK'S COMPANY. (County Unknown.)

Served from April 15, until October 14, 1813.

Lieut. James Black	Ensign, John T. Ireland	Sergt. John Demoss
Sergt. James Quinn	Corp. William Bennet	Corp. Jabez Bennet
Privates.	**Privates.**	**Privates.**
Banfill, Thomas	Baker, Lewis	Biers, Isaac
Boyd, James	Beasley, Thomas	Cooper, Samuel
Collins, John	Caro, David	DeMoss, William
Davis, William	Fall, Daniel	Gamble, Samuel
Gordon, Charles	Gordon, James	Hoag, Ensebius
Ireland, Samuel	Jones, William	Landers, Daniel
Milner, William	Martin, William	Nickum, Davis
Pilson, Hugh	Pemberton, Joseph	Riley, John
Ringer, Jacob	Scott, Thomas	Shanks, Jacob
Sallee, Samuel	Street, John	Timmons, George
Wilkinson, Charles	Wilson, John	

Page 1. Vol. 1.

SECOND REGIMENT—FIELD, STAFF AND COMPANIES.
ROLL OF FIELD AND STAFF, WAR OF 1812-1813.
COLONEL JAMES STEWART, THIRD REGIMENT, OHIO MILITIA.

Col. James Stewart	Major, Samuel Waddle	Adjt. Joseph Parrott
Q. M., George Allen	Surg. Samuel Baldridge	Surg. Mate, James B. Webster
Pay Master, Wade Loosborough	Q. M. Sergt. Thomas Clark	Sergt. Major, James Carr
Fife Major, Jacob Bushong	Drum Major, Benjamin Davis	

Page. 2. Vol. I.
COL. CHARLES MILLER, THIRD REGIMENT, DRAFTED OHIO MILITIA.

Rank and Name of Soldier.	Rank and Name of Soldier.	Rank and Name of Soldier.
Col. Charles Miller	Major, Abraham Shane	Major, Solomon Bentley
Adjt. Peter Bryans	Q. M. William Marshall	Q. M. Sergt. E. L. Bonham
Q. M., Samuel Taylor	Sergt. Maj., James E. Wells	Surg. James Wilson
Ass't. Surg. Royal N. Powers	Q. M. Sergt., Jacob Clark	

Pages 3-241-440.
COLONEL WILLIAM RAYEN, THIRD REGIMENT, OHIO MILITIA.

Col. William Rayen	Major, George Darrow	Maj. W. W. Colgreave
Maj. Peter Muster	Adjt. James Mackey	Q. M., Arad Way
Pay Master, John E. Woodbridge	Surg. Henry Manning	Surg. Mate, James Hillman
Sergt. Maj., William Ingersol	Sergt. Maj. Stephen Miller	Q. M. Sergt. Lewis Hoyt
Q. M. Sergt. John Srain	Drum Major, William W. Wright	Fife Major, Aaron Collar

Page 4.
COLONEL ROBERT BAY, THIRD REGIMENT, OHIO MILITIA.

Col. Robert Bay	Maj. Peter Cribs	Maj. Thomas Knowls
Surg. Christian Espich	Surg. Mate, Jacob Espich	Q. M., James Cleud
Pay Master, Christian Deardorf	Adjt., Lloyd Talbert	For. M., Henry Laffer

Page 5.
ROLL OF CAPT. CYRUS BEATTY'S COMPANY.
(From Guernsey County.)
Served from October 23, 1812, until February 22, 1813.

Capt. Cyrus Beatty	Lieut. David Burt	Ensign, Nicholas Stoner
Sergt. William Martain	Sergt. Joseph Pollock	Sergt. Samuel Beymer
Sergt. William Van Horn	Corp. John Meek	Corp. Isaac Stiers
Corp. Andrew Anderson	Corp. Elijah Williams	Drummer, Jacob Wirick

Privates.

Addy, Loid	Anderson, William	Conner, John
Cochran, William	Feticuck, Michael	Gibson, William
Hutchins, David	Havens, James	Henderson, John
Johnston, George	Johnston, John	Kirkpatrick, Alexander
Loury, Robert	Meek, Samuel	Martain, John S.
McKee, John	Nance, Samuel C.	Ogle, George
Reasoner, Ganett	Ross, Daniel	Reamey, Robert
Reasoner, William	Reynolds, Joseph	Stiers, Samuel
Shivel, George	Shipley, James	Shipley, John
Shatto, Nicholas	Sparr, James M.	Stanley, Joseph
Turner, William	Talbot, William	Tolbat, Nathaniel
Ward, Joseph	Work, Samuel	Wirick, Michael
Waddle, James	White, Thomas	

Page 6.
ROLL OF CAPT. JAMES WIMP'S COMPANY. (County Unknown.)
Served from September 20, 1812, until February 20, 1813.

Capt. James Wimp	Lieut. James Parker	Ensign, Thomas Rodgers
Sergt. George Hammet	Sergt. Eli Watts	Serjt. George Moore
Sergt. Daniel Swackhamnar	Corp. Robert Frost	Corp. William Richardson
Corp. David Scott	Corp. Henry Weller	

Privates.

Baro, George	Crooks, Anthony	Condron, William
Collins, John	Dill, Solomon	Foraker, Joshua
Gates, Wilson L.	Lefler, John	McBride, Isaac
McElhiney, Patrick	Moore, William	Paret, Allen
Rose, Robert	Rombo, Tobias	Stover, David
Stinson, John	Peargrin, John	Wiseman, Michael
Walls, Benjamin	Wilson, William	

Page 7.
ROLL OF CAPT. ABSALOM MARTIN'S COMPANY.
(From Guernsey or Belmont County.)
Served from August 26, until November 12, 1812.

Capt Absalom Martin	Lieut. Wyatt Hutchison	Ensign, James Shuman
Sergt. John Broton	Sergt. George Scadan	Sergt. Thomas Mullen
Sergt. William Israel	Corp. Christopher Donouer	Corp. James Edwards
Corp. Edward Davis	Corp. Henry Wolford	Drummer, Thomas DeBatnon
	Fifer, Edward Milner	

Privates.

Atkinson, Michael	Brown, David	Bowers, Jonah
Burys, David	Berry, Thomas	Beard, Thomas
Bowers, Joseph	Bell, Joseph	Beard, Moses
Carnes, William	Cogle, Joseph	Carroll, Henry

Vol. I.

ROLL OF CAPT. ABSALOM MARTIN'S COMPANY. (Continued)

Rank and Name of Soldier.

Privates.

Davis, Henry
Fink, William
Hill, Henry
Launtz, George
Moore, William
McGiffin, William
Pack, Samuel
Reeves, Joshua
Shipley, George
Tetrick, Michael
Warne, Jonothan
Woodbick, John

Rank and Name of Soldier.

Privates.

Delong, Darel
Hart, Jacob
Heage, Aaron
Miller, James
Maple, William
McGiffin, John
Reed, John
Shove, Philip
Salor, John
Tetrick, Richard
Wirick, Andrew
Wanich, Robert
Wirack, Peter

Rank and Name of Soldier.

Privates.

Everett, James
Hanna, William
Lambert, Lewis
Mealman, John
Merrit, Thomas
McWilliams, Phillip
Reed, William
Stites, Jonothan
Tetrick, Jacob
Wilson, David
Wilkins, Thomas
Wanich, James

Page 8.

ROLL OF CAPT. SIMON BEYNER'S COMPANY.
(From Guernsey County.)

Served from August 20, until November 12, 1812.

Capt. Simon Beyner
Sergt. David Slater
Sergt. Robert Ewings
Corp. William Inglehag

Lieut. Stewart Speer
Sergt. George Wine
Corp. Nicholas Bumgavance
Corp. Alexander Barton
Fifer, David Moor

Ensign, Henry Beyner
Sergt. Andrew Dougherty
Corp. William Beyner
Drummer, Frederick Beyner

Privates.

Argo, Morris
Brannan, Thomas
Bates, Ezekial
Clark, Joshua
Dilly, Abraham
Findlay, Collins
Llewellyn, Henry
Larde, James
McConnell, James
Shevel, Samuel
Saterfield, William
Smith, William
Sherman, William
Vanpell, John

Privates.

Beach, Charles
Barnes, Ford
Chance, William
Doughty, David
Dye, George
Frye, Peter
Lynn, Joseph
Lancing, Robert
Rainey, John
Stephenson, Moses
Smith, Thomas
Sickman, Andrew
Sickman, Pressley
Wright, Moses

Privates.

Beaham, John
Bates, William
Cook, William
Dilly, Ichabod
Evans, Elisha
Hawkins, James
Levi, Lewis
McGowan, Andrew
Reed, Joseph
Saltsgiver, Frederick
Sickman, John
Stiers, Henry
Thomas, Jacob
William, Nehemiah

Page 9.

ROLL OF CAPT. LEVI ROSE'S COMPANY. (County Unknown.)

Served from June 1, 1812, until June 1, 1813.

Lieut. Sylvanus Mitchell
Sergt. Orin Granger
Corp. Asa B. Gavit
Musician, Justin Thillyer

Capt. Levi Rose
Sergt. John Rees
Corp. Knowles Linnel
Musician, Thomas Spillman

Ensign, Eleazar C. Clemens
Sergt. Timothy Spillman
Corp. Lester Case

Privates.

Alexander, James
Butler, Levent
Clark, Arunna
Ford, Thomas
Gibbons, William B.
Johnston, Hezekiah
Linnell, Benjamin
Martin, John
Owens, Owen
Rees, Theophilus
Spillman, Spencer
Thrall, Colton M.

Privates.

Avery, George
Clemens, Harry
Cooley, Festus
Gilman, Elias
Gavit, Benjamin F.
Kelley, John
Messenger, David
Messenger, Campbell
Pratt, Calvin
Rose, Ormon
Thompson, William
Thrall, Alexander

Privates.

Brown, Mahalon
Clark, Rowley
Fox, Elijah
Graves, Clodius L.
Hoskins, Titus S.
Kelley, Hugh
Meed, Seth
Murdock, Dan
Rathbone, Elijah
Shephard, James
Thompson, David
Wells, Joel

Pages 10-11.

ROLL OF CAPT. JOSEPH CAIRNS' COMPANY. (County Unknown.)

Served from December 12, 1812, until April 12, 1813.

Capt. Joseph Cairns
Sergt. Henry Ferris
Sergt. William Smith
Corp. John G. Pigman

Lieut. Isaac VanHorn
Sergt. James Nixon
Corp. Matthias Hollinback
Corp. Richard Cairns
Fifer, Ira Cass

Ensign, John Eason
Sergt. James M. Wood
Corp. Samuel Johnston
Drummer, Henry Blake

Privates.

Armstrong, James
Blunt, James
Blake, Nehemiah
Cacheart, William

Privates.

Blake, John
Bland, William
Colly, Benjamin
Craig, William

Privates.

Bland, Thomas
Barren, William
Corberry, James
Coats, John

ROLL OF CAPT. JOSEPH CAIRNS' COMPANY. (Continued)

Rank and Name of Soldier.

Privates.
Cantwell, James
Dennis, Samuel
Fickle, George W.
Futhey, Isaac
Hau, Isaiah
Hare, Joseph
Leckey, Arthur
Lane, Walter
Marshall, Thomas
Moore, Robert
McDonald, Stephen
Pettitt, Joseph
Piatt, Robert
Smith, Alexander
Seabring, Robert
Upp, Francis
Usher, Lloyd
Warson, James

Rank and Name of Soldier.

Privates.
Cares, John
Dowell, John
Fickle, Michael
Groves, Solomon
Harris, George
Johnston, James
Loare, John
Lackey, Hugh
Moore, Petter
McFadden, Neal
McConley, Thomas
Piatt, Stephen
Harvey, Petter
Sutton, Joseph
Shadley, Henry
Verdin, Leary S.
Williams, Littleton
Winner, John

Rank and Name of Soldier.

Privates.
Darrill, Thomas B.
Eddington, Robert
Frey, Isaac
Gilkerson, Jonothan
Hartley, Thomas
Jeffries, James
Lawson, Septemus
Monroe, John
Moore, Thomas
McNeal, Alexander
Parker, Benjamin
Pierce, William
Richards, Jacob
Sherrard, David
Smith, Benjamin
VanWinck, James
Welsh, Moses

Page 12.

ROLL OF CAPT. GEORGE SANDERSON'S COMPANY.
(Fairfield County.)

Served from April 13, 1812, for one year.

Capt. George Sanderson
Sergt. John VanMetre
Sergt. James Larimer
Corp. James White

Lieut. David McCabe
Sergt. John Smith
Corp. Robert Cunningham
Corp. William Wallace

Ensign, Isaac Larrimer
Sergt. Isaac Painter or Winter
Corp. Daniel Hutson or Hudson
Corp. Daniel Huston

Privates.
Baker, Daniel
Coborn, Joseph
Davis, John
Tuchbone, Isaac
Hawwrick, John
Hines, Phillip
Johnston, Jacob
Johnson, Samuel
Mellow, Jacob
Menteenth or Monteith, Jacob
Miller, Daniel
McClung, Lare
Nolan, Samuel
Pyatt, David
Ray, John
Swiler, John
Switer, John
Oborn, Joseph

Privates.
Baker, George
Dagen or Dugan, John
Darnel, Archibald
Faikbone, Jesse
Hiles, Christopher
Huffman, John
Hardy, Thomas
Jenkins, William
Kirby or Kerley, John
Martin, Charles
Martin, Henry
McDonald, William
McClung, William
Nelson, William
Larimer, Robert
Ray, William
Shrimp, George
Smith, David or Daniel
Wright, Spencer
Work, Samuel

Privates.
Collins, John
Darnell, Archibald
Edmind or Edmonds, William
Fitzpatrick, Rees
Highman, John
Hiles, John
Harshman, John
Jenkinson, William
Laefland or Loffland, Joseph
Miller, James
Monteith, Jonas
McIntire, John
Nelson, John
Post, Cornelius
Bimbeck or Brubeck, William
Sharp, Henry or Jacob
Short, Thomas
Turly, John
Whitsen or Whetson, Joseph

Page 13.

ROLL OF CAPT. THOMAS COLLIER'S COMPANY.
(Probably from Adams County.)

Served from July 28, until August 21, 1813.

Lieut. Thomas Collier

Sergt. Matthew Jones
Corp. James Killing

Sergt. William Green

Privates.
Anderson, Nathaniel
Collier, Daniel
Daniels, Joseph
McCormick, James
Stuce, Jacob
Thompson, James

Privates.
Black, Zechariah
Chambers, Elijah
Freeland, Jesse
Osmun, John
Shoup, Henry
Wilcoxen, John

Privates.
Burkitt, William
Davis, John
Helterbrand, Daniel
Peterson, Thomas
Trotter, Elijah
Weaver, George

Page 14.

ROLL OF CAPT. JOHN SHARP'S COMPANY.
(Probably from Washington County.)

Served from May 23, 1812, until———

Capt. John Sharp
Sergt. John H. Simons
Sergt. Otis Reekard
Corp. David Miskgimens

Lieut. William Sawyer
Sergt. Thomas Green
Corp. Joseph Knox
Corp. James Elwell

Ensign, Jacob Trobridge
Sergt. Chester Wilson
Corp. William S. Crain
Musician, Christian B. Smith

ROLL OF CAPT. JOHN SHARP'S COMPANY. (Continued)

Rank and Name of Soldier.	Rank and Name of Soldier.	Rank and Name of Soldier.
Privates.	**Privates.**	**Privates.**
Anderson, William	Benedick, Alvin	Beers, Benjamin
Browning, Baizilla	Black, John	Badgly, Benjamin
Bancroft, Samuel	Clark, Joseph	Dunkin, William
Downing, James	Ellis, Hanis	Frazer, Louis
Fox, Joseph	Goldsmith, William	Geary, James
Kelley, Ezra	Lynch, William	Lyon, Abraham
Langdon, Phillip	Mull, Samuel	Murphy, Samuel
McMullen, Samuel	Nicklow, Jacob	Nevels, Jacob
Nixon, Samuel	Robertson, John T.	Shingler, John
Skinner, John	Rogers, Joseph	Tuttle, Jabez
Ward, John	Williams, David	Wall, James

Page 15.

ROLL OF CAPT. JOHN F. MANSFIELD'S COMPANY.
(Probably from Hamilton County.)
Served from May 2, until September 15, 1812.

Capt. John F. Mansfield	Lieut. Stephen McFarland	Ensign, Thomas Heckweler
	Sergt. James Chambers	
Privates.	**Privates.**	**Privates.**
Armstrong, John	Byers, Israel	Crone, John
Cameron, William A.	Cameron, Robert A.	Ennis, John B.
Englis, Samuel	Everly, Michael	Gillaspey, Robert
Gibson, James	Goodspeed, Gideon	Heighway, John
Hafrer, Henry	Howell, Stephen	Harburt, Asher
Hatch, William S.	Kautz, Jacob	Lawrence, Thomas
Lawrence, John	Madden, Samuel	Mann, Isaac
Marshall, William	Moody, Nathaniel	Minshall, Jacob
McQuelkin, Samuel	Platt, John H.	Rutter, George
Stephens, Henry	Sayre, Elias	Sliezeman, John
Smith, James	Sloo, Thomas, Jr.	Smith, Elias P.
Stephens Blackall	Thompson, Erasmus K.	Williams, James
Williamson, John	Wallace, Robert	Wade, David
	Waring, Henry	

Pages 16-17.

ROLL OF CAPT. BENJAMIN SCHOOLER'S COMPANY.
(Probably from Champaign County.)
Served from February 21, until March 21, 1813.

Capt. Benjamin Schooler	Lieut. John Tulbe	Ensign, George McCullough
Sergt. Solomon McCulloh	Sergt. Andrew Moore	Sergt. Thomas Dickinson
Sergt. Nicholas Stilwell	Corp. Silas McCulloh	Corp. Jacob Slagle
Corp. William Tinnis	Corp. Layton Pollock	
Privates.	**Privates.**	**Privates.**
Asksen, David	Black, Samuel	Cain, Joshua
Coddington, William	Dickinson, Joseph	Dowden, William
Davis, Turner	Daniel, Thomas	Hill, James
Easley, Thomas	Henry, James	Robinson, Thomas
Hatfield, Samuel	Jenkins, Jesse	Lewis, Benjamin
Moore, George	Moore, John	Moore, William
Moots, Conrad	Maggard, Moses	Makenson, John
McDaniel, John	McLane, Charles	Burdett, Booth
Provolt, John	Robinson, Samuel	Rutherford, Evan
Shaw, Henry	Shaw, James	Schooler, William
Schooler, Charles	Tidd, Samuel	Taylor, Henry
Terrel, Mathew	Tong, Thomas	Wolverton, Daniel
Wallace, John	Wilkinson, Ashael	Zane, Isaac

Page 18.

ROLL OF CAPT. JAMES BROWN'S COMPANY. (County Unknown.)
Served from October 20, 1812, until February 20, 1813

Capt. James Brown	Lieut. Amasa Davis	Ensign, Peter Bryan
Sergt. Thomas Sells	Sergt. Isaac Minshall	Sergt. Lewis Steenrod
Sergt. Joseph Hawkins	Corp. Mathias Spangler	Corp. Peter Waterson
Corp. William Fuller	Corp. Samuel Janings	
Privates.	**Privates.**	**Privates.**
Bane, Daniel	Bronkar, Louis	Bowman, Daniela
Chilbey, Moses	Crawford, Joseph	Curtis, Joshua
Chilby, James	Cummins, John	Dains, Jacob
Fulk, Joshua	Gormor, John	Hughes, William
Hammond, Zoeth	Ingalls, Abraham	Jay, George
Lewis, William	Linn, Joseph	Lemon, Stephen
Marshall, Simon	Montoney, Isaac	McCulley, Patrick
McKee, Thomas	Newton, William	Owens, Thomas
Parker, George	Poke, William	Pierce, Jonothan
Rainey, John	Regener, Benjamin	Ross, William
Parkinson, John	Swank, George	Sawyer, George
Taylor, Thomas	Cummins, Samuel	Workman, Benjamin
White, Benjamin	Wright, Robert D.	

ROSTER OF OHIO SOLDIERS IN WAR OF 1812

Page 19. Vol. I.

ROLL OF CAPT. JOSEPH SUTTON'S COMPANY. (County Unknown.)
Served from September 30, 1812, until March 30, 1813.

Rank and Name of Soldier.	Rank and Name of Soldier.	Rank and Name of Soldier.
Capt. Joseph Sutton	Lieut. Wilson Holden	Ensign, Henry Kliever
Sergt. John C. Holden	Sergt. Thomas Barry	Sergt. Jacob Bickell
Sergt. David Moore	Corp. Mathias Kliever	Corp. Hazle Green
Corp. Eli Brady	Corp. Jeremiah Bartholomew	
Privates.	**Privates.**	**Privates.**
Alexander, Henry	Bartholomew, Stephen	Bonham, Elisha L.
Beem, Richard	Barnes, John	Craft, Ridgeway
Conner, Joseph	Carson, Benjamin	Conner, John
Carrol, George	Damans, Thomas	DeWees, Samuel
Edgol, William	Fisher, Levin	Horsey, Henry
Hull, Samuel	Herron, Samuel	Harris, William
Oakwood, Daniel	Hull, George	Hull, Benjamin
Johnston, Robert	Livingston, George	Lianburger, Peter
Miers, Solomon	Morris, John	Motherspaw, Daniel
McDaniel, William	McElvey, Samuel	McCalla, Andrew
Moore, Moses	Neff, George	Parr, Richard
Patter, John	Patter, Hira	Rouson, Jonothan
Statloe, John	Stewart, James	Stotts, Jacob
Wilson, Hyatte	Wilson, Jeremiah	Wilson, Abraham C.

Page 20.

ROLL OF CAPT. ISAAC EVANS' COMPANY.
(Probably from Coshocton County.)
Served from October 18, 1812, until February 17, 1813.

Capt. Isaac Evans	Lieut. Joshua Lemert	Ensign, Eli Shryock
Sergt. Richard Johnson	Sergt. Samuel Gillum	Sergt. Silas Smith
Sergt. Thomas Hunt	Corp. Barney Cantwell	Corp. Nathan Devore
Corp. Peter Carr	Waggoner, William Carr	
Privates.	**Privates.**	**Privates.**
Ammon, Jacob	Butler, James	Baker, Rezin
Biggs, James	Blew, Daniel	Cox, Thomas
Cornelius, Isaac	Chainey, Samuel	Cass, John
Dorn, Cornelius	Freeman, Henry	Gross, John
Helms, Nicholas	Horton, David	Hollenback, George
Hahn, George	Irven, James	Jeffries, Thomas
Adams, Littleton	McLane, John	McGee, James
Nowels, Moses	Rickner, Henry	Reed, James
Snyder, Joseph	Shotwell, William	Sell, David
Sherard, William	Shadley, Daniel	Shurtz, George
Thompson, Smallwood	Thompson, Archibald	Parker, Joshua
Ward, Lewis	Ward, Thomas	

Page 21.

ROLL OF CAPT. (Jesse or JOHN D. COURTRIGHT'S COMPANY.
(From Fairfield County.)
Served from September 27, 1812, until February 26, 1813,. Part served from October 22, 1812.

Capt. John D. Courtright	Lieut. John List	Ensign, John Glick
Sergt. David Egbert	Sergt. Peter Hartsock	Sergt. Isaac Hardin
Sergt. Thomas Pullen	Corp. John Smother	Corp. John Foust
Corp. Pressley Priest	Corp. Daniel Escol	Fifer, Isaac Stephens
Privates.	**Privates.**	**Privates.**
Allen, Samuel	Bochard, Jacob	Buzzard, William
Buzzard, David	Boyles, Thomas	Burke, Jacob
Buzzard, George	Bradley, John	Carlisle, Bazil
Chaina, John	Chestnut, Elisha	Glick, Solomon
Gessele, Jacob	Howitt, Richard	Kirk, George Sr.
Kirk, George Jr.	Linback, George	Lutz, John
Long, William	Marshall, John	Moore, Peter
Missmore, John	Paier, John	Plotner, Daniel
Proudfoot, John	Punchos, Peter	Russell, Jacob
Doult, James	Shoup, Jacob	Shawhan, Thomas
Silvers, William	Stripes, William	Steel, Lemuel
Torrance, John	Winterslam, Nicholas	Waite, George
White, William	Welshhous, Jacob	Willits, Elias
	Wright, Jeremiah	

Page 22.

ROLL OF CAPT. JOSEPH JOHNSON'S COMPANY. (County Unknown.)
Served from October 18, 1812, until February 18, 1813.

Capt. Joseph Johnson	Lieut. John Gard	Ensign, George Sluthower
Sergt. George Gibson	Sergt. William Henderson	Sergt. Lemuel Johnson
Sergt. James O'Donald	Corp. Jacob Blotzley	Corp. William Hogland
Corp. Jacob Kline	Corp. Jesse Foster	Fifer, David Waggoner

Vol. I.
ROLL OF CAPT. JOSEPH JOHNSON'S COMPANY. (Continued)

Rank and Name of Soldier.
Privates.
Armstrong, James
Beymer, John
Baker, George
Cummins, William
Forman, Jacob
Green, Thomas
Hill, William
Griffin, Johnson
Lacoy, Thomas S.
Lafferty, Edward
Ray, John
Vanamon, Edward
Weaver, Frederick

Rank and Name of Soldier.
Privates.
Burroughs, John
Bell, Robert
Carson, Samuel
Doty, Arthur
Gibbs, James
Guesbach, Henry
Haversback, Conrad
Johnson, John
Lanman, John
Miller, Jacob
Runk, Michael
Vanande, Aaron
Williams, Thomas

Rank and Name of Soldier.
Privates.
Burroughs, Samuel
Boltzley, John
Carson, John
Eakin, David
Gibbs, William
Hand, Cornelius
Jones, Elijah
Kale, George
Lamb, Lawrence
McGarvey, Alexander
Sodours, Frederick
Williams, Levi
Williams, Benjamin

Page 23.
ROLL OF CAPT. JOSEPH KIRKWOOD'S COMPANY.
Served from October 22, 1812, until February 22, 1813. Part served from December 1, 1812.

Capt. Solomon Bentley
Ensign, Joseph Grimes
Sergt. Hugh Brown
Corp. David Dille
Corp. Israel Day

Capt. Joseph Kirkwood
Sergt. James Kyle
Sergt. John Boyd
Corp. Dennis Forest
Drummer, Evan Rogers

Lieut. George Love
Sergt. Samuel Nixon
Sergt. William McCoy
Corp. Joseph Rankin

Privates.
Duddle, Caleb
Didzler, John
Brill, Michael
Campbell, Dougal
Cluny, Alexander
Fryman, George
Gilliland, Morgan
Grimes, John
Haniman, David
Kyzor, Thomas
Long, Michael
Meek, Samuel
McMahan, Dennis
Russell, John
Shepherd, Isaiah
Tarrier, John
Watson, Robert

Privates.
Dallas, John
Devore, John
Dark, James
Coss, Abraham
Carrington, Nicholas
Gaston, John
Gilliland, Thomas
Herd, William
Irwin, George
Keen, Henry
Lashley, Hezekiah
Marquis, William
Robinson, John
Starr, James
Shannon, John
Thompson, John
Wright, Coleman S.

Privates.
Dillon, Samuel
Davis, Jacob
Coles, Jeremiah
Carpenter, John
Erskine, Thomas
Goosehorn, Leonard
Graham, Thomas
Howell, William
Jaques, John
Long, Adam

Masters, Richard
Ryder, Obed
Shepherd, Arnold
Sturgeon, Reuben
Tuttle, James
Vandine, George

Page 24.
ROLL OF CAPT. CALVIN SHEPARD'S COMPANY. (County Unknown.)
Served from August 9, until October 9, 1812.

Capt. Calvin Shepherd
Sergt. Nathan Newson
Sergt. Joseph Vandenbenen
Corp. David S. Grayum

Lieut. John Roadarmour
Sergt. John Gibson
Corp. Joseph Ganyum
Corp. Solomon Haywood
Fifer, John Rutherford

Ensign, John Boston
Sergt. John Phillips
Corp. Charles Budenot
Drummer, Moses Everett

Privates.
Aleshire, John
Amen, David
Berry, Malachier
Bellar, Elias
Cavin, William
Domly, John
Clifford, John
Entringer, David
Fulton, John
Hubbell, Roland
Graham, Gabriel
Mathews, Thomas
Mannay, James
Martin, James
Ross, Joseph W.
Shaw, John
Sweett, John

Privates.
Aleshire, William
Aleshire, Ephraim
Bailey, Robert
Bray, William
Clark, Samuel
Donaldson, Ebenezer
Durst, Joseph
Ellison, John
Gardner, Joshua
Hill, Jesse
Killen, James
Miller, Martin
McMillin, Joseph
Odell, Isaac
Robinson, Ephraim
Smith, John
Yates, Jacob

Privates.
Atkinson, Wiley
Browbaker, David
Bailey, John
Chitwood, James
Donnolly, Andrew
Denny, William
Entringer, John
Ellison, Joseph
Hubbell, Jesse
Hipkins, Benjamin
Littleton, William
Moreton, John
McCarty, George
Patton, Mathew
Rutherford, Evans
Smith, Constantine
Wadkins, Johnson V.

Page 25.
ROLL OF CAPT. ZADOC MARKLAND'S COMPANY
(Probably from Adams County.)
Served from July 28, until August 28, 1813.

Capt. Zadoc Markland
Corp. Andrew Ellison
Drummer, Charles Olden

Lieut. Thomas Lytle
Sergt. Allen Pucket

Corp. Samuel Naylor
Corp. John Baldwin

ROLL OF CAPT. ZADAC MARKLAND'S COMPANY. (Continued)

Rank and Name of Soldier.

Privates.
Barrett, John
Eastburn, Jesse
Miller, William
Pennecolt, Reuben
Thatcher, Charles

Rank and Name of Soldier.

Privates.
Copaz, Isaiah
John, Thomas
Myers, Abraham
Raider, George
Wasley, Jonothan

Rank and Name of Soldier.

Privates.
Casperson, Tobias
Lovejoy, David
Mellow, Henry
Sutterfield, David
Wood, John

Page 26.

ROLL O FCAPT. PETER WIKOFF'S COMPANY.
(Probably from Adams County.)

Served from July 28, until August 21, 1813.

Capt. Peter Wikoff

Sergt. James Wikoff

Corp. Lavan Robinston

Privates.
Antis, John
Cain, Jesse
Moore, John
Smolly, David

Privates.
Boldman, James
Dillion, Isaac
Newman, James
Williams, William

Privates.
Baker, John
Jones, Andrew
Stephenson, Charles
Young, David

Pages 27-76.

ROLL OF CAPT. EDMUND WADE'S COMPANY. (County Unknown.)

Served from July 28, until August 28, 1813.

Capt. Edmund Wade
Sergt. John Frazier
Corp. Daniel Smith

Sergt. James Baldwin
Sergt. James Cole
Corp. Robert January

Sergt. Arthur McFarland
Corp. Mathew Campbell

Privates.
Acton, William
Baldridge, James
Cavin, John
Edgerton, Joshua
Gutridge, Charles
Harper, George
Kirkpatrick, James
Montgomery, Andrew
Maddox, William
McCayne, Thomas
McClenahan, John
McRight, James
Page, David
Roush, John
Tucker, Elwin
Wade, Joseph

Privates.
Burnes, James
Baird, Robinson
Depue, John
Edginton, Joseph
Glasgow, William
Hayslip, John
Lawrence, Jacob
Montgomery, John
McCormick, Adam
McFadden, Moses
McCulloch, Alexander
McClennahan, John
Patton, Thomas
Shepherd, John
Thompson, James
Wheatley, Walter
Waldron, John

Privates.
Balls, Jemcil
Connell, John R.
Ellison, Robert
Elliott, Robert Sr.
Glasgow, Joseph
Johnston, Elisha
Milligin, William
Mahaffey, John
McLaughlin, John
McCague, William
McClelland, Thomas
Nouelman, Richard
Roe, George
Smiley, James
VanPelt, John
Waldron, Henry

Pages 28-29-436-437-438.

ROLL OF CAPT. CONRAD FLESHER'S COMPANY.
(Probably from Ross County.)

Served from July 28, until September 5, 1813, and from March 12, until April 16, 1814.

Capt. Conrad Flesher
Ensign, John L. Corn
Sergt. Henry Rogers
Sergt. William Hankins
Sergt. Nicholas Young
Corp. Martin Hire
Corp. John Haselton
Corp. William Borland
Musician, Elijah Johnston

Lieut. James Crusan
Ensign, Reuben Pursell
Sergt. Peter Harper
Sergt. Robert Hoddy
Sergt. John Williams
Corp. John Nuland
Corp. Sylvester Root
Fifer, Henry Bevington
Musician, Samuel H. Timmons

Lieut. Perceval Adams
Ensign David Jones
Sergt. Thomas Moore
Sergt. James Carpenter
Corp. John Roebuck
Corp. Samuel Blair
Corp. Robert McElhiny
Drummer, Jeremiah Smith

Privates.
Ayres, Richard
Blue, Peter
Briant, George
Blair, Thomas
Ballinger, Joseph
Correy, John
Cunningham, Thomas
Cochran, Abraham
Dines, William
Dungelbarger, Frederick
Everett, Samuel
Fennymore, Joseph
Gooley, Jacob
Hinkle, David
Hopkins, James
Hurst, James

Privates.
Anderson, John
Brown, Jacob
Brooks, James
Blue, Jacob
Brant, John
Cain, Richard
Chill, Thomas
Chapman, David
Day, Basil
Decker, James
Eymon, Abraham
Featheringill, George
Goddard, Robert D.
Hill, William
Harper, Cochran
Holloway, Thomas

Privates.
Brunhed, Joseph
Blue, John
Bush, Daniel
Brown, Thomas
Bennet, Darius
Collins, Absalom
Cochran, John
Dickinson, Jacob
Davis, Adam
DeWitt, Martin
Figgins, Edward
Gilbert, Thomas
Hurley, Henry
Hopkins, John
Haggard, William
Hover, George

ROLL OF CAPT. CONRAD FLESHER'S COMPANY (Continued.)

Rank and Name of Soldier.

Privates.

Humphrey, Lemuel
Jones, Amos
Kerr, John
King, Charles
Moore, Ezekial
Michael, John
Myers, John
McDonald, Thomas
McCan, Thomas
McKune, John
Olds, Benjamin
Pew, Thomas
Roberts, Charles
Rose, Cornelius
Starr, Henry
Stafford, Young
Sebern, Francis
Southard, Hudson
Thomas, Joseph
Thompson, Edward
Timons, Henry
Vaughn, James
White, Christopher L.
Williams, Amon
Ward, John

Hoskins, William
Jones, William
Kilgore, John
Lane, William
Miller, Henry
Moots, John
Meanaugh, Hugh
McCafferty, James
McGinnis, James
Newman, John
Orr, Joseph
Rogers, John
Rogers, Peleg
Sidney, Stephen
Skinner, James
Scoby, William
Stratton, Charles
Thompson, James
Thompson, John
Tuller, Orson
Vaughn, Seborn
Wood, Benjamin
Wilson, George
Windle, Abraham
Weeks, John

James, Dawson R.
King, Isaac
Knight, Orena
Lock, Jesse
Miller, Solomon
Myers, Jacob
Matheny, Nathan
McNeal, Archibald
McCafferty, David
Neal, John P.
Pool, William
Rosal, James
Smith, John
Simpson, Thomas
Stout, Peter
Stagg, Michael
Smith, Amos
Timmons, Eli
Tuttle, Erastus
Vestal, John
Warren, Moses
Weeks, William
Winsett, Joseph
Westfall, Joseph
Wilcox, Edward

Page 30.

ROLL OF LIEUT. JAMES KINSEN'S COMPANY. (County Unknown.)

Served from July 27, until August 16, 1813.

Capt. James Kinsen
Sergt. John Hall
Corp. Francis Waddle
Corp. Jacob Caylor

Ensign, Phillip Gossard
Sergt. Thomas Moore
Corp. James Blair
Musician, Jesse Arnold

Sergt. John P. Neal
Sergt. William Hawkins
Corp. John Newland

Privates.

Ayers, Richard
Dunn, James
Feaganz, Edward
Hopkins, David
Moore, Ezekial
Rupard, George
Thompson, Edward

Burnet, Thomas
Downard, James
Gilbert, Thomas
Hopkins, James
Orr, Joseph
Snider, Henry
Wright, David
Workman, John

Brooks, James
Foster, Thomas
Hopkins, John
Jameson, Charles
Pool, Edward
Snider, Jacob
Wright, John

Pages 31-32-33-34.

ROLL OF CAPT. CLARK PARKER'S COMPANY.
(Probably from Geauga County.)

Served from August 22, until October 2, 1812. Part served from December 1, until February 27, 1813.

Capt. Clark Parker
Sergt. William P. Scott
Sergt. Jonothan Russell
Sergt. Moses Allen
Corp. Ephraim Morrison
Corp. Chester Dean

Lieut. Caleb G. Foges
Sergt. Jared Nicholson
Sergt. Stephen Worthington
Sergt. Stephen King
Corp. Lewis Smith
Drummer, Joseph Burke

Ensign, Caleb Baldwin
Sergt. Theodore Royes
Sergt. Jonothan Hill
Corp. Charles H. Paine
Corp. Henry Fitch
Fifer, Avery Button

Privates.

Adams, Sebastion
Abot, Josiah
Bacon, Dexter
Baker, Noah
Bradley, Corner
Buchanan, John
Cranny, John
Coleman, Jacob
Crocker, Frederick D.
Craft, Thomas
Dillingham, John
Eckman, James
Fowler, Henry
Goldsmith, Jonothan
Gunn, Elijah
Hayes, Ebenezer
Hudson, Silas F.
Hill, David
Harding, Jacob

Andrews, Amos
Arthur, William
Barker, Samuel
Bates, Caleb
Burdet, Rurand
Calhoun, Amos
Chase, Daniel
Clapp, Orris
Crossman, Abner
Crooks, James
Dustman, Jacob
Field, Wawing
Frank, Jacob
Granger, John
Gilbert, Henry
Harvey, Luther
Harper, John R.
Herrington, John
Hoel, John

Arnes, Isaac
Archer, William
Barker, William
Bradby, Selah
Burgess, Robert
Chandler, David
Craw, Henry
Carlton, Guy
Crawford, William
Dunn, Elijah
Dennison, David
Fight, Jacob
Gun, Christopher
Granger, Samuel
Gilbert, Samuel
Hooton, John
Hayes, Seth
Hamilton, Hugh
Iles, Jeremiah

ROSTER OF OHIO SOLDIERS IN WAR OF 1812

Vol. I.

ROLL OF CAPT. CLARK PARKER'S COMPANY. (Continued.)

Rank and Name of Soldier.   Rank and Name of Soldier.   Rank and Name of Soldier.

Privates.

Privates.	Privates.	Privates.
Johnson, William	Johnson, Samuel	Jones, Olive
John, Elliott	James, John	Jack, James
Knopp, Christian	Kinney, Manvah	Landon, Henry
Love, William	Leonard William	Love, Samuel
Morley, Isaac	Minor, Phil	Moore, Isaac
Maxum, John	Miller, Theodore	Marlatt, George
Moore, Henry S.	Murphy, John	McMillen, James
McCreary, William	McCombs, Thomas	McCreary, John
McMullin, Charles	McMullen, James	Newton, James
Norton, Simon	Nye, Ebenezer	Olds, Daniel
Olds, James	Pain, Franklin	Prentice, Robert
Parker, Henry	Parsons, Horace	Paris, John
Park, Solomon	Patterson, Richard	Parker, Calvin
Pratt, Harvey	Paxton, John	Peterman, Jacob
Potter, Samuel Y.	McCloud, Francis	Russell, Ralph
Rawlins, James	Rathbone, John	Rusage, James
Russell, Eliakim	Rumage, Thomas	Rose, Robert
Reed, William	Sebastian, Freeman F.	Spencer, Allen
Smith, William	Smith, Francis	Spencer, Allen Sr.
Simons, Adam	Stall, Andrew	Spargo, George
Sell, John	Townsley, John	Thomas, Levi
Turner, Samuel	Turner, Conrad	Moore, Henry T.
Thompson, William	Upton, Benjamin	VanNorman, Joseph
Webster, Elijah	Wood, Benjamin	Wright, Alexander
White, John	White, James	Young, John

Page 35.

ROLL OF CAPT. HORACE FLOWERS' COMPANY. (County Unknown.)

Served from August 24, until August 28, 1812.

Capt. Horace Flowers   Lieut. William Jones   Sergt. Philo Borden
Sergt. Daniel B. Rushnell   Corp. Lewis Bushnell   Corp. Liston Bushnell

Privates.	Privates.	Privates.
Andrews, Richard	Bates, Liman	Borden, Asahel Jr.
Brockway, Aaron	Bushnell, Alexander	Brockway, Philemon
Brockway, Jesse	Dugan, Thomas	Ellis, William
Fultz, Francis H.	Ganyard, Martin	Hull, John
Hull, George	Hull, John Jr.	Hayes, Listin
Jones, Seldin	Kepnoe, John	McFarland, Thomas
McFarland, Archibald	Phonts, John	Quigle, Michael
Shull, Frederick	Stilwell, Jeremiah	Thompson, Seth
	Woolford, Elijah	

Page 36.

ROLL OF CAPT. CLEMENT TRIFORD'S COMPANY.
(Probably from Fayette County.)

Served from July 26, until August 16, 1813.

Capt. Clement Triford   Lieut. Bazzel Cleavenger   Sergt. David Hayes
Sergt. John Cooper   Corp. John Grubb   Corp. Jacob Pallman
    Drummer, John P. Newman

Privates.	Privates.	Privates.
Alexander, David	Blue, John	Blue, Peter
Blue, Jacob	Cradle, John	Compton, George
Gragg, George	Gragg, Reuben	Hayes, William
McDonald, Thomas	McArthur, John	Parker, Nathan
Pool, Thomas	Wilcox, Edward	

Pages 37-38-39-39½

ROLL OF CAPT. JOSHUA T. COTTON'S COMPANY.
(From Trumbull or Mahoning Counties.)

Served from August 26, until November 8, 1812.

Capt. Joshua T. Cotton   Lieut. George Monteith   Lieut. Edmond O. Fanner
Ensign Jacob Irwing   Sergt. John Cotton   Sergt. John Myer
Sergt. George Wintermate   Sergt. Abraham Wintermate   Corp. John Carlton
Corp. Boardman Robins   Corp. John Russell   Corp. George Ounsbury
    Fifer, Daniel Wick

Privates.	Privates.	Privates.
Ague, Nathan	Andres, Samuel A.	Boyd, Andrew
Brunsteter, Henry	Bradford, Joel	Bradon, John
Blackman, Simion	Buchanan, Walter	Bradford, William
Brockway, Romant	Craft, Thomas	Crum, Samuel
Carter, Joseph	Calhoun, Samuel	Cummings, Thomas
Cawer, Seneca	Cowden, John	Cummings, Joseph
Curtin, Zenas	Demel, James	Duc, Jacob
Dillon, William	Fisher, Isaac	Foos, Henry

ROLL OF CAPT. JOSUA T. COTTON'S COMPANY. (Continued)

Rank and Name of Soldier.

Privates.

Fankle, William
Goodspeed, Nathaniel
Harvey, Francis
Hamilton, William
Kerr, Robert
Long, Robert
Leach, Abraham
Moore, Sampson
Morris, Archibald
McClellan, David
McMahon, Susan
Irwin, Thomas
Osborn, Joseph
Powers, Jacob
Peny, Levi
Ramage, James
Smith, Daniel
Shatts, Daniel
Veneman, Nicholas
Storm, Michael
Woolcut, Joseph
Whittersbey, Anthony

Gilbert, George
Hayes, John
Hull, Jacob
Henry, Peter
Luts, Daniel
Lyon, Isaac
Moor, John
Maxwell, Robert
Mann, Samuel
McCollom, John
McConnal, Richard
North, Samuel
Parkhurst, Isaac
Prudden, David
Phillip, Kimmel
Swager, Adam
Saxton, John
Smith, George
Stoke, Jacob
Walden, Jonothan
Winans, James
White, John
Zedechai, John

Guy, Mathew
Hover, Abraham
Higgins, Silas
Johnson, Anson
Lyons, John
Leonard, Nicholas
Moore, John, Sr.
Munns, William
McEnery, Thomas
McLaughlin, John
McCreery, William
Osborn, Conrad
Parkhurst, John
Poyens, John
Roll, Benjamin
Shields, William
Simons, Abraham
Steward, Daniel
Thorn, Henry
Wilson, John
White, Samuel
Young, John

Pages 40-41.

ROLL OF CAPT. ICHABOD PLUM'S COMPANY.
(Probably from Delaware County.)

Served from May 4, until May 27, 1813. Part served from July 26, until August 13, 1813.

Capt. Ichabold Plum
Sergt. Thomas Brown
Sergt. David Butler
Corp. Joseph Carrin
Corp. James Carpenter

Lieut. John Milligan
Sergt. Adison Carver
Corp. Joel Taylor
Corp. Gilbert Weeks
Musician, Sylvester Drake

Ensign John Brundage
Sergt. Benjamin Carpenter
Corp. Ezra Olds
Corp. Robert Carpenter

Privates.

Alden, Daniel
Bishop, Elisha
Foust, David
Hull, Nathaniel
Heath, Samuel
Keys, Isaac
Manvil, Eli
Landon, David
Olds, Comfort
Roth, Nathan
Slack, Ralph
Shoemaker, Benjamin
Wyatt, William

Armstrong, David
Day, Charles
Fisher, George
Harper, James
Jones, Solomon
Kepler, Samuel
Moles, James
Osterhout, Gideon
Patterson, John
Ridgeway, William
Steward, Solomon
Trindle, James
Welit, Isaac

Brown, Ezekial
Foust, Henry
Gregory, David
Hatch, Nathaniel
Jones, Richard
Main, Eleazar
Munson, Michael
Olds, Benjamin
Patrick, Joseph
Sharp, William
Steudervant, George
Wilson, James

Page 42.

ROLL OF LIEUT. ADDISON GARVER'S COMPANY.
(Probably from Delaware County.)

Served from July 26, until August 13, 1813.

Lieut. Addison Garver
Ensign David Butler
Sergt. Joseph Steward

Privates.

John Leonard
Daniel J. Carpenter
Atkin, Russell
Carpenter, Henry
Holt, George
Longwell, Robert
Phipps, Jacob
Slack, John

Crandell Rosecrans
Moses Carpenter
Adams, Johnson
Heaver, William C.
Lewis, John, Jr.
Lewis, Joseph
Rosecrans, John
Stark, James
Young, Andrew

Benjamin Patrick
Mathias Nauloon
Carpenter, William
Helt, Michael
Lewis, Chester
Phipps, William
Slack, Ezekial
Taylor, Nathan

Pages 43-44.

ROLL OF CAPT. JOHN FOOS' COMPANY.
(Probably from Delaware County.)

Served from July 26, until August 18, 1813. Part served from September 1, until September 15, 1813.

Capt. John Foos
Sergt. John Davis
Sergt. Robert Perry
Corp. James Carpenter

Lieut. Thomas Driver
Sergt. William Baker
Sergt. Abraham Lookingbell

Ensign Benjamin Warren
Sergt. James Hopkins
Corp. David Shoup

ROLL OF CAPT. JOHN FOOS' COMPANY. (Continued)

Rank and Name of Soldier.

Privates.

Adams, Elijah
Cellar, George
Dilden, Ralph
Foos, William
Gallant, Allen
Hoskins, John
Munroe, Isaac
Fibert, Richard
Pugh, Thomas
Shaw, Samuel
Taylor, Benjamin
Wolf, John
Whiters, Isaac

Rank and Name of Soldier.

Privates.

Cooper, Samuel
Cothren, John
Driver, John
Evins, Edward
Gillies, James
Kyle, Hugh
Marks, David
Roderick, Jacob
Stephens, Reuben
Sloper, Charles
Taylor, Richard
Wison, Frederick
Whittenger, Nicholas

Rank and Name of Soldier.

Privates.

Cellar, John
Davis, David
Delsever, Michael
Gallant, James
Hushow, Phillip
Kepler, Samuel
Mickson, James
Perry, David
Smith, John
Tyler, Samuel
Wright, George
Wilson, John

Page 46.

ROLL OF CAPT. BENJAMIN M. FAIRCHILD'S COMPANY.
(Probably from Delaware County.)

Served from July 26, until August 10, 1813.

Capt. Benjamin Fairchilds
Sergt. Sherman Fairchilds
Sergt. William Hendrichs
Corp. Nathaniel Hatch

Lieut. Gilbert Weeks
Sergt. William Williams
Corp. Barak Weeks
Corp. Lorrin Hills

Ensign Markus Curtis
Sergt. Daniel Lane
Corp. William Smith

Privates.

Andrews, Thomas
Budd, John
Faucher, Samuel
Lock, Jesse
Rogers, Philemon
Schovey, John

Privates.

Bennet, James
Budd, William
Hills, Zimri
Plum, Parysek
Robinson, John W.
Smuthers, Christian

Privates.

Baughman, Adam
Faucher, Henry
Jenkins, David
Pelton, Johnson
Roberts, John
Sebring, Francis

Pages 45-73.

ROLL OF ISRAEL P. CASE'S COMPANY.
(Probably from Franklin County.)

Served from August 24, until October 4, 1812, and from May 4, until May 27, 1813.

Capt. Israel P. Case
Ensign, Timothy Lee
Sergt. Obediah Blakely
Sergt. William Hall
Drummer, Samuel Beach

Lieut. Cruger Wright
Sergt. George Osborne
Sergt. Charles Thompson
Sergt. Ebenezer Goodrich
Fifer, Jeremiah Boardman

Lieut. Abiel Case
Sergt. Job W. Case
Sergt. Herman Wheeler
Sergt. Edward Phelps

Privates.

Andrews, Waren
Bristol, Adna
Cochrin, Harper
Case, Henry
Deckron, Daniel
Goodrich, Levi
Morrison, William
Millington, Peter
Palmer, Luther
Twadel, Joseph
Whitford, John B.

Privates.

Brown, Gilbert
Beech, Samuel
Cochrin, Glass
Clark, Oliver
Denton, Justus
Holmsted, Philo
Morrison, Henry
Parmento, Erastus
Perry, Levi
Vining, William
Wallace, Herman

Privates.

Bisett, William
Bardsley, Ebenezer
Case, Orin
Cooper, Thomas
Goodrich, Bela
Ingham, Abraham
Mitchell, Joseph
Pratt, Lemuel
Rees, Caleb
Wever, John W.
Wilcox, Tracey

Page 47.

ROLL OF CAPT. HENRY SLACK'S COMPANY.
(Probably from Delaware County.)

Served from October 27, until November 19, 1812.

Capt. Henry Slack
Sergt. David Skeels

Lieut. Samuel Maynard
Sergt. Shearman Fairchild
Sergt. Joel Taylor

Ensign, David Butler
Sergt. Ethan Palmer

Privates.

Adams, Samuel
Barker, Joseph
Johnson, Stafford
Marvin, Jesse
Rosecrans, Abraham
Roberts, John
Steudevant, Ira
Show, Jonothan
Welsh, Isaac

Privates.

Brundage, Nathaniel
Cowan, Levi M.
Kyrk, John
Peny, Henry
Roberts, Amar
Rugg, Orn
Swetland, Artemus
James Preston

Privates.

Bishop, Elisha
Foust, John
Lewis, Isaac
Patrick, Benjamin
Rogers, Philemon
Shover, James
Taylor, Nathan
William, Heaver C.

Page 48.

ROLL OF CAPT. SAMUEL MYERS' COMPANY.
(Probably from Fayette County.)

Served from July 26, until August 16, 1813.

Rank and Name of Soldier.

Capt. Samuel Myers
Sergt. Arnold Richards
Sergt. Solomon Parker
Corp. Michael Hawk

Privates.

Allen, Elijah
Campbell, Joseph
Dickison, Jonothan
Harrod, Samuel
McCafferty, James
Smith, John
Thomas, Joseph

Rank and Name of Soldier.

Lieut. David Allen
Sergt. John Harrod
Corp. Shreve Pancoast
Corp. Charles White

Privates.

Allen, James
Campbell, Runey
Dickison, Jacob
Henderson, James
Page, John
Stout, William
Thompson, James

Rank and Name of Soldier.

Ensign, John Popejoy
Sergt. James Harvey
Corp. James Davis
Drummer, Armsted Carder

Privates.

Busick, George
Dickison, Isaac
Hinckle, Daniel
McGowan, James
Rozell, James
Stutch, Jesse
Westfall, Joseph

Page 49.

ROLL OF CAPT. ROBERT McELWAIN'S COMPANY.
(Probably from Ross County.)

Served from July 16, until August 15, 1813.

Capt. Robert McElwain
Sergt. Aaron Archer
Corp. John Sowards

Privates.

Allen, Jeremiah
Bragg, John
Gansel, Michael
Gilmore, William
Flick, William
LeValley, John
Kerr, John
McClever, William
Rankin, John
Reader, Amos
Smith, Alexander
Wibright, John

Lieut. Jacob Jones
Sergt. John Hayes
Corp. David McElwain

Privates.

Biggs, John
Callison, James
Gaskill, John
Harrison, Joseph
Applegate, William
Lee, John
Maxwell, Ephraim
Plyman, James
Reed, William
Rodgers, Benjamin
Sample, Nathaniel
Warwick, James

Sergt. William Devlon
Corp. Benjamin Salmon
Corp. William Hayes

Privates.

Black, William
Chidester, Elias
Gow, Daniel I.
Hannaman, John
Kent, Penin
Lafford, Young
Mowberry, Reuben
Redden, Mathew
Reeder, Joseph
Runkin, William
Taylor, David

Page 50.

ROLL OF CAPT. ADAM KIOUS' COMPANY.
(Probably from Ross County.)

Served from July 28, until August 16, 1813.

Capt. Adam Kious
Sergt. Peter Harper
Corp. Levi Bavington

Privates.

Blair, Samuel
Brown, Jacob
Day, Bazel
Hill, Stephen
McLaughlin, William
Pool, William
Seylor, George
Warren, Humphrey

Lieut. John L. Chorn
Sergt. Addison Day
Corp. Martin Hyer
Corp. Daniel Happis

Privates.

Boyd, George
Bryan, George
Dickson, Robert
Hill, William
Painter, George
Orr, Samuel
Timmons, Eli
White, John

Sergt. Samuel Chorn
Sergt. Wicks
Corp. Bazil Mysett

Privates.

Burnet, David
Carter, Isaac
Finney, Alexander
Mussett, John
Punn, Abraham
Rodgers, Pilique
Waddle, John
Whetston, George

Page 51.

ROLL OF CAPT. THOMAS ROBINSON'S COMPANY. (County Unknown.)

Served from July 28, until August 12, 1813.

Capt. Thomas Robinson
Sergt. Risdon McDonald
Corp. William Kendal

Privates.

Ballinger, Thomas
Green, Solomon
Horney, James
Price, John

Lieut. Patrick Kerne
Sergt. Daniel Honey
Drummer, Obediah William

Privates.

Bison, Joseph
Kilgore, John C.
Steady, John
Wiley, William

Sergt. William C. Scott
Corp. William Holloway

Privates.

Carr, Michael
Kellip, John M.
Steady, William

Page 52.

ROLL OF CAPT. JAMES CROTHER'S COMPANY.
(Probably from Ross County.)

Served from July 27, until August 16, 1813.

Capt. James Crothers
Sergt. Richard Davis
Sergt. William Row
Corp. David McDonald

Lieut. Isaac Saunders
Sergt. William Priddy
Corp. John Row
Corp. John Draper

Ensign, James Row
Sergt. Phillip Olinger
Corp. Robert Adams

ROLL OF CAPT. JAMES CROTHER'S COMPANY. (Continued)

Rank and Name of Soldier.

Privates.
Arnold, John
Buck, John
Howe, Jacob
Lines, William
Meeny, Hugh
McCoy, Jesse
Tracy, Solomon

Privates.
Babbit, Job
Clark, David
Hand, Lemuel
Garrison, Abner
Moon, William
Pearson, William
Tracey, William
Vaughn, John

Privates.
Barley, William
Gorby, Ebenezer
Knadler, George
Cochran, Barnabus
Mitchell, Jacob
Shroyer, George
Tracey, Wornel

Page 53.

ROLL OF CAPT. PETER COOLEY'S COMPANY.
(Probably from Adams County.)
Served from July 28, until August 28, 1813.

Capt. Peter Cooley
Corp. Thomas Bowman

Sergt. James Heslet
Drummer, John Gillman

Sergt. Nathan Rounsavell

Privates.
Donaldson, Israel
Kimble, Elijah
Riggs, John
Yerden, John

Privates.
Fetters, Charles
Montgomery, Nathaniel
Smith, William

Privates.
Henderson, Thomas
Robb, John
Thomas, Moses

Pages 54-55.

ROLL OF CAPT. JOSHUA FOBES' COMPANY (County Unknown.)
Served from August 24, until November 2, 1812.

Capt. Joshua Fobes
Lieut. Nathaniel Hopkins
Sergt. James W. Foster
Corp. William Clever
Corp. John Burwell
Fifer, Nathan Fobes, Jr.

Lieut. Thaddeus Selby
Ensign, Augustus Smith
Sergt. Jehiel Bidwell
Corp. Jabes Fobes
Corp. Daniel Davis
Drummer, Walter Thorrington

Ensign, Simon Fobes, Jr.
Sergt. Iddo Bailey
Sergt. William Randall
Corp. John Randall
Corp. Justice Fobes

Privates.
Andrews, Marquis
Burnett, Silas
Cone, Lester
Drake, Jesse
Fobes, Justice
Foster, Samuel
Fobes, Elias
Gildersleiver, Bayley
Hulbart, Nathaniel
Hoover, Isaac

Privates.
Ballard, Ezekial
Burnett, Uriel
Coleman, Noah
Daughter, David
Falsone, Noah
Falsone, Moses
Foot, Levi
Fobes, Nathan
Hart, Joseph
Harris, John
Inman, Daniel N.

Privates.
Bidwell, Riverius
Coleman, Nathaniel
Cone, Rabzabon
Duer, John
Folsome, David
Fobes, David
Farrow, Isaac
Hayes, Titus
Hough, Henry
Hannah, Thomas

Pages 56-74.

ROLL OF CAPT. JACOB ULP'S COMPANY (County Unknown.)
Served from August 24, until August 28, 1812.

Capt. Jacob Ulp
Sergt. Henry Hull
Corp. Mathias Swatsweler
Corp. James Thompson

Ensign, Joseph Reeves
Sergt. George Tribey
Corp. David Wheeler
Drummer, William Burnett

Sergt. James Montgomery
Sergt. George Bentley
Corp. Thomas Patton

Privates.
Briggs, John
Burnett, John
Groscost, John
Hughes, John
Kinney, James
Love, Robert
McMarrow, Thomas
Quiggle, Phillip
Swatseller, Martin
Wilson, James

Privates.
Burnett, William, Sr.
Crawford, Alexander
Harson, Robert
Hisley, Daniel
Kerr, Jonothan
Mizner, James
Patrick, John
Rothburn, Amos
Waldorf, Phillip
Yarnal, Job

Privates.
Bradon, John
Cunningham, William
Hughes, James
Huff, Adam
Lake, Constant
Montgomery, Robert
Quiggle, Peter
Strubel, George
White, William
Alderman, Manty

Pages 57-58.

ROLL OF CAPT. JOHN R. REED'S COMPANY (County Unknown.)
Served from August 23, until November 30, 1812, and from January 1, until March, 1813.

Capt. John R. Reed
Sergt. Joseph Kerr
Sergt. Daniel Castle
Corp. Epaphras Lyman
Artificer, Benjamin Hanks

Lieut. Alexander Harper
Sergt. John C. Chase
Corp. David Burrough
Corp. David Doughton
Drummer, William Morrison

Ensign, Samuel Johnson
Sergt. Sebastian Adams
Corp. William Harper
Corp. William Jones
Fifer, David Bartram

ROLL OF CAPT. JOHN REED'S COMPANY. (Continued)

Rank and Name of Soldier. | Rank and Name of Soldier. | Rank and Name of Soldier.

Privates.

Privates	Privates	Privates
All, Adam	Beach, Luman	Bartholomew, Peter
Bartholomew, John	Bartholomew, Joseph	Brooks, James
Brown, Samuel	Baldwin, William	Curtis, James
Crosby, Calvin	Coon, David	Curtis, Jairns G.
Chapman, Comfort	Cleveland, Asahel	Dunbar, Thomas
Griffin, Sullivan	Gordon, John	Gould, John
Gage, John R.	Gordon, Thomas	Hall, Joseph D.
Houghton, Rufus	Hanington, Eldad	Harmon, Anan
Hubbard, Manoah	Healy, Ezra	Hitchcock, David
John, Murray	Joslin, John G.	Kent, Batus
Kent, Elisha	Lamberton, Amos	Lamont, Robert
Laughton, Abijah	Montgomery, John H.	Maranvil, Jabez D.
Morgan, James	Mann, Warner	McElvy, James G.
Napier, Benjamin A.	Norton, John	Noyes, Daniel
Naper, William	Parker, Andrew	Pain, Orin F.
Proctor, Jonas	Rockwell, Joshua	Rogers, Phinehas
Silverthorn, Thomas	Strong, Jabez	Spooner, John
Swift, Philip	Spencer, Edward P.	Stone, Merit
Sweet, Peleg, Jr.	Shepherd, Peletiah	Strong, Samuel
Stewart, Ambrose	Sweet, Lewis	Strong, Nathan Jr.
Shepherd, Marquis	Tappen, Abraham	Vidite, Jaspar
Whetmore, William	Wood, John	Wright, John
Wright, Solomon	Walkly, Jonothan	Widner, John L.
Widner, Benjamin	Wilder, Oliver	Wallen, Joseph
White, Josiah	Watrous, William	Whetmore, Collins
	Yates, Benjamin	

Page 59.

ROLL OF LIEUT. ROSWELL FULLER'S COMPANY.
(Probably from Delaware County.)

Served from August 23, until September 24, 1812.

Lieut. Roswell Fuller	Ensign, Joseph Higgins	Sergt. Nathan King
Sergt. Martin Pace	Sergt. David Buell	Sergt. Darius Bardsley
Corp. Truman Case	Corp. Norman Case	Drummer Nathaniel Carpenter
	Fifer, John Hardin	

Privates.	Privates.	Privates.
Benjamin, Daniel	Carpenter, Alfred	Case, Ralph
Davis, Eleazar	Ely, Peter	Gibson, Samuel
Higgins, Josiah	Higgins, Ebenezer	Herrick, Septemus
Keys, Talmon	Millhiser, Phillip	Patton, William
Pierce, Ariel	Powers, Luther	Ryan, Edward
Skeels, Reuben	Scribner Elias	Shaw, Benjamin
Tuller, Roswell, Jr.	Vinning, Elver	Watson, William
	Zimmerman, Henry	

Pages 60-61.

ROLL OF CAPT. JOHN SNELBEKER'S COMPANY.
(Probably from Licking County.)

Served from January 30, until March 4, 1815.

Capt. John Snelbeker	Lieut. Jeremiah Doty	Ensign, John Dixon
Sergt. William Martin	Sergt. Thomas Merritt	Sergt. Jesse Patterson
Sergt. Mark Anderson	Corp. Michael B. Miller	Corp. Philip Foreman
Corp. Jeremiah Guard	Corp. John Belair	Musician, Frederick Beyner

Privates.	Privates.	Privates.
Armstrong, James	Arnold, John	Boyd, John
Barnhart, Jacob	Brokes, Jonothan	Bloss, Adam
Bowan, Constant	Ball, Cyrus	Burge, Henry
Butler, Joseph	Craig, Jonothan	Cassman, Joseph
Critz, Andrew	Denney, Daniel	Dennen, William
Corbet, Robert	Enos, John	Engle, John
Daine, Asa	Fussel, William	Green, Thomas
Enslow, David	Gabriel, Reason	Herron, Phillip
Gibbs, William	Hines, Phillip	Irwin, George
Halfhill, Abraham	Johnson, Samuel	Kenistrick, Henry
Jesse, Hutchins	Miller, Michael	Miers, Jacob
Miller, John	Nagal, Andrew	Pardo Richard
McHenry, Richard	Rees, Thomas, Jr.	Rolins, William
Penticost, James	Shew, David	Stout, George
Rolston, John	Smith, David	Stockwell, William
Shrayer, Abraham	Tylers, Isaac	Thomas, Cornelius
Torrence, Aaron	Williams, James	Whan, John
Watson, Abraham	Wolford, Andrew	Wiggins, Robert

Page 62. Vol. I.

ROLL OF LIEUT. SAMUEL COOPER'S COMPANY.
(Probably from Delaware County.)
Served from August 24, until September 10, 1812.

Rank and Name of Soldier.	Rank and Name of Soldier.	Rank and Name of Soldier.
Lieut. Samuel Cooper	Ensign, David Marks	Sergt. Isaac Keys
	Sergt. Samuel Harding	
Privates.	**Privates.**	**Privates.**
Cooper, John	Driver, John	Driver, Thomas
Davis, David	Davis, John D.	Dunn, Andrew
Evans, Edward	Gallant, Allen	Gallant, James
Hoskins, John	Jones, Richard	Kepler, Samuel
Lookingbell, Abraham	Peny, Robert	Phillips, John
Penny, David	Shannon, George	Scribner, John
	Warner, Thomas	

Page 63.

ROLL OF CAPT. JOAB NORTON'S COMPANY.
(Probably from Delaware County.)
Served from June 2, until September 19, 1812.

Capt. Joab Norton	Sergt. Ira Carpenter	Lieut. John Aye
Ensign, Jonothan Hatch	Sergt. M. McLoeland	Sergt. John Depson
Sergt. Erastus Rowe	Corp. Francis Beebe	Corp. James Miller
Corp. Harlock Dunham	Drummer, Jonothan Dunham	Corp. Samuel Scribner
	Fifer, Silas Denham	
Privates.	**Privates.**	**Privates.**
Aye, Jacob	Brown, John	Curtis, Asa D.
Cocheran, Harper	Crosby, Rhederick	Conner, Joseph
Dickey, John	Duncan, James	Diminck, Daniel
Godfrey, Samuel	George, Thomas	Hatch, Nathaniel
Heaviilors, Barnett	Erwin, William	Erwin, James
Leonard, Amos	Maker, William	Minter, John, Jr.
Monroe, Lemuel F.	Minter, Valentine	McFilly, Thomas
Little, William	Lemon, David	Olds, Benjamin
Root, Azariah, Jr.	Price, John	Rickey, Joseph
Smith, Solomon	Vox, Rufus	Welch, Aurora
Walters, James		

Page 64.

ROLL OF CAPT. WILLIAM S. DRAKE'S COMPANY.
(Probably from Delaware County.)
Served from August 24, until September 25, 1812.

Capt. William S. Drake	Ensign Daniel Wyatt	Sergt. Ira Wilcox
	Corp. John Foust	
Privates.	**Privates.**	**Privates.**
Brundage, Nathaniel	Dundleberger, Frederick	Dundleberger, Peter
Ely, Peter	Foust, Jacob	Shaw, Jonothan
Tuboss, Isaac	Welsh, Isaac	Wilcox, Hera

Page 65.

ROLL OF CAPT. JESSE D. JACKSON'S COMPANY. (County Unknown.)
Served from August 23, until September 4, 1812.

Capt. Jesse D. Jackson	Lieut. John Rudd, Jr.	Ensign John Brooks
Sergt. Erastus Rudd	Sergt. Samuel Vinton	Sergt. Ira Parker
Sergt. Chauncey Tinker	Corp. Nathan Russell	Corp. Daniel Sawtell
Corp. Samuel Brown	Drummer, Leonard H. Niles	Fifer, Horace Pearsons
	Fifer, Silas Tinker	
Privates.	**Privates.**	**Privates.**
Allen, Merritt	Brooks, James	Brooks, Hananiah
Blackmer, Stephen	Bates, David	Coles, David
Cook, Rosswell	Drennen, John	Fox, Sinkler
Ferguson, Jonothan	Harrington, Eldad	Harring, Samuel
King, Peter, Jr.	Leavitt, James	Lewis, Caleb
Lewis, Jonas	Marainville, Jabez D.	Moore, John
Miranville, Stephen D.	McNear, Thomas	Noble, Aaron
Stuntz, George	Smith, Chester	Spooner, John
Scovill, Linus	Tubbs, Morgan	Talbot, Daniel
Widner, John L.	Withrow, Hugh	Wooden, Joel

Page 66.

ROLL OF CAPT. WARHAM GRANT'S COMPANY. (County Unknown.)
Served from August 23, until September 4, 1812.

Capt. Warham Grant	Lieut. Harvey Rockwell	Sergt. John Shook
Sergt. Daniel Webster	Sergt. Edward B. Spencer	Corp. Joseph Miller
Corp. Nicholas Miller	Musician, Martin Huntley	Musician, John Gee
Privates.	**Privates.**	**Privates.**
Benjamin, Reuben	Benjamin, Mathew	Asahel, Cleveland
Dewey, Rodolphus	Ensign, Orrin	Griggs, Solomon
Gee, Salmon	Hills, Ira	Huntley, Ezekial
Jones, Robert	Peck, Josiah	Peck, William
Peck, Ansel	Strickland, Joshua	Randall, David
Smith, Platt	Webster, Michael	Wrench, William

Page 67. Vol. I.

ROLL OF CAPT JACOB BARTHOLOMEW'S COMPANY. (County Unknown.)

Served from August 23, until September 2, 1812.

Capt. Jacob Bartholomew
Sergt. Lorrin Cowles
Lieut. Benjamin Montgomery

Ensign Uriah Bertram
Sergt. Truman Watkin
Corp. George Hewins

Sergt. Jonothan Hill
Corp. Daniel I. Bartholomew
Fifer, Benjamin Bartholomew

Privates.

Allen, David
Bartholomew, Samuel
Burnum, Enoch
Cowles, Adna
Cook, Stephen
French, Squire B.
Gregory, Daniel
Hartwell, John
Harper, Archibald, Jr.
Heniman, Stephen
Johnson, Otis
Morrison, Strawbridge
Noyes, John
Smith, Stephen A.
Williams, Havel
Wright, Samuel
Ward, Elisha

Privates.

Bartholomew, Abraham
Brown, I. Zadoc
Bartholomew, Isaac
Cowley, Alpheus
Colhoun, Reynolds
Gaylord, Levi, Jr.
Gaylord, Elihu S.
Hale, Jacob
Houghton, Rufus
Jackson, Walter
Kingsley, John
Moore, Henry I.
Parker, Calvin S.
Spencer, Barzilla
Wood, John
Wright, James, Jr.
Webster, Abraham

Privates.

Bartholomew, John B.
Bachman, Ludwick
Cunningham, Cyrus
Cahoon, Reynolds, Jr.
Custin, Benjamin
Gay, Harding
Hewin, William
Harper, William A.
Hill, John
Jones, Billy
Miller, William
Montgomery, Eli
Phelps, Isaac H.
Turney, Daniel
Williams, Joseph
Williams, Samuel
Webster, Norman

Page 68.

ROLL OF CAPT. ROSWELL AUSTIN'S COMPANY. (County Unknown.)

Served from August 23, until September 6, 1812.

Capt. Roswell Austin
Sergt. David J. Stone
Musician, Joseph Cade

Lieut. Aaron Leyon
Sergt. Josiah Atkin
Musician, Obed Didell

Sergt. Edson Phelps
Corp. William Willams

Privates.

Dibble, John, Jr.
Knapp, Elihu
Robbins, Samuel
Rider, Samuel

Privates.

Goff, Benjamin
Lyman, Joshua
Squires, Daniel
Thorp, Alpha

Privates.

Knap, Roswell
Phelps, Stephen K.
Skinner, Ashbel
Wood, Samuel, Jr.

Pages 69-70.

ROLL OF CAPT. CHANCEY BARKER'S COMPANY.
(Probably from Franklin County.)

Served from August 24, until September 15, 1812. Part served from May 4, until May 27, 1813.

Capt. Chancey Barker
Sergt. Eliphalet Barker
Sergt. Silas Barlow
Corp. William Derrickson

Lieut. Samuel Maynard
Sergt. Ethan Palmer
Corp. William Thompson
Corp. Isaac Harrison

Ensign Hector Kilbourn
Sergt. Berkley Comstock
Corp. Abraham Phelps
Musician, Andrews, Noah

Privates.

Allen, Isaac
Crippin, John
Cochrane, Nathaniel
Chapman, Albert
Faulkner, Joshua N.
Hone, Henry
Impson, William
Kirk, John
Maynard, Amos, Jr.
Moore, Simeon, Sr.
Puntney, Aquilla
Smith, John
Skeels, Belias H.
Turbee, Mathias
White, William
Wheeler, Herman

Privates.

Benedict, Asahel
Crippen, Joseph
Case, Orlando
Derickson, John
Glasby, Enos
Hoffman, Jacob
Knight, Oreno
Lee, Asa
Maynard, Moses
McCutchan, Robert
Phelps, Abraham
Sharp, Ganit
Tolland, Thomas
Wilcox, Asa
Willard, Windsor
Yonel, John

Privates.

Brient, Jeremiah
Cooper, John
Crosby, Charles
Fisher, Isaiah
Griswold, Isaac
Hills, James H.
Kilbourn, John
Maxfield, Amos
Mitchell, Newman
Olmsted, Francis
Rugg, Origen
Stanberry, Recompense
Toppin, Zopher
Wilson, Samuel
Weaver, Asa, Jr.

Page 71.

ROLL OF LIEUT. SILAS FLEMING'S COMPANY. (County Unknown.)

Served from August 30, 1812, until February 28, 1813

Lieut. Silas Fleming
Sergt. John Bishop
Drummer, Hugh Smith

Ensign Isaac Sutton
Corp. William Bunch
Fifer, Joseph Smith

Sergt. Charles Johnston
Corp. George Kelley

Privates.

Allen, John
Crowel, Michael
Highly, John
Holdeman, Christian
Ireland, William
LeDruell, John
Melling, Thomas
Purviance, Levi
Railsback, Jacob
Summers, John
York, Jeptha

Privates.

Bridge, John
Douglas, Samuel
Hewit, Israel
Hole, Charles
Irwin, Thomas
Lewallen, Thomas
Michael, Jacob
Powell, Hezekiah
Ringen, Jacob
Swisher, William

Privates.

Childer, Thomas
Davis, George
Hudlow, John
Hapner, Abraham
Keaston, Samuel
Lewallen, Phillip
Pain, Isaac
Reesley, Thomas
Summers, James
Tullinger, William

Page 72. Vol. I.

ROLL OF CAPT. JOHN FLEMING'S COMPANY. (County Unknown.)

Served from August 23, 1812, until February 22, 1813.

Rank and Name of Soldier.	Rank and Name of Soldier.	Rank and Name of Soldier.
Capt. John Fleming	Lieut. George Richardson	Ensign Henry Mann
Sergt. James W. Maxwell	Sergt. George Hardy	Sergt. William Williman
Sergt. Daniel Knop	Corp. John Morris	Corp. Thomas Morris
Corp. Martin Vance	Corp. Josiah Clawson	

Privates.

Alred, Thomas	Allen, John	Atkinson, Ison
Allved, Isaac	Burnes, Barnabus	Boyd, Andrew
Bond, Exum S.	Brown, James	Brown, Nathan
Cristler, Aaron	Caldwell, Joseph W.	Doharty, Edward
Defree, Archibald	Dingman, Daniel V.	Elliott, Ebenezer
Frederick, Christian	Goldsmith, John	Gorman, James
Gearhart, William	Hewitt, David	Hayes, John
Homero, Jacob	Helm, Christian	Ingersom, Benjamin
Gilbert, John	Jones, William	Lindsley, Dennis
Lennox, James	Maundey, Jacob	Marsham, Mathew
Maiers, Jacob	McCoy, Daniel	McComb, Andrew Y.
Nelson, William	Pilson, Hugh	Russel, Charles
Richardson, William	Singer, Thomas	Smith, John
Shackelford, James	Swartword, Abraham	Sumption, Charles
Simpson, Samuel	Studibaker, David	Shackelford, William
Woodward, Jacob	Williams, John	Worle, Samuel, Sr.
	Worle, Samuel, Jr.	

Page 424.

ROLL OF CAPT. GEORGE RICHARDSON'S COMPANY. (County Unknown.)

Served from August 29, until October 29, 1812.

Capt. George Richardson	Lieut. Gottfreid Westhofer	Ensign Peter Johnston
Sergt. Jacob Houck	Sergt. William Kemp	Sergt. Robert Sparks
Sergt. Mathias Waggoner	Drummer, Robert Caples	

Privates.

Bumtrager, John	Bartlett, Peter	DeLong, Solomon
Davis, Joseph	Davis, David	Everett, Henry
Engle, Levi	Frederick, Peter	Graham, Ebenezer
Griffith, Nathan	Hayes, Samuel	Huston, Michael
Johnson, William	Kinder, John	Knight, Michael
Miller, Henry	Moore, George	Moninger, George
McMullan, David	McDonough, Hugh	Parker, Andrew
Roysher, Daniel	Rebstock, Martin	Sells, Jonothan
Spiker, Phillip	Smith, John	Thompson, Michael
Wycoff, William	Wieland, Peter	Watson, James

Pages 268-269-270-271.

ROLL OF CAPT. JEDEDIAH BURNHAM'S COMPANY. (County Unknown.)

Served from August 24, until November 10, 1812, and from January 1, until February 28, 1813.

Capt. Jedediah Burnham	Lieut. Benjamin Allen	Lieut. Nathaniel Hopkins
Ensign Alexander Mathews	Lieut. Lewis Dill	Ensign Dexter Clinton
Ensign Augustin Smith	Sergt. Aaron Rice	Sergt. James Laughlin
Sergt. Robert Henry	Sergt. Henry Bignel	Sergt. Amzi Webb
Sergt. Gurden Hutchins	Sergt. Iddo Bailey	Sergt. William Randall
Sergt. Justis Fobes	Sergt. William Cleaver	Corp. Daniel Bewen
Corp. Samuel Randall	Corp. Ebenezer Weber	Corp. John L. Cook
Corp. James King	Corp. Michael Rutledge	Corp. Alexander Mathews
Corp. John Burwell	Corp. Samuel Tuthill	

Privates.

Adams, Augustus	Allen, Chester	Alexander, Joseph
Anderson, William	Adkinson, Enoch	Andrews, Michard
Alderman, Eber	Alderman, Jonothan	Andrews, Asa
Andrews, Sherman	Brackin, Ezekial	Braklin, David
Buel, Ezra	Burnes, Jacob	Broadwell, Henry
Babcock, Silas	Brainard, Solomon	Barnes, Ebenezer
Burnes, George	Ballard, Ezekial	Brockway, Jesse
Burnham, Joshua	Breden, John	Bates, Dennis
Christy, William	Christy, Andrew	Cossit, Eli
Calvin, Luther	Chapman, Comfort	Carlton, John
Crawford, Alexander	Daly, John	Davis, Walter
Dodge, Samuel	Dickinson, Elisha	Dillon, Asa
Doyle, Anthony	Dillon, Samuel	Ford, Joseph
Ford, Jacob	Ford, Shadrach	Foss, Cotton
Fisher, Benjamin	Folsom, David	Fowler, Chester
Findlay, John	Fobes, Elias	Foot, Levi
Farrow, Isaac	Furgeson, Horace	Folsom, Moses
Giddings, Joshua R.	Giddings, Warren	Goodrich, Gideon
Green, Ebenezer	Galloway, James	Hungerford, Henry
Hutchinson, Daniel	Hill, James	Hough, Henry
Hannah, Thomas	Hill, James, Sr.	Harberson, Robert
Jackson, William	Jones, Silven	Keeler, Ezra

Vol. I.

ROLL OF CAPT. JEDTDITH BURNHAM'S COMPANY. (Continued)

Rank and Name of Soldier.	Rank and Name of Soldier.	Rank and Name of Soldier.
Privates.	Privates.	Privates.
King, Robert	Kinney, Hutchens	Kerr, William
Kerr, Thomas	Long, Isaac	Leffingwell, William
Lewis, Oliver	Lillie, Hen.y	Lyon, William
Lafferty, William	Langley, John	Lake, Constant
Laughlin, Robert	Mathews, Alexander	Mathews, Thomas, Jr.
Morse, Ansel	Mathews, John	Moses, Azariah
Moses, Eldred	Meeker, Andrew C.	Mapes, Henry, Jr.
Moses, Abner	Moss, Simion	Morey, Hosea
Munson, Calvin	McLaughlin, Patrick	McKey, William
McClerg, David	McFarland, William	Nye, Joshua
Newton, Lemuel	Nelson, Hugh	Noys, Samuel
Ogden, Benjamin	Potter, Thomas	Perkins, Seth
Perkins, Enoch	Patrick, John	Pelton, Harvey
Pelton, Julius	Price, Archibald	Reeve, Jeremiah
Roberts, Thomas	Randall, John	Sutliff, Plumb
Scovill, David	Scott, William	Shull, Frederick
Smith, Joel	Splitstene, Henry	Splitstene, Adam
Scott, William	Scovill, Reuben	Scovill, Ansel
Smith, Amos	Smith, James	Spillhouse, Martin G.
Tidd, Martin	Tidd, Charles	Tuttle, Jonothan
Tuttle, Samuel	Tyrell, Judson	Trusedale, James, Jr.
Taylor, John	Woodworth, Ebenezer	Westbay, James
Woodworth, Divdate	Waid, Robert	Wald, Alexander
Woodworth, Albigence	Wolf, Oratio D.	Wakeman, Silliman
Waldorf, Philip	Wood, John	White, William
Worters, Lester	Yelman, Peter	Fifer, Nicholas Little
Fifer, Nathan Fobes	Drummer, Lemuel Clark	Drummer, Levi Mathews

Page 143, Vol. I.

ROLL OF FIELD AND STAFF, WAR OF 1812-1813.
LIEUT. COL. RICHARD HAYES, ———— REGIMENT, OHIO MILITIA.

Lt. Col. Richard Hayes	Maj. Zopher Case	Maj. Samuel Frazier
Adjt. Sterling G. Bushnell	Q. M. John Andrews	Q. M. Clerk Elan Jones
Q. M. Sergt. Nathaniel Coleman	Surg. Peter Allen	Surg. Mate Erastus Goodwin
Sergt. Maj. William Hull	Sergt. Maj. Henry Bignell	Sergt. Maj. Luman Beech
	Fife Maj. Amos Jones	
	Drum Maj. Davis Fuller	

Page 195.

COLONEL LEWIS CASS, ———— REGIMENT, OHIO MILITIA.

Col. Lewis Cass	Maj. Robert Morrison	Maj. Joseph Morrison
Surg. Charles Lester	Surg. Mate, James Reynolds	Adjt. H Northrop
Pay Master Abner Dent	Q. M. Elias Gilman	Q. M. Sergt. James Sharp
Sergt. Maj. Thomas Foster	Drum Maj. G. Goodspeed	

Page 202.

LIEUT. COL. NATHAN KING, ———— REGIMENT, OHIO MILITIA.

Lieut. Col. Nathan King	Maj. Zadoc Thompson	Adjt. Josiah W. Brown
Q. M., I. A. Robinson	Q. M. Clerk, James A. Harper	Surg. Orestes H. Hawley
Surg. Mate, Elijah Coleman	Q. M. Sergt. Robert Harper	Drum Maj., David Bertham
Fife Maj., Silas Tinker		

Page 203.

LIEUT. COL. MILLS STEPHENSON, ———— REGIMENT, OHIO MILITIA.

Lieut. Col. Mills Stephenson	Maj. Anthony Pitzer	Maj. Thomas Moore
Adjt. Alexander Bourne	Pay Master Neville Redmon	Surg. Joseph Keith
Surg. Mate, John L. McCullough	Q. M. Tingley Sutton	Q. M. Sergt. James Finley
	Fife Maj. James K. Caldwell	Drum Maj. William Smith
	Sergt. Maj. Isaac Burkellow	

Page 242.

COLONEL ROBERT SAFFORD, ———— REGIMENT, OHIO MILITIA.

Col. Robert Safford	Maj. Nathaniel Beasley	Maj. Jehiel Gregory
Capt. Nehemiah Gregory	Capt. Calvin Shephard	Lieut. John Rader
Lieut. John Roadamour	Ensign John Bootom	

Page 251.

COLONEL DANIEL COLLIER, ———— REGIMENT, OHIO MILITIA.

Col. Daniel Collier	Maj. Isaac Dawson	Adjt. John Kincade
Q. M. Seth Shoemaker	Pay Master, James Allen	Surg. Mate Clayton Tiffin
Sergt. Maj. John Mathews	Q. M. Sergt. John Cavin	Drum Maj. Jacob Metts

ROSTER OF OHIO SOLDIERS IN WAR OF 1812   87

Page 425. Vol. I.

Rank and Name of Soldier.	Rank and Name of Soldier.	Rank and Name of Soldier.

LIEUT. COL. JEDEDIAH BEARD, ———— REGIMENT, OHIO MILITIA.

Lieut. Col. Jedediah Beard	Maj. Samuel Jones	Maj. Elezor Hecox
Adjt. Eleazor Patchin	Q. M. Samuel W. Phelps	Pay Master Samuel S. Baldwin
Clerk, Peter Hitchcock	Surg. William Kennedy	Surg. Mate Erastus Goodwin
Fife Maj. David Hill	Q. M. James Strong	Sergt. Maj. Hendrick E. Paine
	Drum Maj. Stephen Bond	

Page 201.

MAJ. SAMUEL CONNELL, ODD BATTALION, OHIO MILITIA.

Maj. Samuel Connell	Adjt. Anthony Wayne	Pay Master Henry H. Evans
	Surg. Henry H. Evans	

Page 294.

MAJ. BENJAMIN DANIELS, ODD BATTALION, OHIO MILITIA.

Maj. Benjamin Daniels	Adjt. William Barnes	Pay Master James Sergeant
Q. M. Joseph I. Martin	Q. M. Sergt. John Stewart	

Page 430.

MAJ. JOSEPH RHODES, ODD BATTALION, OHIO MILITIA.

Maj. Joseph Rhodes	Adjt. Samuel Criswell	Q. M. Lewis Hoyt

Page 315.

MAJ. ALEXANDER C. LANIER, FOURTH DETACHMENT, OHIO MILITIA.

Maj. Alexander C. Lanier	Surg. Mate Walter Buell

Page 75.

THE ROLLS OF THE FOLLOWING COMPANIES DO NOT STATE TO WHICH REGIMENT THEY BELONG.

ROLL OF CAPT. WILLIAMS. (Incomplete.) County Unknown.)

Served from ——————————.

Capt. Williams	Private, Ballinger, Joseph

Page 77.

ROLL OF CAPT. JARED STRONG'S COMPANY.
(Probably from Ross County.)

Served from July 27, until August 19, 1813.

Capt. Jared Strong	Lieut. Samuel Gallespie	Ensign William How
Sergt. William Givens	Sergt. John Lake	Sergt. David Mitchell
Sergt. Phillip Strather	Corp. Salmon Goodenough	Corp. Alexander Hill
Corp. Joseph Lake	Corp. William Hillenbohker	Drummer, Harris, Perry
	Fifer, James Markey	

Privates.

Aldride, Samuel	Burn, Samuel	Baly, Stephen
Black, William	Casdele, Thomas M.	Clemens, Joseph
Elliton, William	Hensete, William	Higginbothom, James
Ogg, John	Phillips, James	Robben, Joseph
Rout, Henry	Skelinge Jacob	Sergant, John
	Watson, Jesse	

Pages 78-79.

ROLL OF CAPT. JAMES MORROW'S COMPANY.
(Probably from Greene County.)

Served from May 10, until May 19, 1813

Capt. James Morrow	Lieut. Christopher Sroupe	Ensign George Townsley
Sergt. Joseph Kyle, Jr.	Sergt. James Colliers	Sergt. Samuel Galloway
Sergt. John McCullough	Corp. George Logan	Corp. Robert Stephenson
Corp. William McCoy	Corp. Arthur McFarland	

Privates.

Andrew, James	Andrew, Hugh	Baldwin, David
Barnes, John	Bishop, Solomon	Bull, John
Bull, James	Beatty, William A.	Cannon, Anthony
Confer, George	Chambers, David	Cohagen, John
Currie, William	Dean, Robert	Dermitt, Isaac
Galloway, James N.	Galloway, John	Gant, Robert
Gibson, John	Gibson, Montelion	Gowdy, John
Goldsby, John	Gowdy, Robert	Goldsby, George
Goldsby, Briggs M.	Hivling, John	Ibers, Richard
Jolly, John	Junken, George	Johnston, Arthur
Kendall, John	Moore, Charles	Miller, George
Moore, James	Moodie, Robert	Miller, John
Miller, Daniel	McCarthen, James	McCulley, William
McCulley, James	McCoy, Alexander	McCoy, James
Owings, James	Quinn, Amos	Sparks, Leonard
Stephenson, John	Scott, William	Srouf, David
Sroupe, Lewis	Sterrett, Joseph	Steele, John
Todd, James	Townsley, Thomas	Vancaton, John
Ward, Hervey	Wilson, George	Waltburn, Robert
Woodward, Henry	Winget, Hugh	White, Joseph

Vol. I. Page 81.

ROLL OF CAPT. ISAAC WALKER'S COMPANY. (County Unknown.)

Served from February 10, until April 5, 1813.

Rank and Name of Soldier.	Rank and Name of Soldier.	Rank and Name of Soldier.
Capt. Isaac Walker	Ensign Benjamin Cook	Sergt. Robert Huston
Sergt. Isaac Buchanan	Sergt. Allen Loury	Corp. Robert Watson
	Corp. John Patton	
Privates.	**Privates.**	**Privates.**
Bell, William	Burnett, John	Carter, John
Cross, Nathan	Duncan, John	Deneen, James
Dawson, William	Gerodelle, John	Hany, James
Hyatt, Elisha	Kerr, Nathan	Maxfield, William
Morrison, James	Nye, Joshua	Park, Elijah
Prior, Thomas	Slover, Samuel	Swager, John

Page 82.

ROLL OF CAPT. DANIEL ABEL'S COMPANY. (County Unknown.)

Served from August 24, until August 27, 1812.

Capt. Daniel Abel	Lieut. Elijah Tarnill	Ensign Nathan Webb
Sergt. Abner Fowler	Sergt. George Lilly	Sergt. Ariel Bradley
Sergt. Furzi Webb	Corp. William Deraa	Drummer, John Jackson
Privates.	**Privates.**	**Privates.**
Adams, Augustus	Barnes, Ebenezer	Dickinson, Elisha
Dickerson, Friend	Fisher, Benjamin	Fowler, Chester
Foot, Levi	Fanagh, Isaac	Green, Joseph
Hunt, Ezra	Hungerford, Hervey	Hill, Jared
Jackson, William	Lille, David, Jr.	Lille, Henry
Loury, David	Meeker, Andrew	McKee, William
Nicholson, James	Perkins, Enoch	Perkins, Seth
Silaman, Wakeman	Zeril, Jackson	

Page 83.

ROLL OF CAPT. AMBROSE PALMER'S COMPANY. (County Unknown.)

Served from August 25, until August 28, 1812.

Capt. Ambrose Palmer	Ensign Tensard R. DeWolf	Sergt. Calvin Palmer
Sergt. Samuel Banning	Sergt. Henry Bignol	Sergt. Calvin Smith
Corp. James Bates	Corp. Nathan Chesrey	Corp. Michael Rutledge
Drummer, Stephen Calvin	Fifer, Charles Trunkey	
Privates.	**Privates.**	**Privates.**
Akins, Henry C.	Adkinson, Enoch	Anderson, William
Burnes, Andrew	Brown, William	Brown, James
Calvin, Luther	Case, Ira	DeWolf, Horatio
Gibbs, Isaac	Lewis, Oliver	Linsley, Elan
Langly, John	Moses, Abner	Mowery, Hosea
McClong, David	Scovil, David	Sheldon, Berry
	Yetman, Peter	

Pages 84-85.

ROLL OF CAPT. ASA HUTCHINS' COMPANY. (County Unknown.)

Served from August 24, until November 11, 1812.

Capt. Asa Hutchins	Lieut. William Bartholomew	Ensign Dexter Clinton
Ensign Joseph Reeves	Sergt. Gurden Hutchins	Sergt. Ambrose Hart
Sergt. Silden Scovil, Jr.	Sergt. Aruna Alderman	Sergt. Henry Hull
Corp. Samuel L. Gleason	Corp. Joel Humason	Corp. Lister Bashnell
Corp. Mathias Swatsweller	Corp. Charles Woodruff	Corp. David Wheeler
Privates.	**Privates.**	**Privates.**
Andrews, Asa	Bates, Dennis	Braden, John
Bates, Talcott	Burnett, William	Crawford, Alexander
Crosby, Ezra	Clark, Joseph L.	Clark, Timothy
Clinton, William	Chew, Thomas	Chatfield, William
Alderman, Chauncy	Deming, Phineas	Groscoss, John
Humison, Isaac	Hutchins, Samuel	Heckcox, Chauncy
Hull, John	Hilton, Richard	Hughes, James
Hayes, Lester	Jones, Seldon	Kerr, Thomas
Johnson, Rausen	Kinney, James	Kepner, John
Lowery, Isaac	Lafferty, William	Lowery, Samuel, Jr.
Lewis, Lambert W.	Patrick, John	Smith, James
	Trusdill, James J.	

Page 86.

ROLL OF CAPT. CALEB BALDWIN'S COMPANY. (County Unknown.)

Served from August 23, until September 16, 1812.

Capt. Caleb Baldwin	Ensign Joseph Porter	
Privates.	**Privates.**	**Privates.**
Anderson, James	Burgess, Robert	Beard, John
Barkley, Francis	Cronnan, Abner	Chub, John
Dennison, David	Dustman, Jacob	Dinwiddie, Thomas
Fitch, Henry	Fitch, Andrew	Foulk, Henry
Frank, Jacob	Gilbert, Samuel	Gibson, James
Gilbert, Henry		

ROLL OF CAPT. CALEB BALDWIN'S COMPANY. (Continued.)

Rank and Name of Soldier. | Rank and Name of Soldier. | Rank and Name of Soldier.

Privates.

Privates	Privates	Privates
Hoyls, Nicholas	Hartinger, Jacob	Hayden, Samuel
Love, William	Lowery, Robert	Miller, John
Mears, Joseph	McCreary, John	McMullin, John
McFall, Malcolm	Ormsby, George	Onarwert, John
Peterman, Jacob	Rose, Robert	Rose, David
Spargo, George S.	Sell, John	Simon, Adam
Stout, Jonothan	Swager, Isaac	State, Andrew
Turner, Samuel	Upton, Benjamin	White, James
Whitsell, Jacob	Wilson, Edward	Willey, Frederick

Pages 87-88.

ROLL OF CAPT. DANIEL DULL'S (Deceased) COMPANY. (County Unknown.)
(This Company was Under the Command of Lieut. Robert Earl.)

Served from August 22, until August 28, 1812, and from January 1, until March 8, 1813.

Capt. Daniel Dull	Lieut. Robert Earl	Ensign John Shifelton
Sergt. Eber W. Brooks	Sergt. Benjamin Sutherland	Sergt. Ira Prescott
Sergt. Joseph Allen	Corp. Levi Patman	Corp. John Allen
Corp. William McKonkey	Corp. George Shufelton	Corp. John Colbraith
Fifer, Harmon Deen	Drummer, Michael Peltz	

Privates	Privates	Privates
Allen, William	Alderman, Frederick	Adams, Shubal
Austin, Calvin	Bowen, Lott	Bales, Samuel
Brown, John	Bartholomew, Charles	Caldwell, John
Crooks, Robert	Carlisle, David	Custard, Jacob
Campbell, Alexander	Craige, John	Cale, William
Cale, Thomas	Davison, Benjamin, Jr.	DeCorsey, Isaac
Dixon, Walter	Davidson, William	Earl, Joseph
Earl, Jacob	French, William	Freeman, Robert J.
Fish, Abner	Gibson, Samuel	Hemming, Jacob
Hutson, Mathew	Hill, Alpheus	Hart, Alva
Hall, William	Hulk, Henry R.	Hampton, John
Harmon, Hiram	Hickman, Timothy	Hawey, John
Johnson, Abraham	Kelso, Robert	Lingo, Joseph
Loveless, Samuel	Lumis, Andrew	Miller, Jacob
Marshall, Isaac	More, Joseph	McComb, James
McKelvy, William	McKenzie, Robert	Norton, Michael
Norton, Robert	Porter, Thomas	Robert, Joseph S.
Rook, James	Rawley, Constant	Reed, Hezekiah
Stillman, John D.	Storey, Henry	Scott, Joseph
Stanley, Marshall	Sacket, Gany	Spoony, Elias
Snyder, Benjamin	Snyder, William	Stow, Chester
Trescott, Ira	Turner, Samuel B.	Trescott, Russell
Van Wye, Isaac	Woodward, John	Wilson, David
Walder, Jonothan	Winins, Jacob	Williams, Benjamin
Windle, Francis	Young, William	

Page 89.

ROLL OF CAPT. JAMES STONE'S COMPANY. (County Unknown.)

Served from August 23, until September 5, 1812.

Capt. James Stone	Lieut. Quintus F. Adkins	Ensign Daniel Hall
Sergt. David Wright	Sergt. John Crowell	Corp. Erastus Flower
Corp. Roswell Stephens	Drummer, Samuel Knowlton	

Privates	Privates	Privates
Baily, Benjamin	Clieveland, Orison	Crosby, Calvin
Griffin, Sullivan	Hinman, Arad	Hall, Joseph
Humprey, Guy	Knowlton, Stephen	Luman, Beach
Merrels, Neh	Osborn, Lewis	Trall, Luman
Tuttle, Ara	Walkly, Jonothan	Walkly, David
	Walkly, Seth	

Page 90.

ROLL OF CAPT. ALLEN GAYLORD'S COMPANY.
(Probably from Cuyahoga County.)

Served from August 22, until October 24, 1812.

Capt. Allen Gaylord	Lieut. Walter Strong	Ensign, Elijah Nobles
Sergt. William W. Williams	Drummer, Simon Smith	Fifer, Almon Wolcott

Privates	Privates	Privates
Abbott, Josiah	Blinn, Richard H.	Chase, Daniel
Cahoon, Amos	Comstock, Peter	Ensign, Ira
Frazier, Stephen	Gunn, Christopher	Gunn, Charles
Hungerford, Asa	Johnson, Samuel	King, William, Sr.
King, William, Jr.	Prentiss, Robert	Prentiss, James
Morton, Clark	Porter, Amaziah	Remington, Justus
Rois, Silas	White, Charles	

Page 91. Vol. I.

ROLL OF CAPT. JAMES THOMPSON'S COMPANY.
(Probably from Geauga County.)
Served from August 22, until August 29, 1812.

Rank and Name of Soldier.	Rank and Name of Soldier.	Rank and Name of Soldier.
Privates.	*Privates.*	*Privates.*
Capt. James Thompson	Lieut. Samuel Hardy	Ensign John Hopkins
Sergt. Lewis Smith	Sergt. Benjamin Wells	Sergt. Theodorus Miller
Sergt. Heathman Thomas	Corp. Seth Risley	Corp. William Thompson
Corp. James Heathman	Corp. Elijah Webster	Drummer, John Granger
	Fifer, Joseph Young	
Privates.	*Privates.*	*Privates.*
Brown, Benoni	Dustin, John	Granger, Samuel
Hanchell, Nathan	James, John	Pomroy, Stephen
Russell, Eliakin	Reed, John	Wilcox, Elnathan
White, Holden	Wallace, Robert	Townsley, John

Page 92.

ROLL OF CAPT. NORMAN CANFIELD'S COMPANY.
(Probably from Geauga County.)
Served from August 22, until August 30, 1812.

Capt. Norman Canfield	Lieut. Allen Humphrey	Ensign Horace Taylor
Sergt. Chandler Pears	Sergt. Benjamin Andrews	Corp. Ichabod Pomeroy
	Corp. Elijah Douglas	
Privates.	*Privates.*	*Privates.*
Bond, Joseph	Elwell, John	Elliott, Chester
Hale, Jesse	Hasher, John R.	King, Hosea
King, Isaiah	Kellog, Aranda	King, Nathaniel
Peare, Menick	Spencer, Halsey	Spencer, Allen
	Spencer, Nathaniel	

Page 93.

ROLL OF ENSIGN PETER HUBER'S COMPANY. (County Unknown.)
Served from October 13, until October 27, 1813.

Ensign Peter Huber	Sergt. Roberson Fletcher	Sergt. Reuben Williams
Corp. Joshua Cole	Corp. John Morehart	Corp. George Harrison
	Corp. Thomas Durris	
Privates.	*Privates.*	*Privates.*
Abraham, John	Bush, Martin	Brooks, Joseph
Clark, Oratio	Crumley, John	Death, William
Daubert, John	Faulkner, Martin	Godman, William
Greybill, Christopher	Harman, Jacob	Hood, Robert
Long, Thomas	Long, John	Miller, Daniel
Morehart, Jacob	Measomore, John	Measomore, Henry
McFarland, Walter	Sirk, David	Vandamark, Daniel
Wotring, Abraham	Wells, Thomas	Whitehous, Jacob
	Whitehous, James	

Page 94.

ROLL OF CAPT. RICHARD HOOKER'S COMPANY.
(Probably from Franklin and Fairfield Counties.)
Served from May 7, until September 5, 1813.

Capt. Richard Hooker	Lieut. Valentine Raber	Cornet, James Reed
Sergt. Joseph Hodges	Sergt. Robert Wilson	Sergt. Moses Sowers
Sergt. George Harrison	Corp. Abraham Middlesworth	Corp. Thomas Duddleson
Corp. Arthur Stotts	Corp. Abraham Cole	Trumpeter, Joseph Wright
Privates.	*Privates.*	*Privates.*
Busbee, John	Busbee, George	Cameron, Alexander
Cline, Andrew	Cromby, Christ	Cloughburg, Abraham
Carlisle, Thomas	Delshaver, Jacob	Delshaver, John
Earnman, Frederick	Gessel, John	Glick, George
Hamilton, Orange	Harrison, Alexander	Hayes, Peter
Highland, Edward	Johnston, John	Long, William
Milton, Isaac	Moore, William	Moore, Henry
Milison, Barnett	McVay, John	Nigh, Michael
Nye, George	Propeck, Thomas	Ridenhour, Henry
Reat, Hugh	Stewart, Joseph	Stotts, Absalom
Sowers, John	Sprader, Jacob	Shull, Solomon
Wilson, Samuel	Winders, Daniel	

Page 95.

ROLL OF CAPT. JOHN McCORD'S COMPANY (Probably from Champaign Co.)
Served from September 6, until September 22, 1812.

Capt. John McCord	Sergt. Joseph Low	Sergt. Alexander Allen
	Corp. Joseph O. Lemon	
Privates.	*Privates.*	*Privates.*
Armstrong, Thomas	Byars, David	Evans, Edward
Fitzpatrick, John	Ford, Joseph	Lemon, Laurence V.
Lutser, Henry	McCarthy, William	Neally, William
Powell, Enoch	Powell, Elijah	Powell, Timothy
Patrick, Anthony	Rhodes, Sandford	Largent, Abraham
Robertson, Isaac	Tharp, Jonothan	Tharp, Andrew
Taber, Robert	Vincy, John	Whitaker, Josiah

Page 96. Vol. I.
ROLL OF CAPT. JOHN LINGLE'S COMPANY (Probably from Champaign Co.)
Served from October 15, until November 15, 1812.

Rank and Name of Soldier.   Rank and Name of Soldier.   Rank and Name of Soldier.

Capt. John Lingle
Sergt. John Crosly
Sergt. William Patten
Corp. William Kirkpatrick

Lieut. Cyrus Ward
Sergt. Nicholas Prickett
Corp. Robert Reid
Fifer, John Richards

Ensign, James Humphreys
Sergt. David Crahill
Corp. George Arbogast
Drummer, Newton Bourroughs

Privates.

Audrick, Christopher
Cleveland, Martin
Goble, Thomas
Harnett, Elijah
Murphy, John
McBeth, William
Reynolds, James
Radish, Nathan
Sparrow, Ferdinand
Walker, George

Privates.

Coventon, Henry
Dougherty, John
Gayne, Charles
Hargadine, William
Meenach, William
Nicholson, James
Rankin, George
Reed, Thomas
Shall, Peter
Wilson, Charles

Privates.

Cowen, John
Goble, Daniel
Gamble, Robert
Lewis, John
McBeth, Andrew
Reid, James
Richards, Elijah
Russell, James
Taylor, John

Page 97.
ROLL OF CAPT. JOHN R. LEMMON'S COMPANY
(Probably from Champaign County).
Served from November 12, until December 12, 1812.

Capt. John R. Lemmon
Sergt. Richard Robinson
Corp. Daniel Wren

Ensign, Joseph Coffey
Sergt. Isaac Elsworth
Corp. Joseph Runyon
Corp. Jacob Elsworth

Sergt. William Hunt
Sergt. Charles Irwin
Corp. Mathew Shaul

Privates.

Arbogast, Henry
Botkin, William
Bombgarden, Andrew
Curl, William
Crantrall, Joshua
Dawson, Richard
Hodge, Andrew
Hunter, Jonothan
Lee, James
Marris, William
Runyon, Abraham
Smith, David
Sergant, John
Tuttle, John
Wren, Thomas

Privates.

Baldwin, Joshua
Boyer, Samuel
Collins, Joseph
Cartmell, Nathaniel
Dickeson, Joseph
Frost, William
Hunter, John
Hunter, James
Marsh, Malon
McKonkey, Archibald
Roberts, James
Smith, James
Tunks, Thomas
Van Cultz, David
Ward, Richard

Privates.

Beezly, Isaac
Banes, Oratio
Clemmings, Job
Chance, Samuel
Dawson, James
Graham, David
Hunter, William
Jones, Jonothan
Moss, John
McKinnon, Daniel
Segar, David
Smith, Benjamin
Tunks, Phillip
Van Meter, Solomon

Pages 98-99-100.
ROLL OF CAPT. JOHN R. LEMMON'S COMPANY (Probably from Ross Co.)
Served from January 30, until April 11, 1815.

Capt. John R. Lemmon
Sergt. William Patrick
Sergt. Joshua Williams
Corp. James Tucker

Lieut. James McArthur
Sergt. Ellis S. Baldwin
Corp. Joshua Spry
Musician, Briton Wright

Ensign, David Henderson
Sergt. Phillip Sampson
Corp. John Fitzgerald
Musician, John Clark

Privates.

Albogast, Silas
Borden, James
Brewer, Jesse
Bane, Oratio
Croy, Jacob
Collison, John
Davis, John
Foust, Abraham
Green, William
Hill, William R.
Huff, Charles
Huston, James
Jamison, Charles
Krein, Adam
Missimore, Henry
McFarland, Daniel
Russell, Robert
Smith, Sherman
Townsley, John
Watson, Lewis
Willis, Hugh
Whitesel, John

Privates.

Bagea, Jacob
Buskirk, Lewis D.
Badger, James P.
Crossley, Conrad
Codington, William
Campbell, John
Earl, James
Griffin, Daniel
Goddard, Robert D.
Hird, Thomas
Hood, Edward
Jovin, William
King, William
Lloyd, John
Missimore, John
McHan, William
Stout, Benhon
Shanks, Peter
Tharp, James
Watson, Eli
Wallace, Thomas
Van Amburgh, Abraham

Privates.

Bell, Alexander
Borer, Peter
Bulger, Elijah
Collins, Mathias
Clawson, Abraham
Dum, Henry
Fisher, Jonothan
Glass, James
Hickson, Enoch
Haines, Thomas
Hopkins, James
Jones, Robert
Konklin, John
Minor, Moses
McIntosh, William
McCartney, Isaac
Shrofe, David
Tuttle, Simon
Watson, Paschal
Williams, Isaac
Williams, Lewis

Page 101. Vol. 1.

ROLL OF CAPT. A. HEMPHILL'S COMPANY (County Unknown).
This Company Under the Comman dof Lieut. Aaron Foster.
Served from July 28, 1813, ————

Rank and Name of Soldier.	Rank and Name of Soldier.	Rank and Name of Soldier.
Lieut. Aaron Foster	Corp. William Brown	
Privates.	**Privates.**	**Privates.**
Connal, William	Campbell, William	Eli, William
Fischer, Jacob	Griffin, Samuel	Given, William
Keenor, John	Little, John	Latta, Moses
Latta, John	Latta, James	McMahon, Joseph
McNeel, Archibald	Turnipseed, Christian	Toughman, Peter
Ryan, Joshua	Stewart, Archibald	Shanor, Henry
	White, Merryman	

Pages 102-118.

ROLL OF CAPT. GEORGE GIBSON'S COMPANY (Probably from Ross County).
Served from December 31, 1814, until February 23, 1815.

Capt. George Gibson	Lieut. Mathew Littleton	Ensign, Henry Gutches
Sergt. Mathew Mitchel	Sergt. John Armstrong	Sergt. James McColister
Sergt. George Watson	Corp. Thomas Binton	Corp. Thomas Richardson
Corp. Richard Bradley	Corp. William Seeds	Musician, Jacob Croghan
	Musician Thomas Littleton	
Privates.	**Privates.**	**Privates.**
Anderson, James	Argo, Abraham	Biviton, Basil
Benjamin, William	Campbell, Hugh	Culbertson, Robert
DeWitt, George	Davidson, John	Elder, Thomas
Edward, John	Fewel, John	Fullnig, Alexander
Francisco, Joseph	Hamilton, James	Heaston, Martin
Hoselton, Jacob	Harrison, James	Helsel, Daniel
Haverlow, William	Igo, Daniel	Jaram, William
Jones, Abel	King, Joshua	Ken, James
Lock, John	Lafferty, John	Martin, David
Macklin, Thomas	Morris, Richard	Mann, Reuben P.
Mason, James	McCartney, Duke	McFadden, William
McCoy, John	McArthur, Duncan	McCollum, Archibald
Richey, Andrew	Rodgers, Philemon	Stultz, Jacob
Sweet, Stephen	Swegert, Daniel	Simpson, Richard
Tway, John	Wolf, Phillip	Marshall, Thomas

Pages 103-104.

ROLL OF CAPT. WARREN BISSELL'S COMPANY
(Probably from Trumbull and Mahoning Counties).
Served from August 26, until November 30, 1812.

Capt. Warren Bissel	Lieut. Caleb Baldwin	Lieut. Alexander Reany
Ensign, Nicholas McConnel	Ensign, Joseph Porter	Sergt. George A. Stilson
Sergt. Asa Baldwin	Sergt. Simon Hall	Sergt. John Dowlin
Sergt. Parkis Woodruff	Sergt. Philarmon Stilson	Sergt. Andrew Stull
Sergt. Isaac Blackman	Corp. Abner Crossman	Corp. William McCreary
Corp. John Murphy	Corp. Henry Fitch	Drummer, Michael Pelts
Privates.	**Privates.**	**Privates.**
Arrels, John	Burgess, Robert	Buchanan, John
Beggs, Joseph	Buchanan, William	Buchanan, Walter
Brothers, John	Beardsley, Josiah	Crossman, Abner
Crawford, William	Chaircher, David	Cowden, John
Cowden, Reynolds	Cunningham, James	Craze, Alexander
Craft, Thomas	Crooks, James	Dennison, David
Dustman, Jacob	Diers, Jacob	Dawson, Aaron
Dix, John	Eckman, James	Fitch, Henry
Fight, Jacob	Fowler, John	Foulk, Henry
Franks, Jacob	Fankles, William	Fish, Abner
Gilbert, Henry	Graham, Jesse	Goucher, Robert
Gilbert, Samuel	Hamilton, Hugh	Hamilton, William
Hardinger, Jacob	Hoyles John	Hampton, John
Hardy, John	Johnson, Abraham	Jack, James
Kline, Phillip	Leonard, William	Landon, Henry
Love, Samuel	Liddle, John	Murphy, John
Love, William	Marchant, Joseph	Malcom, Fall
Mears, Joseph	Mokeman, George	Manchester, Benjamin
Maxwell, Robert	McCombs, Thomas	McMillen, Charles
McCreary, William	McCreary, John	McCombs, David
McMullen, John	McGill, Robert	McGill, William
McGill, Joseph	McConnel, Phillip	McCrary, Thomas
McConnel, Richard	Onansweat, John	Rose, Robert
Noble, David	Rummage, Thomas	Rose, David
Reed, William	Spargo, George	Spargo, George S.
Stall, Andrew	Sharon, Hugh	Shields, William
Sell, John	Simons, Abraham	Rose, John
Simons, Adam	Turner, John	Peterman, Jacob
Turner, Samuel	Upton, Benjamin	Willey, Frederick
Potter, Samuel Y.	Walker, Josiah	Wilson, Peter
White, James	White, James, Sr.	Zedeker, John
Whitezell, Jacob		

Page 105. Vol. I.

ROLL OF CAPT. HARVEY MURRAY'S COMPANY.
(Probably from Cuyahoga County.)

Served from August 21, until November 30, 1812.

Rank and Name of Soldier.	Rank and Name of Soldier.	Rank and Name of Soldier.
Capt. Harvey Murray	Lieut. Lewis Dille	Ensign, Alfred Kelley
Sergt. Ebenezer Green	Sergt. Simion Moss	Sergt. Seth Doan
Sergt. Thomas Hamilton	Corp. John Lauterman	Corp. James Rost
Corp. Asa Dille	Corp. Martin Shellhous	Fifer, Adolphus Carlton
	Drummer, Daniel Kielor	
Privates.	**Privates.**	**Privates.**
Burk, Aretas	Burk, Joseph	Branden, Charles
Bishop, John	Bradley, Moses	Burk, Silas
Beacher, Sylvester	Bills, James S.	Clark, Mason
Carlton, John	Doyle, Anthony	Dille, Luther
Dille, Samuel	Ewart, Samuel	Eldred, Moses
Fish, Ebenezer	Freeman, Zebulon R. S.	Harberson, Robert
Judd, Daniel S.	James, John	James, Jackson
Guy, Lee	King, Stephen	Mingus, Jacob
McHuth, Thomas	McConkey, William	Noyes, Samuel
Prentiss, Robert	Ogden, Benjamin	Read, David
Sumey, John	Shadrick, Parker	Stearns, Luther
Thorp, Bazaleel	Taylor, John	Thomas, Thomas
Vanduzen, Heartman	Williams, Joseph	Wighteman, John
White, William	Williamson, Mathew	

Page 106.

ROLL OF CAPT. JAMES HEZLEP'S COMPANY (County Unknown.)

Hezlep's Company served from January 1, until March 9, 1813.

Capt. James Hezlep	Lieut. David Clendenin	Ensign, William Trusdale
Sergt. Joseph McCombs	Sergt. William H. Wright	Sergt. James Strain
Sergt. Merriden Bixby	Corp. Isaac McCombs	Corp. Henry Mathews
Corp. Adam Rallston	Corp. Johnson Lowry	Sergt. Joseph Applegate
Privates.	**Privates.**	**Privates.**
Ague, George	Andrews, Samuel	Brown, William
Bissell, John	Baldwin, Bryan	Bixby, Willis
Castle, Joseph	Dean, Elijah	Decker, Abraham
Ellis, John	Foster, Henry	Foster, John
Foster, Ross	Fitch, Samuel	Garner, Hiram
Graham, William	Jones, David	Kirkpatrick, Andrew
Lowry, Robert	McFarland, William	McFarland, Andrew
Russell, James	Reed, John	Ragers, Reuben
Ray, Andrew	Struthers, Alexander	Stephen, John F.
Truesdale, Hugh	Trusedale, James	Trusedale, John
Walters, James	Watson, William	Strain, John
	Kyle, Joshua	

Pages 107-108-109.

ROLL OF CAPT. JOSEPH KRATZER'S COMPANY (County Unknown).

Served from July 29, until September 8, 1813.

Capt. Joseph Kratzer	Lieut. Barnett Ristine	Ensign. Robert Breckenrige
Sergt. John Askren	Sergt. Benjamin Griffith	Sergt. Thomas Shrow
Sergt. Robert Patton	Sergt. Isaac Lucas	Lieut. Benjamin Purdon
Corp. Thomas Grogen	Corp. David McLaughlin	Corp. Uriah Higginbothom
Corp. Caleb Shreve	Corp. William Line	Drummer, Simion Gardner
Privates.	**Privates.**	**Privates.**
Boatman, Henry	Baty, David	Bonor, John
Cowen, Levi	Coulter, William Sr.	Coulter, William Jr.
Crofford, William	Cowen, Levi, Sr.	Cross, James
Davidson, Daniel	Denny, William	Davis, Isaac
Evans, Hugh	Ewing, Robert	Forbs, Thomas
Fomb, Mathew	Fenton, William	Glaze, Alexander
Gilgus, John	Howland, Levi	Higginbothom, John
Johnson, James	Jolley, Thomas	John, William
John, Daniel	Kendall, Aaron	Kinnett, Arthur
Kindall, James	Long, Joseph	Lucas, John
Lucas, William	Lucas, Robison	Bare, William
Miller, Hugh	Mortain, William	Moore, William
Murphy, Thomas	McKehon, Daniel	McLaughlin, Patrick
Marshall, James	McIntire, Samuel	Hains, Joseph
Pindal, John	Pettijohn, Amos	Phillips, Valentine
Prichert, Jacob	Patin, John	Pettijohn, Edward
Parish, Joshua	Reeves, Thomas	Reed, William
Record, Josiah	Strane, Thomas	Scott, Robert J.
Springer, Uriah	Stroaph, George	Thomas, Rus
Washburn, Isaac	Walker, James	Wilson, David
	Whey, James	

Pages 110-111-112. Vol. I.
ROLL OF CAPT. DAVID HINE'S COMPANY (From Trumbull & Mahoning Cos.)
Served from August 23, until September 17, 1812.

Rank and Name of Soldier.	Rank and Name of Soldier.	Rank and Name of Soldier.
Capt. David Hine	Lieut. Edmond P. Tanner	Lieut. George Monteith
Ensign, Thomas McCune	Ensign, Nicholas McConnel	Sergt. Julius Fanner
Sergt. Silas Johnston	Sergt. Daniel Fish	Sergt. John Huston
Corp. Christopher Razon	Corp. Joseph Bruce	Corp. Linus Tracy
Corp. Whitney, Smith	Fifer, Jacob Osborn	Drummer, Zuah Cook

Privates.	Privates.	Privates.
Anderson, Arthur	Ague, Nathan	Boyd, Henry
Brunstetter, Henry	Bartholomew, Asahel	Camp, John
Chul, Henry	Calhoon, Samuel	Carver, Seneca
Carter, Joseph	Crumb, Henry	Cummins, Thomas
Crays, Alexander	Condera, Ranels	Tharp, James H.
Fisher, Isaac	Ford, Isaac	Green, Samuel
Godsped, Nathaniel	Guild, Jairus	Hile, John
Hiter, George	Houck, Henry	Hewey, Francis
Henry, Francis	Harting, John	Hull, Jacob
Hayes, John	Hoover, Abraham	Jack, James
Kimmel, Phillip	Kerr, Robert	Landon, Henry
Leonard, William	Leonard, George	Lach, Abraham
Leonard, Nicholas	Manchester, Benjamin	Moore, James
Munns, William	Marshall, William	McMullin, John
McCreary, Robert	McConnal, John	McCulley, John
McConnaughy, James	McCollon, John	McDonald, James
McKinney, Henry	McClane, Robert, Jr.	McKinney, William
McKee, John	McLaughlin, John	Irwin, Thomas
Noble, David	Osborn, Conrad	Osborn, Joseph
Pollock, James	Packert, Garret	Parker, Jacob
Parker, John	Powers, Jacob	Parkhurst, Isaac
Ripley, Harvey	Roll, Benjamin	Shook, Jacob
Steel, William	Saxton, John	Storm, Michael
Stephenson, Elijah	Stump, Henry	Stewart, Daniel
Smith, George	Turner, John	Thomas, William
Taft, Aaron	Taylor, Simons	Venamor, Nicholas
White, John	Young, John	

Pages 113-114.
ROLL OF CAPT. JAMES KILGORE'S COMPANY (Probably from Ross Co.)
Served from October 1, until November 5, 1812.

Capt. James Kilgore	Lieut. William Johnston	Ensign, William Niblack
Sergt. John Galaspy	Sergt. James How	Sergt. Hugh Dolshon
Sergt. Adam Stewart	Corp. William Malone	

Privates.	Privates.	Privates.
Arthers, Samuel	Alexander, Francis	Alcutt, Israel
Beall, Phillip	Butte, Thomas	Cartright, Nathaniel
Corkin, Thomas	Campbell, Jonothan	Chenowith, Elijah
Chenowoth, Joseph	Dyer, Gasper	Eckenbarger, Stephen
Fields, Peter	Hanson, Hollis	Kelley, Samuel
Little, James	Lytle, Hugh	Miller, Watson
Moler, Jacob	Poor, George	Rawles, Elijah
Ridgeway, David	Reed, James	Stanholt, George
Thomas, Webster	Vial, John	Wells, Absalom

Page 115.
ROLL OF CAPT. GEORGE KESLING'S COMPANY (Probably from Warren Co.)
Served from September 27, until October 20, 1812.

Capt. George Kesling	Lieut. William Slaiback	Lieut. John T. Ross
Sergt. William Ellis	Sergt. Stephen Minor	Sergt. John McCormac

Privates.	Privates.	Privates.
Aldridg, Joseph	Blackford, John	Boosoe, Henry
Bilderback, Gabriel	Bordman, John	Cassairt, Henry
Carvell, Jacob	Cornell, Sylvanus	Ellis, Isaac
Foley, William	Hatfield, Clark	Headley, William
Long, John	Lowen, James A.	Long, Minor
Montford, David	Mullin, William	Mansfield, John
Mays, Samuel	Mays, John	Morehead, John
Morgan, Jesse	Moore, Nathan	McLean, Aaron
McManis Robert	McCann, Alexander	McCall, Robert S.
Noble, Joshua	Richardson, Daniel	Ray, William
Stires, Ralph	Steel, Joseph	Stonebraker, Jacob
Trimble, Daniel	West, Hugh	West, William
Watson, Robert	White, Thomas	

Pages 116-117. Vol. I.
ROLL OF CAPT. PHILLIP KISER'S COMPANY
(Probably from Champaign County).
Served from September 19, until October 19, 1812, and from August 12, until September 21, 1813.

Rank and Name of Soldier.	Rank and Name of Soldier.	Rank and Name of Soldier.
Capt. Phillip Kiser	Lieut. William Rumple	Lieut. John Rhodes
Lieut. James Toomer	Ensign, Daniel Kilbinger	Sergt. Patrick McKinley
Sergt. Peter Pence	Sergt. Benjamin Pence	Sergt. Nathan Dannall
Sergt. William Steel	Sergt. Colon, Moore	Sergt. John Fitch
Sergt. George Crosby	Corp. John Tofflenoyer	Corp. Edden Jenkins
Corp. John West	Corp. Nelson Lansdell	Corp. William Haltz
Corp. John Pyatt	Corp. Ebenezer Rhodes	Corp. Nathan Adamson
Drummer, Joseph Jones	Drummer, Edward Tarbutton	Fifer, Pressley Ross
	Fifer, Henry Armacush	

Privates.	Privates.	Privates.
Baker, Samuel	Baker, John	Boswell, George
Beatty, John	Beacon, William	Blue, John
Bags, William	Bozier, Isaac	Bacer, Isaac
Bradford, Charles	Barnes, William	Bates, John
Barnes, Horatio	Colbert, John	Crafton, Ambias
Cirkel, Abraham	Cowhick, Thomas	Chapman, Elijah
Cox, Joseph	Clark, Absalom	Cowen, Joseph S.
Davis, Andrew	Darnell, Roswell	Darnell, David
Diltz, Samuel	Dillon, William	Dawson, John
Dawson, James	Dudley, Jabez	Dudley, John
Edgar, Andrew	Elliott, Mills	Forman, William
Flemming, Henry	Foley, William	Godard, Jesse
Gray, David	Grafton, James	Hall, Joseph
Herd, Thomas	Huls, Henry	Howell, Joshua
Humble, Valentine	Hunter, James	Holler, John
Idol, Jacob	Jones, Stephen	Jones, David
Jones, Isaac	Jenkins, Russell	Jackson, Daniel
Kiblinger, Adam	Kelley, Sampson	Kirkpatrick, George
Kelley, Thomas	Largent, John	Lansdale, Nelson
Lansdale, Thomas	Loudeback, Daniel	Little, John
Maggert, Isaac	Martin, Isaac	Moody, John
McBeth, Andrew	Nason, Daniel	Nelson, Thomas
Protsman, David	Prince, Adam	Pence, Daniel
Pence, Henry	Pence, Abraham	Pence, Samuel
Reid, John	Rouse, Levi	Rouse, John
Rose, John	Rector, Samuel	Smith, David
Smith, John	Sibert, Henry	Segar, David
Smith, David, Jr.	Swanger, John	Steele, Joseph
Snodgrass, James	Syms, Joseph	Stephens, Abraham
Smith, Peter	Stranbarger, John	Sills, Michael
Stepelton, John	Speace, Daniel	Shockey, Abraham
Taylor, John	Taber, Robert	Tunks, Phillip
Tarbutton, Eli	Wilson, Robert	West, Stukell
Welch, George	Wells, Thomas	West, Edmund
Walker, George W.	West, Thomas	West, John

Page 119.
ROLL OF SERGT. JAMES EAKINS' COMPANY (County Unknown).
Served from July 28, until August 13, 1813.

Sergt. James Eakins	Sergt. Jacob Cox	Corp. James Ferren
Corp. Jacob Newland		

Privates.	Privates.	Privates.
Brewer, Jacob	Beckman, Gabriel	Beaver, Mathias
Beaver, Michael	Chapman, Henry	Horn, James
Horn, Joseph	Herdman, John	Mershon, Solomon
Mershon, Daniel	Mershon, Timothy	Mershon, Henry
Smith, John	Smith, William	Thomas, Nathan
Thomas, Phillip	Thompson, Henry	Thoroman, Charles
	Williams, William	

Pages 120-121-122.
ROLL OF LIEUT. JOHN DEVAULT OR DEVALL'S COMPANY
(Probably from Washington County).
Served from January 31, until April 10, 1815.

Lieut. John Devault or Devall	Sergt. Isaac House	Sergt. Thomas Devault
Sergt. Levi Bevington	Corp. Gilbert Harley	Corp. Morris Baker
	Corp. James Plymell	

Privates.	Privates.	Privates.
Aye, Henry	Chad, George	Callender, John
Doty, Ephraim	Dyer, William	Doty, William
Dunkle, Jacob	George, Ephraim	Harrison, William
Hobaugh, Phillip	Harter, John	Hurley, William
Hayes, David	Harrison, Phillip	Holbough, John
Hotter, Benjamin	Long, Benjamin	Long, Robert
Mitchell, Robert	Moore, Samuel	Mitchell, Samuel
Moore, Benjamin	Neely, George	Neely, Benjamin
Rhodes, George	Rhodes, Richard	Roebuck, Benjamin
Sharoertz, Daniel	Shackles, Richard	Sanders, John
Sanders, Ezra	Kerr, William	Kile, Oliver
Chaver, Joseph	Roebuck, George	Travis, Ezra
Thompson, Davis	Wright, Caleb	Winder, Joseph
Yates, Maurice	Yates, Horace	

Page 123. Vol. I.

ROLL OF CAPT. DAVID DANIELS' COMPANY (County Unknown).

Served from July 28, until August 28, 1813.

Rank and Name of Soldier.	Rank and Name of Soldier.	Rank and Name of Soldier.
Capt. David Daniels	Lieut. Abraham Bonnet	Ensign, Henry Slaven
Sergt. James Buckman	Sergt. William Rea	Corp. David Miller
	Corp. Joseph Boiler	

Privates.

Bumgarner, John	Brown, William	Brown, John
Collison, Moses	Chinworth, Eli	Cheny, Isaac
Downing, William	Guthrie, John	Gallagher, Mansfield
Guthrie, George	Hotsenpiler, Jacob	Foster, Isaac
Kelleson, John	Morrison, James	Nessel, George
	Pry, Jacob	

Pages 124-125-126-127.

ROLL OF CAPT. ADAM BERRY'S COMPANY (From Pickaway & Ross Cos.)

Served from April 11, until May 12, 1813, and from April 11, until May 12, 1814.

Capt. Adam Berry	Lieut. Arthur McPhee or McKee	Ensign, John Thompson
Ensign, John Thebus	Sergt. John Beavens	Sergt. Jacob Smith
Sergt. George Spangler	Sergt. Thomas Powell	Sergt. John Spores
Sergt. Blain	Sergt. George Fry	Sergt. Adam Zehrung
Sergt. John Clark	Sergt. John Shoup	Corp. Phillip Least
Corp. Hugh Caul	Corp. John Knight	Corp. Stephen Stewart
Drummer, Jacob Smith	Fifer, George Shaugler	

Privates.

Alcot, Israel	Andrew, Thomas	Burben, Edward
Beck, Alexander	Ballinger, Joseph	Brown, Joshua
Bellote, Walter	Ballard, Linsey S.	Blane, John
Barber, Edward	Bagley, Thomas	Clark, John
Cobb, Hugh	Cogley, Thomas	Crum, Thomas
Coaley, James R.	Chenworth, Thomas	Clark, Robert
Cheneworth, George	Chambers, John	Dungan, Titus
Dod, Adam	Dunn, Zephaniah	Erwin, William
Evans, Aldridge	Fullen, Alexander	Frye, George
Graham, Joseph	Grant, William	Garratt, Russell
Hurst, Thomas	Hall, James	Harmon, Samuel H.
Harbert, Richard	Haynes, Henry	Harpster, Peter
John, Thomas	Johnson, Jacob	Johnston, Joel
Kimble, Jacob	Kinser, George	Kennison, Reuben
Laurence, Henry	Lunback, Henry	Lambart, Isaac
Linn, Jacob	Lewis, William	Miller, George
Mathew, John	Marsh, Titus	Mounts, Humphrey
Myers, John	Munday, John	Martz, George
Moore, James	McCord, Thomas	McFadden, William
Nubegal, William	Nease, Abraham	Noland, William
Newman, William	Knight, John	List, Phillip
Odle, Stephen	Pertee, George	Petty, Absalom
Pervolt, Thomas	Peters, Jacob	Reed, Samuel
Ritchie, Andrew	Redden, Reuben	Ratcliff, Charles
Redden, Robert	Southviord, Henry	Sidenbender, John
Strawser, David	Sewel, David	Sowder, John
Snodgrass, John	Steward, Stephen	Suthard, Henry
Sodden, John	Thomas, Andrew	Troy, Jacob
Timons, Henry	Trulling, Abraham	Turly, Andrew
Timmers, Samuel	Vangundie, John	Vestle, Nathan
Winland William	White, Peter	Warren, Moses
Waldron, Phillip	Waldron, George	Wykoff, John
	Wiggins, John	

Page 128.

ROLL OF CAPT. ALEXANDER BROWER'S COMPANY (County Unknown).

Served from February 12, until May 23, 1813.

Capt. Alexander Brower	Ensign, Samuel Cresswell	Sergt. Isaac West
Corp. William Aldridge	Drummer, John Moore	Fifer, Samuel Coburn

Privates.

Campbell, Joseph	Eakin, John	Figley, Simeon
Knatt, James	Hurt, John	Hoffmer, Daniel
Harvey, Christopher	Hammond, David	Pugh, Aaron
Rose, Ephraim	Smith, Jacob	Shiveley, Christopher
Smallwood, Richard	Stephenson, John	Yarnell, Abraham

Pages 129-130-131-132. Vol. I.

ROLL OF CAPT. ROBERT GILMORE'S COMPANY (County Unknown).

Served from August 24, until August 28, 1812, and from February 10, until August 15, 1813.

Rank and Name of Soldier.	Rank and Name of Soldier.	Rank and Name of Soldier.
Capt. Robert Gilmore	Lieut. John Reddin	Lieut. Frederick Harmon
Lieut. William Barkheimer	Ensign, William Ross	Sergt. Robert Young
Sergt. Horace Ladd	Sergt. Ephraim Rose	Sergt. John Sharard
Sergt. William Maxwell	Corp. John Smith	Corp. John Gardner
Corp. William Coburn	Corp. Thomas Greenfield	Corp. Samuel Whitney
Fifer, Thomas Thornbaugh	Drummer, Virgil Moore	

Privates.

Asburn, William	Augustine, George	Armstrong, Benjamin
Augustine, Henry	Bailey, Joshua	Bowlen, John
Belet, Mathew	Burns, Peter	Bricker, John
Bower, David	Bell, William	Burnes, Harvey
Burk, Gains	Baldwin, Amzi	Cellers, George
Cradds, Phillip	Craigin, John	Clark, John
Coss, Nathaniel	Campbell, Samuel	Carter, John
Cross, Thomas	Carroll, Phillip	Doop, John
Dunlap, John	Denun, James	Dawson, William
Deigreis, John	Downard, James	Bennet, Conrad
Endsey, Andrew	Ewing, Samuel	Flemming Patrick
Freet, George	Gilmore, John	Gotthalls, Johann
Gotthalls, William	Gossage, Thomas	Golloway, James
Grier, David	Hoover, Jacob	Heany, Jacob
Hammond, Jacob	Hall, James	Hannon, John
Hopkins, Benjamin	Hart, Lewis	Holmes, Stephen
Haley, Joseph	Judd, Daniel S.	Kuntz, John
Knap, Caleb	Leech, Benjamin	Leaper, Samuel
Lee, Lemuel	Mapel, David	Mellinger, John H.
Merker, James	McComis, James	McKinley, James
McClelland, Thomas	McMillen, James	McClorg, Joseph
McKonkey, William	McLaughlin, George	McElwin, Robert
Pagle, Mordecai	Peterman, Jacob	Patton, John
Palmer, Jesse	Pond, Phineas	Pettibone, Henry S.
Pettibrook, Morton	Reed, Thomas	Rose, Asa
Ray, James	Rogers, Samuel	Rogers, Richard
Ranson, Abide	Robbins, Joseph	Ross, Adams
Stone, Jeremiah	Steele, Jacob	Smith, Adam
Saint, John	Steward, Samuel	Shull, Adam
Saint, Joseph	Switzer, John	Shultz, Henry
Spidle, John	Shenefelt, John	Seelye, Abner
Sike, Phillip	Shively, Christian	Smith, Zepheniah
Saint, Lewis	Stephens, John	Stewart, David
Sipe, Phillip	Stevens, Daniel	Taylor, George
Tulley, James	Underwood, Joseph	Van Horn, Peter
White, Ira	Wyant, Burget	Woods, George
Ward, Robert	Wall, Joseph	Warner, Chauncey
Watson, Robert	Woodward, Daniel	Williams, John
Williams, Charles	Young, Seth	Zuver, George

Pages 133-134-135.

ROLL OF CAPT. WILLIAM DOUGLAS' COMPANY
(Probably from Knox and Richland Counties).

Served from August 26, until October 10, 1812, and from May 4, until May 19, 1813.

Capt. William Douglas	Lieut. John Wheeler	Lieut. Daniel Ayres
Lieut. Samuel Everett	Sergt. Daniel Cooper	Sergt. John C. Gilkison
Sergt. Joseph Berry	Sergt. Henry Markley	Sergt. Cyrus Langworthy
Sergt. William McCartney	Sergt. Abel Cook	Corp. Thomas Axtell
Corp. Edward Wheeler	Corp. Levi Sutton	

Privates.

Ashley, Abel	Adams, James	Burns, Jabez
Bartlett, David	Barney, Charles	Bevans, William
Baptist, John	Cooper, Jacob	Cooper, Elias
Coe, Luther	Chambers, William	Casper, William
Durphy, Freeman	Durbin, Scott	Downs, William
Dowds, William	Corwin, Benjamin	Forsythe, James
Fishback, Richard	Gilkison, James M.	Giberson, Joseph
Hall, William	Irvin, James	Jackson, John
Kimble, Daniel	Johnston, Levi	Layland, John
May, Chison	Mazers, Peter	Mazers, John
Mazers, Nathan	Macaber, John	Loveridge, James
Ogle, Enoch	Peoples, David	Peoples, Robert
Rodgers, Joseph	Ridal, John	Spry, Perry
Smith, James	Shurr, William	Strong, Harley
Sawyer, John	Yeoman, Samuel	

Page 136. Vol. I.

ROLL OF LIEUT. ICHABOD NYE'S COMPANY (Probably from Knox County).

Served from October 27, until December 27, 1812, and from May 4, until May 19, 1813.

Rank and Name of Soldier.　　Rank and Name of Soldier.　　Rank and Name of Soldier.

Lieut. Ichabod, Nye, Sr.

Privates.
Barrell, Joseph
Jackson, Zeba
McGoing, Charles
Pool, John

Privates.
Hinthorn, John, Sr.
Laylin, Charles
McCartney, William
Tegardson, George

Privates.
Hinthorn, John, Jr.
Miller, Andrew
Pierce, Lewis

Page 138.

ROLL OF CAPT. THOMAS CLAUSON'S COMPANY (From Montgomery County).

Served from August 23, until September 17, 1812.

Capt. Thomas Clauson　　Lieut. John Archer, Jr.　　Ensign Benjamin Luce
　　　　　　　　　　　　Sergt. William Blair

Privates.
Allen, Jeremiah
Codington, William
Covolt, Ephraim
Dunkin, John
Gerrard, John
Lunderland, Peter
Loy, Peter
Majors, David
Shanks, John
Watkins, Daniel

Privates.
Bigger, Thomas
Clauson, Abraham
Day, William
Dunken, Peter
Hatfield, Owen
Luce, Moses
Mills, James
McKinney, John
Snowden, James
Watkins, John

Privates.
Baltimore, Phillip
Clauson, Peter
Dill, William
Ewing, Garner
Hufferd, John
Lee, Henry
Majors, James
Shanks, Peter
Sanders, John

Page 139.

ROLL OF CAPT. ABNER AYRES' COMPANY (County Unknown).

Served from May 4, until May 19, 1813.

Capt. Abner Ayres
Sergt. Jacob Mitchell
Corp. George Ayres

Ensign Amos A. Royce
Sergt. John Trimble
Corp. John Brown

Sergt. William Smith
Corp. Isaac Williams
Drummer, John Haldemer

Privates.
Aker, Andrew
Boles, Thomas
Johnston, Daniel
McGown, James
Roberts, William F.

Privates.
Brown, Thomas
Day, Josiah B.
Light, Celeste
McIntire, James
Thompson, Andrew

Privates.
Joseph, Bland
Grant, Josiah
Manning, Alfred
Pinkley, John

Page 140.

ROLL OF CAPT. GEORGE ZIEGLER'S COMPANY (County Unknown).

Served from May 6, until May 20, 1813.

Capt. George Ziegler
Sergt. Charles McCormick
Sergt. Henry Donaldson
Corp. Jacob Collars

Lieut. John Donaldson
Sergt. Heck, John
Corp. David Crossin
Corp. Thomas Martin

Ensign Abraham Pickering
Sergt. William McIntosh
Corp. Jacob Claws

Privates.
Alexander, James
Bugh, John
Finck, George
Lassley, Peter
McCollum, Samuel
Overmire, Peter
Pence, Jacob
Raver, William
Trout, John

Privates.
Allen, Jedediah
Cablien, Caleb
Fickel, Daniel
Miller, James
Newel, John
Prickets, Clement G.
Reed, William
Styers, John
Taylor, John

Privates.
Babb, Jonothan
Donaldson, Aaron
Kitsmiller, Andrew
Millholland, Thomas
Neysemauger, David
Peppus, John
Ricketts, William
Smith, Hezekiah

Page 141.

ROLL OF CAPT. JOSEPH COLEMAN'S COMPANY (Probably from Miami Co.)

Served from May 4, until May 19, 1813.

Capt. Joseph Coleman
Sergt. Jacob Martin

Lieut. Thomas McKee
Corp. Nathan Mages

Sergt. Thomas Erwin
Corp. George Downs

Privates.
Asheraft, Jonothan
Spry, Perry
Wilson, John

Privates.
Lalin, John
Smith, James

Privates.
Marquis, William
Thompson, Uriah

ROSTER OF OHIO SOLDIERS IN WAR OF 1812

Pages 144-145. Vol. I.
ROLL OF CAPT. LEMUEL CONNELLY'S COMPANY (County Unknown).
Served from July 28, until September 5, 1813.

Rank and Name of Soldier.	Rank and Name of Soldier.	Rank and Name of Soldier.
Capt. Lemuel Connelly	Lieut. Joseph Paset, Sr.	Ensign John Parratt
Ensign Samuel Holladay	Sergt. Joseph Creamor	Sergt. James Sanderson
Sergt. William Blackmore	Sergt. William Young	Sergt. Daniel Saward
Corp. Samuel Wicke	Corp. Stephen Hunt	Corp. George Wilson
Corp. William Tracy	Corp. Abraham Workman	Musician, Robert Smith
	Musician, William Kift	
Privates.	**Privates.**	**Privates.**
Antus, John	Arnold, John	Baldwin, William
Bates, William	Bentley, Jonothan	Creamer, David
Day, Bazel	Devitt, George	Cochran, Barnabus
Garrison, Abner	Grady, James	Godfrey, Thomas
Hance, Lemuel	Howe, Jacob	Jones, Oliver
Kirkpatrick, James	Kilgore, Clark	Limes, William
Moon, William	Michael, Jacob	Miller, John
McKay, Jesse	McChandless, Hugh	McFarland, John
Pauley, David	Popejoy, William	Pool, Edward
Rankin, Hugh	Ruport, George	Rankan, Thomas
Sanderson, Alexander	Sawyer, George	Short, Henry
Studiman, William V.	Stanfar, Pierce	Somerville, John
Tracy, Solomon	Tracy, William	Tharp, William
Vann, John	Wilson, George	Wright, Hosea
Witty, William	Wright, David	Workman, John

Page 146.
ROLL OF CAPT. ZECHARIAH P. DEWITT'S COMPANY.
(Probably from Butler County).
Served from September 20, until November 19, 1814.

Capt. Zechariah P. DeWitt	Lieut. John Freeman	Ensign, Henry Watts
Sergt. Samuel Pressley	Sergt. Philip Wiggins	Sergt. John Garard
Sergt. George Kirkpatrick	Corp. Henry Riggs	Corp. Abraham Ansman
Corp. Clement Bostwick	Corp. William H. Lloyd	
Privates.	**Privates.**	**Privates.**
Albartson, William	Albertson, Nathaniel	Black, David
Bridgford, William, Sr.	Bridgford, William, Jr.	Bridgford John
Beedle, Simeon	Coe, Joseph	Cantwal, Hugh
Dollahan, John	Dunn, George F.	Devore, John
Ewing, Matthew	Fowler, James	Fowler, Jeremiah
Freeman, John	Hall, Peter	Hancock, James
Harper, Joseph	Jones, Jonas	Johnson, John
Morris, Enoch	Milan, John	Morris, William
Morris, Jacob	Sloan, Richard	Seward, Isaac
Tilson, Leonard	Jones, John	Taylor, Robert
Taylor, William	Truman, John	Whilavre, John

Page 147.
ROLL OF CAPT. JACOB BELL'S COMPANY (County Unknown).
Served from September 14, until October 14, 1812.

Capt. Jacob Bell	Lieut. William Kerr	Ensign, Thomas Powers
Sergt. James H. Martin	Sergt. John Brady	Sergt. Reuben Ryan
Sergt. John Clark	Corp. William Denman	Corp. Joseph Hand
Corp. William Curry	Corp. John Lingle	
Privates.	**Privates.**	**Privates.**
Allen, Jacob	Andrews, Isaac	Bryan, James
Brown, Aaron	Bell, Abel	Baird, John
Codington, William	Craig, Daniel	Edwards, Elijah
Griffin, David	Hand, Aaron	Kelly, William
Keeter, John	Morris, William	Miller, Elias
Morris, Enoch	Moxer, Ebenezer	Martin, William
Mott, John	Rowe, Joseph	Rowe, Abraham
Stogdon, William	Spencer, Joseph	Snyder, Samuel
Simpson, Allen	Vanblaugher, Peter	Vanmater, Abraham
Welsh, William	Weaver, Henry	Whittaker, Daniel

Page 148.
ROLL OF CAPT. JAMES BARNETT'S COMPANY. (County Unknown.)
Served from August 23, until September 19, 1812.

Capt. James Barnett	Lieut. James McElven	Ensign, David Steel
Sergt. Henry Gagany	Sergt. William Patterson	Sergt. John Tucker, Jr.
Corp. Mathew M. Dodd	Corp. John Kelley	Corp. Robert Young
	Drummer, Cyrus Thartan	
Privates.	**Privates.**	**Privates.**
Allen, Moses	DuPriest, Charles	Gott, John
Hinner, John	Buckhannon, James	Jones, Isaac
Lowrey, Joseph	Musselman, John	McLucas, Samuel
McLucas, William	McGrew, William	Neff, Christopher
Osborn, David	Parson, Lewis	Robb, Johnson
Shepherd, Thomas	Tucker, John Sr.	VanSkogk, Joseph
Wilson, Samuel	Wolf, Conrad	Wade, James
Veale, Samuel	Wagner, Michael	York, Jeremiah

Page 149. Vol. I.

ROLL OF CAPT GEORGE BUCHANAN'S COMPANY (Probably from Miami Co.)
Served from May 5, until August 13, 1812.

Rank and Name of Soldier.	Rank and Name of Soldier.	Rank and Name of Soldier.
Capt. George Buchanan	Lieut. James C. Caldwell	Ensign, Gardner Bobo
Sergt. Andrew Tilford	Sergt. Joseph Hale	Sergt. Benjamin Saunders
Sergt. James Barnett	Sergt. David McClung	

Privates.

Allen, Nathan	Brown, James	Black, Jacob
Beedle, Abraham	Bimgardner, Jacob	Balbee, William
Blue, Michael	Beedle, Jacob	Beedle, Joseph
Duprey, Stephen	Freeman, Noah	Fulkirth, William
Fugate, Edward	Foster, Elijah	Garard, John
Hamer, George	Haney, Jacob	Hurley, Cornelius
Huston, Joseph	Hickman, David	Hurley, Zechariah
Johnson, Giles	Jenkins, George	Jackson, Jacob
Jackson, John	Knoop, John	Leonox, Richard
Lupton, John	Montgomery, Robert	Millhouse, John
Mackey, Samuel	McClary, John	McPhaddon, James
North, William	Prillaman, Christian	Prillman, Daniel
Potts, James	Polset, John E.	Shepherd, Elijah
Thompson, Andrew	Tullis, Aaron	Shoaf, George
Stetler, Abraham	Stedler, John	Shaw, Thomas

Pages 150-151-152.

ROLL OF CAPT. JOHN CLARK'S COMPANY (Probably from Green County).
Served from October 18, until November 20, 1812, and from August 10, until September 5, 1813.

Capt. John Clark	Lieut. John Blessing	Lieut. Samuel Jenkins
Ensign, Boston Hoblit	Ensign, Robert Breddy	Sergt. James Buckles
Sergt. William Knight	Sergt. John Long	Sergt. Edward Allen
Sergt. James Ross	Sergt. Isaachar Pepper	Sergt. John McElvey
Sergt. Perry Timmons	Corp. James Rowe	Corp. Robert Demis
Corp. Arthur Lavis	Corp. John Dysert	Corp. John Biddle
Corp. James Stephenson	Corp. Thomas Cason	Corp. Benjamin Allen

Privates.

Armstrong, John	Amos, Pleasant	Biddle, Henry
Buckles, David	Brown, William	Blue, Daniel
Brown, Zechariah	Cully, Thomas	Cramer, Solomon
Clark, William	Cully, Joseph	Carroll, Samuel
Caldhoon, John	Cook, James	Cox, John
Dureavida, Samuel	Dougherty, Samuel	Dunwida, John
Davis, James	Dennis, Mathias	Dennis, Jonothan
Dennis, Samuel	Ennis, Samuel	Earl, James
Flowers, Aaron	Griffith, Benjamin	Hibbs, Abner
Howard, Nicholas	Hamilton, William	Jones, Joshua
Jones, Lewis	Buckles, Henry	Lewis, Joel
Logue, John	Lewis, Jesse	Lackey, John
Meriman, Joshua	Miller, Charles	Mills, Constantine
Merriman, Aaron	Jones, Thomas	Miniar, Phillip
Miniar, Stephen	Meekins, John	McKnight, Robert
McKee, Joseph	McArthur, Duncan	Porter, James
Rice, Pitch	Rayburn, William	Rodgers, John
Ridley, James	Sackett, Joseph	Smith, Jacob
Sanders, Jesse	Smith, Thomas	Lanime, William
Thorn, Jacob	Whickear, Asa	Warfield, Richard
Worthington, John	Wiley, Jesse	Williams, Gammage
Worthington, Ephraim	Walker, Charles	

Page 153.

ROLL OF CAPT. SAMUEL CALDWELL'S COMPANY (Probably from Warren County).
Served from August 23, until September 18, 1812.

Capt. Samuel Caldwell	Lieut. John C. Death	Lieut. Thomas Covenhoven
Cornet, Robert Young	Sergt. Stephen Reeder	Sergt. Daniel Storms
Sergt. Joseph Crane	Sergt. James Death, Jr.	Q. M. Sergt. James W. Lanier
Corp. Samuel Campbell	Corp. William Harrison	Corp. Christian Petfish
	Corp. Joseph Parks, Jr.	

Privates.

Abbott, John	Allen, John	Bowersack, David
Baldwin, William	Bell, Benjamin	Barnett, John
Craig, Obediah	Death, Bazil	Death, James E.
Death, Samuel	Debrock, Alexander	Ferris, Joseph
Flinn, Daniel	Galbraith, Joseph	Gordon, George
Hammel, Joseph	Irwin, David	Jordan, John
Keslin, Peter	Lang, Charles	Miller, James
McFreen, John	McCord, John	McMeen, Josiah C.
McClure, Ezekial	Orr, Samuel	Perry, William
Potter, Hiram	Payen, Stephen	Robison, Robert
Ross, John	Squires, Timothy	Trimble, James
Vanott, Samuel	Wer, Alexander	Walker, Gracon
Ware, Phillip	Young, Jacob	Troxel, Joseph

Page 154. Vol. I.
ROLL OF CAPT. THOMAS WILLIAMS' COMPANY (County Unknown).
Served from August 29, until September 9, 1812.

Capt. Thomas Williams
Sergt. Samuel Rose

Lieut. Isaac Chambers
Sergt. Edward Haskney

Ensign, Aurelius Thrall

Privates.
Andrews, Isaac
Barret, Stephen
Collins, John
Dush, John
Faunbaker, John
George, John
Hannon, James
Lane, Dutton
Leach, Nehemiah
Moore, Cyrus
Mark, John
Mapes, Thomas
Potter, Jacob
Russell, Phillip
Simpson, Samuel L.
Tharp, Josiah
Warner, Lyman
Welkiger, Abraham

Privates.
Alexander, William
Bennett, Isaac
Collins, Woodgate
Duffey, Hugh
Gray, William
Hedley, Samuel
Hoover, John
Loran, John
Lane, Benjamin
Miller, William
Matson, William
Neselrode, Christopher
Priest, Levi
Spray, John W.
Tipton, Solomon
Thrailkield, Thomas
Walker, Daniel
Williamson, John

Privates.
Arnold, John
Cook, Alexander
Deaver, Walter
Funk, Jacob
Gray, Samuel
Hill, Pressley R.
Kidd, William
Longley, George
Morris, Jesse M.
Many, Michael
Mills, John
Norman, James
Russell, James
Sheldon, Thomas
Twitzer, John
Tharp, Joel
Woodward, William
Whitaker, Isaac

Pages 155-156-157.
ROLL OF CAPT. HENRY BRUSH'S COMPANY (Probably from Ross County).
Served from July 20, until October 4, 1812.

Captain Henry Brush
Ensign, William S. Hutt
Sergt. Robert Stockton
Sergt. Samuel Swearingen
Corp. Richard Snyder
Corp. John Buck

Lieut. William Beach
Ensign, John Stockton
Sergt. Craighead Ferguson
Sergt. Jacob Cryder
Corp. Henry May
Corp. Frederick Fisher
Corp. Matthew Simpson

Lieut. John Entricken
Sergt. William Robinson
Sergt. Henry L. Prentice
Sergt. William Armstrong
Corp. James McDougal
Corp. Joseph Cissna

Privates.
Armstrong, William
Buchanan, Henry
Brown, Peter
Baker, Henry
Cissna, James
Campbell, William
Dougherty, Levi
DuSouchel, Francis
Downs, William
Eastwood, Isaac
Frazer, Malilon
Ferguson, John
Huston, James
Hall, James
Immell, Israel
Johnston, David
Bayley, Thomas
Mitchell, John
Morris, Priestly
McArthur, Duncan
McRoberts, William
Peebles, John
Robinson, James
Shaffer, Jacob
Simpson, Oliver
Stockton, John
Tiffin, Joseph
Willett, Samuel
Watson, John
Williamson, Thomas

Privates.
Andrews, Hugh
Bailey, William
Brush, Edmond
Chew, Colby
Cissna, Stephen
Cunningham, Samuel
Davison, William
Davis, Samuel
Dribler, George
Devault, Lemuel
Fulton, William
Hoffman, Adam E.
Hoffman, John
Hughes, Alexander
Johnson, William
Leister, Peter
Langham, John S.
Mitchell, James S.
McGrim, William
McCann, John G.
Orr, Samuel
Pierce, Edward W.
Russell, James
Stewart, Archibald
Steel, John
Thompson, Nathan
Trewitt, Solomon
Watson, John
Williams, Samuel
Young, George

Privates.
Beverly, Michael
Bready, Robert
Barber, Uriah
Cissna, Joseph
Creighton, William
Curry, James
Davis, Lewis
Dill, Robert
Evans, Horatio
Essex, Jesse
Finnemore, Ebenezer
Holmes, Robert
Hall, John
Hutcheson, Ezekial
Langham, Elias
Hutt, William S.
Miller, Joseph
Monroe, Jonothan
McCollough, Samuel
McGregor, Daniel
Petty, Ebenezer
Rust, George
Shaver, James
Smith, Adam
Sherlock, Edward
Taylor, Isaac
Thompson, John
Wallace, Cadwallader
Williams, Abraham

Page 158.
ROLL OF CAPT. DAVID KASEBEER'S COMPANY (County Unknown.)
Served from August 1, until October 31, 1812.

Capt. David Kasebeer
Sergt. George Stout

Lieut. Samuel Kniseley
Corp. Jacob Snyder

Ensign, John Hornish
Corp. John Stiflor

Privates.
Beavar, Jacob
Butt, Benjamin
Bickle, Thomas
Eakin, James
Fruckler, Henry
Gomer, David
Heaton, Joseph
Kollar, Adam

Privates.
Bess, Isaac
Butt, Joseph
Bickle, David
Flickenger, John
Foreman, David
Hurst, Samuel
Hubaugh, Frederick
Kasebeer, Samuel

Privates.
Baker, George
Baker, John
Cross, Isaac
Foreman, Philip
Gibbs, Isaac
Henney, Frederick
Jackson, Edward
Luninger, George

Vol. 1.

ROLL OF CAPT. DAVID KASEBEER'S COMPANY (Continued).

Rank and Name of Soldier.
Privates.
Long, Joseph
Neal, Andrew
Robnett, James
Shook, Valentine
Shanaman, Henry
Taylor, John
Willard, Ludwig

Rank and Name of Soldier.
Privates.
Misor, John
Robinet, George
Shull, Frederick
Sodoris, Frederick
Snelbecker, John
Williams, Henry
Winkelock, Philip

Rank and Name of Soldier.
Privates.
Mills, Samuel
Roop, Jacob
Snyder, Adam
Sullivan, John
Sweeny, Jacob
Williams, Benjamin

Pages 159-160.

ROLL OF CAPT. JAMES ANDREWS' COMPANY (County Unknown).

Served from September 4, until December 31, 1813, and From January 1, until March 2, 1814.

Capt. James Andrews
Sergt. William Vandervourt
Sergt. William B. Hamilton
Corp. Joseph Arthur

Lieut. Ledowick Weller
Sergt. William Milspaugh
Corp. John Brown
Corp. William Drake

Ensign, Henry Sly
Sergt. Joseph Gossett
Corp. Elias Porter
Fifer, Robert Ross

Privates.
Arthur, James
Badger, Daniel
Bull, Abraham
Boone, Bramfield
Brummingham, Elias
Collins, George
Cooper, James
Davis, Azariah
Degraft, Joseph
Edinger, Philip
Fisher, David
Hand, David
Hughes, Isaac
Knott, Joseph
Moore, Samuel
Morning, John
McAdams, Scutler
Porter, John
Robb, Peter
Stewart, Hall
Smith, Jacob
Thompson, Barnard
Vandervourt, John
Wiland, John

Privates.
Armstrong, William
Brown, Daniel
Buchanan, John
Brannon, John
Cooper, George
Clements, Greer
Conner, Hugh
Davis, William
Deuey, John
Fisher, John, Sr.
Galbreath, Samuel
Hewey, Joseph
Holladay, Joseph
Lewis, Walcut
Melott, Isaac
Marquith, John C.
McKee, William
Powers, Thomas
Roudibash, Daniel
Stouder, William
Shumard, Thomas
Thompson, James
Wood, Richard
Willis, Levi

Privates.
Barkley, George
Brown, Michael
Bull, Walter
Bennet, Benjamin
Christy, John D.
Crichfield, Philip
Douglass, Oliver
Eberhardt, Andrew
Fisher, John Jr.
Hill, Knotley
Hand, Thomas
Hewitt, John
Morris, Clement
Melott, Richard
Miller, Burgher
Nash, John
Brindola, Jacob
Reeves, James
Strickland, William
Strickland, Henry
Tubb, Jesse
Willis, John

Pages 161-162-163-164.

ROLL OF CAPT. SAMUEL ASHTON'S COMPANY (County Unknown.)

Served from February 21, until August 21, 1814.

Capt. Samuel Ashton
Sergt. William Cornell
Sergt. Bromfield Boone
Corp. Owen Davis

Lieut. John Burget
Sergt. Levi Walter
Corp. Joseph McGinniss
Corp. Elijah Deneen
Corp. Elijah Duncan

Ensign, Azor Skillman
Sergt. John Morris
Corp. John Heaton
Corp. John Barton

Privates.
Andrews, Robert
Arbaugh, Peter
Bates, Amos
Bradberry, James
Bingland, Joseph
Castaller, John
Chambers, Samuel
Campbell, John
Dungan, Joseph
Davis, Daniel
Davis, John
Elliott, John
Fisher, Jacob
Granden, Samuel
Harris, Joshua
Harland, Israel
Heaton, John
Kelly, John
Jackson, John
Martin, James
McStanus, Isaac
Noble, Anthony
Roseboom, Henry
Rairde, Jonothan
Sterbaugh, Peter
Stites, Stephen
Shields, Patrick
Shivy, George
Titsworth, William
Vanclef, Tunis
Wilcox, William H.

Privates.
Awwick, Christian
Bell, James
Bracken, Thomas
Bally, John
Boles, William
Carr, James, Jr.
Carr, James, Sr.
Carley, Justus
Dickey, James
Dickey, George
Denon, John M.
Elly, Joseph
Gray, William
Garrison, Jonothan
Howard, James
Hammer, Joseph
Harlin, Ishmael
Keyboone, Henry
Mann, Richard
Moore, Leban
McClure, William
Parker, Samuel
Richmond, Jonothan
Huntsman, George
Shields, John
Smith, Elias
Snider, John
Seward, Brian
Veal, Samuel
Vail, John C.
Whittesay, Joseph

Privates.
Abbott, Jeremiah
Bunker, John
Berry, Benjamin
Blackford, Laamon
Bailey, John
Chestnut, Thomas
Clark, James
Deneen, Samuel
Deneen, John M.
Dougherty, Nathan
Early, Justus
Frakes, Nathan
Gates, John
Gustin, Samuel C.
Howard, Aaron
Horr, James
James, John
Lane, Anisney
Meeker, Peter
Mott, Jeremiah
McMannin, Isaac
Ringland, Joseph
Roseboom, Gilbert
Smith, Thomas
Spiny, George
Shoemaker, Michael
Smith, Thomas
Thomas, Cornelius
Vaughn, Garner
William, James
York, Abram

Pages 165-166. Vol. I.
ROLL OF CAPT. JOHN KELLEY'S COMPANY (Probably from Scioto County).
Served from July 28, until August 28, 1813.

Rank and Name of Soldier.

Capt. John Kelley
Sergt. William Jones
Sergt. John Cannon
Corp. William Wilson

Privates.

Brown, Aaron
Bell, Isaac
Drury, Lawson
Furgeson, James
Hewey, George
Limbarger, Peter
Neal, Walker
Suitor, William

Rank and Name of Soldier.

Lieut. Joseph Kell
Sergt. Christian Yingling
Fifer, Charles Kelley
Corp. George Baker
Corp. Joel Church

Privates.

Bannagar, John
Clark, Cornelius
Davison, Nathaniel
Gibruth, James
Henry, James
Lambart, Isaac
Osborn, Morgan
Stover, John

Rank and Name of Soldier.

Ensign, William Carpenter
Sergt. Jonothan Lambert
Drummer, John Brown
Corp. Pressley Gillilan

Privates.

Barles, Frederick
Cunningham, William
Furgeson, John
Halley, Andrew
Henry, Samuel
Melville, Jonothan
Speary, James
Yingling, Andrew

Pages 167-168.
ROLL OF CAPT. ISAAC MERIDITH'S COMPANY
(Probably from Coshocton County).
Served from August 26, 1814, until February, 1815.

Capt. Isaac Meridith
Sergt. Samuel Stephens
Corp. Thomas Allen
Corp. Ephraim Thayer

Privates.

Brown, Joseph
Bryant, William, Sr.
Crazier, James
Cullins, John
Cummings, James
Debarton, Thomas
Jennings, Bailies
Henry, George
Johnson, George
Lane, Benjamin
Lefler, George
Mealman, John
Miller, Phillip
McMallon, John
Parker, Nathaniel
Stephenson, Moses
Sugner, John

Lieut. Andrew Wharton
Sergt. Elijah Collins
Corp. Samuel Elson
Musician, Jacob D. Brown

Privates.

Brown, William
Bryant, William, Jr.
Culver, Levi
Croy, Alexander
Cosner, William
Edwards, John
Greenfield, John
Hardy, Thomas
Ketcham, Zepheniah
Lane, Dutton
Long, Joseph
Mathews, Noah
McClung, Thomas
Newman, George
Ray, John
Sanderson, Robert
Thompson, David
White, Thomas

Ensign, Henry Kidner
Sergt. Lemuel Steel
Corp. William Heburn
Musician, Edward DeLong

Privates.

Benedict, Alvin
Bingit, William
Cass, Ira
Corson, John
Caterman, Michael
Gillum, Samuel
Gibson, John
Hyet, Moses
Kidner, John
Lawrence, Thomas
Moore, William
Meridith, Henry
McGiffin, John
Phillips, Adam
Stafford, Richard
Sanderson, William
Workman, Thomas

Page 169.
ROLL OF CAPT. CHARLES F. MASTIN'S COMPANY
(Probably from Scioto County).
Served from July 28, until August 28, 1813.

Capt. Charles F. Mastin
Sergt. David Murphy
Corp. Richard Trimmer
Corp. Henry Crull

Privates.

Beauchamp, David
Blower, John
Daniels, Samuel
Johnson, Isaac
Smith, Robert
Travice, Joseph

Lieut. Samuel Darlington
Sergt. William Crull
Corp. James McAuley
Sergt. Abraham Barrett

Privates.

Beloat, George
Armstrong, Aaron
Green, Charles
Reed, Samuel
Swamm, Linsey Z.

Ensign, William McDonald
Sergt. Jesse Cockrell
Corp. James Clark

Privates.

Beloat, Walter
Crull, John
Glaze, Abraham
Shoemaker, Jacob
Scott, Joseph

Pages 170-171-172.
ROLL OF CAPT. SAMUEL ROSS' COMPANY (County Unknown).
Served from March 23, until August 23, 1814. Part served from February 17, until May 17, 1814.

Capt. Samuel Ross
Sergt. William Holmes
Sergt. Robert Bennet
Corp. Elijah Nichols

Privates.

Allen, Nicholas
Cahill, Thomas
Doughty, Hugh
Davidson, John
Douthman, Daniel
Edmonds, Louis, Sr.
Ferguson, Thomas

Lieut. Hugh Ferguson
Sergt. Robert Blair
Corp. James Lamb
Corp. William Taylor
Musician, Andrew Smith

Privates.

Bonner, Reuben
Couch, Isaiah
Dunford, William
Doyle, John
Edmonds, Louis, Jr.
Evans, Louis, Sr.
Fletcher, Jacob

Ensign, Obediah Wimans
Sergt. Benjamin McEvans
Corp. Robert Doughty
Musician, William Lane

Privates.

Bonner, Jacob
Doyall, Charles
Dunham, Charles
Chalmers, William
Evans, Lewis, Jr.
Field, Benjamin S.
Fried, Jacob

Vol. I.

ROLL OF CAPT. SAMUEL ROSS' COMPANY (Continued).

Rank and Name of Soldier.   Rank and Name of Soldier.   Rank and Name of Soldier.

Privates.

Gibson, Alexander
Holton, Tilley
Lindsey, Elijah
Muir, John
McCall, Robert
Parker, James
Porter, Phillip
Quick, John
Rubarts, John
Smith, Jonothan
Stone, William
Taylor, John
Turner, James
Virden, Jedediah
Williams, Elijah
Wheeler, Benjamin

Privates.

Guard, William
Henderson, Joseph
Lanham, Clement
Moore, Anthony
McMillan, James
Parker, Robert
Porter, George
Rounds, James
Rardin, Timothy
Smith, Jacob
Simon, Frederick
Tannyhill, Vivian
Taylor, William
Watson, Jacob
Ward, James
Westerfield, Samuel

Privates.

Hunyval, Asa
Keithler, Joseph
Lyon, William
Miller, Lewis
Merchant, Joel
Parker, George
Orr, William
Richardson, William
Smith, George
Sigman, John
Simmerman, Frederick
Talliferro, Jones
Virden, Josiah
Whitaker, Henry
Walsur, Nicholas
Wrey, George

Page 173.

ROLL OF CAPT. JOSEPH WALKER'S COMPANY (Probably from Knox Co.)
Served from August 8, 1812, until June 10, 1813.

Capt. Joseph Walker
Sergt. John Beving
Sergt. Barney John
Corp. George Dickinson
Drummer, Henry Clemens

Lieut. Richard M. Brown
Sergt. Archibald Crafford or Crawford
Corp. Joliah Trimly
Fifer, Rowley Clark

Sergt. John Elliott
Sergt. Peter Kile
Corp. Samuel Evirt
Corp. Lewis Grinstaff

Privates.

Barton, Michael
Emmet, Abraham
Haun, Emmanuel
King, Joseph
Munsen, Alexander
Rogers, Isaac
Strong, Harley
Simpkins, Benjamin
Wolf, Jacob
Wood, James
Wallace, William

Privates.

Davidson Robert
Enos, Alexander
Kile, Jacob
Linn, Adam
McConnell John
Ryan, John
Smith, John
Swigart, David
Walker, Phillip
Welker, Powell
Welker, Paul
Yoman, Samuel

Privates.

Davy, Michael
Elwell, David
Kile, Nicholas
Mifford, John
Newel, Reverent
Sunderland, John
Stewart, Benjamin
Sprague, Perez
Welker, Andrew
Walker, Alexander
Welker, Andrew

Pages 174-175-176.

ROLL OF CAPT. JAMES RIGHTMIRE'S COMPANY
(Probably from Licking Co.)
Served from May 4, until May 19, 1813, and from September 8, 1814, until March 5, 1815.

Capt. James Rightmire
Sergt. John Wells
Sergt. Samuel Dunlap
Corp. William Starner
Corp. Elijah Harris
Musician, Valentine Dial

Lieut. George Hull
Sergt. Burwell
Sergt. Daniel Dial
Corp. John Harbert
Fifer, David Cox
Musician William Spig

Ensign, Wadly Smith
Sergt. Jonas Frye
Sergt. Thomas Merit
Corp. Joshua Downs
Drummer, Joseph Beckwith

Privates.

Alspaugh, Adam
Barlow, Abraham
Bigsby, Titus
Botton, John
Channel, Isom
Chapman, Timothy
Dison, Turner
Doty, Thrazey
Dial, Phillip
Goodrich, Stephen G.
Holt, James
Hull, Uriah
Harris, Jesse
Harrod, John
Miller, Henry
Mix, Justice
McGowan, James
McMillen, Robert
Potter, Nathan
Robinson, Joel
Night, William
Stitwell, Stephen
Stripe, Warner
Smith, James
Thompson, Rennold
Vansarsdol, Cornelius
Winsett, Joseph
Wills, William
Woodrow, William

Privates.

Agg, Frederick
Bashford, Thomas
Baker, John
Brown, Ebenezer
Cunningham, Joseph
Culverson, Jeremiah
Damaval, Edward
Dial, George
Evans, Joshua
Green, John
Harris, Isaac
Howard, Charles S.
Harrod, Levi
Ireland, Nobel
Morris, William
Mains, William
McCrary, Benjamin
Nemerick, Jacob
Priest, Hankey
Rupp, Jacob
Shillinbarger, Isaac
Stotts, Daniel
Strobe, William
Spirgin, James
Trimbly, Josiah
Vance, Joseph
Wist, James
Wilkin, John

Privates.

Boner, James
Brister, Jacob
Brown, Jeremiah
Claybough, William
Chapman, William
Drumple, Charles
Darrie, Ezziah
Davies, Nathaniel
Fortner, John
Hull, James
Hilman, Daniel
Harris, William
Harris, Enoch
Low, James
Merrit, John
McCormick, Moses
McMillen, Ephraim
Ogden, James
Pumpey, Joshua
Regah, John
Shump, William
Stephens, Chester
Strobe, James
Smith, Phillip
Thomas, William
Woodward, Ashel
Woodruff, Ogden
Walker, Robert

Page 177. Vol. I.
ROLL OF CAPT. WILLIAM M. BURK'S COMPANY (County Unknown).
Served from July 28, until August 28, 1813.

Rank and Name of Soldier.	Rank and Name of Soldier.	Rank and Name of Soldier.
Captain William M. Burk	Lieut. George Salladay	Sergt. John Cook
Sergt. Thompson Sebring	Sergt. Matthew Curran	Sergt. John Sallada
Corp. William Conchlin	Corp. Jacob Woodring	Corp. Reuben Chaflin
	Corp. George Bradshaw	
Privates.	**Privates.**	**Privates.**
Bentley, Joseph	Barcus, James	Brady, William
Berry, James	Bonsor, Joseph	Bradshaw, Isaac
Colegrove, William	Haes, James	Hues, Henry
Louderbach, Peter	Moore, Samuel	Moore, John
Louderbach, Conrad	Louderbach, John	Nicholas, William
Osborn, James	Patton, Samuel	Patton, Thomas
Sikes, Edward	Stockham, Aaron	Saladay, Daniel
Sikes, Levi	Wate, James	Wickson, Barnabus
	Wolford, Frederick	

Page 178.
ROLL OF CAPT. ELIJAH COCKRELL'S COMPANY (Probably from Scioto Co.)
Served from July 28, until August 28, 1813.

Capt. Elijah Cockrell	Ensign James Delag	
Privates.	**Privates.**	**Privates.**
Millar, John W.	Bowers, Solomon	Black, John
Barnes, John	Bumgainer, Reuben	Currie, Henderson
Conway, Simon	Chinworth, Richard	Howard, Amos
Howard, Samuel	Kenney, John	Lewis, Abraham
Mustard, William	Mustard, Samuel	McAuley, Henry
Richmond, R. R.	Slater, Ezekial	Sailor, Jeremiah
Smith, William	Vinson, Jesse	Walls, James
Walls, Levin	Walls, Joshua	

Page 193.
ROLL OF CAPT. JOHN CAMPBELL'S COMPANY (Probably from Portage Co.)
Served from July 1, 1812, until June 30, 1813.

Capt. John Campbell	Lieut. Alva Day	Ensign Aaron Waston
Sergt. Louis Day	Sergt. Ralph Buckland	Sergt. John Wright
Sergt. Louis Ely	Corp. Charles Chittenden	Corp. John Harmon
Corp. Daniel Burroughs	Corp. John Turner	
Privates.	**Privates.**	**Privates.**
Amadown, Abiscan	Allen, Miles	Buckley, Ebenezer
Campbell, Robert	Carter, Charles	Cross, Nathan
Coleman, William	Caris, John	Day, Seth
Harmon, Enos	Harmon, Zacheus	Hartle, Samuel
Jones, David	Jacobs, John	Moore, Mark
Moore, David	Mayfield, William	McGill, James
McCartney, Edward	McManus, John	Newberry, Chaney
Pettibone, Henry	Roos, Henry	Ray, James, Jr.
Reading, Richard	Reading, George G.	Rowley, Thomas
Redfield, Samuel	Smith, John	Turrel, Peter
Tuthill, Samuel	Thompson, Job	Thompson, Samuel
Thornton, William	Underwood, Joel	Ward, William
Williams, John	Williard, Phillip	

Page 194.
ROLL OF CAPT. DANIEL F. REEDER'S COMPANY (County Unknown).
Served from September 14, until October 14, 1812.

Capt. Daniel F. Reeder	Capt. Robert Hays	Lieut. Samuel Yeoman
Lieut. Bratton Crawford	Ensign Henry Loziere	Sergt. William Snook
Sergt. Nathaniel Fitchner	Sergt. John Galbraith	Sergt. Richard Gimanton
Privates.	**Privates.**	**Privates.**
Andrews, William	Blackburn, Benjamin	Bunnel, Henry
Cowen, James, Jr.	Constant, Thomas	Crain, Daniel
Coil, Samuel	Case, Samuel	Crawford, John
Case, Thomas	Clement, Isaac	Colier, James
Drake, Samuel	Ewen, William	Gowdy, James
Gowdy, Alexander	Hatfield, Franz	Hayse, Robert
Hayse, Caleb M.	Dunbar, Joseph	Lamiston, Eleazor
Laurens, Jonothan	Miller, George	Magan, Evan
Maloy, James	Montford, Henry	McMann, James
McCall, James	Rawl, Mathew	Rawl, Week
Robinson, James H.	Pope, William	Shawhaney, James
Spinning, Benjamin	Symonton, Cyrus	Van Pelt, Alexander
Wickersham, John		

Pages 196-197. Vol. I.
ROLL OF CAPT. JOSEPH C. HAWKINS' COMPANY (County Unknown).
Served from September 30, 1813, until March 29, 1814.

Rank and Name of Soldier.	Rank and Name of Soldier.	Rank and Name of Soldier.
Capt. Joseph C. Hawkins	Lieut. John Saylor	Ensign Peter Painer
Sergt. Thomas Nubet	Sergt. William Stephens	Sergt. Ezekial DuWees
Sergt. John Quinn	Corp. Thomas Foster	Corp. William Curry
Corp. Joshua Cloyd	Corp. Jesse Smith	
Privates.	**Privates.**	**Privates.**
Aikins, Benjamin	Aply, John	Allen, James
Arby, Abraham	Alred, James	Black, Frederick
Biers, Isaac	Brannin, Samuel	Brown, John
Brummet, Spencer	Christman, Jacob	Clark, John
Coble, Eli	Cladwell, Train	Creeson, Isaac
Dickey, John	Davis, Robert	Davis, David
Dollyheid, Jesse	Ellis, John	Fox, John
Gamble, John	Gordon, Charles	Gordon, Samuel
Hopkins, Lemuel	Hawkins, Byrd	Harter, William
Hamilton, Alexander	Hayes, Robert	Housten, Thomas
Hel, John	Haworth, Jehu	Hawkins, John
Ireland, Peter	Kenut, Henry	Kellum, Joseph
Keek, Henry	Landers, Daniel	Lenar, Samuel
Lenen, Peter	Lincoln, Thomas	Listre, Elephas
Mash, William	McElvey, Alexander	McClure, John
Matney, Elias	Niekum, Michael	Niekum, Johu
Nelson, John	Quinn, James	Russle, Charles
Niekum, Peter	Shoemaker, Daniel	Stone, William
Rian, James	Smith, Thomas	Saxon, James
Stephens, David	Stephens, David	Sproule, John
Smith, Zadoc	Worle, Samuel	Smith, Thomas
Tharp, Hiram	Williams, Joseph	Wier, John
Williamson, John	York, Newberry	Wiley, Samuel

Pages 199-200.
ROLL OF CAPT. WILLIAM MILLER'S COMPANY (County Unknown).
Served from ———— 16, until March 16, 1814.

Capt. William Miller	Lieut. Owen T. Reeves	Ensign David Coon
Sergt. James Jackson	Sergt. John Stephens	Sergt. Jeremiah Shoppell
Sergt. Archibald Thompson	Corp. John Wilmouth	Corp. John Heckethorne
Corp. William Shaynefelt	Corp. Jacob Rush	Fifer, Daniel Bowsher
Privates.	**Privates.**	**Privates.**
Bowhan, Adam	Beck, James	Bishop, William
Beatty, Samuel	Cummins, William	Cox, William
Conner, Aaron	Cox, Benjamin	Davis, John
Davis, John	Defenbaugh, Joseph	Dukes, Jacob
Duvall, Mareen H.	Falkner, John	Greenho, Andrew
Grimm, George	Graham, Thomas	Haines, Peter
Harbut, George	Ice, William	Ice, William
Justice, John	Kennedy, James	Kanada, James
Kent, James	Kent, Daniel	Krider, George
Kirk, John	Molatt, John	Morris, Joseph
Miller, Hugh	McQuay, James	McCinna, Henry
Puntenney, Aquilla	Pontius, Solomon	Pomewell, John
Pomewell, Thomas	Parton, Andrew	Purtee, Joseph
Purtee, James	Rabourn, Hugh	Rodgers, Lewis R.
Reed, Jacob	Smith, Charles	Shepherd, Peter
Swaggart, Daniel	Spees, Mathias	Shambaugh, Phillip
Stayner, John	Trulinger, Phillip	Wright, Joseph
Williams, Enoch	Walker, Daniel	Walter, Jacob
Williams, Isaac	Young, Daniel	Zimmer, Phillip

Pages 216-217.
ROLL OF CAPT. REZIN SHELBY'S COMPANY (County Unknown).
Served from July 23, until September 6, 1813.

Capt. Rezin Shelby	Lieut. David Frazier	Ensign Jacob Frazier
Sergt. Enoch Ballak	Sergt. David Craig	Sergt. John Augustine
Sergt. Jacob Hellum	Corp. Dorman Cade	Corp. Thomas Wolverton
Corp. Moses Morris	Corp. John Cade	
Privates.	**Privates.**	**Privates.**
Albin, Samuel	Bashford, Francis, Sr.	Bashford, Francis, Jr.
Bending, James	Bradley, William	Creviston, John
Cruver, Christie	Caldwell, William	Coon, Jacob
Essex, Isaac	Essex, Milcay	Gibson, Robert
Huston, John	Harber, Richard	Hardie, Henry
Long, Andrew	Morris, James	Morris, Joseph
Myers, George	Morris, John	Metgar, John
Newhous, Abraham	Phillips, William	Richeson, John
Ryason, Samuel	Rogen, Jonothan	Smith, William
Sisco, Joseph	Stonecock, John	Silivan, James
Vinson, John	Yagar, John	

Pages 210-211-212-213-214-215. Vol. I.

ROLL OF CAPT. LUTHER SHEPHERD'S COMPANY (Probably from Ross Co.)
Served from February 16, until June 16, 1814, part served until August 16, 1814.

Rank and Name of Soldier.	Rank and Name of Soldier.	Rank and Name of Soldier.
Capt. Luther Shepherd	Lieut. John Mulligan	Lieut. William Kirker
Ensign Samuel Mansfield	Ensign Thomas Smith	Ensign Samuel Bliss
Sergt. James Bliss	Sergt. Nyel Nye	Sergt. John Dyer
Sergt. Thomas Compton	Sergt. Arthur McFarland	Ensign Henry Bayne
Sergt. Peter Daily	Sergt. Nathan Chany	Sergt. Moses Warren
Sergt. John Enismyer	Corp. John Ensminger	Corp. Thomas McCime
Corp. Caleb Cox	Corp. John Buck	Corp. John Dolbay
Corp. Abraham McGinnis	Corp. Archibald Raborn	Corp. Thomas McCline
Fifer, Varnum G. Wilson	Drummer, John McKinley	Drummer, Elijah Johnson

Privates.

Anway, George	Amos, Pleasant	Anderson, Cornelius
Barkley, Samuel	Barker, William	Bardman, Samuel
Brooks, Samuel	Barruk, John	Batey, Samuel
Baily, James	Blue, Frederick	Baker, John
Buck, John	Butt, Rignal	Buntin, Alexander
Baker, George	Boner, James	Buckley, Samuel
Chipp, John	Cokenour, John	Cox, John
Comer, Emanuel	Coon, Jacob	Clay, Mathews
Cormick, James	Cooper, John	Clearwaty, Thomas
Clay, Thomas	Cissna, Stephen	Cockmour, John
Conner, Emanuel	Dolbay, John	Device, Henry
Dayton, Spencer	DeWitt, George	Dorman, Jesse
Davis, Henson	Frost, Hemon	Frost, Marcus
Fremont, Luke	Fulen, William	Foster, John
Flinn, Thomas	Fuller, Alexander	Frazier, John
Fuller, William	Goff, Salithiel	Greenfield, John
Hatfield, Thomas	Hutchinson, William	Harper, James
Harper, Robert	Hoop, John	Hamilton, John
Herrin, Timothy	Henderson, John	Hixon, John
Herrold, Jesse	Hughey, Isaac	Jones, William
Jones, Thomas	Jones, Asa	Jack, Andrew
Keon, Jacob	Kirkpatrick, Andrew	Kendall, William
Kirk, Elisha	King, Charles	Landen, Lewis
Linscott, John	Lewis, James	Long, Thomas
Loverton, Daniel	Landin, Levin	Lewis, William
Mowers, Henry	Maddon, Dennis	Mershon, Timothy
Mahaffy, Robert	Mayse, Little Berry	Murray, Benjamin A.
McLain, Moses	McEntire, Robert	McNeal, Joseph
McKinley, John	McKee, John	Nash, Azor
Otinger, William	Parish, John	Phipps, David
Partlow, Amos	Pinkerman, John	Porter, Aquila
Pendell, Thomas	Puckett, Martin	Parker, William
Rowland, Samuel	Rice, Mordecai	Robertson, William
Redmond, Joseph	Ross, Isaiah	Ross, Samuel
Russell, Alexander	Stedman, Abel	Swigg, Jesse
Simmons, William	Smedley, George I.	Sawyer, George
Sanderson, William	Twigg, Jesse	Turner, John
Thompson, John	Thorn, Jacob	Vigus, Paul
Wallace, Austin	Wether, James	Wyekoff, Nicholas
Williams Nathan	Waters, Jacob	White, John
Wyekoff, John	Walden, William	Wirt, James
	Williams, Thomas	

Page 216.

ROLL OF SERGT. JACOB SINN'S COMPANY (Probably from Ross County).
Served from August 22, 1814, until February 21, 1815.

Sergt. Jacob Sinn   Musician, Richard Price

Privates.

Dollarhide, Jesse	Downing, William	Bacon, Ira
Fort, Francis	Hammersley, George	Hews, Robert
Hammett, George	Krein, Adam	Kunn, James
Lowins, Hyatt	Lowman, Joseph	Liston, George
Miller, John	Markin, Thomas	Murray, Daniel
Smith, David	Smith, Thomas	Syphers, George
Sellers, Jacob	Slawson, James	Tuttle, Isaiah
Sissions, Benjamin	Vanmetre, Henry	Winn, William S.
Williams, Joseph		

Pages 221-222-223-224. Vol. I.

ROLL OF CAPT. CALEB HOSKINS' COMPANY (Probably from Ross County).

Served from July 28, until September 7, 1813, part served from January 3, until April 10, 1815.

Rank and Name of Soldier.	Rank and Name of Soldier.	Rank and Name of Soldier.
Capt. Caleb Hoskins	Lieut. Seth Vanmater	Lieut. Aaron Foster
Ensign Andrew Smalley	Ensign Hugh Cook	Sergt. John Moore
Sergt. David Coblar	Sergt. Christopher Beekman	Sergt. Nathaniel Chapman
Sergt. William Hartell	Sergt. Joseph Ross	Sergt. John McCord
Corp. Morwin Williams	Corp. William Hanes	Corp. Simon Shumaker
Corp. John Pollard	Corp. John Highley	Corp. Levin Right
Corp. John Anderson	Corp. Isaac Rockhold	Musician, Henson David
	Musician, William Davis	

Privates.	Privates.	Privates.
Adams, William	Beekman, John	Beddle, George
Beekman, James	Burnes, Robert	Bamfield, John
Braley, James	Bodkins, George	Bowman, John
Burk, James	Carson, Joseph	Cloud, Thomas
Corn, Jonothan	Cross, James	Cross, Thomas
Carter, Samuel	Carter, Daniel	Cummins, Thomas
Cauchy, Samuel	Crouch, William	Cooper, John
Clines, George	Crow, David	Corkwell, Henry
David, James	Downing, John	Danes, Daniel
Davison, Benjamin	Dungen, William	Florow, Joshua
Freeland, Jacob	Guthridge, Thomas	Gilmore, John
Grogan, James	Hurdman, Henry	Hurdman, Michael
Hamilton, Samuel	Hibbs, Jacob	Harmon, Henry
Hughes, Samuel	Izard, Eli	Ivans, John
Johnston, John	Kingery, Berry	Kimble, William
Kuder, George	Kees, Cane	Lockhart, Thomas
Lowderbeck, Zach	Mines, James	Mustard, Samuel
Markland, William	Myers, Jacob	Morrison, James
Miller, George	Michael, George	Mulford, Ezekial
McGarah, William	McGee, John	McDonald, James
McWhorter, Henry	Ouley, Nicholas	Porter, James
Pucket, Redman	Pike, Jarviss	Dickup, Frederick
Raller, Adam	Shard, Nathanial	Satterfield, William
Spears, William	Strope, Harvey	Treber, Jacob
Thomas, Asia	Suderfield, Charles	Shelah, George
Suderfield, James	Taylor, William	Roads, Aden
Jackson, Jesse	Travis, Robert	Tansey, Eli
Towers, William	VanBuckerk, Thomas	Van Nule, Absalom
Watson, Loren	Wilson, John	Weak, George
	Wilson, James	

Pages 225-226.

ROLL OF CAPT. GEORGE BRYAN'S COMPANY (Probably from Ross County).

Served from July 28, until September 9, 1813.

Capt. George Bryan	Lieut. William Smith	Ensign Jesse Edwards
Sergt. John Haslip	Sergt. Samuel Edwards	Sergt. Jonothan Passmore
Sergt. Andrew Davidson	Corp. Elias Hatheney	Corp. Skinner Bloomfield
Corp. John Stephens	Corp. Jacob Edginton	Drummer, John Smith
	Fifer, Henry Malone	

Privates.	Privates.	Privates.
Bowman, William	Blake, James	Baird, Robertson
Cochran, William	Clark, James	Chips, John
Clark, Robert	Carroll, Robert	Cartright, William A.
Cheesman, John	Crawford, William	Edmondson, Samuel
Eginton, Joshua	Edgington, Abraham	Edgington, Isaac
Gordon, Basil	Guthridge, Charles	Hurst, Abraham
Holmes, Thomas	Johnston, Elisha	King, Barlett
Leedom, John	Morford, Thomas	Matheney, Charles
Moore, Daniel	Moore, James	McGoony, Thomas
McClure, Ralph	McClanehan, William	McGin, Robert
McGin, Daniel	Noleman, Richard	Page, David
Preston, Luther	Paterson, John	Reynolds, James
Rulolson, Mathias	Paul, John	Viqus, Paul
Wade, John	Wine, John	

Page 227.

ROLL OF LIEUT. SETH VAN MATRE'S COMPANY. (County Unknown.)

Served from August 25, 1814, until January 24, 1815.

Lieut. Seth Van Matre	Sergt. Nathaniel Chapman	Sergt. Charles Beekman
Corp. John Russell	Corp. James Mines	

Privates.	Privates.	Privates.
Alexander, John	Gibson, James	Hayes, John
Harbaugh, Fred	Hill, Joseph	Jack, James
Jordan, John	Lewis, James	Lewitz, Curtis
Langweld, Robert	Mershore, Solomon	Mershore, Daniel
McLaughlin, ——	McFarland, James	Petty, John Richard
Park, Daniel	Paul, Benjamin	Rodes, Aden
Scott, John C.	Sharp, William T.	

Pages 228-229-230. Vol. I.

ROLL OF CAPT. JOHN VAN METER'S COMPANY (County Unknown).

Served from July 29, until August 17, 1813, part served from August 23, 1815, until February 22, 1816.

Rank and Name of Soldier.	Rank and Name of Soldier.	Rank and Name of Soldier.
Capt. John Van Meter	Lieut. Samuel Jones	Ensign Jacob Hickle
Ensign John Keys	Sergt. Aaron Jones	Sergt. James Dempsey
Sergt. Joseph Doty	Sergt. John May	Sergt. Aaron James
Sergt. George L. Crockett	Corp. Martin Doty	Corp. Humphrey Mounts
Corp. Peter Throckmorton	Corp. Peter Straser	Corp. John Russell
Corp. Nathan Hicks	Drummer, Richard Price	

Privates.	Privates.	Privates.
Austin, Thomas	Barcus, Jacob	Barcus, Joseph
Brown, Henry	Burdington, Aeneas	Creechbarme, George
Cade Robert	Cyphers, George	Dumm, Christian
Deresbach, Benjamin	Dresbach, Henry	Dresbach, Martin
Downs, Thomas	Ezra, Jonothan	Flinn, Joshua
Grafton, Ambrose	Hayes, Solomon	Harper, John
Hickle, Tevault	Hayes, John	Henry, James
Hill, Joseph	Jones, Jabez	Irwin, Andrew
Guthrie, William	Jones, Henry	Jones, Moses
Guess, Anthony	Keller, George	Kirk, John
Lyons, Morris	Malatt, John	DeMars, Thomas
Oliver, John	Pontius, Jacob	Plummer, Jacob
Pontious, John	Paull, Benjamin	Rogers, Lewis R.
Reedy, Conrad	Reedy, John	Reedy, Michael
Reid, John	Ross, Solomon	Strazer, Solomon
Straser, John	Sapeins, Gabriel	Sutton, John
Scott, John C.	St. Muels, Gabriel	Vallequette, Christopher
Throckmorton, John	Vinson, Cuthbert	
Weider, Henry	Webster, George	

Pages 231-232-233.

ROLL OF CAPT. SAMUEL DENISON'S COMPANY
(Probably from Trumbull and Mahoning Counties).

Served from August 26, until November 16, 1812.

Captain Samuel Denison	Lieut. David Augustus Adams	Ensign William Swan
Sergt. Benjamin Armitage	Sergt. Amos Gray	Sergt. William Carlton
Sergt. David Dunwoodie	Sergt. Jesse Alderman	Sergt. Nathaniel Cook
Corp. James Walton	Corp. Robert Stewart	Corp. Matthew J. Scott
Corp. David Raner	Drummer, William Moon	Fifer, Joseph McGill

Privates.	Privates.	Privates.
Armitage, Ephraim	Amiestein, Daniel	Anderson, James
Arrel, John	Boyd, Andrew	Baggs, Joseph, Sr.
Bredon, John	Bell, William	Beard, John
Brothers, John	Barsley, Josiah	Buchanan, William
Crawford, William	Carlton, Peter	Carr, John
Cowden, William	Cowden, Ranels	Crays, Alexander
Day, John	Dinwiddie, John	Dinwiddie, Thomas
Dawson, Aaron	Dickson, John	Eckman, James
Fight, Jacob	Fight, Jacob, Jr.	Ferguson, Samuel
Fowler, Thomas	Gwahe, Robert	Hits, George
Henry, Francis	Howard, William	Kays, David
Kimmel, Philip	Lyon, Isaac	Linn, James
Leonard, John	Liddle, John	Moore, John
Mann, Samuel	Moore, Sampson	Miller, Conrad
Moon, James	McClellan, David	McMurray, John
McMurray, William	McConnal, David	McKnit, William
McConnal, Philip	McGill, Robert	McConnal, John
McGill, William	McKinney, Henry	McDonald, James
McKinney, William	Nelson, John	Noble, David
Oswal, Jacob	Poyers, John	Poly, John
Rose, John	Rummel, Henry	Ripple, George
Stewart, David	Swazer, Isaac	Stephenson, Elijah
Storm, Michael	Stout, Jonothan	Tully, John
Walter, Robert	Wilson, Thomas	Wilson, David
Wilson, Edward	Yost, John	

Page 234.

ROLL OF LIEUT THOMAS C. NUTTER'S COMPANY.
(Probably from Ross County.)

Served from July 29, until August 17, 1813.

Lieut. Thomas C. Nutter	Sergt. Anthony Morton	

Privates.	Privates.	Privates.
Dawson, David	Donnely, James	Crouch, Joseph
Goodman, Peter	Goule, George	Goodman, Samuel
Goodman, Daniel	Haynes, Andrew	Hall, William
Carshner, Daniel	Carshner, Jacob	Stein, George
Tents, Lawrence	Webster, Stewart	White, James

Pages 243-244. Vol. I.

ROLL OF CAPT. ELIHU MOSES' COMPANY (County Unknown).

Served from August 24, until September 5, 1812. Part served from September 19, 1814, until February 23, 1815.

Rank and Name of Soldier.	Rank and Name of Soldier.	Rank and Name of Soldier.
Capt. Elihu Moses	Lieut. Lewis Walcutt	Lieut. Hezekiah Hine
Ensign Robert Gault	Ensign Sheldon Osborn	Sergt. Levi Ormsbury
Sergt. Ephraim White	Sergt. David Curtis	Sergt. Levi Armsby
Sergt. Daniel Burroughs	Sergt. Lyman Hine	Sergt. Thomas Reed
Corp. George Barnes	Corp. Griswold Gillett	Corp. Conrad Turner
Corp. Rhoderick Norton	Corp. Asa Waldon	Corp. Willis I. Walcott
Corp. Smith Hurd	Fifer, Mark Oviatt	Drummer, Ezra Curtis
Drummer, Joy Hurd	Fifer, Comfort Hurd	

Privates.

Adams, Subel	Boyd Thomas	Bartholomew, Charles
Bartholomew, Jacob	Bronson, Elisha	Bradford, Joel
Bradford, William	Brockway, Romanty	Barklor, John
Bristol, Thomas	Carpenter, Lewis	Curtis, Sheldon
Cummings, John	Cummings, William	Cox, John
Curtis, Lewis	Dunlap, William	Daniel, James
Fausler, John	Fish, Abner	Higgins, Silas
Heart, Gad	Higley, Thompson	Krigler, Michael
King, Nathan	Koigler, Jacob	May, Charles
Martial, William	Marshall, James	Moore, Frederick
McCombs, Robert	Norton, George	Norton, Zacheus
Norton, Henry	Norton, John	Osborn, Gilbert
Reed, William	Rook, James	Stillman, John D.
Stacey, Mathew	Southwortt, Joseph	Turk, Ephraim
Trescott, Ira	Upton, Benjamin	Van Vey, Isaac
Walker, Jonothan	Wilson, Elijah	Walcott, Josiah
Walcott, Horace	Wilson, John	Witts, Zepheniah
Waid, Alexander	Williams, Allen	Bushnell, Alexander
Adkins, John	Buck, James	Bailey, David
Beebe, Samuel	Burk, Onin	Clow, Daniel
Crawford, Alexander	Curtis, Calvin	Hamilton, William
Clark, Elijah	Dickenson, Elijah	Hart, Alva
Harrington, Zenas	Hum, Samuel	Hutson, Andrew
Hunt, Ezra	Hutson, Mathew	Haney, James
Hutson, Thomas	Hofsteater, David	Knapp, Andrew
Harper, Archibald	Johnson, Chandler	Little, James
Linkin, William	Lary, Isaac H.	Phelps, Spencer
Murphy, James	McKnit, William	Reed, Benjamin
Quiggle, Peter	Ring, William W.	

Pages 245-246.

ROLL OF CAPT. RIAL McARTHUR'S COMPANY (County Unknown).

Served from August 22, until October 29, 1812. Part served from April 27, until May 22, 1813.

Capt. Rial McArthur	Lieut. Wiley Hamilton	Ensign Charles Powers
Sergt. Joshua King	Sergt. Alpha Wright	Sergt. David Kenny, Jr.
Sergt. Lunar Bishop	Sergt. Samuel Cheeney	Corp. Edmund Strong
Corp. Drake Fellows	Corp. Justice Barnes	Corp. Justin E. Frink
Drummer, Stephen W. Butler	Fifer, Ara Griltt	

Privates.

Adams, Philander	Allen, Samuel	Allen, Miles
Arthur, Aaron	Ayres, Asa	Atkins, Samuel, Jr.
Bierin, Henry	Bradley, James	Baldwin, Eliakin
Bissel, Orris	Blackman, Elijah, Sr.	Baldwin, James
Bellows, Ithamar	Bradley, Justice	Boosinger, John
Baird, Robert	Baird, William	Butler, Henry
Adams, Moses, Jr.	Cacklin, Christy	Campbell, John
Collins, John	Castle, John	Chapman, Titus
Chaney, Samuel	Cook, David	Darrow, Nathaniel
Decker, Aaron	Draper, Asa	Ellet, Thomas
Ellet, David	Eggleston, Moses	Ellet, George
Fogger, Samuel	Furgeson, Samuel	Granger, Horace
Gaylor, Stewart	Green, Abner	Hall, James
Heart, William	Heyns, Samuel	Haymaker, George
King, Henry	King, Charles	Kent, Zardus
Kent, Zeno	Kennedy, David	Lowrey, Shubal H.
Liverton, Dixon	Lindley, Jesse	Lappin, William
Lappin, John	Neal, Jesse	Norton, Peter
Nighman, George	Perkins, Elisha	Perkins, Stephen
Powers, David	Preston, Samuel	Preston, David, Jr.
Preston, John S.	Preston, Lott	Prior, William
Pease, Ebenezer	Perkins, Grant	Pelton, John
Powers, George	Prior, David	Russel, Samuel
Blair, Bohan	Ridlake, Daniel	Spicer, Amos, Jr.
Sacket, Norman	Singletary, John C.	Strong, David
Tousley, Joseph	Tupper, Hezekiah	Thompson, James
Vanhyning, Thomas	Wright, John, Jr.	Wilcox, David
Woolcott, Alfred	Williams, Barnabus	Woodward, Stephen
Wyatt, Ezra	Williams, John	Sacket, Leander

Page 247 Vol. I.

ROLL OF CAPT. WILLIAM N. HUDSON'S COMPANY
(From Geauga or Portage Counties.)
Served from August 24, until August 31, 1812.

Rank and Name of Soldier.	Rank and Name of Soldier.	Rank and Name of Soldier.
Capt. William N. Hudson	Ensign Erastus Creary	Corp. Ashbel Gilmore
Privates.	**Privates.**	**Privates.**
Archer, William Sr.	Archer, William Jr.	Eames, Isaac
Gilmore, Samuel	Kent, Elihu L.	Lacey, George B.
Lacey, Jaspar B.	Minor, John	McConnaughey, Porter D.
Osborn, Alexander	Singletary, Uriah I.	Sheffield, Leroy
	Sheffield, Alpheus	

Pages 248-249-250

ROLL OF CAPT. ROBERT McELWAIN'S COMPANY. (County Unknown.)
Served from September 28, until October 25, 1812, and from April 20, until July 16, 1813.

Capt. Robert McElwain	Lieut. Robert Tate	Ensign Jacob Funk
Sergt. Andrew Knox	Sergt. John Jewett	Sergt. Andrew Richards
Sergt. William Devlon	Sergt. Aaron Archer	Sergt. John Funk
Sergt. John Hayes	Corp. Benjamin Salmon	Corp. John Sowards
Corp. David McElwain	Corp. William Hays	
Privates.	**Privates.**	**Privates.**
Applegate, William	Allen, Jeremiah	Archer, John
Allen, George	Buck, John	Bell, Isaiah
Bell, Charles	Biggs, Joseph	Black, William
Black, Samuel	Bragg, John	Baldwin, Uriah
Biram, William	Carden, Armstrong	Croze, John
Calliston, James	Chichester, Elias	Freeland, Luke
Funk, John	Flick, William	Gilbert, Henley
Gilner, William	Gunsol, Michael	Gaskill, John
Harper, Alexander	Hurley, Zedick	Harrison, Joseph
Harrison, L. B.	Gone, David I.	Ellis, Henry
Jolymill, James	Kennedy, Robert	Kerr, John
Kerns, Samuel	Kent, Terren	LeVally, Jacob
March, David	Maxwell, Ephraim	Mowberry, Reuben
McDonald, William	McElvain, David	McClure, William
Odle, William	Plyman, James	Pendegrass, James
Rollins, Samuel	Rankins, John	Rankins, William
Reed, William	Roback, George	Riddle, David
Runion, John	Rodgers, Henry	Redden, Mathew
Redden, Edward	Reed, William	Rodgers, Benjamin
Smith, William	Stephenson, Thomas	Taylor, George
	Webster, James B.	

Page 252

ROLL OF CAPT. JOEL BEREMAN'S COMPANY (Probably from Highland Co.)
Served from March 28, until September 28, 1812.

Capt. Joel Bereman	Lieut. Hugh Rodgers	Ensign Peter Cooley
Sergt. James Heslet	Sergt. William Black	Sergt. Nathan Roansevell
Corp. Jesse Williams	Corp Robert Fitzpatrick	Corp. Jacob Metzgar
Corp. William Rion	Corp. John Hoop	
Privates.	**Privates.**	**Privates.**
Beard, John R.	Burns, James	Bryan, Jesse
Cosby, Stith	Coe, Joseph	Dick, Quintin
Edgington, Joseph	Eavans, Samuel	Gibson, Samuel
Hoop, John	Hoffman, Phelix	Fitzpatrick, John
Haigh, Job	Hilderbrand, David	Hix, Nathan
Kelso, Michael	McGowan, John	McRight, James
Strain, William	Steward, Willson	Shoomaker, Solomon
Sturin, Thomas	Watts, Thomas	

Page 253

ROLL OF CAPT. REUBEN WESTFALL'S COMPANY
(Probably from Miami County.)
Served from May 1, until May 15, 1812, and from October 24, until November 13, 1812.

Capt. Reuben Westfall	Lieut. Amos Petite	Sergt. Jesse Miller
Sergt. Moses Garard	Corp. Elias Garard	
Privates.	**Privates.**	**Privates.**
Alexander, James	Arnold, David	Bennett, Benjamin
Brown, John	Ballinger, Even	Ballenger, Daniel
Coats, James	Cothran, James	Curtis, James
Edwards, James	Hunter, William	Kern, Henry
Kern, John	Kyle, Samuel	Layton, Joseph
McJimsey, Robert	McJimsey, William	North, Richard
Swailes, Rice	Smith, Jonathan	Smith, Henry
Trader, Tegal	Thomas, Samuel	Thornsburg, Uriah
Thomas, Adam	Westfall, Levi	Westfall, Joel
White, Robert	Orbison, John	Richardson, John
Robbins, Richard		

Pages 254-255 Vol. I.

ROLL OF CAPT. RICHARD SLOAN'S COMPANY (County Unknown).

Served from October 8, 1812, until April 7, 1813.

Rank and Name of Soldier.	Rank and Name of Soldier.	Rank and Name of Soldier.
Capt. Richard Sloan	Lieut. John Hawkins	Ensign John Harter
Sergt. William McCreary	Sergt. Charles Hole	Sergt. Simon Cassiday
Sergt. Michael Straw	Corp. William Hendricks	Corp. Andrew Spaight
Corp. Tetrach Fall	Corp. William Davis	Drummer, Thomas M. Dill
	Fifer, John Byers	

Privates.	Privates.	Privates.
Abbott, James	Abshire, James	Allen, William
Bloomfield, Samuel	Banfill, John	Bloomfield, Nathaniel
Bloomfield, John	Blackley, Littleberry	Bennet, James
Banfill, Enoch	Abshire, Isaac	Cox, James
Cloyd, Joshua	Faris, James	Faris, David
Foster, Thomas	Harris, Benjamin	Hopkins, Lemuel
Hollowell, Adam	Hamilton, Samuel	Harris, John
Huston, James	Hayes, William	Hill, Thomas
Hawkins, Joseph	Highlander, William	Killough, James
Loy, Jacob Jr.	Lyons, David	Martin, Andrew
Masee, James	Minigs, William	Morphew, James
Minigs, John	Mitchell, John	McNitt, John
McGano, James	Ozias, Jacob	Payton, John
Phillips, William	Worl, Joseph	Shoemaker, Christian
Small, James	Shetler, Jacob	Sidfen, Andrew
Smith, Samuel	Singer, Joseph	Shanks, Jacob
Sanders, Robert	Sutton, James	Sprowl, Robert
Stephens, David	Stone, Andrew	Strader, George
Swaney, James	Ramsey, Nathan	Riley, John
Thompson, George	Utt, John	Wolf, John
Woodward, Asahel	Woodward, Eli	Wright, William
	Wright, Levin	

Page 256

ROLL OF CAPT. ZECHARIAH FERGUSON'S COMPANY
(Probably from Green County).

Served from September 23, until October 30, 1812.

Capt. Zechariah Ferguson	Lieut. Peter Borden	Ensign, James Popenoe
Sergt. Samuel D. Kirkpatrick	Sergt. Andrew Hawker	Sergt. Isaac Morgan
Sergt. George Hittle	Corp. Peter Hoy	Corp. Jacob Cosler
Corp. Abraham Cosler	Corp. Samuel Bowen	

Privates.	Privates.	Privates.
Anderson, Seth	Ashby, Lawrence	Borders, George
Birely, William	Coy, Jacob	Coy, Adam
Cyphers, John	Davis, David	Engle, Isaac
Freeman, William	Gott, John	Givens, James
Gibson, Robert	Hill, James	Hames, Jacob
John, James	John, Joseph	Judy, John
John, Lemuel	Kiser, John	Kingerly, Martin
Key, George	Morgan, Joshua	Manning, Benjamin
Maxwell, William	Noble, Joshua	Owens, Thomas
McClure, William	Palmer, Joseph	Poag, William
Powell, Joseph	Russell, Adam	Swigerd, John
Rose, William	Steele, David D.	Shoe Phillip
Solinger, Adam	Tucker, John	
	Vance, Daniel	

Page 256.

ROLL OF CAPT. JOHN S. WALLACE'S COMPANY
(Probably from Hamilton Co.)

Served from August 23, until September 4, 1812.

Capt. John S. Wallace	Lieut. William Stanley	Ensign, George G. Terrence
Sergt. Joseph B. Robinson	Sergt. John Humes	Sergt. John Hilton
	Sergt. William Berry	

Privates.	Privates.	Privates.
Barker, Thomas	Biger, John	Bowl, Robert, Jr.
Boal, James	Blanchard, William	Bird, Richard
Bruin, Isaac	Clark, John	Cary, Chris
Chase, L. Homadine	Carr, Francis	Davison, Thomas
Eson, Alexander	Finice, John	Greenlie, Will
Gibson, John	Garner, Alexander	Gard, Seth
Horne, David	Horne, Ebenezer	Hall, Stephen
Henderson, Thomas	Hogan, Niles	Hardy, Richard
Irwin, William	Jessup, John	Kemper, Stephen
Karr, Robert	Levensworth, Seth M.	Lining, John
Layre, Samuel I.	Leward, Jacob	Meek, Edward
Malson, John	Pierce, Eli	Pancoast, Jonothan
Rodgers, William	Rogers, Samuel	Stone, Ethan
Sayre, Leonard	Snider, David	Sears, Benjamin
Stites, Thomas	Thompson, Thomas	Van Benkton, Daniel
Wilson, James	Woodworth, Daniel	Watson, John

Page 258.
ROLL OF CAPT. PETER BACUS' COMPANY (Probably from Scioto County).
Served from July 28, until August 28, 1813.

Rank and Name of Soldier.	Rank and Name of Soldier.	Rank and Name of Soldier.
Capt. Peter Bacus	Lieut. Peris Thompson	Ensign, John Thompson
Sergt. John Cutright	Sergt. Jonothan B. Hand	Sergt. Henry Sumner
Corp. David Stumbough	Drummer, William Burt	
Privates.	**Privates.**	**Privates.**
Abbott, Jeremiah	Abbott, Eben	Bell, Benjamin
Bowin, William	Blithe, Thomas	DeWitt, W.
Furst, Francis	Fulson, Samuel	Fetzer, John
Gillilan, William	Humbough, Adam	Hall, John
Kindall, Booton	Kimbol, William	Louis, William
Link, Jacob	Malone, Richard	Miller, Abraham
Osborn, William	Proebster, I. Adam	Powell, William
Stewart, George	Woolf, Andrew	

Pages 259 260.
ROLL OF CAPT. ANDREW HEMPHILL'S COMPANY (County Unknown).
Served from July 28, until September 5, 1813.

Capt. Andrew Hemphill	Lieut. James McConnel	Ensign, Jacob Hare
Sergt. James Latta	Lieut. Aaron Foster	Ensign, Gutham Anderson
Sergt. George McCann	Sergt. Robert Hurley	Sergt. Conrad Vanderman
Sergt. Merit Jameson	Corp. William Brown	Corp. John Baird
Corp. Jacob Caylor	Corp. Jacob Hire	Corp. Joshua Smithson
	Drummer, Moses McKensie	
Privates.	**Privates.**	**Privates.**
Andrews, Gibson	Anderson, Samuel	Clark, James
Fisher, John	Fruet, Gilly	Goldsberry, Jonothan
Gossom, William	Gossard, Jacob	Grubb, Daniel
Harris, Amos	Hire, Daniel	Hire, George
Hoskins, John	Johnston, William	James, William
Killough, William	Kerr, George	Lease, John
Kor, Christian	Michie, Mathew	Mitchell, Frederick
Myers, John	Near, James	Newlain, Jacob
McCracken, Isaac	Rambo, Michael	Powell, Emery
Roads, George	Spikes, Francis	Streebey, Peter
Platt, Henry	Shanor, Henry	Turner, James B.
Shoemaker, David	Vanderman, Henry	Vanderman, Mathias
Turnipseed, Christian	Williams, Calvin	

Pages 261-262.
ROLL OF CAPT. ISAAC PANCAKE'S COMPANY (Probably from Ross County).
Served from July 28, until September 5, 1813.

Capt. Isaac Pancake	Ensign, Arthur McCarty	Sergt. William Staggs
Sergt. John Down	Sergt. Richard V. Hoddy	Corp. James Corey
Corp. George Seavers	Corp. John Clossen	Musician, Samuel Mark
	Musician, Amsted Carson	
Privates.	**Privates.**	**Privates.**
Adams, John	Brown, Edward	Brittenham, Aaron
Brittenham, Mathias	Brown, Phillip	Chamberlain, Jacob
Chamberlain, William	Cochran, James	Fields, William
Goldsberry, Thomas	Haggert, Daniel	Henderson, Daniel
Gimmons, Amos	Jones, Amos	Long, George
Lowery, Solomon	Mahone, Joshua	McCarty, James
McQua, James	Parish, John	Parish, William
Parish, James	Porter, Henry	Porter, William
Roseboom, Abraham	Stothard, Septimus	Stumbe, Adam
Timmons, George	Templain, John	

Page 266.
ROLL OF CAPT. BENJAMIN GOLDSBERRY'S COMPANY (County Unknown).
Served from July 28, until August 15, 1813.

Capt. Benjamin Goldsberry	Ensign, Henry Hester	Sergt. John Ireland
Sergt. Cornelius Johnston	Sergt. Michael Summerman	Corp. Francis Tully
Corp. John Hamilton	Corp. William Bell	Corp. Joshua Smithson
	Fifer, Samuel Edwards	
Privates.	**Privates.**	**Privates.**
Cunningham, Samuel	Davis, William	Devorse, Joseph
Denfinger, Cornelius	Essex, Jesse	Gipson, Andrew
Gradless, William	Jamison, Samuel	Jameson, Ment
Leigore, Joseph	Pick, William	Pereu, William
Stookey, Abraham	Vanderman, Conrad	Wilson, Stephen

Page 278. Vol. I.

ROLL OF CAPT. NATHANIEL BEASLEY'S COMPANY (County Unknown).
Served from August 22, until October 22, 1812.

Rank and Name of Soldier.	Rank and Name of Soldier.	Rank and Name of Soldier.
Capt. Nathaniel Beasley	Lieut. William Russell	Ensign, Abraham Colven
Sergt. William Marsh	Sergt. Thomas Wright	Sergt. George Harrison
Sergt. Elijah Redmon	Corp. Andrew Davidson	Corp. Joseph Brownfield
Corp. Benjamin Griffith	Corp. John Reed	Fifer, George Ramsey

Privates.

Boatman, John	Boggess, William	Brooks, Adolphus
Cline, Daniel	Compton, John	Chambers, Elijah
Cole, Lewis	Criswell, David	Clark, Samuel
Duffey, William	Evans, Samuel	Evans, Thomas
Haynes, William	Killen, James	Lane, James
Munay, Joseph	Moore, John	Murphy, John
McKittrick, James	Osler, Charles	Peterson, Thomas
Pollard, Robert	Roads, Israel	Roads, Thomas
Stout, John	Sullivan, John	Storay, John
Shevalier, William	Sargent, James	Sroph, John
Smith, Walter	Smith, John	Shirely, Timothy
Stephenson, Ralph	Swisher, John	Thompson, John
Trotter, Elijah, C.	Woods, Tobias	Wilson, Gustavus

Pages 263-264-265.

ROLL OF CAPT. JOSEPH ROCKHOLD'S COMPANY (Probably from Ross Co.)
Served from July 28, until September 5, 1813.

Capt. Joseph Rockhold	Lieut. Abraham Pebble	Lieut. Joseph O'Brian
Ensign, Amaziah Morgan	Ensign, Joseph Heistand	Sergt. James Mahan
Sergt. Levi Wells	Sergt. Isaac Rockhold	Sergt. John Barton
Sergt. John Hendershot	Sergt. Iadeth Tully	Corp. Samuel Logan
Corp. Adam Gilfillen	Corp. Charles O'Brian	Corp. Benjamin Bromley

Privates.

Brakeman, William	Beekman, Abraham	Briant, Elijah
Briant, Peter	Beekman, Aaron	Blackstone, John
Black, Abraham	Benona, Christian	Bonner, Henry
Clay, William	Cochran, David	Chafford, Solomon
Cameron, Alexander	Demoss, James	Dunlap, Robert
Ewing, Samuel	Elliott, Burgiss	Eubanks, Mathew
Eubanks, David	Beekman, Christopher	Freshour, Daniel
Freshour, Abraham	Foster, Lawrence	Grove, Frederick
Goodman, James	Gant, Jacob	Hartley, John
Hartley, Obijah	Johnston, John	Gray, John
Layton, Asher	Lowman, Joseph	Layton, Elias
Mason, Samuel	Minna, Bonna	Marquis, Isaac
Merrman, Enoch	McDonald, John	Nicely, Henry
Nevan, Alexander	Ogle, Joseph	Pendrill, Gabriel
Patterson, John	Price, Robert	Pherron, Phillip
Rowley, Alpheus	Roberts, Asa	Reeves, John D.
Stockton, William	Stockton, Thomas	Sleter, Jeremiah
Slater, James	Shepley, Peter	Scartler, Alexander
Cowden, Samuel	Straton, Charles	Senter, George
Thompson, Joseph	Wheaton, Humphrey	Wyckoff, Isaac
Williams, Robert	Williamson, Charles	

Page 267.

ROLL OF CAPT. CLAYTON WEBB'S COMPANY
(Probably from Hamilton County).
Served from August 24, until September 20, 1812.

Capt. Clayton Webb	Lieut. John Armstrong	Ensign, Nathan Hatfield
Sergt. James Jones	Sergt. Peter Bell	Sergt. David Kelley
Sergt. James Armstrong	Corp. William Landen	Corp. Stephen Cobley

Privates.

Askron, Thomas	Burrows, Joseph	Black, Peter
Black, David	Burdsall, Josiah	Crichfield, Phillip
Clark, Ichabod	Cross, Ignatius	Crosson, Benjamin
Christ, George	Davis, William	Earhart, Samuel
Ferris, John	Gordon, James	Greenwood, Will
Huff, John	Hawkins, Reson	Hawkins, Richard
Hosbrook, Archibald	Johnson, Charles	Jenkins, Henry
Jones, John T.	Knopper, Jacob	Lee, Louis H.
Miller, Jacob J.	Keely, John	Martin, John
Mawhinny, James	Martin, William	Mack, Erastus
Moln, John	Mail, George	Nicely, Abraham
Orr, Andrew	Parker, Jacob	Robinson, Edward
Riggs, Henry	Welch, Robert	Schillinger, William

Page 279. Vol. I.

ROLL OF LIEUT. JOHN McARTHUR'S COMPANY (Probably from Ross Co.)
Served from July 28, until August 27, 1813.

Lieut. John McArthur
Sergt. James Riley
Corp. Robert Miler

Sergt. John Sample
Corp. James Dean
Corp. Joseph Morton

Sergt. James Larkins
Corp. Ezra Lucas

Privates.

Blane, Thomas
Blain, James
Caldwell, James
DeVoss, Isaac
Logan, John
Milligan, Hugh

Brackney, Benjamin
Cannon, Handy
Cassel, John
Kelley, Mathew
Morton, John
McClure, William
Young, Silas

Burkley, John
Cunningham, Adam
Clark, Daniel
Kerr, Adam
Morrow, Richard
McCracken, Alexander

Pages 275-276.
ROLL OF JACOB YOUNG'S COMPANY (From Knox and Richland Counties.)
Served from August 26, until October 31, 1812.

Capt. Jacob Young
Ensign, John Parcel
Sergt. Ziba Jackson
Sergt. Peter Wolf
Sergt. Henry George
Corp. James Johnston
Corp. Noah Young

Lieut. George Sapp
Ensign, Amos H. Royer
Sergt. Jesse Inlow
Sergt. John Logan
Corp. William Evans
Corp. Peter Johnston
Drummer, John Halderman

Lieut. Insly Johnston
Ensign, Daniel Ayres
Sergt. Andrew Kirkpatric
Sergt. Joseph Denman
Corp. William Tucker
Corp. Daniel Conger
Fifer, Mathew Merrit

Privates.

Austin, David
Brown, Benjamin
Bal' Hiram
Beers, Jabez
Davis, Azaniah, Jr.
Denman, Uriah
Dickson, Miron
Herrod, William
Huffmire, William
Irwin, James
Knight, William
Lyon, Benjamin
Mirick, Higgins
Melick, David
Ostin, James
Robinson, William
Slater, John
Strong, Truman
Talmage, Joseph
Williams, Thomas

Austin, James
Barcus, James
Bue, Samuel
Cremer, John
Day, Josiah D
Davis, David
Fitting, Castar
Harris, Elijah
George, Richard
Johnston, Samuel
Lepley, George
Lyon, Absalom
Morrison, John
McCreary, James
Ogden, James
Rush, Peter
Shaw, David
Shur, Jacob
Thomas, William
Woodruff, Stephen
Walker, John

Arbuckle, Samuel
Bryan, Eliab
Brown, John, Jr.
Conger, Thomas
Dalrymple, Israel
Drake, William
Herrod, John
Holt, James
Inlow, Isaac
Kimbel, Daniel
Lewis, Samuel
Lindley, John P.
Mitchell, Nathaniel
Nuffmore, Wilson
Pierce, George
Spurgeon, James
Sams, Andrew
Peoples, David
Welker, Solomon
Walker, Alexander

Pages 285-286.
ROLL OF CAPT. STEPHEN HORSEY'S COMPANY.
(Probably from Pickaway County.)
Served from July 28,, until August 26, 1813.

Capt. Stephen Horsey
Sergt. John Pancake

Lieut. James Nevill
Sergt. Balitha Linch
Sergt. Pierce Atchison

Ensign, Cornelius Mikel
Sergt. Daniel Justice

Privates.

Atchison, Fielding
Campbell, Robert
Diver, James
Foresman, Henry
Hubbard, John
Henderson, James
Johnson, Richard
Leonard, Charles
Moore, Fergus
Randle, Tibble
Rively, Daniel
Seabourn, Doress
Van Waggoner, John
Wanaughmaker, Phillip

Beavins, Josiah
Chipman, John
Dumond, Isaac
Flemming, John
Henderson, David
Henderson, John
Knight, Enos
Lacount, Charles
McGroos, Isaac
Romine, Abraham
Smith, Henry
Shuff, Frederick
Van Horn, Walter
Whitsell, Daniel

Benedict, James
Dodd, Isaac
Devenport, Wesley
Galbraith, John
Horsey, Edward
Hanaman, George
King, William
Moore, James
Nicholas Christian
Ridman, James
Sullivan, Aaron
Shephard, William
Waples, Derixson

Pages 280-281-282-283-284.
ROLL OF CAPTAIN WILLIAM MUNN'S COMPANY (County Unknown).
Served from July 28, until August 28, 1813, and from February 16, until March 16, 1814.

Capt. William Munn
Ensign, Abraham Stewart
Sergt. Richard Johnson
Sergt. William G. Robinson
Sergt. John Cannon
Corp. Jesse Martin
Corp. William Holland
Fifer, Elijah Jacobs

Lieut. Joseph Kelley
Ensign, John Clemens
Sergt. John Ruke
Sergt. James Gilbruth
Corp. Samuel Crull
Corp. Henry Crull
Corp. Yoel Church

Lieut. Tapley White
Sergt. Thomas Phillips
Sergt. John Bennet
Sergt. Briar Griffin
Corp. John Bennet
Corp. Eli Rogan
Drummer, Charles Bennet

ROLL OF CAPT. WILLIAM MUNN'S COMPANY (Continued).

Privates.

Anderson, Jacob
Barret, Elijah
Buck, James
Crookham, George L.
Cline, George
Dener, John
Dawson, Othe
Farney, John
Graham, John
Gillilan, Hugh
Gilmore, William
Gunies, James
Hadley, George
Hubbell, Rowland
Graham, Joseph
Lewis, Abraham
Munroe, Charles
Monroe, Solomon
Mounts, Enoch
McKenney, William
Perry, Isaac
Runkle, George
Star, John
Shane, Daniel
Sherlock, John
Satherland, John
Utt, Adam
Waggoner, James

Anderson, Mark
Brewer, James
Bowser, Adam
Cox, William
Cartmell, Samuel
Duncan, John
Davis, Nathaniel
Fry, Joseph
Goodin, Daniel
Gunies, John
Gibson, John
Hill, John
Hollingshead, William
Johnson, James
Kuby, Nathan
Linton, William
Monroe, Barnabas
Martin, Hugh
Miller, William
McKenney, Theadore
Pemil, Enoch
Reynolds, James
Sierot, John
Seberell, Nicholas
Strange, William
Timmonds, John
Utt, Jacob
Walker, John
Wilson, Alexander

Alkin, John
Bonner, Abraham
Copias, John
Cross, Robert
Calhoun, William
Craig, Thomas
Fleming, Andrew
Finley, James
Grubb, Joseph
Gilmore, Robert
Glisten, James
Haddox, William
Howard, Lewis
Jones, William
Kennedy, Robert
Linch, Samuel
Martin, John
Mercer, Levi
Morrison, Robert
Nelson, Jonothan R.
Radcliffe, Daniel
Sappington, Thomas
Stigalls, Frederick
Satterly, Isaac
Stewart, Jeremiah
Thomas, Jacob
Walker, John D.
Wells, Absalom

Pages 287-288.

ROLL OF CAPT. HENRY SLACK'S COMPANY (Probably from Delaware Co.)

Served from August 24, until September 25, 1812. Part served from July 26, until August 13, 1813.

Capt. Henry Slack
Sergt. Gilbert Carpenter
Corp. Daniel Alden
Corp. Henry Love
Corp. Sylvester Drake

Lieut. Gilbert Weeks
Sergt. Mathew Marvin
Corp. Benjamin Shoemaker
Corp. Robert Carpenter
Fifer, Mathias Vanloon

Lieut. Benjamin Carpenter
Sergt. Alexander Smith
Corp. Leonard Jones
Corp. James Carpenter

Privates.

Anway, George
Budd, John
Bonnet, Isaac
Day, Charles
Gregory, David
Hess, George
Heath, Samuel
Jones, David
Landon, David
Leonard, Samuel
Morehous, Philemon
Perfect, Truman
Phipps, William
Slack, John
Scoby, John
Shoemaker, Benjamin
Williams, William

Armstrong, David
Brown, John
Carpenter, Moses
Fairchild, Benjamin
Harris, Samuel
Hills, Louis
Jones, Richard
Keys, Isaac
Lewis, John
Longwell, Ralph
Munson, Mishael
Perfect, Thomas
Rosecrans, John
Skeels, Jonothan
Steward, Solomon
Patrick, Joseph
Young, John

Bishop, Daniel
Barr, Alva
Closson, Jacob
Ford, Augustus
Harper, James
Helt, Michael
Johns, Francis C.
Kepler, Samuel
Lane, Daniel
Manvill, George
Osterhout, Gideon
Phipps, John
Ross, John
Smith, William
Studevant, George
Waters, Nehemiah
Young, Andrew

Page 289.

ROLL OF CAPT. JAMES NISBET'S COMPANY (County Unknown.)

Served from April 28, until August 12, 1812.

Capt. James Nisbet
Sergt. Daniel Kenselo
Sergt. Isaac Harral
Corp. Peter Shidler

Lieut. Joseph Lower
Sergt. James W. Maxwell
Corp. Frederick Utt
Corp. Willis Copland
Fifer, William D. Williams

Ensign Henry Johnston
Sergt. Bestly M. Burris
Corp. James Taylor
Drummer, Jacob Parker

Privates.

Allen, John
Beard, Paul
Banfield, Thomas
Caster, William
Davis, Silas
Gard, Levi
Howard, Thomas
Kircheval, Samuel
Larsh, Paul
Michael, Frederick
McDowell, James

Aldred, Isaac
Bell, John
Bishop, William
Case, Samuel
Demoss, Charles
Gamble, Robert
Harton, Isaac
Kircheval, John
Lease, Daniel
McDaniel, John
Nelson, William

Ashby, Abraham
Butt, Phillip
Clap, Tobias
Dooley, Abner
Flemming, Mitchel
Grisom, George
Hendricks, William
Krieger, Jacob
Moore, Jesse
McKnutt, Alexander
Purviance, David P.

ROLL OF CAPT. JAMES NISBET'S COMPANY (Continued).

Rank and Name of Soldier.	Rank and Name of Soldier.	Rank and Name of Soldier.
Privates.	Privates.	Privates.
Penlan, Alexander	Pierce, Eros	Reed, Adam
Russel, Charles	Snider, Baltzer	Smith, Charles
Stephens, David	Sprowl, Robert	Shannon, James
Van Aarsdal, Peter	Vanwickle, Daniel	West, Jeptha
	Winich, Daniel	

Page 290.
ROLL OF CAPT. HUGH FLINN'S COMPANY (County Unknown).

Served from July 28, until August 13, 1813.

Capt. Hugh Flinn	Sergt. William Hackney	Sergt. John Perril
Sergt. James Wheaton	Corp. Henry Carter	Corp. Edwin H. Smith
Corp. Jacob Chenewith	Corp. Robert Montgomery	Musician, Richard Chenewith
	Musician, Uriah Chenewith	
Privates.	Privates.	Privates.
Chenewith, Isaac	Chenewith, John	Chenewith, Elijah
Chenewith, Abraham	Carter, Thomas	Chenewith, Joseph
Burk, Michael	Davis, John F.	Howard, Cornelius
Keen, James	Moore, William	Montgomery, John
Sewell, David	Tucker, Levi	Thomburgh, William
Travis, Asa	Wiley, Thomas	

Page 291.
ROLL OF LIEUT. MARTIN NUNKEEPAR'S COMPANY.
(Probably from Ross County.)

Served from July 29, until August 7, 1813.

Lieut. Martin Nunkeepar	Ensign John O'Neal	Sergt. Joseph Fermon
Sergt. Joshua Hall	Sergt. Zedekiah Dawson	Corp. Joseph Porter
Corp. Moses Wiggins	Drummer, Joseph Polem	
Privates.	Privates.	Privates.
Abanatha, John	Bensher, Jacob	Cremeon, John
Evet, John	Frye, Henry	Godfrey, Lewis
Hall, James	Hartman, Philip	Halderman, David
Larrick, Isaac	Ramy, Presley	Stanley, Thomas
Worley, Daniel	Williams, Enoch	

Pages 292-293.
ROLL OF CAPT. ISAAC DAWSON'S COMPANY (Probably from Ross Cunty).

Served from August 22, until September 24, 1812, and from May 6, until May 18, 1813.

Capt. Isaac Dawson	Lieut. John Perkins	Lieut. John McCollough
Ensign, John McCoy	Ensign, John Caldwell	Sergt. Mathias Enge
Sergt. James McCoy	Sergt. John Rodgers	Sergt. Oratio Walker
Sergt. James Bunn	Sergt. John Vanmeter	
Privates.	Privates.	Privates.
Armstrong, Thomas	Burnes, John	Cochran, James
Cochran, John	Corbett, David	Collins, Samuel
Corbett, Joseph	Clarridge, Edmon	Crouch, James
Dunn, Peter	Dyer, William	Dawns, James
Eschine, Daniel	Fisher, John	Gibson, John
Goodin, John	Guthrie, William	Green, Charles
Hicks, Willis	Hinton, Thomas	Hanes, Peter
Justice, John	Kerr, William	Kerr, John
Lee, Parker	Loveless, Joseph	Moreland, William
Massie, Thomas	Mace, John	Morris, Jeremiah
Mullin, Joseph	Mounts, Humphrey	McCafferty, David
McMahon, Robert	Niece, George	Ogden, John
Perkins, John	Perkins, John Sr.	Phillips, William Jr.
Parish, Meredith	Potts, Nathan	Purtee, James
Enger, Mathias	Rodgers, Benjamin	Rogers, Mathew
Sommers, William	Stockton, George	Stockton, William
Smith, John	Stone, Daniel	Seath, William
Timmons, John	Thweeks, Elijah	Timmons, George
Thimons, Edmon	Will, George	Will, David
Will, David, Sr.	Williams, Isaac	Walker, Thomas

Page 294.
CAPT. JAMES DAVIS' COMPANY (Probably from Ross County).

Served from July 30, until August 30, 1813.

Capt. James Davis	Ensign, Abraham Stewart	Sergt. Curtis Berry
Sergt. Prior Griffith	Corp. Eli Ragoon	Corp. Richard Heath
Privates.	Privates.	Privates.
Clark, Daniel	Clark, James	Cordrey, Shepherd
Goodwin, John	Heath, Amos	Hibben, Samuel
James, John	Luzador, Thomas	Miller, Warrick
Mathews, Isaac	Murphy, Andray	Martin, William
McMullen, John	Longshow, James	Summers, William
Scott, Peter	Tenebaugh, Jacob	Wilson, Caleb

Pages 295-296. Vol. I.

ROLL OF CAPT. DANIEL MUSSELMAN'S COMPANY
(Probably from Ross County).

Served from July 27, until August 18, 1813.

Rank and Name of Soldier.	Rank and Name of Soldier.	Rank and Name of Soldier.
Capt. Daniel Musselman	Lieut. Christopher Bickle	Ensign, Jacob Whitzel
Sergt. Valentine Engle	Sergt. Michael Heater	Sergt. Adam Bowhan
Sergt. Mensil Ellis	Corp. Jonas Marble	Corp. Robert Caldwell
Corp. Abraham Davis	Corp. John Wilson	

Privates.

Brink, Robert	Coon, Jacob	Chambers, John
Claypool, Isaac	Clayton, William	Engler, Jacob
Fink, Henry	Ferron, Daniel	Glover, William
Goodman, John	Hammersley, George	Hivley, Jacob
Holarstat, Jacob	Ingam, Isaiah	Johnson, George
Jones, Moses	Migers, Mathias	Myres, Abraham
Markle, John	Myers, Jacob	Mosey, Jacob
McKin, John	Nayhart, Peter	Piper, Phillip
Sipes, Mathias	Smith, Thomas	Shaw, Samuel
Tittle, Jacob	Whitsel, Samuel	Wiley, John
	Wright, Thomas	

Page 297.

ROLL OF CAPT. ARCHIBALD STEWART'S COMPANY (County Unknown).

Served from March 26, until April 26, 1813.

Capt. Archibald Stewart	Lieut. William Williams	Sergt. Daniel Downs
Sergt. William Stewart	Sergt. Alexander Numan	Sergt. Jeremiah Bowen
Corp. Samuel Morecraft	Corp. Isaac Hughes	Fifer, Hamilton Rogers

Privates.

Binley, James	Burton, Thomas	Brown, David
Boyd, George	Bousman, Nichodemus	Claypool, James
Davis, John	Fitzpatrick, Daniel	Gratridge, Joseph
Lee, Benjamin	Mason, Mathew	Norton, David
Martin, Archer	Norton, Giles	Mason, Isaac
Stephens, Robert	Stewart, Thomas	Spencer, Beverly
Tharp, Levi	Tharp, William	Tharp, Abner
Thomas, Joel	Taylor, William	Reed, John
Rutledge, William	Williams, Henry	Williams, James
	Walters, Levi	

Page 298.

ROLL OF CAPT. ABNER BARRETT'S COMPANY
(Probably from Champaign County).

Served from August 9, until September 9, 1813.

Capt. Abner Barrett	Lieut. Edward Jones	Sergt. John Kelley
Sergt. James Guthridge	Sergt. Jacob Hazel	Sergt. Allen Minturn
Corp. John B. Neal	Corp. Obediah Valentine	Corp. William Kelley
	Corp. Jesse Gutridge	

Privates.

Adams, John	Baker, Aaron	Bracken, Nathan
Britten, Evans E.	Beatty, Miles C.	Britten, Nathan
Binley, James	Chaney, Edward	Chaney, William
Cartmell, John	George, Richard D.	Cory, John
Crage, John	Burnside, William	Frankeberger, John
Gilpin, Elias	Cartmell, William	George, William M.
Hudson, Edward	Harbert, William	Hutson, Abraham
Hendrix, William	Hutsin, James	Hoover, Peter
Hail, Bradford	Jones, Daniel	Lafferty, John
Kain, John	Minturn, George	Jones, Justice
Long, David D.	Kelley, Gilbert	Minturn, Bunnel
Mathews, James	Neally, Mathew	Oppy, Abraham
Runyon, John	Piper, John	Price, William
Pierce, Andrew	Reese, Maurice	Rathburn, John
Runyon, John Jr.	Sitzer, Henry	Sayre, Thomas
Tucker, Isaac	Thompson, John	Thompson, Joshua
Tucker, Samuel	Rees, Jacob	Valentine, David
Vanse, Solomon	Ward, Obed	

Pages 299-300.

ROLL OF CAPT. ENOCH GEST'S COMPANY (County Unknown).

Served from February 17, until March 17, 1813.

Capt. Enoch Gest	Lieut. Elijah Stout	Ensign, Richard Phillips
Sergt. James Moon	Sergt. James Winters	Sergt. Benjamin B. Cox
Sergt. Joseph Vanhat	Corp. Samuel Robertson	Corp. Jacob Jones
Corp. Joseph Ferris	Corp. Robert Bennet	

Vol. 2.
ROLL OF CAPT. ENOCH GEST'S COMPANY (Continued).

Rank and Name of Soldier.   Rank and Name of Soldier.   Rank and Name of Soldier.

Privates.

Andrews, James
Burk, Elisha
Clark, Mathew
Compton, Abraham
Creglon, Christian
Davis, Thomas
Fridley, John
Gwrin, Silas
Gray, Martin
Harper, Mathew
Johnson, William
Kimble, Henry
Job, Archibald R.
Leonard, Cory
Moorehead, William
McGunnegle, John
Roney, James
Smith, Jacob
Simpson, Alexander
Tarrens, Samuel
Wing, Ebenezer
Wolverton, Daniel
Wing, Silas

Privates.

Allison, Alexander
Boyer, William
Croyes, William
Cameron, William R.
Coplon, Willis
Dennis, Benjamin
Ferguson, James
Guerin, Elias R.
Huston, Joseph
Howard, Abner
Jones, Jonothan
Jackson, John
Lilly, John
Meeker, David
Northan, Walter B.
Ross, John
Shoman, Jacob
Tumbleson, John
Tucker, Ephraim
Watson, John
Wilkinson, John L.
Wheeler, Thaddeus
Johnson, William

Privates.

Burrel, John
Connet, Henry
Campbell, Andrew
Carson, David
Coleman, Thomas B.
Earley, John
Ford, Elijah
Gorman, Hugh
Hill, James M.
Irwin, John
Jessup, Isaac
Kibby, Ephraim
Meeker, John
McGee, William W.
Nichols, Leicester
Riggle, Benjamin
Shots, John
Tousley, Amos
Vaneaton, Levi
Winters, John
Wade, John
Probus, Henry
Johnson Eleazar

Page 301.

ROLL OF CAPT. SAMUEL McCORMICK'S COMPANY
(Probably from Hamilton County).

Served from September 1, until September 30, 1813.

Capt. Samuel McCormick
Sergt. William G. Serviss
Sergt. Abner Garard
Corp. Calvin Ward

Lieut. John Hopkins
Sergt. Owen Todd
Corp. John Farquer
Corp. David Ayers

Ensign, John Knox
Sergt. William Dixon
Corp. Ephraim Munthan

Privates.

Baldwin, Thomas
Biddle, Solomon
Conner, Luke
Campbell, James
Eastwood, Benjamin
Fitzwater, Thomas
Hopkins, John
Hopkins, John Sr.
Johnson, John M.
Miller, William
McCollum, Thomas
Riley, Ely
Shaw, Daniel
Smith, James
Smith, Jacob
Ward, Luther
Watson, William

Privates.

Burroughs, James
Cawer, William
Cunningham, Richard
Bostwick, Clement
Flinn, William Jr.
Fordeck, Christopher
Hudson, Shadrach
Hurley, Joel
Marsh, Isaac
Mounts, Providence
McCollister, Michael
Ramsey, George
Stewart, William
Sunderland, Die
Todd, Paxton
Ward, Ashbel
Westfall, William

Privates.

Bush, Jacob
Cook, Thomas
Chambers, James N.
Depriest, Charles
Flinn, William Sr.
Havens, William
Havens, Benjamin
Gordon, John
Marsh, Joseph
McKinney, Anthony
McCollister, Frederick
Reeder, Benjamin
Shaw, Isaiah
Smith, Thomas
Vanscoyke, Joseph
Watson, Isaac
Wood, Robert

Page 305.

ROLL OF CAPT. WILLIAM LINDSEY'S COMPANY
(Probably from Hamilton County).

Served from August 25, until September 25, 1812.

Capt. William Lindsey
Sergt. James Robb
Sergt. Isaac Ferguson
Corp. Timothy Riddler

Lieut. John Shaw
Sergt. George Rinker
Corp. Elijah Lindsey
Corp. Isaac Ford

Ensign Isaiah Ferguson
Sergt. John Beltt
Corp. Robert Donham

Privates.

Beezley, William
Donham, Amos
Ferguson, Hugh
Gray, Andrew
Morris, Joseph
Rinker, George
Welsh, Thomas
White, David

Privates.

Brown, Joshua
Donham, Abel
Gray, John
Moring, Redham
McCord, Richard
Rardin, Jacob
Wood, James

Privates.

Conner, Timothy
Fitzpatrick, James
Gray, Neeley
Morris, Benjamin
Rardin, Timothy
Snyder, John
Williams, Samuel

Pages 302-303-304. Vol. I.

ROLL OF CAPT. ROBERT McCLELLAND'S COMPANY
(Probably from Greene County).
Served from August 22, until September 22, 1812, and from May 25, until November 24, 1813.

Rank and Name of Soldier.	Rank and Name of Soldier.	Rank and Name of Soldier.
Capt. Robert McClelland	Lieut. James McBride	Lieut. Elisha Leslie
Ensign David Douglas	Ensign William Erwin	Sergt. Samuel Snodgrass
Sergt. Isaac Miller	Sergt. Jacob Hozier	Sergt. John McDaniel
Sergt. John Barnes	Corp. Samuel Lawrence	Corp. Henry Webb
Corp. William Sutton	Corp. John Alexander	Corp. John Hacker
Corp. Jacob Beals	Corp. William Constant	Corp. Adam Wolf
Fifer, Robert Snodgrass	Musician, William Harrison	Musician, Daniel DeWitt

Privates.	Privates.	Privates.
Alexander, Francis	Allen, William	Burney, Thomas
Benitt, James	Bias, Isaac	Bowen, Ephraim
Benham, John	Benjamin, Thomas	Benjamin, Lewis
Buchanon, James	Babcock, Thomas	Collier, Moses
Campbell, William	Currie, Robert	Cain, Samuel
Cain, Joseph	Casebolt, Robert	Concleton, David
Cruson, Cornelius	Cox, Israel	Cunningham, John
Cottrell, John	Dean, Robert	Dickensheets, William
Devore, John	Douglas, James	Downey, William
DeWitt, Isaac	Eatton, Joseph	Edge, George D.
Fallows, Isaac	Follist, John	Griffy, Daniel
Gott, John	Griffith, Benjamin	Glenn, William
Hamilton, William	Holmes, John	Hufford, John
Hoop, John	Hibbs, Abner	Hutchison, George
Huse, John	Haddox, Nimrod	Jones, Benjamin
Junkins, James	Johnson, William	Knight, William
Kune, Hugh	Knight, Samuel	Laird, Benjamin
Kendall, William	Mitchell, James	Miller, William Poog
Martin, Samuel	Murphy, John	Moore, William C.
Moreland, John	Meninghall, William	Mitchell, Jesse
Murphy, John	McFarlin, John	McKaig, Benjamin
McCoy, John	McDaniel, Demesy	Neely, James
Nimerick, John	Noble, Joshua	Page, James
Perry, Allen	Poage, William	Rich, Jacob
Paige, William	Russell, Moses	Reagon, Reason
Reed, William	Snodgrass, William	Snodgrass, James
Sutton, William G.	Sparks, Thomas	Smith, Thomas
Saunders, Aaron	Sheley, Benjamin	Shelinger, George
Smith, John	Smith, Spencer	Snodgrass, Robert
Smith, William	Shoe, Phillip	Todd, John B.
Vance, James	Vaughn, William	Vaneaten, John
Vaughn, Thomas	Vance, John	Vance, Joseph C.
Whicker, John	Wilson, Joseph	Wilson, David
Watson, James	Wolff, Jacob	White, William
	Weaver, Christian	

Page 306.
ROLL OF LIEUT. GARNER BOBO'S COMPANY (Probably from Miami Co.)
Served from September 26, 1812, until March 26, 1813.

Lieut. Garner Bobo	Sergt. Jonothan Couch	Corp. David Knight
	Corp. Thomas Green	

Privates.	Privates.	Privates.
Adams, Joseph	Ballinger, James	Bedle, Daniel
Dickson, Nicholas	Dye, Samuel	Baker, Peter
French, Ezekial	Harrison, Richard	Mann, Barnabus
Mellinger, John	Mason, Peter	McConnoughey, David
Mann, John	Redinger, Andrew	Simons, Adam
Shaver, Simon	Statler, Christopher	Stranbarger, Joseph
Vaneman, James	Woodruff, Hampton	

Page 307.
ROLL OF CAPT. EZEKIAL KIRTLEY'S COMPANY (County Unknown).
Served from May 27, until November 27, 1813.

Capt. Ezekial Kirtley	Sergt. Samuel Reed	Sergt. Sampson Coats
Corp. Barnabus Blue	Corp. Samuel Williams	

Privates.	Privates.	Privates.
Brown, William	Carson, David	Childers, John
Folkerth, William	Goble, Daniel	Goble, John
Haney, Jonas	Hudson, John	Ingle, John
Jenkins, Isachor	Lowery, Fielding	Miller, Joseph
Mendenhall, William	Moore, Samuel	Dye, John B.
Overfield, Benjamin	Price, John	Stewart, Joseph
Stockstill, Thomas	Saunders, George	Stinchcomb, David
Sharp, David	Woodbourne, Robert	

ROSTER OF OHIO SOLDIERS IN WAR OF 1812

Pages 308-309. Vol. I.

ROLL OF CAPT. HENRY ZUMALT'S COMPANY (From Hamilton County).
Served from August 22, until September 30, 1812.

Rank and Name of Soldier.	Rank and Name of Soldier.	Rank and Name of Soldier.
Capt. Henry Zumalt	Lieut. Henry Chapman	Ensign Thomas Connel
Sergt. John Ross	Sergt. William Pangburn	Sergt. Samuel Ross
Sergt. Robert Allen	Corp. Robert Davidson	Corp. William W. Daniel
Corp. Chinley Mitchell	Corp. Noah Ellis	Fifer, John Allen
Privates.	**Privates.**	**Privates.**
Archer, Johnson	Alexander, Benjamin	Blair, John
Burget, Abraham	Burget, Valentine	Brunden, Andrew
Burget, Aaron	Bingerman, Frederick	Criss, Frederick
Calvin, James	Currey, William	Durand, Nicholas
Davis, Thomas	Ellis, Abraham	Evans, Duncan
Fee, Elisha	Gibson, James	Gibson, Andrew
Grogan, James	Hill, John	Hesler, George
Hall, Charles	Gould, William	Hillman, Joseph
Hall, Edward	Hicks, Robert	Jennings, Thomas
Jolley, Samuel	Jennings, Israel	Kerchival, Daniel
King, Victor	Landson, George	Lindsey, John
Lucas, Jacob	Leming, William	Leming, Samuel
Leming, Abraham	Little, George	Moore, Andrew
Mackland, John	Minor, Ephraim	Myers, Francis
McCurdy, Robert	Parker, James	Pangburn, Lype
Preston, Daniel	Reynolds, Daniel	Rees, Abel
Ross, William	Springer, Job	Shingle, George
Sellars, Peter	Stapleton, Joseph	Smith, James
Skedman, Ralph	Shick, John	Thompson, George S.
Thompson, Samuel	Woodruff, John	Woodruff, Jacob
Woodruff, William	Woodruff, William, Jr.	Wolars, Samuel
Williams, Isaac	Wright, George	Wood, James

Page 311.

ROLL OF CAPT. WILLIAM B. JONES' COMPANY (County Unknown).
Served from September 14, until October 14, 1812.

Capt William B. Jones	Lieut. Simon Phillips	Ensign Abraham R. Caldwell
Sergt. John Elliott	Sergt. John Drybread	Sergt. William Morris
Corp. Alexander Grant	Corp. Samuel Hardin	Corp. David Bell
	Corp. Perry Orndorf	
Privates.	**Privates.**	**Privates.**
Bett, Henry	Bears, John	Barnfield, Thomas
Blackburn, William	Campbell, Samuel	Cooper, Justice
Evans, David	Howard, James	Howard, Stephen
House, Andrew	Hardin, Charles	Jones, William
Montgomery, Hugh	Montford, Aaron	Montgomery, Thomas
Montgomery, William	Montgomery, Henry	Price, Michael
Pottinger, Dennis	Pickle, Thomas	Pickett, Joseph
Ralph, Louis	Stokes, Joseph	Sallee, William
Shaw, Knowles	Sallee, Samuel	Thompson, John
	Wyne, James	

Page 312.

ROLL OF CAPT. GARVIN JOHNSTON'S COMPANY (County Unknown).
Served from August 23, until September 18, 1812.

Capt. Garvin Johnston	Lieut James Norris	Ensign Thomas Barber
Sergt James Brown	Sergt William Gillespie	Sergt. James Johnston
Sergt Jonathan Baldwin	Fifer, William Williamson	Drummer, Isaac Covenhover
Privates.	**Privates.**	**Privates.**
Brown, William	Caldwell, Joseph	Elliott, Robert
Fossett, Thomas	Gillis, John	Gillis, Reuben
Griffies, John	Harrison, Isaac	Holinshade, James
Johnston, William	Johnston, Alexander	Lowery, Abraham
Linhing, Michael	McCord, James	McCord, Robert
Phillips, Lemuel	Ratcliffe, Daniel	Russell, Findley
Ross, John	Ross, David	Trowsdale, Samuel
Williams, Lewis	Woodruff, Hempton	Ward, Daniel W.

Page 313.

ROLL OF CAPT. DANIEL KAIN'S COMPANY (County Unknown).
Served from August 24, until September 24, 1812.

Capt. Daniel Kain	Lieut Samuel Irwin	Ensign William Sloan
Sergt James Perrine	Sergt Oliver Lindsey	Sergt Rodger W. Waring
Sergt. Benjamin Tingley	Corp William South	Corp. John Boyd
	Corp G. S. Bryan	
Privates.	**Privates.**	**Privates.**
Arthurs, James	Blair, John	Blair, Robert
Beck, Levi	Beck, Samuel	Boyd, William
Cran, Davis	Cade, Thomas	Dole, Joshua

ROLL OF CAPT. DANIEL KAIN'S COMPANY (Continued.)

Rank and Name of Soldier.

Privates.

Dole, Joseph
Ellis, Benjamin
Fountain, Mathew
Fletcher, William
Gould, Jesse
Hall, John
Knott, William
Laaghlin, James
Morris, Thomas
McCollum, Hugh
Prickett, Josiah
Stephens, Jesse
Sanders, Isaac
Thornburgh, Thomas
Vanosdole, James
Williams, William

Rank and Name of Soldier.

Privates.

Danberry, Spencer
Earhart, John
Flitcher, Jesse
Foot, Thomas S.
Glaney, William
James, Isaac
Knott, Joseph
Moorehead, John
McClure, Richard
Nuber, Jacob
Reeves, John
Schroder, John F.
Snider, Adam
Townsley, William
Vanosdole, Robert
Wilson, Peter

Rank and Name of Soldier.

Privates.

Dunn, Robert
Ellison, Jackson
Foster, Israel
Frambus, Joseph
Huling, Isaac
Jinkings, Zephaniah
Leeds, Robert
Lattermore, John
McKnight, John
Osborn, John
Rust, Thomas
South, Isaac
Smith, Joseph
Shotwell, John
Wagaman, John
Wood, Vincen

Page 314.

ROLL OF CAPT. JOSEPH LUCAS' COMPANY (Probably from Green County).

Served from January 20, until March 2, 1813.

Capt. Joseph Lucas

Sergt. Isaac Garard
Corp. Abraham Lucas

Sergt. Henry Bone

Privates.

Brewin, William H.
Beales, Jacob
Downey, John
Foster, Samuel
Price, William
Shillinger, George
Thornbury, George

Privates.

Bales, John
Beason, Thomas
Ellis, Jacob
Harris, Steward
Price, George
Turner, Joseph
Thornbury, James

Privates.

Beales, Jonothan
Copeland, William
Murphy, David
Fair, Thomas
Ross, John
Townsend, Zephaniah

Page 316.

ROLL OF LIEUT. CRAIGHEAD FERGUSON'S COMPANY (County Unknown).

Served from April 19, until October 18, 1813.

Lieut. Craighead Ferguson
Sergt. Jacob Shaffer
Corp. Benjamin Short

Ensign Alexander Gray
Sergt. John Myers
Corp. Thomas Johns

Sergt. James T. Hutton
Corp. Benjamin Hoff
Corp. Thomas H. Colivet

Privates.

Abraham, Israel
Butler, John E.
Conner, Aaron
Dalson, Peter
Kent, Davis
McDonald, Enoch
Slawson, James H.
Wright, Moses

Privates.

Bagley, Thomas
Baker, James
Cisna, Stephen
Ferree, Henry
King, Charles
Sibral, Nicholas
Sands, Joseph
Williamson, Thomas

Privates.

Buck, William
Craighton, William
Dayton, Spencer
Hall, James
Lindsey, Andrew
Slaughter, William
Stuick, Peter

Page 317.

ROLL OF CAPT. JOHN PATTERSON'S COMPANY (Probably from Warren Co.)

Served from July 6, until July 23, 1814.

Capt. John Patterson
Sergt. Alexander Johnston
Corp. John Gillis

Ensign William S. Crain
Sergt. Thomas Phillips
Corp. Henry Williamson
Fifer, Isaac Conover

Sergt. William Gillespie
Sergt James Johnston
Drummer, Henry Catick

Privates.

Conner, John
Dawson, John
Griffis, John
Johnston, William
Moore, John
Oiter, Phillip
Phillips, John
Sutton, Absalom

Privates.

Chambers, John
Forough, Robert
Gillespie, John
Kennedy, Robert
McCord, Robert
Phillips, Samuel
Sawyer, John
Ross, David

Privates.

Crane, George
Commin, Martin
Hormel, John
Landon, John
Norton, Joseph
Pates, Michael
Shephard, Joseph

Pages 318-319.

ROLL OF CAPT. DAVID OLIVER'S COMPANY (County Unknown).

Served from July 5, until August 18, 1814.

Capt. David Oliver
Sergt. Andy Dripes
Sergt. John Dunsath
Corp. Peter Trout
Fifer, Henry Reisingson

Lieut. James Wilmoth
Sergt. William T. Starkes
Corp. Peter Stull
Corp. John Smith

Ensign Nathaniel Williams
Sergt. James Mansfield
Corp Freeman Rittenhouse
Drummer, Christian Oblinger

Vol. I.
ROLL OF CAPT. DAVID OLIVER'S COMPANY (Continued).

Rank and Name of Soldier.   Rank and Name of Soldier.   Rank and Name of Soldier.

Privates.

Adams, James
Brightwell, William
Cornwell, John
Ewing, John
Gannon, Abner
Graham, Thomas D.
Harris, Elisha
Hindes, John
Jackson, Samuel
Lord, John P.
Millen, Anthony
McCowen, George
Nelson, Thomas W.
Oldham, Thomas
Provost, Joseph
Richey, Stephen
Smith, John J.
Laberto, John
Sutton, Tingley
Stotten, John
Salman, Daniel
McConnell, Jeremiah
Teetley, Joseph
Templeton, John
Vanhook, William B.
Wallace, William
West, James

Privates.

Bailey, Barzilla
Clark, Lemuel
Eaverson, George
Force, Whitfield
Gillis, William
Gant, John
Horn, Ellis
Hantin, Arthur
Legg, John
Moore, William
Moore, William, Jr.
McDonald, Joseph
Nevis, Tillman
O'Neele, James
Patt, Lemuel
Radley, John
Stephens, Moses
Strong, Zebulen
Sloop, John
Stewart, William
Salman, James
Eve, Tillman
Teetley, James
Templeton, David
Wise, Solomon
White, Alexander
Wallin, Edward

Privates.

Bildenbeck, Daniel
Clark, Thompson
Evans, Robert
Greene, Alevicious
Gannon, William
Gaunt, Robert
Hanley, John
Irwin, John
Lockhart, John
Milton, Benjamin
Miller, John
McOnde, Jeremiah
Nevis, Daniel
Oldham, Nathaniel
Ponder, Jesse
Richey, John
Steele, John
Sellers, Peter
Smith, Daniel
Sale, Clayton
Sutton, English
McReynolds, Joseph
Tweedy, Robert
Taylor, George W.
Wilmouth, Warren
Wheeler, William
Woodcock, John

Pages 320-321.
ROLL OF CAPT. JOHN SPENCER'S COMPANY, OHIO SPIES
(Probably from Licking County).

Served from August 27, until September 25, 1812, and from September 4, 1813, until March 4, 1814.

Capt. John Spencer
Cornet, Jacob Mann
Sergt. John Peck
Sergt. John C. Spencer
Sergt. Isaac Dougherty
Corp. Enoch Smith

Lieut. Abraham Bennet
Ensign John Benham
Sergt. Jesse Sutton
Sergt. Robert B. Covert
Corp. Enoch Wilkin
Corp. James Patten
Musician, Richard Baker

Lieut Henry Goode
Sergt. Daniel Eaton
Sergt. Martin Robinson
Sergt. Abner Meek
Corp. Isaac Good
Musician, Daniel Crane

Privates.

Anderson, William
Blackburn, James
Brewin, Thomas
Carnal, Silvanus
Cul, Joel
Codington, Isaac
Colter, William
Deane, John
Clyne, George
Fox, David
Garner, Job
Hogan, James
Hinkston, Benjamin
Jackson, Samuel G.
Linsey, John
Lassee, John
Lynn, Samuel
Mills, John
Mullin, James
McCray, Daniel
Morrow, Lewis
Payne, Absalom
Rycraft, Joseph
Sheafe, George
Spragg, James
Whitmore, Miles

Privates.

Allen, John
Blackford, J. K.
Blackford, William
Cahill, Daniel
Cline, John
Copeland, Joseph
Cawthorn, William S.
Daugherty, William
Evans, David
Freeman, James
Griffin, James
Holmes, John
Gill, John
Kirkpatrick, William
Swailes, Rue
Lawrence, George
Linsey, Leonard
Morton, Benjamin
Mills, Daniel
McDaniel, William
McDowell, Demsy
Parkhill, John
Ruble, Samuel
Silsby, David
Thompson, James
Wallace, John

Privates.

Alexander, John
Bedunnah, Ebenezer
Conklin, William
Cahill, Isaac
Codington, Freeman
Clark, Abraham
Cummins, Andrew
Death, George
Elliott, Wright
Garner, Henry
Hamilton, Isaac
Hoblet, David
Fugus, Clement
Kennear, James
Lee, John
Lyttle, John
Meek, Abner
Murphey, John
Mossburgh, Henry
Newkirk, Jacob
Ogler, John
Patterson, John
Sawyer, John
Scott, Joseph
Whitaker, John
Young, John

Pages 322-323.
ROLL OF CAPT. JOHN WILLIAMS' COMPANY (County Unknown).

Served from October 6, until October 26, 1812, and from August 25, 1813, until January 4, 1814.

Capt. John Williams
Sergt. William Hickman
Sergt. Phillip S. Williams
Corp. James Harvey
Corp. Peter Price
Musician, William Kennedy

Lieut. Jesse Edward
Sergt John Shidaker
Sergt. Daniel Rowzer
Corp. Stephen Davis
Corp. John Shell
Musician, Abraham Myers

Ensign Samuel Clappen
Sergt. John Johnston
Sergt. Adkinson, Henry
Corp. Zebulan Wallace
Corp. Israel Price

ROLL OF CAPT. JOHN WILLIAMS' COMPANY (Continued).

Privates.

Cramer, Abraham
Corey, John
Euhart, Jacob
Harvey, James
Hickman, William
Lennon, James
Mitchell, William
Manson, David
Price, Michael
Rouzer, John
Stafford, Joseph
Sailor, Philip
Stafford, James
Saunders, William

Clingan, James
Croy, Peter
Fritz, Christian
Helvie, John
Johnston, John
Lowthain, Absalom
Myers, Lewis
Cory, Daniel W.
Price, Israel
Sunderland, Francis
Stafford, Ralph
Shell, Christian
Woodburn, Joseph
Wisehart, Benjamin

Clingan, Edward
Davis, Stephen
Fraze, James
Helvie, Adam
Lowthain, George
Madden, William
Mann, Isaac
Price, Jeremiah
Rouzer, Daniel
Sunderland, Peter
Shell, James
Songer, Adam
Wallace, John

Pages 324-325.

ROLL OF CAPT. HIRAM RUSSELL'S COMPANY (County Unknown).

Served from February 8, until May 23, 1813.

Capt. Hiram Russell

Sergt. Thomas Star
Corp. Lewis Hoyt

Sergt. O. C. Dickinson

Privates.

Andrews, Richard
Arnold, William
Buell, Ezra
Caughey, Joseph
Findley, John
Galloway, James
Hough, Henry
Lafferty, William
McKnight, Robert, Jr.
Nelson, Hugh
Russell, Job
Shaler, John
Stephens, Daniel
Pond, Phineas
Warner, Chancy
Waldorff, Phillip

Andrews, Sherman
Baker, Hubbard
Burnham, Joshua
Doyle, Anthony
Fowler, Chester
Graham, Jesse
John, James
Mapes, Henry
McFarland, William
Queen, John
Rodgers, Richard, Jr.
Scoville, Reuben
Smith, James
Tuttle, Samuel
Willetts, John

Alderman, Eber
Bailey, Iddo
Ballad, Ezekial
Dickinson, Elisha
Ferguson, Hans
Henning, Jacob
Laughlin, Robert
McKonkey, William
Newton, Lemuel
Ray, James
Sweet, Amos
Sessions, James
Spitstone, Adam
Turner, Conrad
Woodworth, Albigence

Page 326.

ROLL OF CAPT. JOHN DAVIS' COMPANY (Probably from Green Co.)

Served from May 3, until May 20, 1813.

Capt. John Davis
Cornet, Henry Barnes
Sergt. David Hanes

Lieut. David M. Laughead
Sergt. John B. Todd
Sergt. John John

Lieut. Stephen Commwell
Sergt. Adam Shigley

Privates.

Blue, Davis
Clifford, Thomas
Gibson, John
Lamm, Josiah
McFarland, John
Shanks, Thomas
Watson, James

Black, Peter
Devone, John
Glum, Thomas
Mitchell, James
Shaw, Amos
Taylor, John A.
West, William

Barker, Joseph
Elam, John
Gill, Hugh
Munthoud, Ephraim
Talbert, Josiah G.
Vance, John
White, John

Page 327.

ROLL OF CAPT. ROBERT GOWDY'S COMPANY (Probably from Green Co.)

Served from August 23, until September 21, 1813.

Capt. Robert Gowdy
Sergt. William Sutton
Corp. William Sterrett
Corp. David Conkelon

Lieut Thomas Constant
Sergt Joel Hixon
Corp. John Loid
Drummer, William Allen

Sergt Samuel Gray
Sergt. James Fire
Corp. William Simpson
Fifer, Samuel Simpson

Privates.

Aldreedezr, Littleberry
Bruce, James
Conkelon, Samuel
Gawley, Ryan
Hummer, Peter
Joiner, Charles
Larew, Abraham
Maxey, Stephen
Seaman, Peter
Thornberry, George
Vanard, Francis

Barber, John
Barnes, Alexander
Curtis, Wiley
Gill, John
Hoop, Andrew
Jones, Jacob
Moore, James
Oemm, Samuel
Salsberry, James
Thornberry, John
Wright, Josiah

Beales, Jonothan
Bell, Daniel
Gibson, John
Hough, Joseph
Gibson, Thomas
John, William
Maxey, Martin
Sutton, William G.
Townsley, George
Turner, Henry

Pages 328-329. Vol. I.
ROLL OF CAPT. SAMUEL HERROD'S COMPANY (County Unknown).
Served from September 15, until October 15, 1812, and from August 1, until August 16, 1813.

Rank and Name of Soldier.

Capt. Samuel Herrod
Ensign Thomas Constant
Sergt. David Lawhead
Sergt. David Garrison
Sergt. Reuben Johnson
Corp. Thomas Watson

Lieut. Robert Gowdy
Ensign Samuel Musick
Sergt. William Andrews
Sergt. Anthony Cannon
Sergt. Andrew Douglas
Corp. James Andrews

Lieut. Christopher L. Sroupe
Sergt. William Buckles
Sergt. William Campbell
Sergt. Evan Brock
Sergt. Thomas Kelso
Corp. James Bouls

Privates.

Andrews, Hugh
Bromagem, James
Beason, Thomas
Cuswell, James
Cutright, Peter
Durraugh, John
Frazier, James
Galloway, James
Hanna, Robert
Husted, John N.
Johnston, Isaac
Jenkins, William
Ladd, John
Lamme, James
Maxwell, William
Moore, Charles A.
Mitchell, Forgis
McFarland, John
McClellan, William
Norris, Nathan
Paullin, Joseph
Buckles, Robert
Donaldson, Alexander
Radgsdale, Alexander
Sutton, Jesse
Shaw, Amos
Stout, Bonem
Stout, Isaac
Townsley, Thomas
Thompson, James
Watson, Thomas
Wright, John

Ash, Adam
Bransen, Eli
Bromagem, Samuel
Collier, James
Callander, William
Edgar, William
Ferguson, Zechariah
Guin, Amos
Hornback, Samuel
Henderson, Joseph
Johnson, Aaron
Johnson, Reuben
Ladd, Christopher
Lamme, David
Mendenhall, John
Miller, John
McFarland, Arthur
McFarland, Robert
McCulley, John
Ogden, William
Hoop, Andrew
Paullin, Jacob
Kain, Thomas
Rodgers, William
Sterett, Joseph
Sutton, Garner
Sharp, William
Shanks, Thomas
Turner, John
Thomas, Indian
Wright, Hugh
Wolf, John

Adams, Samuel
Best, Elias
Borders, George
Campbell, John
Duley, Samuel
Feris, James
Goff, John F.
Gawen, Johnson
Hartman, Peter
Jenkins, Lancelot
Johton, Benjamin
Kent, James
Long, Thomas
Long, John
Morton, John
Mullen, Charles
McCoy, William
McBride, Henry
McCoy, William
Palmer, Joseph
Parris, Joseph
Pickering, Henry
King, Richard
Reed, John
Sutton, John
Selvey, James
Sroupe, David
Turner, Robert
Turner, Allen
Thornberry, John
Watson, John
Wilson, Joseph

Page 330.
ROLL OF CAPT. JOHN HUMES' COMPANY (Probably from Clermont Co.)
Served from January 30, until April 10, 1814, and from January 11, until April 10, 1815.

Capt. John Humes
Sergt. John Steel
Sergt. John Meeks
Corp. Edward Gandy

Lieut. James Turner
Sergt. Thomas Holland
Corp. Joseph Anderson
Corp. Robert Evans
Fifer, William Lane

Ensign Levi Moore
Sergt. Charles Troy
Corp. William Congar
Drummer, George Smith

Privates.

Arthur, William
Bunald, John
Bell, William
Bigg, Isaac
Crosson, William
Coleman, Isaac
Davis, Noah
Fossett, William
Gates, Uriah
Higbee, Amasa
Kirgen, David
Little, David
McKee, Thomas
Shull, Phillip
Smith, Burris
Shaw, Solomon
Test, William

Ayers, Henry
Boreland, James
Burg, Richard
Cutright, Aaron
Couch, Isaiah
Carroll, John
Debruler, Reason
Frambes, Peter
Gibb, John
Hamel, Thomas
King, Leonard
Moore, John
Powers, Isaac
Sellers, Peter
Tillatson, Luther
Vold, Henry
Wheeler, Benjamin

Burke, James
Beam, David
Bushman, David
Coleman, Leroy
Clinton, Archibald
Chance, John
Floro, Thomas
Griffin, Ebenezer
Gard, William
Hinde, John
Leonard, John
Mallott, Zedekiah
Stalo, John L.
Storey, Washington
Thomas, Ephraim
Washburn, Josiah

Page 331.
ROLL OF CAPT. ALEXANDER BLACK'S COMPANY (County Unknown).
Served from August 18, until August 26, 1812.

Capt. Alexander Black
Sergt. Samuel Wilson
Sergt. Eli Wilson

Lieut. Alexander Snoddy
Sergt. Robert Clark

Ensign John Moore
Sergt. John Tites

Vol. I.

ROLL OF CAPT. ALEXANDER BLACK'S COMPANY (Continued.)

Rank and Name of Soldier. Rank and Name of Soldier. Rank and Name of Soldier.

Privates.

Alexander, Joseph
Crow, Joseph
Elliott, John
Lockridge, James
Martin, Job
McIlvain, Moses, Sr.
Newell, Hugh
Petty, Ezekial
Smith, Henry
Tipton, John

Privates.

Baird, John
Clark, Thomas
Gunn, John
Moore, Samuel
Moviele, Batiece
McIlvain, Moses, Jr.
Newell, Thomas
Smith, Joel
Simes, John
Wace, Stephen
Workman, John

Privates.

Boyd, William
Dunn, John
Kirkwood, William
Moore, Raphael
McCloud, William
McDonald, Ebenezer
Newell, William
Shields, David
Server, Jacob
Wall, John

Page 332.

ROLL OF CAPT. JAMES CAMPBELL'S COMPANY (County Unknown).
Served from October 20, 1812, until April 20, 1813.

Capt. James Campbell
Sergt. David Henderson
Sergt. Richard Copeland
Corp. Thomas Dille

Lieut. John Nichols
Sergt. Thomas Thompson
Corp. John H. Smith
Corp. Jeremiah Russell

Ensign Zepheniah Bell
Sergt. Isaac Coleman
Corp. Joshua Russell

Privates.

Archer, John
Bundy, Joseph
Coleman, Nathaniel
Crampton, Henry
Evans, Garrett
Goness, David
Hunter, Joseph
Hisket, Benjamin
Lewis, Samuel
Moore, Daniel
McConnell, James
Pool, John
Shekan, Joshua
Swart, Jacob
Stoner, Henry
Tipton, Thomas
Workman, William
Workman, Amos

Privates.

Beatty, William
Barton, Michael
Coleman, Samuel
Diven, John
Ferguson, James
Gorley, John
Harris, Simon
Kirk, Joseph
Lewis, Stephen
McKittrick, John
Price, William
Pearce, George
Stephens, Benjamin
Smith, Bazel
Swanny, George
Tagert, Isaac
Wilkins, Thomas
Wheeler, William

Privates.

Burvit, Benjamin
Conner, Robert M.
Clark, Jacob
Elrue, Burned
Fonda, Lawrence
Gant, Reuben
Hopny, Samuel
Kincaid, Joseph
Martian, John
McConnell, Robert
Porter, Reason
Roberts, Jacob
Slater, John
Stackhous, Jacob
Stephenson, John
Vanwey, Burrus
Wilkins, Andrew

Page 333.

ROLL OF CAPT. NICHOLAS DAVIS' COMPANY (County Unknown).
Served from August 18, 1814, until February 25, 1815.

Capt. Nicholas Davis
Sergt. David Mulligan
Sergt. John Mulligan
Corp. John Humphrey

Lieut. Abraham Layfert
Sergt. John Rankin
Corp. George Duffield
Corp. Silas Roose

Sergt. Robert Gooke
Sergt. William Boyles
Corp. William Guttery

Privates.

Bell, Adam
Bunyon, Henry
Freete, George
Guilinger, Martin
Muney, James
Niles, Sanford
Patrick, Robert
Russell, Joseph
Smith, David
Wilson, David

Privates.

Bashford, Joseph
Bur: m, William
Force, Thomas
Kling, John
Maynard, Ezra
Ogel, Mordecai
Roberson, Walter
Smith, Andrew
Springer, William
West, Thomas

Privates.

Buneyer, Daniel
Clinton, Charles
Gurwell, William
Lockerd, Eleben
Maides, William
Pool, Conrad
Rerigh, Andrew
Sample, James
Sanderlin, Thomas

Page 334.

ROLL OF CAPT. JAMES FLAGG'S COMPANY
(Probably from Washington County).
Served from October 20, 1812, until January 11, 1813.

Capt. James Flagg
Sergt. Lary Ford
Sergt. Peletiah White
Corp. Joseph Witten

Lieut. Benedie Hutchinson
Sergt. John Greenman
Corp. Jacob Lane
Corp. John G. Askell

Ensign, Nathaniel Olney
Sergt. David Trobridge
Corp. Charles Thomas

Privates.

Alpha, Daniel
Anderson, James
Baker, John
Coalman, Daniel
Cady, Philip
Dennis, Thomas
Emerson, Asa
Goodwin, James
Hutchinson, James
Ingles, John
Morris, Nehemiah
Priest, Richard D.
Witten, James

Privates.

Abbott, George
Burbank, Seth D.
Burchet, Jonah
Castle, George
Chapman, Simon
Dougherty, George
Ewing, James
Gosset, John
Harris, George
Kidd, John
Olds, Gilbert
Starke, Pardon

Privates.

Adams, James
Britton, Nathan
Barrett, John
Coverton, Henry
Cline, William
Donahue, Daniel
Fordice, Stanton
Hutchins, James
Heinman, Curtis
Knight, James
Mallary, Elisha
Walker, James B.

Page 335. Vol. I.
ROLL OF CAPT. JEREMIAH SIMMS COMPANY (County Unknown).
Served from February 20, until March 20, 1813.

Rank and Name of Soldier.	Rank and Name of Soldier.	Rank and Name of Soldier.
Capt. Jeremiah Simms	Lieut. William Buckley	Ensign, Joseph Clevinger
Sergt. James McIntire	Sergt. Abner Martin	Sergt. Arthur Collison
Sergt. James Morris	Corp. John A. Swearinger	Corp. Alexander Hayes
Corp. Andrew Sparks	Corp. Jacob Smith	
Privates.	**Privates.**	**Privates.**
Bailey, Michael L.	Bailey, Amos	Callison, John, Sr.
Callison, John, Jr.	Elliott, William	Elliott, Thomas
Frantz, Jacob	Hallin, Joseph	Kellar, John
Ludlow, Cooper	Lintz, Peter	Minnick, John
Mesate, James	Morris, Richard	Morris, Benjamin
Martin, Jacob	Martin, Isaac	Miller, Martin
Olinger, Philip	Olinger, Jacob	Overpeck, William
Palmer, Elias	Seffel, Samuel	Stewart, Stephen
Thompson, Francis	Tamplin, John	Wickerly, William
	Waggoner, John	

Page 336.
ROLL OF CAPT. JOSEPH EVANS' COMPANY (Probably from Ross County).
Served from February 24, until March 24, 1813.

Capt. Joseph Evans	Lieut. Joseph Stokes	Ensign, Samuel Haines
Sergt. William Green	Sergt. Thomas Segar	Sergt. Job Sharp, Jr.
Sergt. Thomas Marshel	Sergt. Benjamin Smith	Musician, David Henly
	Musician Thomas Atha	
Privates.	**Privates.**	**Privates.**
Branson, Robert	Brown, John	Bishop, William
Curl, Samuel	Downs, Joseph	Garwood, Lott
Green, John	Haines, Thomas	Haines, William
Inskup, Lewis	Pope, Nathaniel	Painter, Abraham
Marmon, Richmon	Reams, Caleb	Reams, Jeremiah
Pickerell, Nicholas	Sharp, Allen	Sharp, William
Rea, John	Sharp, Jesse	Warner, Jack

Pages 337-338-339.
ROLL OF CAPT. WILLIAM WILSON'S COMPANY (Probably from Ross Co.)
Served from March 3, until August 15, 1814.

Capt. William Wilson	Lieut. Cornelius Stringer	Ensign, William Miller
Sergt. Samuel Lamberson	Sergt. Stephen Mahaffey	Sergt. John Oslin
Sergt. Benjamin Stephenson	Corp. Joseph Watson	Corp. James Armstrong
Corp. Thomas Owens	Corp. James Tulk	Fifer, Thomas Mathews
Privates.	**Privates.**	**Privates.**
Allfather, Adam	Anderson, Mark	Bronkart, Louis
Bowen, Constant	Babb, Bell	Beyner, George
Beamer, Adam	Black, Adam	Beers, Thomas
Coss, David	Cline, Phillip	Carr, Peter
Cockrill, Joseph	Dunkin, James	Davis, John H.
Dowl, John	Bontsong, Jonothan	Daugherty, David
Foreman, David	Fareare, John	Gibbs, Isaac
Gardner, Isaac	Henell, Christopher	Hall, John
Barbaugh, Samuel	Holmes, Thomas	Harding, Israel
Hilhouse, John	Jefferrs, Thomas	James, David
Kasebeer, Samuel	Kruger, John	Long, William
Longley, George	Morris, George	Maple, David
Mathews, James	McHufens, James	McHenry, David
McKee, John	Nixon, Andrew	Norris, Charles
Prewith, William	Parr, William	Parr, Thomas
Romine, Abraham	Sreak, Jacob	Sickman, Luke
Smith, John	Stent, George	Swyer, George
Sly, John	Sullaven, George	Summers, Isaac
Turel, John	Taylor, Samuel	Wilson, James
Williams, James	Woodward, William	Waggoner, David
	Watson, Robert	

Page 340.
ROLL OF CAPT. FRANCIS PATTERSON'S COMPANY (County Unknown).
Served from October 17, 1812, until December 22, 1813.

Capt. Francis Patterson	Lieut. David Scott	Ensign, James Merris
Sergt. William Patterson	Sergt. George Bradford	Sergt. Michael Lennon
Sergt. Archibald Campbell	Corp. Eliza Griffith	Corp. Jacob John
Corp. Daniel Houser	Corp. Robert Kiddle	
Privates.	**Privates.**	**Privates.**
Blue, Frederick	Bedele, Calvin	Christian, John
Clark, Solomon	Beard, John	Croy, Peter
Culbertson, Robert	Dye, Andrew	Duncan, Robert
Frane, William	Greer, John	Garard, Isaac

ROLL OF CAPT. FRANCIS PATTERSON'S COMPANY (Continued.)

Rank and Name of Soldier.   Rank and Name of Soldier.   Rank and Name of Soldier.

Privates.

Privates.	Privates.	Privates.
Guthrie, James	Hurley, Robert	Haines, Ephraim
Hosier, Isaac	Hannah, Thomas	Jackson, Jesse
Kiser, John	Kirby, John	Lehman, Henry
Meeker, John	Moyer, Isaac	Morgan, Cornelius
Maloy, James	Neff, Lewis	Newman, William
Perry, Orin	Shaffer, John	Seth, George
Shover, Jacob	Shephard, Thomas	Sprague, Stephen
Tanner, Edward	Rogel, Jacob	Underwood, John
Vinyard, Rezin	Woolfe, Conrad	Wilson, Samuel
Weaver, Peter	Wollaston, George	

Page 341.

ROLL OF CAPT. JAMES STEELE'S COMPANY (Probably from Fayette Co.)

Served from August 22, until September 30, 1812.

Capt. James Steele	Lieut. George Grove	Ensign, James McClure
Sergt. Maj. Joseph H. Crane	Sergt. John Folkirth	Sergt. Ralph Wilson
Sergt. John Strain	Sergt. James Henderson	Corp. Matt Patton
Corp. Alexander Grimes	Corp. George Harris	Corp. David Henderson

Privates.	Privates.	Privates.
Brier, James	Brier, David	Bay, James
Bay, William	Collins, Jeremiah	Devor, John
Enoch, John	Fryback, William	Gordon, Lewis
Guy, Alexander	Holderman, John	Hatfield, Moses
Jennings, Henry	King, Samuel M.	Green, Joshua
Lowe, John	Montgomery, William	Miller, James
McCain, James	McNair, Moses	McCormick, William
McCarter, Simpson	McCleary, Robert	Maybroll, Jonothan
McCabe, John	Newcom, George	Newcom, John
Petticrew, James	Robinson, Andrew	Riffle, David
Rowan, John	Smith, Ira	Smith, Abraham
Sunderland, Daniel	Vanscoys, William	Vanasdel, William
Worley, Caleb	Ward, George	Watton, Samuel
Wallaston, George		

Page 342.

ROLL OF CAPT. THOMAS STRETCH'S COMPANY
(Probably from Champaign County).

Served from November 27, until December 27, 1812.

Capt. Thomas Stretch	Lieut. Ezekial Arrowsmith	Ensign, Walker Johnston
Sergt. James McLaughlin	Sergt. George Faulkner	Sergt. William Sargent
Sergt. Frederick Stonebager	Corp. Joseph Hill	Corp. John Long, Sr.

Privates.	Privates.	Privates.
Comer, David	Comer, Peter	Clark, Marcus
Clark, Reuben	Colbert, Jesse	Dils, Samuel
Humphries, Robert	Hufman, Jeremiah	Hanback, Lewis
Harber, Elisha	Kite, Benjamin	Kite, Samuel
Longfeller, Joseph	Lyon, John	Long, John, Jr.
Metz, Emanuel	Monroe, James	Moody, John
Maggeat, Adam	Mitts, Samuel	Mitchell, James
Mitchell, John	Megill, John	McAlexander, James
McIntyre, Thomas	Smith, James	Slegle, Jacob
Stephens, Christian	Runkle, Peter	Stephens, John
Whiteman, John	Wilson, William	

Pages 343-344-345.

ROLL OF CAPT. WILLIAM STEPHENSON'S COMPANY
(Probably from Green County).

Served from October 24, until December 22, 1812, and from Sept. 20, 1813, until March 20, 1814.

Capt. William Stephenson	Lieut. Samuel Stites	Ensign, John McCally
Lieut. Edward Jones	Ensign, Daniel Kebbinger	Sergt. Alexander Ireland
Sergt. Thomas Sleeth	Sergt. Moses McNair	Sergt. Peter Pence
Sergt. William Kelley	Sergt. William Harper	Corp. Peter Stephenson
Corp. James McKaig	Corp. William Wilson	Corp. Nelson Lansdell
Corp. William Price	Corp. Elias Gilkin	Fifer, Jonothan Claton
Fifer, Henry Steenbarger	Drummer, John Gillelan	Drummer, Joseph Jones

Privates.	Privates.	Privates.
Adams, John	Babcock, Simon	Benet, Francis
Bradley, John	Beeth, James	Bennett, George
Black, John	Bates, John	Babcock, William
Benson, Thomas	Browder, Wesley	Casad, John
Cleton, William	Campbell, John	Criswell, David
Davis, Zebe	Dunn, Simon	Carpenter, Joseph
Davis, Noah	Ditz, John	Evans, George
Ellis, William	Forbes, George	Follis, Isaac

ROLL OF CAPT. WILLIAM STEPHENSON'S COMPANY (Continued.)

Privates.

- Garlough, Adam
- Gregory, Daniel
- Hussey, Christopher
- Hopkins, Richard
- Hodge, John
- Hale, Bradford
- Jones, Thomas
- Kiser, John
- Loomon, Joseph
- Myers, George
- Meed, Daniel
- Miles, Christian
- McManime, William
- Oppy, David
- Roberts, John
- Smith, William
- Skilliland, Lewis
- Stephenson, John
- Thomas, John
- Waggoner, George
- Wilson, John

Privates.

- Grose, William
- Hardman, Henry
- Hussey, Nathan
- Hustide, Aaron
- Harstock, William
- James, Thomas
- Kendle, John
- Loomon, Ralph
- Miller, Charles
- Martin, Jacob, Sr.
- McAuly, William
- Norman, Jacob
- Read, William
- Steeth, James
- Snip, Abraham
- Strain, John
- Tatman, Edward
- Turner, James
- Wilson, James
- Walbourne, Robert
- Ward, Obediah

Privates.

- Gibson, Monteleon
- Harker, John
- Harris, Stewart
- Hammell, Valentine
- Ivens, Richard
- Krigler, Jacob
- Lippingcot, Obediah
- Lambert, John
- Moody, James
- Mills, Lewis
- McKaig, John
- Olinger, Jacob
- Rose, William
- Smith, Caleb
- Stephenson, James
- Spuce, Daniel
- Thomas, Abraham
- Vaughn, William
- Winget, Caleb
- Winget, Hugh
- Wolf, Jacob

Pages 346-347.

ROLL OF CAPT. AARON STRONG'S COMPANY (County Unknown).
Served from October 7, until December 15, 1812.

- Capt. Aaron Strong
- Sergt. Bulkey Comstock
- Sergt. Ira Wilcox
- Corp. Samuel Hayden

- Lieut. Chaney Barker
- Sergt. Roswell Tuller
- Corp. Joseph Heath
- Corp. Norman Case
- Fifer, Mathias Vanloon

- Ensign, Aaron Welsh
- Sergt. Nahum King
- Corp. Isaac Harrison
- Drummer, Sylvester Drake

Privates.

- Benjamin, Daniel
- Barker, William N.
- Carpenter, Nathan
- Calkins, Lovewell
- Dickey, John
- Dunham, Walter
- Evans, Edward
- Fischar, Josiah
- Fisher, George
- Foust, Abraham
- Gale, Jesse
- Hilt, Daniel
- Hare, John
- Lewis, John
- Main, Cloyer
- Mitchell, Samuel
- McCutcheon, Robert
- Napp, Thomas D.
- Patterson, John
- Rath, Nathan
- Reed, Daniel
- Strong, Daniel
- Silbee, David
- Slate, Valentine
- Teedell, Joseph
- Olds, Ezra, Jr.
- Welsh, Orora
- Welsh, Samuel
- Young, Andrew

Privates.

- Bardsley, Darius
- Bety, Francis
- Case, Orlando
- Cooper, John
- Denton, Justice
- Davis, John D.
- Flige, Daniel
- Foltner, Joshua N.
- Fancher, Henry
- George, Thomas
- Hall, William
- Hilt, Jacob
- Judd, Liman
- Maxfield, Amos
- Manville, John
- Mitchell, Moses
- McGinnis, Samuel
- Nelson, Robert
- Perry, Samuel
- Royee, Nijad
- Robinson, Thomas
- Sharp, Gant
- Stark, James
- Scribner, John
- Tylor, Richard
- Van Loon, Jacob
- Wallace, Heman
- Wallis, Solomon
- Zimmerman, Henry

Privates.

- Bixby, Appleton
- Brown, Thomas
- Case, Nathan
- Davis, Elezer
- Dixon, Myron
- Dunlebarger, Frederick
- Foose, William
- Foust, Henry
- Fancher, William
- Griswold, Isaac
- Humphrey, Lemuel
- Helt, John
- Keyes, Tolman
- Millington, Peter
- Manville, Flemming
- Milliken, John
- McCumber, Jeremiah
- Pultney, Aquila
- Phillips, John
- Reed, Samuel
- Scott, Asa
- Simmers, Ephraim
- Kent, Daniel
- Tuttle, Rosswell, Jr.
- Tarboss, John
- Watson, William
- White, James H.
- Wyatt, Nathaniel

Page 348.

ROLL OF CAPT. ROBERT RUSSELL'S COMPANY (Probably from Scioto Co.)
Served from July 28, until August 22, 1813.

- Capt. Robert Russell
- Sergt. William Cole
- Corp. Andrew Beles

- Lieut. William Russell
- Sergt. Joseph McKee
- Corp. Thomas Clerk

- Sergt. John Eakins
- Sergt. William Murpny

Privates.

- Beles, Peter
- Green, Nathaniel
- Lard, John S.
- Ralston, Robert
- Stout, Isaac

Privates.

- Colvin, George
- Killin, John
- Marvin, Silas
- Roberts, Lewis
- Stout, Jesse

Privates.

- Colvin, Jacob
- Kinyon, Jonothan
- McCall, William
- Severingham, Duke
- Stitts, William

Pages 349-350. Vol. I.

ROLL OF CAPT. JOSEPH CURTIS' COMPANY (County Unknown).

Served from February 23, until March 28, 1814.

Rank and Name of Soldier.

Capt. Joseph Curtis
Sergt. Henry Shuey
Sergt. John Mathias
Corp. John Woods

Privates.

Aughe, William
Brian, George S.
Clevenger, Samuel
Cornell, Heli
Crosson, Columbia
Dunkin, William
Fendley, William
Gustin, Samuel N.
Hathaway, Samuel
Herner, Jacob
Lesenea, Samuel
Laird, David
Merrit, Joseph
Potter, Hiram
Reed, John
Ree, Charles
Shank, Jacob
Sentmire, George
Seamon, Jaconiah
Benard, Jesse
Willas, William

Rank and Name of Soldier.

Lieut. Isaac Clements
Sergt. William P. Andrews
Corp. John Sedgwick
Corp. Hugh Stephenson

Privates.

Bryan, Ebenezer
Bearnheart, Benjamin
Cox, John
Clements, John
Cox, William
Duterrow, Jacob
Fox, Frederick
Gray, Amos
Hines, John
Hayes, Caleb W.
Long, Robert
Montgomery, Elisha
McDonald, James
Penticost, Simion
Reed, Leonard
Reagin, Daniel
Sweeney, William
Stephenson, Thomas
Sutpir, John
Benard, Stephen
Wilkins, William
Young, Jacob

Rank and Name of Soldier.

Ensign Joash Edwards
Sergt. David Hayes
Corp. Stephenus Clark
Drummer, Joseph Stephenson

Privates.

Brandenburgh, Jacob
Carter, Joshua
Cattlan, Harris
Cummins, Robert
Death, Aaron
Elberhart, Samuel
Griffith, Benjamin
Holley, Daniel
Hester, Jacob
Kelsey, Daniel
Long, Joseph
Merrit, Abraham
McReynolds, William
Reed, Ezra
Rase, Benjamin
Reagin, Reason
Snyder, Henry
Smith, Obediah
Thorn, Eli
Wells, Benedict
Wilson, Peter A.

Page 251.

ROLL OF CAPT. SIMON PHILLIPS' COMPANY (County Unknown).

Served from July 22, 1813, until January 25, 1814.

Capt. Simon Phillips
Sergt. Ethelred Delk
Sergt. John Huit
Corp. William Douglas

Privates.

Atkins, John
Cassady, William
Gift, Peter
Harter, Philip
Moss, Jacob
McGriff, John, Jr.
Pickle, Henry
Phillips, Valentine
Scott, Thomas C.
Webb, Adron

Lieut. Wear Cassady
Sergt. James Hole
Corp. George Miller
Corp. Thomas Pickle
Musician, John Wepp

Privates.

Biers, John
Griffin, John
Garrett, William
Kerrie, Dennis
Moss, John
Phillips, Daniel
Phillips, Lewis
Ross, Benjamin
Shelton, Joel
Whitsel, George

Ensign, Patrick McGriff
Sergt. Jacob Miller
Corp. Christian Frederick
Musician, Anthony Atchison

Privates.

Cassady, Thomas
Guntle, Jacob
Hill, Jacob
Michael, Jacob
McGriff, John Sr.
Phillips, Hezekiah
Pickle, Tobias
Rape, Lewis
Tanner, James
Winegardner, John

Page 352.

ROLL OF CAPT. SAMUEL BRIER'S COMPANY (County Unknown).

Served from April 12, until October 11, 1813.

Capt. Samuel Brier
Sergt. William Miller
Sergt. Joseph R. John
Corp. David Heaston

Privates.

Arnte, George
Branburg, George
Cox, William
Cronn, Daniel
Dice, Paul
Coblentz, Jacob
Henry, George
Kader, Phillip
Lechlider, George
McCreary, Nathan
Pettit, James
Reed, William
Studebaker, John
Swart, John
Wood, Ashbury
Wood, Samuel

Lieut. Jacob Lighty
Sergt. Cornelius Ganasdol
Corp. Mathew M. Dodds
Corp. Daniel Hatch
Drummer, Isaac Walker

Privates.

Bay, William
Bucken, Michael
Crull, Daniel
Cox, William
Enoch, John
Gelelant, Emanuel
Harshman, Jacob
Kelsen, Daniel
Haman, Solomon
Overholser, Jacob
Phlweyn, Charles
Rickey, John
Statler, William
Shively, Isaac
Wolf, Jacob
Woodhouse, Henry

Ensign, Daniel Hearton
Sergt. Samuel Arnold
Corp. Joseph Blair
Musician, Conrad Slagle

Privates.

Blair, James S.
Cofman, Jacob
Casdy, Simon
Deiterick, Peter
Edomes, Edmond
Heister, George
Jones, Price
Lawrose, John
McDonald, Archibald
Phillips, Thomas
Pickles, Simon
Shelly, Jacob
Parks, Joseph
Talburt, James
Westfall, John

Pages 353-354.   Vol. I.
ROLL OF CAPT. WILLIAM McCONNELL'S COMPANY (County Unknown).
Served from April 5, until July 26, 1813.

Rank and Name of Soldier.
Capt. William McConnell
Sergt. John Handle
Sergt. Benjamin Walters
Corp. Lawrence Wisecamere

Privates.
Bowers, Jacob
Bice, John
Degarmore, William
Gaumer, Daniel
Justice, James
Keeler, James
Moore, John
McCully, Patrick
Rough, Peter
Stots, Jacob
Varnon, Samuel
Woods, Thomas

Rank and Name of Soldier.
Lieut. Jacob Wisecamere
Sergt. Robert Wilson
Corp. John Bowers
Corp. John Schelberry
Drummer, Mathew Robins

Privates.
Boggs, Robert
Cooksey, Josiah
Finkbone, John
Haire, John H.
Kenney, Thomas
Kirk, Jesse
Mace, Daniel
McKune, William
Robison, David
Stump, Abraham
Walters, John

Rank and Name of Soldier.
Ensign, John Brown
Sergt. Joseph McConnell
Corp. Robert Hawk
Fifer, George Slack

Privates.
Barret, Henson
Courts, Thomas
Fickle, Benjamin
Hart, David
Kain, John
Moore, Robert
Mires, Charles
Over, Jacob
Slack, Jacob
Varnon, Joseph
Watson, John

Pages 355-356.
ROLL OF CAPT. WILLIAM MORROW'S COMPANY (County Unknown).
Served from April 29, until August 7, 1813.

Capt. William Morrow
Sergt. Alexander Harper
Corp. John Hollyday

Privates.
Blair, Benjamin
Blair, John
Callamber, Richard
Finch, Joseph
Harper, Benjamin
Huffman, Henry
Keanier, Adam
King, Reuben
Montgomery, Humphrey
McMann, William
Peterson, Jacob
Roberts, Moses
Shannon, Thomas

Lieut. James Harper
Sergt. Daniel Hare
Corp. Samuel W. McConnell
Corp. John Harper

Privates.
Bellinger, Joshua
Carr, Thomas
Davis, Jacob
Frame, George
Hemphill, John
Irwin, William
Kirkendall, Jeremiah
Miller, Ferdinand
McConnell, John
McConnell, William
Ramsey, Lyle
Stookey, Samuel
Taylor, William

Ensign, Daniel Robins
Sergt. Joseph Boggs
Corp. Henry Pittenger

Privates.
Blair, William C.
Cowler, John
Dear, John
Griffith, Evan
Hemphill, Mathew
Jones, Abner
Kennedy, Robert
Miller, Stephen
McMann, Samuel
Pummel, James
Robbins, Phillip
Stephenson, Thomas
Wilson, James

Page 357.
ROLL OF CAPT. DAVID EWING'S COMPANY (From Fairfield County).
Served from April 8, until July 16, 1813.

Capt. David Ewing
Sergt. Nathaniel Reed
Sergt. John Abrams
Corp. George Rodabough

Privates.
Culps, Jacob
Foster, Frederick F.
Hume, John
Mentzer, David
Shiang, William
Smither, George
Trumph, John

Lieut. Thomas Ewing
Sergt. William Springer
Corp. George Hollenback
Corp. Jacob Eversol

Privates.
Cunningham, Daniel
Gunder, Henry
James, Kirke
Post, Russell E.
Smither, John
Smither, Daniel
Weaver, Jacob

Ensign, John Burton
Sergt. George Carpenter
Corp. John Rees
Drummer, John Beaver

Privates.
Connkle, Adam
Hollenback, John
Kirby, John
Rodabough, Jacob
Stewart, James
Tripe, William

Page 358.
ROLL OF CAPT. ANDERSON SPENCER'S COMPANY (County Unknown).
Served from June 4, until December 5, 1813.

Capt. Anderson Spencer
Sergt. Patrick Cassiday
Sergt. Jonothan Pierson
Corp. Ephraim Elkins

Privates.
Alston, Benjamin
Clifton, Nathan
Davis, John
Hesley, Henry
Mahan, John
Martin, Robert
McDonald, William
Simons, John
Smith, James
Vinadge, David

Lieut. Ephraim Cattlen
Sergt. John Wells
Corp. Joel Drake
Corp. David Alexander
Musician, Harris Cattleton

Privates.
Bradberry, Hezekiah
Davis, Richard D.
Freeman, Elijah F.
Knox, William
Mitchell, Parker
Martin, William
McDaniel, Joshua
Sanders, John
Stine, Christian
Woodruff, Jesse

Ensign, Benjamin D. Davis
Sergt. David Line
Corp. John Hunter
Musician, William Sheley

Privates.
Bramon, Henry
Davis, Daniel
Gordon, Ross
Line, Moses
Murphy, Edward
Miller, Daniel
Spivey, John
Seward, Caleb
Thompson, John
Whitaker, Daniel

Page 359   Vol. I.

ROLL OF CAPT. JOSEPH JENKINSON'S COMPANY
(Probably from Hamilton County.)
Served from August 11, 1812, ——————

Rank and Name of Soldier.	Rank and Name of Soldier.	Rank and Name of Soldier.
Capt. Joseph Jenkinson	Lieut. Stephen Gano	Lieut. Alexander Gibson
Sergt. William Kerr	Sergt. John Cox	Sergt. John Craven
Sergt. John S. Ludlow	Corp. Sampson Mooney	Corp. Joseph Weekley
Privates.	**Privates.**	**Privates.**
Ayres, John	Avery, Coleman	Baum, Jonas
Blooker, Samuel	Bonnel, Samuel	Corn, Peter
Clark, John S.	Crow, Thomas S.	Coppin, Joseph
Clark, William	Donnell, James	Drips, Andrew
Engle, Phillip	Evens, Robert	Hanley, John
Gardner, Robert	Garret, Curtis	McDonald, James
Leadam, Jacob	McMaster, William	Pike, Richard M.
Nelson, Robert	Norris, Richard	Smith, Thomas B.
Pots, Charles	Satterly, Isaac	Wheeler, Alvin
Smith, John H.	Shunk, John	Whiteside, William
White, Joseph	White, John	Zains, Adam

Page 360

ROLL OF CAPT. WILLIAM LUCE'S COMPANY (Probably from Miami Co.)
Served from August 23, 1812, until February 22, 1813.

Capt. William Luce	Lieut. John McClary	Ensign John Dodds
Sergt. Edward Dyer	Sergt. Benjamin John	Sergt. John Brown
Sergt. Robert McElhaney	Corp. Robert Elliott	Corp. Jeremiah Collins
Corp. Abraham Corrall	Corp. Peter Rodebaugh	Drummer, Samuel Buck
	Fifer, Peter Musselman	
Privates.	**Privates.**	**Privates.**
Bull, Amos	Bowman, Gilbert	Boles, John
Brown, John	Blair, William	Creviston, Henry
Coleman, George	Catro, Charles	Clark, Andrew
Cofman, Jacob	Cofman, Henry	Cook, John
Deem, John	Fall, Hanteter	Green, John
Houser, John	Hannason, Samuel	Long, Jesse
More, Samuel	McGraw, James	McGrew, Samuel
McGrew, Archibald	Rial, Jaq	Robbins, John
Scott, David	Stitter, Daniel	Tinckle, Nicholas
Westfall, Job	Wead, John	

Page 362.

ROLL OF CAPT. WILLIAM RAMSEY'S COMPANY (Probably from Preble Co.)
Served from October 11, 1813, until April 7, 1814.

Capt. William Ramsey	Sergt. James Newton	Corp. Samuel Douglas
Drummer, William Dailey	Fifer, Henry Newton	
Privates.	**Privates.**	**Privates.**
Bobebrake, John	Beeson, James	Baley, Gough
Clawson, Josiah	Dougherty, Thomas	Dougherty, Edward
Dailey, Dennis	Green, David	Harlin, John
Hammon, Philip	Hammon, William	Hamilton, Andrew
Kester, Paul	Kays, John	Killough, John
Kirkham, Mikel	Lambert, Jonothan	Lesh, Henry
Morris, William	McGaw, Moses	Pressley, John
Pressley, Joseph	Pressley, Robert	Stephen, Richard
Stephen, William	Smith, Robert	Smith, Phillip
Wead, Andrew	Wright, John	White, Johab

Pages 363-364

ROLL OF CAPT. JOSEPH EWING'S COMPANY (County Unknown).
Served from August 9, 1813, until February 8, 1814.

Capt. Joseph Ewing	Lieut. John Archer	Ensign Truman Munger
Sergt. Joshua Burk	Sergt. John Windslow	Sergt. Ezra Kellog
Sergt. Daniel Watkins	Corp. Samuel Ewing	Corp. Lewis Lorris
Corp. John Garrard	Corp. Joseph Hancock	Drummer, Henry King
	Fifer, Thomas Hatfield	
Privates.	**Privates.**	**Privates.**
Bonta, Henry	Brown, Conrad	Brooks, Jacob
Baldwin, Ezekiel	Butt, Henry	Butt, John
Brown, William	Branblossom, Abraham	Cox, Elijah
Cortner, John	Cortney, William	Cunningham, William
Coffman, Henry	Delop, William	Douglas, Robert
Gallahan, Jonas	Graham, George	Gilbert, Thomas
Holtzklaw, James	Houston, Edward	Haines, Ephraim
Ifert, Jacob	John, Lemuel	Kizer, Rannah
Luce, Benjamin		

Vol. I.
ROLL OF CAPT. JOSEPH EWING'S COMPANY (Continued).

Rank and Name of Soldier.

Privates.
Loveless, Sylvanus
Middal, John G.
Overholster, John
Predy, William
Rodes, Jacob
Scott, Alexander
Scott, William
Thompson, John
Wood, Aquila
Wood, Joshua
Warner, Jacob

Rank and Name of Soldier.

Privates.
Muzzleman, Peter
Mill, George
Pool, George
Quinn, James
Riffle, Jacob
Scribner, Azor
Shell, Joseph
Tennent, Alexander
Whitsell, Henry
Whitaker, John
Webb, John
Zeazel, John

Rank and Name of Soldier.

Privates.
Majors, William
Messenger, Nicholas
Peck, John
Rittenhous, Peter
Rittenhouse, Obediah
Sumption, Charles
Scott, Moses
Van Skike, John
Westfall, Job
Warts, Israel
York, Aaron

Page 365
ROLL OF CAPT. THOMAS MICKEY'S COMPANY (Probably from Franklin Co.)
Served from August 25 until October 10, 1812.

Capt. Thomas Mickey
Privates.
Armstrong, John
Carter, Joseph
Hopkins, James
McElvain, John

Privates.
Brickle, John
Driver, John
Jones, Richard
Newcome, Christopher

Privates.
Congell, Joseph
Fuller, William
Morehead, Thomas
Sells, Peter

Page 370
ROLL OF CAPT. SAMUEL BLACK'S COMPANY (County Unknown).
Served from August 24, 1812, until February 24, 1813.

Capt. Samuel Black
Sergt. John Black
Sergt. James Bruce
Corp. Isaac Ellis

Lieut. James McBride
Sergt. William Smith
Corp. Henry Williams
Corp. William Beason
Fifer, William Harrison

Ensign George Price
Sergt. Myers, John
Corp. Francis Kelley
Drummer, Roswell W. Smith

Privates.
Albin, John
Black, Peter
Bigger, John
Casey, Jacob
Evans, Benjamin
Goble, Daniel
Hushaw, Peter
Hall, Abner
Hamilton, James
Kennedy, John
Loofberrard, Jacob
Minick, Peter
Moore, John H.
McIntire, Joseph
McFarland, John
Price, John
Richard, Conrad
Shirely, Samuel
Venard, Francis
Wood, Zedock
Wood, John

Privates.
Black, James
Buchanon, James
Concklin, John
Dill, William
Elliott, John
Gilliland, Thomas
Hook, Hugh
Hayes, James
Hayes, John
Kelley, Abner
Melvin, Ebenezer
Miller, George
Murphy, Thomas
McClure, James
McWhalen, Hugh
Russell, Robert
Snodgrass, Robert
Smith, Samuel
Vance, Joseph
Williams, Levi
Williams, William

Privates.
Birt, William
Blaney, Robert
Confer, Jacob
Dickensheets, Henry
Elliott, Alexander
Hide, John
Hobbs, Littleton
Gaff, John
Ivers, Richard
Loofberrard, David
Miller, John
Murphy, Oratio
Morris, Henry
McBride, Jesse
Palmer, Layton
Ross, Alexander E.
Sutton, Jesse
Smith, Robert
Whalon, John
Willey, Hugh N.

Page 372
ROLL OF CAPT. SOLOMON BENTLEY'S COMPANY
(Probably from Belmont County)
Served from August 22 until October 22, 1812.

Capt. Solomon Bentley
Sergt. Joseph Grimes
Sergt. James Kyle
Corp. Dennis Forrest

Lieut. Joseph Kirkwood
Sergt. James Nixon
Corp. David Dille
Corp. John Vroyd

Ensign George Love
Sergt. Hugh Brown
Corp. William McCoy
Musican Evan Rodgers

Privates.
Adeidler, Caleb
Dallis, John
Day, Israel
Erskine, Thomas
Gilliland, Thomas
Harriman, David
Kyzer, Thomas
Marques, William
Powel, Joseph
Robinson, John
Simeson, James
Wright, Coleman H.

Privates.
Armstrong, Travis
Carrington, Nicholas
Devore, John
Grimes, John
Gilliland, Morgan
Irvin, George
Long, Adam
McMahan, Dennis
Rankin, Joseph
Shepherd, Arnold
Starr, James
Watson, Robert

Privates.
Cluney, Alexander
Dillon, Samuel
Ditzler, John
Goeshorn, Leonard
Herd, William
Howel, William
Lashley, Hezekiah
Park, James
Rider, Obed
Shepherd, Isaiah
Tarrier, John

Page 373   Vol. I.
ROLL OF CAPT. PETER BACUS' COMPANY (County Unknown).
Served from August 19 until September 18, 1812.

Rank and Name of Soldier.	Rank and Name of Soldier.	Rank and Name of Soldier.
Capt. Peter Bacus	Lieut. Levin Willoughby	Sergt. John Conrad
Sergt. Adam Brinter	Sergt. Nicholas Sibral	Sergt. Thompson Sebring
Corp. Seaburn Hinton	Corp. Thomas Phillips	Corp. George Chad
Corp. William Dean	Drummer, John Stall	
Privates.	**Privates.**	**Privates.**
Byers, William	Barker, Joseph	Black, John
Cutright, Henry	Cassill, Abraham	Curts, John
Dever, John	Extine, Daniel	Fultz, Jacob
Fulk, Henry	Francis, Joseph	Hull, Isaac
Hines, Adam	Husk, John	Harley, Carter
Ice, Jacob	Hornback, John	Knox, Benjamin
Linton, William	Murphy, Redmond	McHenry, Aaron
Overly, Jacob	Overly, David	Rusk, Moses
Ray, William	Rush, George	Rush, Josiah
Shoote, Richard	Strucy, Michael	Swaggert, Daniel
Shane, Henry	Sullivan, William	Smith, Samuel
Sullerback, John	Stewart, James	Strevey, Daniel
Smith, William	Taylor, Nimrod	Vezey, William
Vanmetre, Henry	Wech, John	

Page 374
ROLL OF CAPT. ANDREW DILL'S COMPANY (County Unknown).
Served from May 1, 1812, until May 1, 1813.

Capt. Andrew Dill	Lieut. William Weatherington	Ensign John H. DeLorshmuts
Sergt. Andrew McMahan	Sergt. Robert McElvain	Sergt. Josiah Williams
Sergt. William Mickey	Corp. Jonathan Piper	Corp. Joseph Morgan
Corp. Samuel C. Rayl	Corp. Barnabus McMahan	Musician, Roswell W. Smith
Privates.	**Privates.**	**Privates.**
Abbott Armstrong D.	Bogard, Joseph	Burk, Joseph
Buck, William	Braden, James	Breckinridge, Joseph
Conner, John	Carns, John	Davies, William
Denny, John	Culbertson, Samuel	Dyer, Samuel
Ford, Benjamin	Harrison, James	Hamler, Jacob
Ice, George	Hott, Peter	Lewin, John
Lynn, Lewis	Leonard, John	Martin, Daniel
Mettel, Abel	Monel, Jesse	McNutt, James
Nicherson, Uzziah	Nicherson, Isachar	Parkinson, John H.
Robinson, Daniel	Right, George	Richtes, John
Reid, Charles	Stiers, Henry	Sordan, Jonathan
Shafer, Frederick	Wolf, Charles	Whiteman, James
Williams, Matthew	Walling, Asa	Wyant, John

Page 375
ROLL OF CAPT. GABRIEL COX'S COMPANY (Probably from Champaign Co.)
Served from September 14 until October 16, 1812.

Capt. Gabriel Cox	Lieut. Nicholas Sturm	Ensign Nicholas Van Densan
Sergt. Ezekiel Rice	Sergt. Walker Aldridge	Sergt. James Herd
Sergt. William B. Craghill	Corp. John Reid	Corp. John Bowman
Fifer, Newton Burroughs	Drummer, William Hull	
Privates.	**Privates.**	**Privates.**
Blair, William	Beacon, David	Bendure, William
Blackford, John	Brooks, Thomas	Carter, Israel
Dotson, Thomas	Dean, Barzilla	Dillon, William
Davidson, Stephen	Dillon, Richard	Gerard, Jacob
Green, John	Goodfellow, Moore	Griffith, Azel
Gandy, Abijah	Herd, Thomas	Hutchinson, Thomas
Hunt, John	Heaton, Jonah	Haney, James
Hopkins, Richard	Hanna, David	Jones, Stephen
Jones, David	Keyser, Benjamin	Kennedy, Samuel
Moss, Jacob	Price, John	Patrick, Johnson
Parks, James	Perry, James	Rudesiliy, Jacob
Smith, David	Smith, John	Sturm, Mathias
Spencer, Aaron	Simpson, Alexander	Turner, Robert
White, Benjamin	Williams, Zechariah	White, Joseph

Pages 378-379
ROLL OF CAPT. JEHIEL GREGORY'S COMPANY (Probably from Ross Co.)
Served from July 28 until September 3, 1813.

Capt. Jehiel Gregory	Lieut. Jacob Dunbaugh	Ensign Thomas Ewing
Sergt. Montgomery Perry	Sergt. Andrew Gregory	Sergt. John Bell
Sergt. Elijah Pilcher	Corp. John Cox	Corp. William Rines
Corp. John Jackson	Corp. Edward Pilcher	

Vol. I.
ROLL OF CAPT. JEHIEL GREGORY'S COMPANY (Continued.)

Rank and Name of Soldier.	Rank and Name of Soldier.	Rank and Name of Soldier.
Privates.	**Privates.**	**Privates.**
Ackley, Henry	Abbott, John	Bananes, George
Bananes, Jacob	Davis, Samuel	Goodridge, Timothy
Graham, William	Howtell, Hiram	Kenney, John
Polk, Ciphus	Polk, Eber	Ranul, Daniel
Rabonet, Ezekiel	Rewis, George	Rabb, Johnson
Reynolds, Justice	Richardson, Abraham	Spence, Abraham
Speed, George	Stroud, Joel	Simonton, Jacob
Stedman, Abel	Seloy, Gabriel	Tucker, John
True, Josiah	Wright, John	Waters, Josiah

Page 380
ROLL OF ENSIGN JACOB HOOVER OR HOOBER'S COMPANY
(Probably from Ross County.)
Served from July 28 until August 18, 1813.

Ensign Jacob Hoover or Hoober	Sergt. George Corwine	Sergt. William McKonkle
Sergt. William Stewart	Corp. Michael Robinson	
Privates.	**Privates.**	**Privates.**
Bowman, Daniel	Bowman, Benjamin	Corwine, Samuel
Chenworth, Thomas	Fewell, John	Graham, Robert
Hultz, William	Harrel, Daniel	Jordan, Jones
Mounts, Eli	McMullin, Alexander Jr.	Rhidemeer, Frederick
Stewart, George	Stegall, Frederick	Thomas, Ormes
Vineyard, James	Wilson, George	Wood, Jonothan
Williams, Amos	Wilson, James	Warren, James
Warren, Greenbury	Wells, Peter	Wells, Isaac

Page 381
ROLL OF CAPT. TIMOTHY BUELL'S COMPANY
(Probably from Washington County).
Served from August 1 until September 7, 1813.

Capt. Timothy Buell	Lieut. Peter White	Lieut. Salvanus Olney
Ensign James Leget	Sergt. Nathaniel Hamilton	Sergt. George Nixon
Sergt. Jabez Palmer	Sergt. S. D. Buell	Corp. Samuel Nott
Corp. Edward Corner	Corp. John Barrough	Corp. Nicholas Chapman
Privates.	**Privates.**	**Privates.**
Blackmer, Timothy	Coleman, Daniel	Corns, John
Clark, John C.	Coleman, Elisha	Cuddington, Zechanah
DeLong, Henry	Dunbar, Thomas	Demont, Richard
Dennis, Thomas	Ellis, Benjamin	Gates, Timothy, Jr.
Gates, Stephen	William F.	Havens, Henry
Jennings, Zebulum	Kimball, Titus	Lawrence, R., Jr.
Liget, Robert	Laughey, John	Laughey, William
Miller, Jacob	McGee, Robert	Miller, Samuel
McCoy, Alexander	McConnel, John	Nulton, Jacob
Palmer, Benjamin F.	Perry, John	Porter, John R.
Pruant, William	Quigley, Horace	Rair, Dennis
Ray, James	Scott, John	Smith, Nathaniel
Taylor, John	Wilson, Jonothan	Whitney, Jonothan
Wood, Paulus E.	Zuthinger, Clark	

Pages 382-383
ROLL OF CAPT. JOHN RAMSEY'S COMPANY (County Unknown).
Served from December 1, 1812, until March 9, 1813.

Capt. John Ramsey	Lieut. James Anderson	Ensign, Lindsey Cannon
Sergt Thomas Roseburg	Sergt. James Craighead	Sergt. James Rainsey
Sergt. Samuel Zolly	Corp. John Hunter	Corp. Phillip Fout
Corp. Joseph Fife	Corp. William Hamilton.	
Privates.	**Privates.**	**Privates.**
Augustine, Henry	Anderson, James	Beer, James
Brown, Joseph	Bennet, James	Craig, Robert
Cannon, Thomas	Daugherty, James	Daugherty, Samuel
Earley, James	Earley, David	Fife, James
Fife, Samuel	Frank, Adam	Furney, John
Farmer, Thomas	Graham, John	Guthery, William
Guthery, Samuel	Goss, Mathias	Gardner, Jacob
Geddes, James	Hamilton, Jonothan	Hunter, Samuel
Hayes, David	Hickman, Nicholas	Haggart, William
Hurney, Adam	Jackson, John	Kees, Russell
Lamburn, Josiah	Figgins, Samuel	Campbell, John
Carnes, George	Craig, William	Meek, Samuel
Meek, Robert	Meek, William	McLaughlin, Robert
McLaughlin, William	McDonald, Duncan	McAllily, Samuel
McCullogh, James	McCready, William	Opdyke, Albert
Prince, William	Paul, Benjamin.	Paul, Henry
Pollock, William	Grimm, Jacob	Robinson, Jonah
Rupert, Jacob	Smith, Sampson	Sheets, Jacob
Sheets, John	Simcock, Michael	Thompson, John L
Walls, Richard	Wright, Gilbert	Shirts, Peter
Whitmore, John	Shiver, Samuel	

Pages 384-385 Vol. I.

ROLL OF CAPT. JAMES DOWNING'S COMPANY (County Unknown).

Served from January 1 until March 9, 1813.

Rank and Name of Soldier.

Capt. James Downing
Sergt. John Forsythe
Sergt. Samuel Richards
Corp. John Warden

Privates.
Burke, John
Bair, David
Bower, John
Camp, Henry
Funk, Samuel
Fulks, George
Howman, Isaac
Heffner, David
Knap, Caleb
Mills, Abraham
Mathews, Isaac
Nedeck, Samuel
Powel, John
Pinckney, Adam
Richards, Daniel
Reed, Adam
Stephens, Daniel
Smetts, John
Vaughn, Jonothan
Wike, George

Rank and Name of Soldier.

Lieut. Peter Johnston
Sergt. John Barke
Corp. Abraham Bair
Corp. Joseph Bashford

Privates.
Bower, Henry
Barber, Henry
Boyle, Richard
Dixon, John
Gruble, John
Henning, Jacob
Hiser, Peter
Kepler, Andrew
Mills, Eli
Morrison, James
Nelson, William
Perkins, James
Parker, Thomas
Rodgers, Levi
Ryla, Elijah
Smith, Jacob
Thompson, John
Voyt, James
Winis, Barnabas
Williams, John

Rank and Name of Soldier.

Ensign, Thomas Smith
Sergt. Michael McGowin
Corp. Benjamin Atkinson
Fifer, Jesse Ellis

Privates.
Bair, John
Baird, Andrew
Crites, William
Forsythe, Andrew
Holtz, John
Hartner, Jacob
Kinney, Peter
Leatherman, Peter
Murry, Patrick
McCaughey, Joseph
Patten, Mathew
Painter, Jacob
Parkerson, Jacob
Rodgers, John
Strickland, Edward
Stover, Samuel
Vaughn, Richard
Worley, Thomas
White, Samuel

Pages 386-387

ROLL OF CAPT. WILLIAM BLACKBURN'S COMPANY (County Unknown).

Served from December 1, 1812, until March 9, 1813.

Capt. William Blackburn
Sergt. Benjamin Holm
Sergt. George Wiseman
Corp. Daniel Cross

Privates.
Armstrong, Thomas
Brown, Joseph
Betz, Frederick
Bishop, Joseph
Brinker, Peter
Curl, Charles
Grimes, John
Harwood, Peter
Jumper, Joseph
Kuntz, Emanuel
Mannon, William
Night, Robert
Queen, Samuel
Rodger, George
Sheets, George
Shanke, Jacob
Turnipseed, John
Wolf, George
Willitts, John

Lieut, Samuel Ferguson
Sergt. William Milner
Corp. Andrew Gilson
Corp. Joseph Earl
Drummer, Frederick Blecher

Privates.
Anderson, Andrew
Bootz, George
Britton, Archibald
Bradfield, Joseph
Brown, William
Foulks, Charles
Gibson, David
Hahn, Caleb
Jones, Nicholas
Moody, Joseph
Moss, Phillip
Panner, Jesse
Queen, John
Robinson, John
Stephens, Benjamin
Swardley, John
Wolf, John
Wollem, Jacob
Woolam, Henry

Ensign, George Grimes
Sergt. Samuel Swoy
Corp. Phillip Branderberry
Fifer, Daniel McCaskey

Privates.
Booker, Isaiah
Branderberry, Conrad
Bell, William
Bashan, Ezekial
Canehey, Joseph
Fishel, Frederick
Gibson, John
Helmick, Adam
Kuntz, John
Miller, Stephen
Myers, John
Patterson, Joseph
Redmond, Jacob
Rossell, Job
Sooy, Samuel
Skelton, John
Wolf, Phillip
Welker, William

Pages 388-389

ROLL OF CAPT. JOSEPH K. McCUNE'S COMPANY (County Unknown).

Served from February 12 until August 12, 1813.

Capt. Joseph K. McCune
Sergt. Abraham Pollock
Sergt. John McFarson

Privates.
Bailey, James
Briggs, James
Corningham, Edward
DeLong, Isaac
Deaver, Walter P.
Griffith, William
Hibner, John
Lane, Dutton
McFarland, Samuel
Patterson, Obediah
Rattle, James
Spry, Elijah
Swank, Philip

Lieut. Thomas Kirkpatrick
Sergt. Jonothan Eddington
Corp. William C. Slaughter

Privates.
Baird, Robert
Burch, Zebulum
Chandler, Daniel
Dawson, Henry
Feroson, Robert
Heaton, Joseph
Haddon, William
Mingus, William
Parker, Henry
Ross, John
Switzer, John
Welsh, William

Ensign, John Day
Sergt. Alexander D. Tucker
Corp. Moses Powell

Privates.
Bingham, David
Barnard, William
Deans, George
Cummings, William
Gibson, George
Holt, James
Hutchison, George
Moss, Nehemiah
Parscale, Cornelius
Shepardson, Jared
Snider, Jacob
Waggoner, Mathias

Page 390. Vol. I.

ROLL OF CAPT. WILLIAM GILL'S COMPANY. (County Unknown.)
Served from April 16, 1812, until April 17, 1813.

Rank and Name of Soldier.	Rank and Name of Soldier.	Rank and Name of Soldier.
Capt. William Gill	Lieut. Wynekoop Warner	Ensign Jacob Witt
Sergt. Alexander McBratney	Sergt. Thomas Riddle	Sergt. Titus Shotwell
Sergt. John Gorden	Corp. Parry Hulse	Corp. James Bigley
Corp. Ezekial Boggs	Corp. Asaph Butler	Fifer, John Robinson
	Drummer, Archibald Lafferton	

Privates.

Browny, John	Bryan, Aaron	Butler, Eli
Bright, Nicholas	Boyd, William	Berry, Joseph
Colter, Archibald, Sr.	Crooks, James	Colman, Samuel
Coulter, Archibald, Jr.	Edwards, Walter	Edy, Job
Fairhurst, William	Gassaway, Benjamin	Gardner, John
Hamilton, John	Hardesty, Lewis	Hardesty, John
Holmes, Thomas	Harred, Samuel	Hammerly, Joseph
Lansdown, William	Lamson, John	Mitchell, Henry
Martin, Robert	Montgomery, Robert	Miller, John
McMahon, John	McWilliams, Alexander	Neff, Henry
Piper, Tristan	Porterfield, Robert	Paitens, Christian
Ritchie, William	Ritchie, Robert	Rankin, John
Rouse, George	Fisher, John	Scott, William
Stowden, Jacob	Stewart, James	Stephenson, Arthur
Scott, Joseph	Scott, John	Spurgeon, Nathan
Smith, Robert	Skinner, William	Taylor, James
Willis, William	Wood, George	Watkins, Thomas

Page 391.

ROLL OF CAPT. BENJAMIN MAPEL'S COMPANY.
(Probably from Belmont County.)
Served from February 7 until March 7, 1815.

Capt. Benjamin Mapel	Lieut, Jacob Winnings	Ensign Augustine Andrew
Sergt. James Swindler	Sergt. James Bashford	Corp. James Jobes
Corp. John Sprangler	Drummer, John Marshall	

Privates.

Abrams, Anthony	Alexander, James	Augustine, George
Burk, Moses	Boyles, Nurman	Bennet, Thomas
Bassett, Ebenezer	Brenner, Jacob W.	Cole, Ezekial
Collear, Joseph	Fowler, John	Franks, Michael
Grove, William	Lyle, William	Lewis, Thomas B.
Miller, Samuel	Pinewell, Elias	Russell, Joshua
Russell, David	Rukeson, Jacob	Spedle, William
Swinehart, Daniel	Taylor, Abner	Welsh, John
West, Adam	Welday, Abraham	Yeckne, Charles
Lutchlenwatter, Jacob		

Page 392.

ROLL OF CAPT. JOHN McELROY'S COMPANY.
(Probably from Belmont County.)
Served from October 20, 1812, until January 11, 1813.

Capt. John McElroy	Lieut. Anthony Weizer	Ensign David Rook
Sergt. Alexander Smiley	Sergt. Thomas Gourley	

Privates.

Ault, Peter	Baker, Charles	Burkirk, Isaac
Cucklen, Samuel	Dean, Daniel	Dean, Aaron
Dean, Benjamin	Duff, David	Duff, John
Graham, William	Grubb, Jacob	Hardesty, Robert
Hardesty, Samuel	Hughs, James	Logan, John
Markes, Samuel	McClelland, David	Nillane, James
Renneson, John	Renneson, William	Robertson, Robert
Smith, Anthony	Shipman, Stephen	Tharp, John
Vanwy, Charles	Work, Alexander	Wilson, George
Word, Morcer	Taggert, James	

Page 393.

ROLL OF CAPT. VENE STONE'S COMPANY.
(Probably from Geauga County.)
Served from August 23, until August 30, 1812.

Capt. Vene Stone	Lieut. Eli Fowler	Ensign Gunyon Moss
Sergt. Theadore Royer	Sergt. Stephen H. Worthington	Sergt. John Charter
Sergt. Simon Burroughs	Corp. Solomon Charter	Corp. Simon Speng
Corp. Solomon Harks	Drummer, Jacob Burton	Fifer, Adolphus Coulton

Privates.

Andrews, Amos	Andrews, Leman G.	Brooks, Jonothan
Brooks, Ichabod	Bradley, Bildad	Bradley, Moses
Bradley, Selah	Bradley, Gomer	

Pages 395-396. Vol. I.

ROLL OF CAPT. WILLIAM T. CULLUM'S COMPANY. (County Unknown.)

Served from September 4, 1813, until March 2, 1814.

Rank and Name of Soldier.	Rank and Name of Soldier.	Rank and Name of Soldier.
Capt. William T. Cullum	Lieut. William Misner	Ensign Francis Cullum
Sergt. Purnell I. Reddish	Sergt. Peter Carle	Sergt. William Williamson
Sergt. Solomon Slayback	Corp. James Nicholson	Corp. Morgan Huff
Corp. John Miller	Corp. William Frazee	Corp. Ephraim Earle
Drummer, Thomas Ogdon	Fifer, Joseph Broughard	

Privates.

Argadine, Edward	Broughman, Joseph	Brooks, John
Brewner, Jacob	Bash, William	Brook, Stephen
Cary, Benajah	Cameron, Daniel	Conklin, Joseph C.
Collins, John	Congar, James	Cathers, Robert
Carr, Samuel, Sr.	Carr, Samuel, Jr.	Carr, William
Clark, Thomas	Collier, Hazel	Cramer, John
Falkner, James	Flint, John	Farmer, Tatley
Goldthwaite, Nathaniel	Gray, William	Harrison, Charles
Hope, David C.	Hubard, Vivdate	Henderson, John
Huffman, Jonas	Hunter, James	Harrison, Merines
Hageman, Simon, Sr.	Hageman, Simon, Jr.	Hufner, Thomas
Isrig, Daniel	Irwin, William	Jessup, Walter
Oslin, John	Osgood, Nathan	Kain, Richard
Murphy, Albert	Miller, John	Miller, James
Miller, Samuel	Moore, Samuel	Miller, Silas
Moore, William	Masters, William	Mockridge, Samuel
McKee, Anthony	McKee, James	McFerin, Samuel
McBride, Samuel	McFeally, Thomas	McKee, William
Noble, Henry	Noble, John	Nicholas, Jonothan
Packer, Barnabus	Potts, Charles	Pack, Enos
Park, Israel	Pherris, Joseph	Pack, Nathan T.
Pack, Samuel D.	Robertson, Cuthbert	Russell, Moses
Simson, Alexander	Sands, Daniel	Swim, Ezra S.
Shadley, James	Stell, John	Skull, John
Speere, James	Shiffer, Lambert	Shed, Silas
Shaddak, Shank	Thomas, David	Trisler, Peter
Taylor, Robert	West, John	

Page 397.

ROLL OF CAPT. GEORGE SHEMMELL'S COMPANY. (County Unknown.)

Served from August 7, 1813, ————.

Capt. George Shemmell	Lieut. John Guard	Ensign George Sluthrin
	Sergt. Cornelius Hand	

Privates.

Andreas, Peter	Alwood, Christopher	Biddinger, Henry
Blickensturfer, Jacob	Burnet, Richard	Baker, George
Baker, Peter	Butt, William	Balsly, Jacob
Bales, Abraham	Clum, John	Cline, Henry
Carson, John	Gorpman, John	Deardorf, Isaac
Danner, Jacob	Eakin, Daniel	Foster, Jesse
Flitkinger, John	Forney, Abraham	Gossage, Benjamin
Gibson, George	Hill, Jesse	Harbaugh, Isaac
Hill, Charles	Hogland, William	Hill, William
Haverstock, Conrad	Jackson, Francis	Most, Joseph
Johnston, Lemuel	Minick, Phillip	Price, Thomas
Miller, Jacob	Rutter, Jolly	Rippeth, William
Purcussele, Christian	Shane, Abraham	Sharp, John Jacob
Ridgeway, Thomas	Study, George	Stocker, Trumbow, John
Shark, Valentine	Uhrick, Michael	Vail, George
Thompson, Jacob	Walgamurth, Joseph	Williams, Thomas
Walton, Esse	Walters, Samuel	Walters, Jacob
Williams, Levi	Wetty, John	Young, Jacob

Page 398.

ROLL OF JOHN AUGUSTINE'S COMPANY. (County Unknown.)

Served from September 6 until November 24, 1814.

Capt. John Augustine	Lieut. Peter Conkel	Ensign, Augustine Bushong
Sergt. David Kemp	Sergt. Samuel Crawford	Sergt. John Augustine
Sergt. Phillip Shou	Corp. James Gaff	Corp. Joseph B. Sedball
Corp. Michael C. Homan	Drummer, Jacob Bash	Drummer, Jesse Ellis
	Fifer, Thomas Tidball	

Privates.

Allenton, James	Arnold, John	Bryan, Daniel
Conley, James	Carrington, John	French, Samuel
Geddis, James	Harriman, William	Hall, James
Lester, Christopher	Lewis, Francis	McConnichy, Hugh
McPherson, James	McConnell, Wilson	Palmer, John
Palmer, James	Risher, Daniel	Robinson, Jonothan
Rosberry, William	Swinehart, Samuel	VanArsteen, Frederick

Page 399. Vol. I.
ROLL OF CAPT. JOHN NIMMON'S COMPANY. (County Unknown.)
(Incomplete.)
Served from October 1, 1812, until March 31, 1813.

Rank and Name of Soldier.	Rank and Name of Soldier.	Rank and Name of Soldier.
Capt. John Nimmon	Lieut. Anthony Loustenhiser	Ensign, Felty Shoop
Sergt. John Warden	Sergt. Seldon Woster	Corp. George Almonds
	Musician, John Kuntz	

Page 400.
ROLL OF MARTIN SITTLER'S COMPANY.
(Probably from Columbiana County. Incomplete.)
Served from August 25 until November 5, 1812.

Capt. Martin Sittler	Lieut. Conrad Yarian	Sergt. John Roose
Sergt. Albert Opdyke	Sergt. James Watson	Sergt. Mathias Yearian
Corp. John Forney	Corp. Peter Forney	Corp. Adam Forney
	Private, George Lowfure	

Page 401.
ROLL OF CAPT. SAMUEL WATSON'S COMPANY. (County Unknown.)
Served from September 18 until October 18, 1812.

Capt. Samuel Watson	Sergt. Daniel McMichael	
Privates.	**Privates.**	**Privates.**
Coon, Jacob	Coon, John	Coon, George
Eldfield, Jonothan	Goss, William	McClure, Samuel
McClure, Thomas	McClure, James	McClure, James Jr.
Robbins, Elisha	Riddle, William	Speir, Duncan
Stout, Jacob	Sent, Jacob	Sent, John
Sent, John Jr.	Sent, Daniel	Weyrick, John
Weyrick, Peter	Watson, Amaziah	

Pages 402-403.
ROLL OF CAPT. JOHN GREER'S COMPANY.
(Probably from Knox County.)
Served from August 26 until October 10, 1812.

Capt. John Greer	Lieut. Carey Cooper	Ensign, John Cook
Sergt. John Wells	Sergt. George Low	Sergt. Smith Hadley
Sergt. David Brown	Drummer, Daniel Dial	Fifer, Stephen Butler
Privates.	**Privates.**	**Privates.**
Arnold, John	Ayres, Ashel	Ackre, Adam
Atherton, Francis	Baker, John	Baughman, Jacob
Brown, Jeremiah	Blakeney, Francis	Boyle, John
Brown, Samuel	Carnes, Abraham	Chapman, Timothy
Doty, Frazer	Davis, Alexander	Earleywine, Adam
Craig, Jonothan	Dodd, Judathan	Guinn, John
Garrison, John	Green, John	Harris, Jesse
Harrod, James	Harris, James	Holt, Even
Humphreys, John	Hoglin, George	Harrod, Lerue
Johnston, Samuel	Lepley, Joseph	Lewis, Samuel
Martin, James	McBride, Robert	McBride, Thomas
McKee, Alexander	Pool, John	Pinkley, John
Pumphrey, Joshua	Nail, Henry	Shafer, Benjamin
Spurgeon, George	Shop, Benjamin	Swore, Jesse
Strange, James	Smith, William	Smith, George
Sapp, William	Tallmage, Joseph	Thompson, Andrew
Truax, William	Tawnyhill, Charles	Vanosdoll, Charles
Young, John Jr.	Young, Aaron	Welker, Jacob
Zimmerman, John	Zinn, George	

Pages 411-412-413.
ROLL OF CAPT. GEORGE HOSHER'S COMPANY. (County Unknown.)
Served from February 16 until April 16, 1814. Part served until August 16, 1814.

Capt. George Hosher	Lieut. Michael Walter	Ensign, William Evens
Sergt. Henry Bonsteel	Sergt. Ezekial Joseph	Sergt. John Livingston
Sergt. John Miller	Corp. Massy Climer	Corp. Joshua Evens
Corp. Michael Hively	Corp. Daniel Spohn	Corp. John Hiles
Sergt. William McIntosh	Drummer, William Boan	
Privates.	**Privates.**	**Privates.**
Baker, Joseph	Bold, Henry	Bryan, William
Bixter, Christian	Courson, John	Chambers, James
Chester, George	Clem, Henry	Davis, Aquila
Daniel, John	Demas, Thomas	Fisher, Jacob
Friend, William	Farmer, Samuel	Futhy, Isaac
Friend, George	Gibbs, Daniel	Green, Jacob
Guin, Hezekiah	Green, Robert	Hills, John
Houts, Christian	Hoy, Phillip	Helm, John

ROLL OF CAPT. GEORGE HOSHER'S COMPANY (Continued.)

Rank and Name of Soldier.

Privates.

Hiland, Edward
Hively, Michael
Looker, Jonothan
Lair, Andrew
Lott, George
Lappwine, Gabriel
Miller, Phillip
Meeker, Aaron
Moyer, John
Morris, William
McClung, Thomas
Nutt, David
Parish, John
Ray, Abraham
Shaffer, William
Stephens, Justice
Stevens, Chester
Vandermark, John
Webster, Jacob

Rank and Name of Soldier.

Privates.

Hawey, James
Jenkins, Evan
Love, James
Lobdell, Samuel
Lineburg, Peter
Martin, Joseph
Miller, John
Moore, Thomas
Miller, Othias
Moredeck, William
McCormick, James
Pair, Thomas
Ricketts, John
Ridenour, Martin
Stouter, John
Sutton, John
Thrush, Michael
Westfall, Harvey
Westfall, Henry

Rank and Name of Soldier.

Privates.

Humbarger, Peter
King, Jacob
Limbaugh, George
Larimore, Joseph
Lineburg, William
Meeker, Moses
Messmore, George
Meek, John
Mercer, Robert
McWilliams, Alexander
Nogle, Isaac
Pressler, John
Russell, William
Spicer, John
Sinbary, William
Signer, George
Turner, Benjamin
Williams, William

Pages 404-405-406-407-408-409-410-439.

ROLL OF CAPT. WILLIAM KILGORE'S COMPANY. (County Unknown.)

Served from February 16 until April 16, 1814. Part served until August 16, 1816.

Capt. William Kilgore
Lieut. Aaron Foster
Sergt. Richard Berry
Sergt. William T. Ricords
Sergt. Thomas Nichols
Corp. James Dean
Corp. Charles Green
Corp. Morgan Osburn
Corp. Daniel Reiley
Corp. Samuel Arnold

Privates.

Arman, George
Bowen, Shadrack
Bradon, Robert
Bennett, Isaac
Cooper, William
Clarke, Simon
Cremead, Smith
Cooper, William
Corey, Abraham
Davis, Lewis
Devorss, John
Emery, James
Foulkeson, John
Gray, James G.
Gooden, Daniel
Grimes, John
Hood, Edward
Harris, Amos
Hasselton, David
Hannon, John
Kirkpatrick, David
Laslin, John
Moots, Jacob
Miller, George M.
Mason, Owen
Mathews, Samuel
McCord, John
McCartney, Duke
Pool, Edward
Powers, Michael
Russell, James
Russell, Bazil
Razell, Barzilla
Scroggs, Alexander
Shane, Daniel
Seabrell, Nicholas
Todhunter, Thomas
Williams, Ezekial
Wood, Conley
Webb, William
Wells, Squire
Walker, John
Bush, Daniel
Coil, Thomas
Grady, John
King, John

Lieut. James Krusen
Ensign, Charles Wells
Sergt. George Kerr
Sergt. Martin Peterson
Sergt. James Gilruth
Corp. Mathew Young
Corp. Samuel White
Corp. Thomas E. Johnson
Corp. Handy Cannon
Corp. Shadrack Bowen

Privates.

Arnold, Samuel
Bradley, Owen
Boots, Jacob
Barker, John
Carey, Abraham
Clark, Thomas
Christy, Joel
Crull, Henry
Dearborn, Nathan
Depew, George
Davis, John
Finimore, John
Green, Samuel
Gragg, William
Gilmore, William
Gilliland, Hugh
Hasselton, Daniel
Holt, William
Headley, George
Hoffman, Leonard
Logue, John
Ledmore, Clement
Mathias, Samuel
Mathews, Thomas
Mounts, Joseph
McCandless, Nathaniel
McCandless, Hugh
O'Brien, Charles
Painter, Elias
Prior, Griffith
Reiley, Nathan
Robison, James
Swinney, John
Stingley, Leonard
Swanzy, John
Timmons, Eli
Vandamen, Conrad
Williams, Calvin
West, James
Wright, John
Woodall, Cosby
Blair, Thomas
DeWitt, George
Hayes, Andrew
Lane, William

Ensign, William Holloway
Sergt. James McArthur
Sergt. Samuel Johnson
Sergt. John Haner
Sergt. William Robinson
Corp. Clement Ledman
Corp. John Hoddey
Corp. Nathan Reiley
Corp. George Armon
Corp. Charles Benett

Privates.

Anderson, John
Bowen, Gardner
Brunt, Jonothan
Brewer, James
Coder, Simeon
Campbell, William
Clark, James
Church, Joel
Dooley, Samuel
Davis, Benjamin
Day, Overton
Frye, Joseph
Groves, John
Green, Charles
Gilmore, Robert
Hopkins, David
Hair, Daniel
Hison, Daniel
Holland, William
Jacobs, Elijah
Lafton, John
Moses, Thomas
Mark, John
Mains, William
Mounts, Enoch
McClure, Michael
McLaughlin, William
Peacock, Ezekial
Patterson, John
Ryan, Messack
Rinely, Daniel
Roe, John
Selden, Spencer
Spencer, Seldon
Swine, John
Taylor, Nehemiah
Windall, Joseph
Ware, Daniel
Webb, Jehiel
Wonstaff, Daniel
Webb, John
Corey, John
Fergans, Daniel
Jameson, Jacob
Roi, Zechariah

Pages 414-415-416. Vol. I.
ROLL OF CAPT. MICAH WOOD'S COMPANY. (County Unknown
Served from February 16 until August 15, 1814.

Rank and Name of Soldier.	Rank and Name of Soldier.	Rank and Name of Soldier.
Capt. Micah Woods	Lieut. Samuel Pope	Ensign, Archabel Beckwith
Ensign, William Newel	Sergt. Benjamin Naylor	Sergt. August Richards
Sergt. Isaac Henderson	Corp. John Cruzan	Corp. Alexander Campbell
Corp. Thomas Mays	Corp. Adam Shaffer	
Privates.	**Privates.**	**Privates.**
Adams, William	Andrews, John	Alkire, John
Buzzard, Robert	Bever, Christian	Blaze, John
Bell, Andrew	Boatman, George	Bishop, Samuel
Baldwin, John R.	Bill, Charles	Borer, Adam
Borer, Abraham	Brown, William	Blair, Daniel
Branson, Isaac	Cummings, Robert	Creed, David C.
Camp, Richard	Coffee, Mitchell	Covin, John
Cummings, William	Dutcher, John	Derby, Stephen
Dunlap, William	Duncan, Alexander	Dennis, John
Dawson, Othy	Davis, Nathaniel	Evans, Thomas
Earl, David	Earl, Isaac	Frye, John
Groom, Thomas	Grady, Thomas	Grub, Joseph
Gibson, John	Gibson, James	Hill, Joseph
Hobaugh, George	Henry, John	Hair, William
Holman, Jesse	Hilderbrand, Phillip	Hubble, Rowland
Hill, John	Howard, Lewis	Johnston, John
Jolly, William	Knox, John L.	Kinsely, David
Kessinger, John	Laycock, Peter	Lucas, James
Mears, Samuel	Marshall, James	Montgomery, Andrew
Moore, Elijah	Miller, Rush P.	Miller, Gilbert
Nicely, David	McLaughlin, George	Paine, Thomas
Parker, Joseph	Paige, David	Peny, Isaac
Qirrey, John	Robbins, Joseph	Reynolds, James
Shields, John	Shoemaker, Frederick	Smith, Jacob
Statelar, Joseph	Shepherd, John	Smith, Jeremiah
Summer, Isaac	Sanbach, John	Starr, John
Stigall, Frederick	Satterlee, Isaac	Shaffer, Adam
Talbot, Rhodney	Thormar, Jacob	Timmins, John
Titus, Peter	Taylor, William	Venoy, William

Pages 417-418.
ROLL OF ABSALOM VANMATRE'S COMPANY. (Probably from Ross County.)
Served from September 28 until October 25, 1812, and from July 29 until August 18, 1813.

Capt. Absalom Vanmatre	Lieut. Joseph Vanmatre	Ensign, John Seaman
Sergt. Joseph Vanmatre Jr.	Sergt. William Clavanger	Sergt. George Fedrick
Sergt. Samuel Jones	Sergt. Pierce Vanmatre	Sergt. John Shockley
	Ensign, David Johnson	
Privates.	**Privates.**	**Privates.**
Burger, Christian	Braskny, Hudson	Bowers, David
Bowers, Jacob	Clevenger, Samuel	Cox, William
Clevanger, Abraham	Gillispy, Hugh	Gillispy, Thomas
Gallispie, Jonothan	Hammer, William	Jones, Oliver
Jones, Isaac	Jones, Daniel	Gainer, Enoch
Lane, Peter	Miller, Isaac	Miller, John
Marsh, Peter	Marsh, George	Massee, James
McCulloch, Samuel	McDonald, Robert	McKilbeans, John
Noble, Benjamin	Noble, William	Pitson, Mathias
Rush, James	Stroup, Anthony	Ross, David
VanMatre, Abner	Shockley, Benjamin	Vanmater, Isaac
VanMater, Samuel	Walton, Henry	White, Jason
White, Absalom	Walton, Nathaniel	White, William
White, Isaac	Walton, Aaron	

Page 426.
ROLL OF CAPT. CALVIN HOADLY'S COMPANY. (County Unknown.)
Served from August 27 until November 1, 1812.

Capt. Calvin Hoadly	Lieut. Lathrop Seymour	Ensign, Daniel Bronson
Sergt. Silas Wilmot	Sergt. Elias Frost	Sergt. Samuel Y. Potter
Sergt. David Beebe	Corp. Richard Vaughn	Corp. Noah Warner
Corp. Ephraim Vaughn	Corp. Roswell Scoville	
Privates.	**Privates.**	**Privates.**
Adams, Benoni	Bunnel, Daniel	Beeb, Loman C.
Culver, Martial	Doam, Timothy	Eddy, David
Frost, Lyman I.	Fowls, Abraham	Fowls, John
Fowls, Ephraim	Geer, James	Hoadly, Clark
Hickcox, Eri	Hickcox, Jared	Hickcox, Samuel
Hill, John W.	Morgan, Ira B.	Morgan, Asa
Morgan, Sylvester	Osborn, Thomas	Potter, Zaphna
Pardy, Samuel	Pritchard, Beard	Robinson, Asath
Tyler, Seymour	Terrell, Iryah S.	Terrell, Oliver
Terrell, Wyllys	Terrell, Tillotson	Tunell, Philander
Vaughn, Jonothan	Wilmot, Ebenezer	Wooster, Sheldon

Page 427.   Vol. I.
ROLL OF CAPT. TIMOTHY BISHOP'S COMPANY. (County Unknown.)
Served from August 22 until October 2, 1812.

Rank and Name of Soldier.	Rank and Name of Soldier.	Rank and Name of Soldier.
Capt. Timothy Bishop	Lieut. John Cunningham	Ensign, Abraham Ozman
Sergt. Isaac Ozman	Sergt. Aaron Miller	Sergt. Moses Decker
Corp. Henry Post	Corp. Pliny Brown	Corp. John Galloway
Privates.	**Privates.**	**Privates.**
Bawn, Isaac	Brown, Daniel	Brown, Samuel Jr.
Carter, William	Eddings, Henry	Farran, Leman
Johnston, Andrew	Jordon, James	Maze, John
Mallet, Henry	Matlin, Alexander	Miller, Samuel
Miller, Alexander	Miller, Isaac	Ozman, Israel
Robinson, Abner	Stanford, James	Spaulding, Jesse
Spillman, Charles	Walcott, Alfred	

Pages 428-429.
ROLL OF CAPT. AMOS LUSK'S COMPANY. (County Unknown.)
Served from August 22 until November 30, 1812, and from January 1, until March 9, 1813.

Capt. Amos Lusk	Lieut. George W. Holcomb	Lieut. John Caris
Ensign, Hiram King	Sergt. Charles Miles	Sergt. William Chamberlings
Sergt. Comfort Raney	Sergt. Nathaniel Stone	Sergt. Henry Post
Sergt. Roswell Scoville	Sergt. Alexander Hall	Sergt. Jonothan B. Bissell
Sergt. Moses Jordon	Corp. Amos Chamberlain	Corp. John Gaylor
Corp. Milo L. Hudson	Corp. Myron Huttinson	Corp. Ami Baldwin
Corp. Timothy Holcomb	Corp. Daniel Brown	Corp. Joseph Baird
Corp. Moses Jordon	Drummer, Joseph B. Bishop	Drummer, Asa Rose
	Fifer, Henry Wood	
Privates.	**Privates.**	**Privates.**
Auter, Claron	Allen, Jesse	Allen, Nathaniel
Bostwick, Adna H.	Brown, Daniel	Baird, Joseph
Baird, James	Burdick, James	Ballford, Moses
Baldwin, Caleb	Beach, David	Brian, Robert
Brine, Henry C.	Bishop, David	Croy, Richard
Cackler, John	Chamberlain, Joseph	Cain, Gabriel
Carpenter, Richard	Cannon, George	Cochran, William
Cook, James	Draper, Asa	Drake, Francis B.
Dillingham, John	Ellsworth, Elijah	Fisher, Joseph
Gardner, David	Hall, John	Hill, John
Johnson, Daniel H.	Jordon, James	Johnston, Samuel
Lindley, Abia	Lindley, Jesse	Lindley, Ichabod
Metcalf, Jonothan	Muttin, Alexander	Messenger, Nathaniel H.
Mallet, John	McConoughy, Jarvis	Newton, John
Nye, Joshua	Norton, Lebbeus	Owen, Thomas
Oviatt, John	Oviatt, Herman	Oviatt, Benjamin
Pond, David	Prior, Warden	Pease, George
Pease, Ebenezer	Post, Lina	Richardson, Micaiah
Riley, Julius, Jr.	Robinson, Abner	Spilman, James
Sacket, Harvey	Sweet, Amos	Spaulding, Jesse
Spellman, Charles	Shaw, John	Steel, Alexander
Sutliff, Jesse	Tickner, David	Vanhining, Thomas
Vail, Samuel	Wilcox, David	Walker, James
Walker, Robert	Walker, George	Whitaker, William
Willys, Martin	Whorton, James	Wilson, James
Wills, John	White, Joel	Williams, Jonothan
	Wilcox, Isaac	

Page 431.
ROLL OF CAPT. THOMAS RICE'S COMPANY. (County Unknown)
Served from August 22 until October 3, 1812.

Capt. Thomas Rice	Lieut. Thomas Vallhyning	Sergt. Abel Woodward
Sergt. Theodore Hammon	Sergt. Henry Clark	Sergt. Jonothan Gaylord, Jr.
Corp. Samuel Osman	Corp. Gibson Gates	Corp. William Lappin
Drummer, Zenas Kelsey	Fifer, Thomas Gaylord	
Privates.	**Privates.**	**Privates.**
Baker, Samuel	Cackler, Abraham	Gaylord, Stewart
Haymaker, John	Haymaker, George	Johnston, Nathan
Latta, Moses	Lappin, John	Nighman, George
Owen, Thomas	Powers, George	Rodgers, Constant
Strong, David	Turner, Samuel	Turner, John
Vaner, Abel	Wyatt, Ezra	Wells, John
Woodward, Stephen		

Page 432. Vol. I.

ROLL OF CAPT. SAMUEL HALE'S COMPANY. (County Unknown)
Served from August 22 until October 3, 1812.

Rank and Name of Soldier.	Rank and Name of Soldier.	Rank and Name of Soldier.
Capt. Samuel Hale	Lieut. William Honson	Ensign, Jamin Hulbert
Sergt. Charles Crittenden	Sergt. Ira Hulbert	Sergt. Alexander Hall
Sergt. Martin Kemp, Jr.	Corp. Daniel Culver	Corp. Johan Blakely
Corp. Barnabus Williams	Corp. William Johnson	Drummer, Bradford Waldo

Privates.

Adams, Moses Jr.	Allen, Nathaniel	Allen, Jesse
Baird, Joseph	Baird, William	Beach, James
Buzzard, Henry	Baird, James	Bradford, Moses
Boosinger, George	Boosinger, John	Bellows, Ithmar
Bradley, Ariel	Bradley, Justice	Baird, Robert
Cook, David	Cunningham, Amzi	Chamberlain, Luther
Dunlap, Thomas	DeHaven, Nathaniel	Elliott, George
Fretih John	Hall, David	Hall, James
Hall, John	Hale, John	Hale, Thomas
Hart, William	Holcomb, Timothy	Haines, Samuel
Haines, Benjamin	Haines, John	Kent, James
Moore, Lee	Minard, Daniel	Martin, John
McCormick, James	Norton, Peter	Pelton, John
Spicer, Minard	Sackett, Harvey	Sackett, Leander
Simcock, George	Smith, Robert	Tickner, David
Tickner, John	Tupper, Ezekial	Tupper, Reuben
Upson, Reuben	Upson, Stephen	Van Garden, James
Way, David	Whittlesey, Harvey	Willis, Martin

Page 433

ROLL OF CAPT. EBENEZER HARMON'S COMPANY. (County Unknown.)
Served from August 22 until October 7, 1812.

Capt. Ebenezer Harmon	Lieut. Joseph Eggleston	Ensign, Eber Kennedy
Sergt. Chauncey Eggleston	Sergt. Brainard Spencer	Corp. Jonothan B. Russell
Corp. Eli Cannon	Corp. Warren Squire	Corp. Justice Parrish
	Fifer, Isaac D. Faxon	

Privates.

Ayres, Asa	Blackman, John H.	Bidlake, Daniel
Baldwin, Eliakim	Blair, Behan	Baldwin, James
Blackman, Elijah, Jr.	Blair, James	Baldwin, Sanford
Baldwin, Henry	Baldwin, Caleb	Cannon, George
Cannon, Stephen	Bissell, Orris	Crooks, William
Eggleston, Moses	Ferguson, Samuel H.	Granger, Horace
Eggleston, Martin	Herrick, James W.	Kent, Zeno
Kent, Zardis	Messenger, Ebenezer	Norton, Lebbeus
Kennedy, Zebno	Norton, Seldon	Norton, Eber
McConnekey, Jarvis	McHerdry, James	Plum, James
Perkins, Grant	Peese, Jem	Riley, Julius, Jr.
Richardson, Micaiah	Russell, Samuel	Riley, Eppy
Squire, Aaron	Singletary, John C.	Spencer, George
Sweet, Amos	Sheldon, Gershon	Webb, Lyman
Wheeler, Oliver	White, Joel	

Page 434.

ROLL OF CAPT. PHILLIP McNEME'S COMPANY. (County Unknown.)
Served from August 14 until October 14, 1812.

Capt. Phillip McNeme	Lieut. John Jackson	Ensign, D. Hoffman
Sergt. John Clark	Sergt. Jonothan Corbell	Sergt. Charles Shukley
Sergt. Jacob Crabil	Corp. John Dillman	Corp. Isaac Temple
Corp. John Cook	Corp. William D. Baily	Drummer, John Botts
	Fifer, Noah Downs	

Privates.

Ater, Jacob	Ater, George	Brown, Joseph
Bready, James	Briggs, Walter	Clark, Stephen
Champ, Alexander	Davis, Jeremiah	Davis, Benjamin
Gordy, Thomas	Hammon, William	Hines, Jacob
Leonard, Alexander	McRea, Alexander	Nolin, Thomas
Nier, Jacob	Nolan, Edward	Redman, James
Smith, Jonas	Stothard, Joseph	Shanton, Charles
Thompson, O.	Thompson, Ignatius	Timins, Stephen
Watson, Robert		

Page 435.

ROLL OF CAPT. CHARLES WOLVERTON'S COMPANY.
(Probably from Miami County.)
Served from August 24 until September 23, 1812.

Capt. Charles Wolverton	Lieut. James Blue	Ensign, Reuben Westfall
Sergt. Samuel Kyle	Sergt. Ezekial Kirtley	Sergt. James Morrow
Sergt. James Brown	Corp. John Pelford	Corp. John McClary
Corp. James Marshall	Corp. Nathaniel Garard	

Vol. I.

ROLL OF CAPT. CHARLES WOLVERTON'S COMPANY (Continued.)

Rank and Name of Soldier. Rank and Name of Soldier. Rank and Name of Soldier.

Privates.

Bedle, Solomon
Bull, Thomas
Campbell, John
Dumont, Peter
Garard, James
Gibson, Andrew
Hunt, George
Martin, Corbly
Junkins, Lancelot
Leland, Simon
Marshall, Joseph
McFarland, William
Stephenson, Robert
Westfall, Levi

Privates.

Bedle, Samuel
Bedle, Abraham
Crossley, Joseph
Dye, William
Garard, Henry
Hay, James
Howell, Samuel
Ingerson, Benjamin
Jackson, James
Lloyd, David
McCoy, James
Pollock, John
Stephenson, William
White, Robert

Privates.

Barnes, Robert
Bull, John
Crowder, William
Frost, William
Garard, Abner
Hamil, Hugh
Hayes, James
Junkin, George
Linvill, John
Layton, Joseph
McGallaway, James
Rodgers, Thomas Jr
Thompson, James

Pages 39-40.

ROLL OF CAPT. JAMES GATES' COMPANY.
(Probably from Champaign County.)

Served from August 18 until September 23, 1812, and from July 30 until August 13, 1813.

Capt. James Gates
Sergt. John Boyce
Sergt. Jacob Flemming
Sergt. William Boyce
Corp. Aaron Shall

Lieut. James Munire
Sergt. Aquila Ellsworth
Sergt. James Haney
Corp. Joel Thomas
Fifer, Newton Burroughs

Ensign, John Best
Sergt. Thaddeus Tuttle
Sergt. Samuel Carey
Corp. Henry Harris
Drummer, William Green

Privates.

Bulderach, Gabriel
Boyce, William
Carter, Benjamin
Dugan, John
Ellsworth, Moses
Gable, Thomas
Gates, Henry
Hall, John
Judy, Benjamin
Lockart, John
Morris, Richard
Osborn, Edward
Plummer, James
Reswin, Joseph
Sturd, James W.
Shell, Aaron
Tarbutton, Eli

Privates.

Bright, Edward
Brooks, Thomas
Collins, James
Caldwell, John
Dillon, Isaac
Fee, Lewis
Gable, Robert
Goble, Hiram
Haines, Absalom
Kenton, William
Lewis, Zebulum
McClintock, William
Osborn, James
Richards, Saul
Reagan, William B.
Smith, John
Shaffer, Peter
Wallingford, Benjamin

Privates.

Beizly, Joseph
Carter, Lewis
Caldwell, John
Dimit, James
Goodfellow, Moor
Gates, John
Garwin, William
Judy, John
Kilt, George
Moore, John
Nelson, Thomas
Plummer, Greenbe
Richards, Silas
Shell, Jonah
Sergent, Ezekial
Tuttle, John

Pages 335-336

ROLL OF CAPT. TIMOTHY TITUS' COMPANY.
(Probably from Miami County.)

Served from September 4, 1813, until March 14, 1814.

Capt. Timothy Titus
Sergt. Severs Hudson
Sergt. George Whitmore
Corp. John Devors

Lieut. Daniel West
Sergt. Daniel Mills
Corp. John Fate
Corp. Job Severs
Fifer, William McKee

Ensign, Adam Milmon
Sergt. Philip Everman
Corp. Michael Tierman
Drummer, Ashbel Crane

Privates

Baldwin, Daniel
Bushels, Henry
Bunnel, Noah
Crook, John
Crosin, Edward
Dill, Solomon
Garwood, Williiam
Goodpaster, John
Horner, Samuel
Irvin, Eli
Kriteser, Henry
Lofort, Lewis
Myers, Jacob H.
McDonald, John
Reynard, John
Shight, Peter
Sidels, Israel
Surface, Henry
Van Skike, John
Winnings, Lewis
Yillock, Charles

Privates

Buchels, David C.
Burrows, John
Bunnel, John
Cast, John
Davis, George
Dollison, Rezing
Gray, Thomas
Gaskil, Samuel
Hurst, William
Jones, Joshua
Lacey, John
Linley, Francis
Mills, Michael
Orchey, Job
Stites, John F.
Smith, Obediah
Stipo, George
Settlemyre, William
Vineyard, John
Wells, Abraham

Privates

Baird, George
Buckles, David B.
Boner, Patrick
Cast, Archibald
Downs, David
Emmet, John
Garwood, Hosea
Hilt, William
Hayes, William D.
Kelow, Samuel
Lacey, William
Meed, Isaac N.
McLaughlin, Darby
Phillips, Thomas
Stilley, Elisha
Surface, Andrew
Stanford, Philip
Tittle, John
Waggoner, Michael
Watson, Moses

ROLL OF CAPT. ICHABOD NYE'S COMPANY (CAVALRY).
(Probably from Knox County.)
Served from August 26, until October 4, 1812.

Rank and Name of Soldier.
Capt. Ichabod Nye
Sergt. William Bartlet
Corp. Jonothan Hunt
Farrier, Michael Coliass

Privates.
Ash, David
Bonnet, Isaac
Dunlap, John
Harrod, James
Harrod, Samuel
Inlow, Jesse
Leonard, Amos
Middlemer, John
Morton, Stephen D.
Smelt, Samuel H.
Smith, George
Woodruff, Johab

Rank and Name of Soldier.
Lieut. James Craig
Sergt. Isaac Beam
Corp. Stephen D. Minton
Farrier, Michael Cleck

Privates.
Ayres, James
Berrit, David
Dickinson, George
Holmes, Nicholas
Howard, Samuel
Layton, John
Lyberger, George
Minton, Stephen
Smith, Samuel H.
Smith, James
Walker, James
Walker, Joseph
Walker, John

Rank and Name of Soldier.
Cornet, John Barney
Sergt. Solomon Giller
Trumpeter, John Kizer

Privates.
Adams, Elijah
Davidson, George
Garrison, John
Hunt, Jonothan
Irwin, John
Long, Hughes
Mills, John
Mills, Michael
Stilly, John
Selley, William H.
Waggoner, Ferall
Watson, Noah

ROLL OF CAPT. HENRY COONROD'S COMPANY (CAVALRY).
(Probably from Pickaway County.)
Served from May 9, until May 24, 1813.

Capt. Henry Coonrod
Sergt. Thomas R. Duncan
Sergt. Hane Harrelton
Corp. Jacob Stingly

Privates.
Adamson, Isaac
Grim, George
Johnson, James
Laundry, Simeon
Millson, Bernard

Lieut. William Nicol
Sergt. James Stanley
Corp. David Martin
Corp. Peter Augistean

Privates.
Baum, Jonas
Grim, David
Keller, George
Moore, Isaac
Nevill, Robert

Cornet, Joseph Maurice
Sergt. Thomas Harbert
Corp. Robert Johnston

Privates.
Baum, Jacob
Hossleton, Samuel
Luiby, John
Myer, William
Nichols, John

ROLL OF CAPT. BENONI PEARCE'S COMPANY (LIGHT DRAGOONS.)
(County Unknown.)
Served from November 1, 1812, until January 25, 1813, and part from Aug. 8 until Oct. 8, 1812.

Capt. Benoni Pearce
Sergt. James Bell
Corp. George W. Reynolds

Privates.
Alexander, William
Chandler, Samuel
Evans, David
Frazier, Mahlon
Heap, George
Mercer, Jacob
Meiers, Solomon
Prior, John

Lieut. John Lee
Sergt. Martin Chandler
Corp. Solomon Mayers

Privates.
Betz, John
Carpenter, John C.
Frazier, William
Granstaff, William
Ireland, Thomas
Marshall, Andrew
McLain, Daniel
Prior, Isaac
Woodward, William

Cornet, James Warden
Corp. John Harvey
Trumpeter, George Green

Privates.
Best, Valentine
Bowermaster, Peter
Funk, Jacob
Hawey, John
Mercer, George
Morrow, William
Parkinson, John
Scott, Samuel

ROLL OF CAPT. JOSEPH VANCE'S COMPANY (DRAGOONS.)
(Probably from Franklin County.)
Served from August 24, until October 14, 1812. Part served from August 1, until Sept. 4, 1813.

Capt. Joseph Vance
Lieut Jacob Keller
Sergt. Benjamin Steward
Corp. Daniel McFarland

Privates
Boggs, John
Beasley, Isaac
Dyer, Robert
Davison, Andrew
Edgar, John
Hunter, John
Hereoff, William
King, Samuel
Mark, William
McElvain, James
Parrish, Orris
Reed, Alexander
Shannon, Samuel
Smart, Isaac
Stumpbough, John
Upson, Alfred
Wing, Oliver

Lieut. Joseph Grate
Cornet, Francis Stewart
Sergt. John M. White
Corp. Adam Reed
Trumpeter, Andrew McElvain

Privates
Barr, John
Courtney, Richard
Dillingham, Ajalon
DeLashmutt, Van B.
House, Richard
Hunter, Joseph
Hill, Willard
Kile, John
McKensey, James
McElvain, John
Pinkard, William
Rennick, Asahel
Shron, Joseph
Starr, Joseph
Sullivan, Lucas
Watts, John
Winsel, John

Lieut. Jacob Read
Sergt. Daniel Liggert
Corp. Henry Weston
Corp. William Hunter

Privates
Brown, Henry
Culbertson, Samuel
Dickey, Michael
DeLashmutt, John K.
Goetschins, Nicholas
Hilsel, John
Kean, John
Kern, John
McGowan, John
McElvain, William
Power, Luther
Shannon, John
Simpkins, John
Strain, John M.
Swam, Gustavus
White, Alexander

Page 394 Vol. I.

ROLL OF CAPT. JAMES DOUD'S COMPANY (CAVALRY.)
(County Unknown)

Served from August 22, to November 30, 1812, and from January to March, 1813.

Rank and Name of Soldier.	Rank and Name of Soldier.	Rank and Name of Soldier.
Capt. James Doud	Lieut. Zalman Fitch	Lieut. Ensign Church
Cornet, Joseph Coit	Sergt. William Fitch	Sergt. Linus Brainard
Corp. Russell, Starr	Corp. Comfort Migatt	Corp. Abijah Peck
Corp. Comfort Starr	Musician, Hugh Baird	Musician Daniel Miles

Privates

Brainard, Ira	Benedict, Billy	Bostwick, Adna H.
Brainard, John	Chidester, Hezekiah	Case, Ariel
Chidester, Philo	Davidson, Samuel	Fitch, Cook
Loveland, John	Logan, William	Miles, Samuel
Mann, William D.	Miles, Daniel	Michaels, Moses
Osborn, Elias R.	Pinder, Austin	Ramsey, Hugh S.
Stilson, George A.	Sprague, William	Turner, Samuel
Haydon, Samuel M.	Turner, Conrad	Taft, Aaron
Warner, Elisha	Wetmore, Josiah	

Vol. 2, Page 394.

ROLL OF CAPT. SAMUEL McCORD'S COMPANY (CAVALRY.)
(County Unknown.)

Served from August 16, until September 18, 1812.

Capt. Samuel McCord	Lieut. Thomas Vance	Lieut. James Foley
Cornet, James Shipman	Sergt. James Roberts	Sergt. William McKinnon
Sergt. Sampson Hubbell	Sergt. Conrad Goodlove	Corp. Jeremiah Curl
Corp. David Taylor	Trumpeter, William Eals	

Privates.

Armstrong, Thomas	Anderson, James	Benson, George
Clifford, John	Dawson, John	Frazure, Benjamin
Foley, William	Gibbes, Samuel	Blend, John
Green, John	Hopkins, Richard	Harr, Daniel
Harvey, John	Hunter, George	Hodge, William
Haines, William	Konklin, John	McDonald, James
McCoy, John	Morris, Thomas	McGrew, Mathew
Neihle, Lawrence	Smallwood, Walter	Thompson, John
Vanmeter, Jacob	Welsh, James	Ward, John B.
	Ward, Robert	

Pages 395-396.

ROLL OF CAPT. ELIAS MURRAY'S COMPANY (CAVALRY.)
(Probably from Delaware County.)

Served from September 20, to November 19, 1814.

Capt. Elias Murray	Lieut. Daniel Prince	Lieut. James M. Crawford
Cornet, Robert Jameson	Cornet, Roswell Tulles	Sergt. Cyrus Hubbard
Sergt. Joseph Prince	Sergt. Forest Meeker	Sergt. William Riley
Sergt. David Dix	Sergt. William Patton	Sergt. George Manvill
Sergt. Sylvester Root	Sergt. Aaron Welch	Sergt. James Nugent
Corp. Solomon Steward	Corp. Nathaniel Ulyatt	Corp. James Carpenter
Corp. Ezra Steward	Corp. Adam Shover	Trumpeter, William Lother
Saddler, Abner Root	Farrier, James Harper	

Privates.

Adams, Elias	Agord, James S.	Appleton, Bixbe
Arnold, Calvin	Basker, Orlando H.	Beebe, Chauncy
Bush, John	Carpenter, Alfred	Cherry, John
Conklin, Jacob	Cowgill, Morris	Crawford, David
Creamer, John	Crown, Thomas	Crunkeltin, Joseph
Cunningham, Joseph	Davis, Eleazor	Dixon, Abel
Dixon, Miran	Dunn, Andrew	Eaton, Stephen S.
Friley, Martin	Foust, David	Ford, Augustus
Gabriel, William	Helt, Daniel	Helt, George
Hardin, John	Harper, James	Hillman, Benjamin
Hughes, Joseph S.	Hinton, Levi	Jones, Leonard
Kent, William	Kent, Daniel	Kent, James
Loofbourow, John	Longwell, Ralph	Lewis, Joseph
Munroe, Lemuel F.	Olds, Benjamin	Meeker, Forest
Pufut, James	Phelps, Levi	Pelton, Johnson
Riley, Henry	Root, Azariah	Robinson, Mellen
Slack, John	Smith, William	Thomas, David
Thompson, John	Trindle, James	Wilson, John
Werley, Henry	Vose, Rupert	Williamson, John

Vol.2. Page 398.
ROLL OF CAPT. CHARLES DEVOL'S COMPANY (CAVALRY.)
(Probably from Washington County.)
Served from October 20, to December 18, 1812.

Rank and Name of Soldier.	Rank and Name of Soldier.	Rank and Name of Soldier.
Capt. Charles Devol	Lieut. Isaiah Scott	Lieut. Washington Olney
Sergt. James White	Sergt. William White	Corp. John Clark
Corp. Pardon Cook	Corp. Samuel Reid	
Privates.	**Privates.**	**Privates.**
Brown, Solomon	Browning, Thomas	Finch, Maurice
Olney, Gilbert	Pixley, Argelus	Quigley, John
Shuttleworth, Joseph	Tucker, Joshua	Whittle, Samuel
	Wood, Paulus E.	

Page 399.
ROLL OF CAPT. JOHN McNEAL'S COMPANY (CAVALRY.)
County Unknown.)
Served from August 23, until October 14, 1812.

Capt. John McNeal	Lieut. William Nicols	Lieut. Jacob Markle
Cornet, George Keller	Sergt. Thomas K. Duncan	Sergt. Samuel E. Barr
Sergt. Thomas Harcell	Corp. Robert Hill	Corp. Abraham Stingley
Corp. Thomas Waddle	Corp. John Fonman	Musician, John Williams
Saddler, Charles Coveleer	Farrier, Adam Pence	
Privates.	**Privates.**	**Privates.**
Augustine Peter	Baum, Jonas	Conrad, Adam
Crane, James	Conrad, Henry	Chambers, James
Dolby, John	Ferguson, John	Ferguson, William
Grimm, George	Grimm, David	Graham, James
Hill, Eli	Hahn, Phillip	Johnson, James
Johnson, Robert	Kile, Abraham	Milliser, Barney
Martin, David	Moore, Isaac	McCort, John
Nash, Chester	Rodgers, James	Stanley, James
Stingley, Jacob	Vandorn, Hezekiah	Weaver, Anthony
Weily, John	Wilson, Andrew	Wolf, George
	Wolf, John	

Page 266
ROLL OF LIEUT. EZEKIEL BLUE'S DETACHMENT.
(Probably from Ross County.)
Served from July 28, until August 28, 1813.

Lieut. Ezekial Blue	Ensign Hugh Cook	Sergt. John Beauchant
	Corp. Isaac Johnston	
Privates	**Privates**	**Privates**
Briggs, Robert	Chamberlain, Wyatt	Funk Jacob
Surrals, Mathew	White, Daniel	White, John
	Young, John	

Page 381
ROLL OF CAPT. MOSES PATTERSON'S MOUNTED COMPANY.
(Probably from Highland County.)
Served from September 14, until October 14, 1812.

Capt. Moses Patterson	Lieut. David Strain	Ensign Samuel Evans
Sergt. Augustus Richards	Sergt. James Rodgers	Sergt. Joseph Patterson
Sergt. John McConnel	Corp. John Thornton	Corp. Price Evans
Corp. James Jolly	Corp. Samuel McConnel	
Privates	**Privates**	**Privates**
Adair, George	Buckham, Thomas	Blair, John
Connell, John	Davies, Jacob	Evans, Dan
Flinn, Joshua	Finch, Josiah	Frame, George
Harper, James	Hinton, Evans	Hedd, Bigges
Jolly, David	Keys, William	Lamb, Maxwell
Midseker, David	Monn, William	Morrow, William
McMunn, William	McConnel, James	Pittenger, Nicholas
Rapp, David	Riddick, Samuel D.	Strain, John R.
Smalley, Joseph	Swartz, Sebastian	Swartz, Henry
Tayler, William	Templin, Peter	Wilson, John

Page 393 Vol. 1.

ROLL OF CAPT. G. W. BARRERE'S COMPANY (CAVALRY.)
(Probably from Highland County.)

Served from April 30, 1812, until May 6, 1813.

Rank and Name of Soldier.	Rank and Name of Soldier.	Rank and Name of Soldier.
Capt. G. W. Barrere	Lieut. John Davidson	Ensign John Elliott
Sergt. Sovereign Brown	Sergt. Peter Hoop	Sergt. Robert Hunter
Sergt. Benjamin Eakins	Corp. Henry Addison	Corp. David N. Gardner
Corp. Gideon Jackson	Corp. William Davidson	Bugler, Wm. Stockton
Privates.	**Privates.**	**Privates.**
Bond, Henry	Badgley, Robert	Barnes, Jacob
Boatman, Elias	Barden, George	Bowman, John
Borden, John	Barngrover, George	Borden, David
Borden, Jacob	Charles, Andrew	Campton, William
Colvin, John	Campton, Robert	Duckwall, John
Davidson, John	Eakins, St. Clear	Gibler, John
Gibler, Phillip	Grisley, Levi	Hill, William
Hough, Paton	Hoffman, Jacob	Hair, John
Jackson, James	Losier, John	Morrow, Robert, Sr.
Morrow, Robert, Jr.	Malcom, James	Malcom, Samuel
Moury, Samuel	McKinley, Robert	McQuinty, William
Nelson, William	Nesbit, Robert	Osborn, Enoch
Parkison, George	Robison, William	Robison, George
Roberts, Joshua	Ross, John	Swaim, Joseph
Sanderson, William	Welkins, Abraham	

Page 397 Vol. 2.

ROLL OF CAPT. WILLIAM KENDALL'S COMPANY (CAVALRY.)
(Probably from Scioto County.)

Served from July 28, until August 28, 1813.

Capt. William Kendall	Lieut. George Clengman	Lieut. Allen Moore
Cornet, William Jones	Sergt. Nathan Glover	Sergt. James Collins
Sergt. Samuel G. Jones	Sergt. Joseph Boynton	Corp. Charles C. Boynton
Corp. Samuel Nichols	Corp. John Clengman	Corp. Thomas Brown
Musician, William Lowery	Farrier, Lloyd Johnstin	
Privates	**Privates**	**Privates**
Adams, Francis	Brady, Samuel	Brown, John
Burley, Daniel	Burkles, William	Bennet, Thomas
Barger, Jacob	Byerly, Michael	Conner, Cornelius
Clark, Jonothan	Curtis, Joseph	Fuert, Benjamin
Gunn, Howell	Glover, Elijah	Gharkey, David
Huff, Jesse	Huff, Caleb	Hall, Samuel A.
James, John	King, John	Lock, Benjamin
Margrove, Abner	Munn, James	Moore, Lewis
McKinney, Solomon	Prather, John	Phillips, James
Robey, William	Richert, Henry	Robison, William
Sheley, Henry	Shangler, Jacob	Sappinger, Thomas
Slack, Abraham	Taylor, Nimrod	Welch, Abraham
White, Uriah	Young, Samuel	

Page 400.

ROLL OF CAPT. ALEXANDER GIBSON'S COMPANY (ARTILLERY.)
(Probably from Butler County.)

Served from September 11, until November 30, 1812.

Capt. Alexander Gibson	Lieut. William Karr	Sergt. Andrew Drips
Sergt. John Cox	Sergt. John S. Ludlow	Sergt. Joseph Winkley
Corp. Sampson Mooney	Corp. Richard McPike	Drummer Alvin Wheeler
	Fifer, Samuel Bonnet	
Privates	**Privates.**	**Privates**
Ayers, John	Ayers, Isaac	Baun, Jonas
Clark, William	Cask, John S.	Craven, John
Coleman, Avery	Crow, Thomas S.	Coppin, Joseph
Donald, James	Engle, Philip	Evans, Robert
Fotherzole, Geo. W.	Garret, Curtis	Gardner, Robert
Handley, John	Looker, Samuel B.	Love, Peter
McDonald, James	McMaster, William	Nelson, Robert
Norris, Richard	Satterly, Isaac	Potts, Charles
Smith, Thomas B.	Sedan, Jacob	Smith, John
Shank, John	White, John	White, Thomas
Whiteside, William		

Page 382. Vol. 2.

ROLL OF CAPT. JACOB FUDGE'S MOUNTED COMPANY.
(Probably from Warren County.)

Served from September 27, until October 20, 1812.

Rank and Name of Soldier.	Rank and Name of Soldier.	Rank and Name of Soldier.
Capt. Jacob Fudge	Lieut. Joseph Stephens	Ensign William Campbell
Sergt. John Flester	Sergt. Robert Morris	Sergt. Jacob Woots
Privates.	**Privates.**	**Privates.**
Ayers, Michael	Button, James	Bonta, Peter A.
Chambers, John	Crow, William	Cox, Joshua
Forquer, Thomas	Haynes, David	Harbsell, Abraham
Hartter, George	Jamison, John	Kitchen, Stephen
Lee, Henry	Myers, George	Mills, Joseph
McMahon, Joseph	Newton, Henry	Payon, Jacob
Ridenour, Samuel	Ridenour, Jonothan	Ridenour, Peter
Rabourne, Joseph	Stinson, Alexander	Sellers, John
Toler, William	Trinkle, John	Thompson, James
Welsh, John	Vanest, John	

Page 383

ROLL OF CAPT. JOHN ELLIS' MOUNTED COMPANY.
(Probably from Adams County.)

Served from September 28, until October 28, 1812.

Capt. John Ellis	Lieut. Elijah Martin	Ensign William Dunlap
Sergt. John Evans	Sergt. Peter Wiles	Sergt. Adam McPherson
Privates.	**Privates.**	**Privates.**
Austin, Nelson	Alexander, John	Bland, Micajah
Cutler, Benjamin	Cormick, James	Ellis, Samuel
Fetters, Charles	Flaugher, Jacob	Henry, John
McKenny, Hezekiah	McPherson, David	Reeves, Ila
Reeves, Daniel	Riggs, Zach	Wiles, Christian
	Yates, William	

Page 384.

ROLL OF CAPT. DANIEL COLLIER'S MOUNTED COMPANY.
(County Unknown.)

Served from September 30, until October 28, 1812.

Capt. Daniel Collier	Lieut. Seth Vanmatre	Ensign Isaac Earles
Sergt. Peter Lewis	Sergt. Jonothan Horne	
Privates.	**Privates.**	**Privates.**
Boyd, Jonothan	Biddle, George	Cox, Jacob
Clay, Mathew	Chapman, Nathaniel	Cobbler, David
Davis, William	Downing, Meshach	Killen, John
Metz, Jacob	Mines, James	Mershon, Daniel
Newland, Jacob	Porter, James	Taylor, William
Thompson, James	Wikoff, Samuel	

Page 385.

ROLL OF CAPT. SAMUEL DAVIS' MOUNTED COMPANY.
(Probably from Ross County.)

Served from September 28, until October 28, 1812.

Capt. Samuel Davis	Lieut. Daniel Robbins	Ensign George Teter
Sergt. Daniel Hare	Sergt. Philip Hare	Sergt. Thomas McDonald
	Sergt. Hugh Cochran	
Privates.	**Privates.**	**Privates.**
Boye, George	Boye, Francis	Boggs, Joseph
Blair, William	Canida, Robert	Core, Henry
Caniey, John	Clover, Peter	Dean, James
Davis, Asa	Edmiston, John	Gradless, William
Hester, Henry	Hopkins, Moses	Hare, Jacob
Huston, Joseph	McDonald, Thomas	Pummel, James
Riley, James	Rockhold, Joseph	Robbins, Moses
Shirlock, Edward	Shannon, Thomas	Smithson, Joseph
Waugh, Lemon	Yaren, Adam	

Page 386.

ROLL OF CAPT. THOMAS LEWIS' MOUNTED COMPANY.
(Probably from Ross County.)

Served from September 28, until October 28, 1812.

Capt. Thomas Lewis	Sergt. John Hayslip	Sergt. Peter Shults
Privates.	**Privates.**	**Privates.**
Bayless, John	Bayless, Nathan	Blake, Samuel
Casseldine, John	Campbell, John	Campbell, Samuel
Cain, James	Cain, Jesse	Cormick, James
Earley, George	Earley, Michael	Morehead, Mathew
McBride, James	Saunders, Francis	Scott, Joseph
Redman, George	Washburn, Nathaniel	Wilson, Benoni

Pages 179-180 Vol. 1.

ROLL OF CAPT. WILLIAM HUSTON'S MOUNTED COMPANY
(Probably from Scioto County.)

Served from October 1, until November 1, 1812.

Rank and Name of Soldier.	Rank and Name of Soldier.	Rank and Name of Soldier.
Capt. William Huston	Lieut. Allen Moore	Cornet, Uriah White
Sergt. Nathan Glover	Sergt. Samuel G. Jones	Sergt. James Collins
	Sergt. Ezra Osborn	
Privates	**Privates**	**Privates**
Applegate, Charles	Bartow, Kimber	Brown, John, Jr.
Boynton, Joseph E.	Burk, William M.	David, Elnathan
Dollarhead, William	Davison, Nathaniel	Barkels, Frederick
Chamberlain, Anson	Chamberlain, Hyatt	Chappen, Reuben
Curany, Mathew	Carpenter, William	Cannon, John
Darlington, Samuel	Fuqua, Moses M.	Glover, Asa
Gunn, Zina	Grant, William	Hammett, John
Jones, David	Jones, William	Johnston, John
Kelby, John	Loyd, Johnson	Musgrove, Abner
Moore, Phillip, Jr.	McKenney, Solomon	Pain, Olney
Power, William	Perry, Samuel	Rankin, William
Robey, William	Smith, John	Swords, William
Salada, John	Tomlison, John	Thompson, Robert
Turner, John R.	Thompson, James	Wheeler, Nathaniel
Wheeler, Amos	Wilson, Braden	

Pages 181-182

ROLL OF LIEUT. JOHN HAYSLIP'S MOUNTED COMPANY.
(County Unknown.)

Served from September 13, until December 9, 1814.

Lieut. John Hayslip	Lieut. Isaac Foster	Ensign John Moore
Sergt. Thomas Lockhart	Sergt. James Hayslip	Sergt. William Rowland
Privates	**Privates**	**Privates**
Bayless, Daniel	Browning, Edman	Baird, Robert
Briggs, Thomas	Collins, Elijah	Crawford, George
Carey, Isaac	Dining, Daniel	Ellison, Andrew
Galloway, James	Hubanks, Foster	Hempleman, Jacob
Harris, Thomas	Lambert, Joseph	Moore, John
Murphy, Recompense	Mannan, William	McHenry, Alexander
McCollum, Isaac	Pemberton, Fountain	Paul, James
Paul, John	Pollard, John	Pennington, Obediah
Rader, John	Sparks, George	Stephenson, John
Strict, Joseph	Sutton, William G.	Walker, Joseph
Warren, Peter	Woods, Simon	Walling, William

Pages 183-184

ROLL OF CAPT. JOHN FOSTER'S MOUNTED COMPANY.
(Probably from Ross County.)

Served from September 14, until October 14, 1812.

Capt. John Foster	Lieut. John Woods	Ensign Richard Tomlinson
Sergt. David Lyons	Sergt. Corwin George	Sergt. John Heath
Sergt. William Slaughter	Corp. Abraham Stewart	Corp. William McCorkle
Corp. Samuel Corwin	Corp. Thomas Graham	Corp. Caleb Wilson
Privates	**Privates**	**Privates**
Burke, Paul	Bevens, Philip	Bishong, John
Bogart, Cornelius	Carter, Henry	Debruler, Jacob
Hodges, Daniel	Hoover, Jacob	Hampton, Dudley
Henson, Harrod	Heath, Richard	Hamson, John
Jacks, Gardner	Loney, John	Hulse, William
Leads, Absalom	Longshore, James	Lockhart, Elijah
Mount, Eli	Pancake, John	Scott, Peter
Stewart, William	Switzer, Peter	Wood, Jonathan
Wells, Peter	Wilson, George	

Page 185.

ROLL OF CAPT. WILLIAM LEEDOM'S MOUNTED COMPANY.
(Probably from Ross County.)

Served from September 28, until October 28, 1812.

Capt. William Leedom	Lieut. George Bryan	Sergt. William Smith
	Sergt. Robert Baird	
Privates.	**Privates.**	**Privates.**
Baird, Robinson	Edgington, Isaac	Edgington, Joshua
Ellison, James	Gutridge, Charles	Hoslip, John
Marcus, Jacob	Naylor, George	Waldran, Henry

Pages 186-187. Vol. I.

ROLL OF CAPT. JAMES DUNLAP'S MOUNTED COMPANY.
(Probably from Ross County.)

Served from July 28, until August 17, 1813.

Rank and Name of Soldier.	Rank and Name of Soldier.	Rank and Name of Soldier.
Capt. James Dunlap	Lieut. James McCoy	Ensign John Rodgers
Privates.	**Privates.**	**Privates.**
Benedick, James	Benedick, George	Barton, Jesse
Beal, Philip	Blue, John M.	Blue, John
Boyd, Francis	Brown, James	Corbet, Joseph
Corbett, David	Coon, Henry	Coon, Adam
Clark, James	Dawnard, James	Dyer, William
Currey, William	Dines, James	Gatt, Jacob
Gilfillen, John	Grady, John	Gamble, John
Heness, William	Henderson, David	Innis, William
Jamison, Charles	Johnson, Thomas	Kirkbride, John
Lisney, John	Latta, Moses	May, Henry
Miller, James	Mitchell, John	Miskinens, William
Mace, John	McCoy, Dickson	McCoy, Alexander
McNeal, John	McCafferty, Richard	McKee, Mathew
McCluer, James	McLaughlin, William	McCoy, John
Newman, George	James, Adam	Parrish, Meredith
Parker, Jesse	Reaves, John	Rinley, Daniel
Rosaboom, John	Rayburn, John	Robinson, William
Stone, Daniel	Stanton, Abraham	Shoemaker, Peter
Thompson, Wheeler	Timmens, John W.	Wilcut, John
	Walker, William	

Page 188.

ROLL OF CAPT. JOHN BOGGS' MOUNTED COMPANY.
(Probably from Ross County.)

Served from September 27 until October 14, 1812.

Capt. John Boggs	Lieut. William Miller	Ensign Daniel Musselman
Sergt. Henry David	Sergt. James Roberts	Sergt. Jacob Frazer
	Sergt. Valentine Angel	
Privates.	**Privates.**	**Privates.**
Abbott, Elijah	Baum, Jacob	Campbell, William
Bunsey, John	Ernheart, Jacob	Evans, David
Forsman, Robert	Galbraith, John	Jones, John
Johnston, James	Kooder, John	Kieler, James
Levengood, Jacob	Lobaugh, Daniel	McKinnon, William H.
McKinnon, Daniel	Newhouse, Anthony	Price, James
Pollard, John D.	Phillips, James	Rennels, John
Rooder, Peter	Reid, William	Rowe, George
Simms, William	Smith, John	Willenmyer, Jacob

Pages 189-190.

ROLL OF CAPT. WILLIAM RUTLEDGE'S MOUNTED COMPANY.
(Probably from Ross County.)

Served from May 7, until May 20, 1813.

Capt. William Rutledge	Lieut. William Lamb	Ensign James Reyborn
Sergt. Nathaniel Spencer	Sergt. Daniel Kerr	Sergt. Garnet Lauman
Sergt. John Watson	Corp. John Gilfillan	Corp. James Bramble
Corp. William Baley	Corp. James McCallister	
Privates.	**Privates.**	**Privates.**
Anderson, Levi	Anderson, John	Arrington, David
Brown, Edmond	Brown, Peter	Baitman, William
Clifford, James	Clark, John	Chestnut, William
Crampton, John	Clark, William	Curtis, Drayton N.
Edwards, Edward	Fortimer, Richard	Frye, Joseph
Fultz, Conder	Fortney, Peter	Gibbs, James
Green, George	Hume, George	James, Adam
Kelley, Jonothan	Leister, Peter	Lownes, George
Lacey, John	Mills, Levin	Millar, William
Mayhigh, Levin	McCormick, Samuel	McCollister, Henry
McCollister, Daniel	Onley, Charles	Phillips, James
Pickens, John	Prentice, Henry L.	Reese, Ludwick
Romine, Elias	Romine, Amos	Stoll, Frederick
Smith, Amos	Smith, George	Smith, Green
Snyder, John	Scott, James	Thompson, Abraham
Tucker, John	Tiffin, Clayton	Thompson, William
Thompson, Joseph	Utt, Adam	Utt, Jacob
Walker, John	Williams, William	White, Thornely L.
Wright, Moses H.		

Pages 191-192. Vol. 2.

ROLL OF CAPT. JOHN CAMPBELL'S MOUNTED COMPANY.
(Probably from Ross County.)
Served from September 13, until December 9, 1814.

Rank and Name of Soldier.	Rank and Name of Soldier.	Rank and Name of Soldier.
Capt. John Campbell	Lieut. Samuel Ellis	Lieut. Peter Shaw
Lieut. John Evans	Sergt. David Lawwill	Sergt. Joseph Runnels
Sergt. Jonothan Wisner	Sergt. Charles Larsh	Sergt. James Brownfield
	Musician, James Lawwill	
Privates.	**Privates.**	**Privates.**
Bishop, Peter	Cooper, Thomas	Conn, Robert
Copple, Daniel	Canley, Thomas	Davison, William
Dunlap, Alexander	Ellis, Jeremiah	Ellis, Jesse
Edwards, George	Elsey, Lewis	Elaney, Moses
Greenley, William	Gardner, Simon	Grimes, William
Glendenning, John	Hewitt, Richard	Kratzer, Joseph
Knox, John	Key, Samuel M.	Mahaffey, William
Middleton, William	McPherson, Samuel	Newlen, James
Pricherd, James	Parker, William	Pritchard, Jacob
Payn, Benjamin	Reid, Traves	Rains, Alexander
Runnels, Henry	Rains, John	Springer, Job
Stewart, William M.	Stewart, William	Scott, John
Shreve, Caleb	Stivers, James	Shaw, Russle
Shaw, James	Prickett, William	Turner, John
Wills, William	Wisby, Joseph	Wherry, James
	Wills, James	

Page 198.

ROLL OF CAPT. WILLIAM MILLER'S MOUNTED COMPANY.
(Probably from Pickaway County.)
Served from May 8, until May 20, 1813, and from February 16, until March 16, 1814.

Capt. William Miller	Lieut. Peter Rou	Ensign Jacon Frazier
Sergt. Joshua Miller	Sergt. Henry Wise	Sergt. George Hoffman
Corp. Thomas Spillman	Corp. Benjamin Reynals	
Privates.	**Privates.**	**Privates.**
Bowsher, Anthony	Blair, William	Bryner, John
Bawton, Adam	Brown, Robert	Bothin, George
Colter, Charles	Cade, Dorman	Craig, David
Dickson, George	Funk, Henry	Ferrin, Daniel
Graham, Robert	Gibson, Robert	Hannan, Samuel
House, John	Hively, Jacob	Hardesty, Richard
Hobbs, Richards	Justice, Jesse	Johnston, Henry
Hannady, William	Kenser, Peter	Loofborrow, Peter
Meyres, Jacob	Rush, Josiah	Ross, Jacob D.
Reister, George	Richardson, John	Stoke, Jacob
Spicer, Jonothan	Swaggart, Daniel	Strouse, Philip
Shaw, Samuel	Sullivant, James	Streevy, Joseph
Stoder, Christopher	Neff, Adam	Wolfly, Coonrad
Wollenton, Thomas	Walton, Jacob	Whitsel, Samuel
	Wintin, William	

Pages 204-205.

ROLL OF CAPT. WILLIAM KENDALL'S MOUNTED COMPANY.
(Probably from Ross County.)
Served from September 13, until September 20, 1814.

Capt. William Kendall	Lieut. George W. Clingman	Ensign, Allen Moore
Sergt. Nathan Glover	Sergt. Samuel G. Jones	Sergt. Charles C. Boynton
Sergt. John Knox	Saddler, James Beacham	Farrier, Johnston Loyd
	Musician, William Lowery	
Privates.	**Privates.**	**Privates.**
Andrews, John	Abbot, James	Armstrong, Jeremiah
Brady, Samuel	Barber, Isaac	Bonsor, Samuel
Brown, John	Brickles, William	Bonner, Cornelius
Culp, Jacob	Codot, Lemuel	Collins, John
Culp, Cornelius	Dawson, Abijah	Davison, Nathaniel
Emmons, Case	Ferguson, John	Flanders, Ezekiel
Funk, Jacob	Feurt, Gabriel	Feurt, Thomas
Greaves, George	Gee, Joseph	Hice, Andrew
Hitchcock, James	Hewet, Thomas	Horley, Andrew
Huston, William	Hull, Isaac	Headley, William
Hice, Phillip	Kirkendall, David	Lowderback, Zechariah
Long, Joel	Moore, Philip	Moore, Lucius
McDowell, John	McAuley, Henry	Noel, John
Normon, James	Noel, John, Jr.	Obourn, James
Payton, William	Patten, James	Price, Joseph
Rankins, William	Ritter, Frederick	Sapington, Stephen
Spangler, Jacob	Sheets, John	Timmons, John
Triggs, Thomas	Vincen, Jesse	Wilson, Barnabas
Wheeler, Isaac	Wilson, James	Williams, Robert
Wood, Daniel	White, Copley	

Page 219. Vol. I.
ROLL OF CAPT. NATHANIEL MASSIE'S MOUNTED COMPANY.
(Probably from Ross County.)
Served from May 1, until May 19, 1813.

Rank and Name of Soldier.	Rank and Name of Soldier.	Rank and Name of Soldier.
Capt. Nathaniel Massie	Lieut. James Menary	Ensign Samuel Wilson
Sergt. Alexander Menary	Sergt. John McDonald	Sergt. Gustavus Wilson
Corp. Henry Kiewsley	Corp. Meredith Parish	Corp. John Dunlap
Privates.	**Privates.**	**Privates.**
Armstrong, John	Bukman, Abraham	Blackstone, John
Brown, George	Beckman, William	Bryan, George
Cummins, Hermandez	Cary, Isaac	Cochran, James
Camble, William	Camble, Dunning	Cochran, David H.
Clawson, John	Dunlap, James	Dyer, Robert
Edwards, James	Elliott, David	Ford, William
Gunston, Thomas	Gray, James G.	Goth, Jacob
Hedges, Enoch	Hamilton, John	Hemphill, Andrew
Jank, John	Jenkins, Samuel	Kilgore, William
Kent, William	Loyan, Samuel	Ludlow, William
Morris, John	Mathews, Alexander	Morgan, Amaziah
Montgomery, Hugh	McCraken, Isaac	McArthur, Duncan
McCullough, John	McCoy, Dixon	McLain, Alexander
Parker, William	Porter, George	Russell, Reuben
Rockhold, Joseph	Reeves, Samuel	Rider, Jacob
Storm, John	Shaffer, Menary	Stockton, George
Shields, John	Showden, Samuel	Turner, James B.
Taylor, Joseph	Wilcox, William	Ward, John
Walsh, Joseph	Watts, Hamey	

Page 220.
ROLL OF CAPT. JAMES RENICK'S MOUNTED COMPANY.
(County Unknown.)
Served from May 7, until May 18, 1813.

Capt. James Renick	Ensign Daniel Hoffman	Sergt. John Stephenson
Sergt. James McKinsey	Sergt. David Marsh	Sergt. David Thomas
Privates.	**Privates.**	**Privates.**
Alkire, John	Brown, Zechariah	Burbridge, Benjamin
Barnes, William	Cochran, Alexander	Casler, James
Campbell, Joseph	Crippin, Joseph	Driver, James
Dyer, Robert	Dodd, Isaac	Graham, William
Heath, Asahel	Hollings, George	Hayse, Maurice
Leavell, John	Messick, Nathan	Madden, John
Martin, John	McGroves, Isaac	McKinney, Henry
Renick, Asahel	Stephenson, David	Willetts, John
Ward, Absalom	Wisehart, Henry	Yates, David

Pages 235-236-237-238.
ROLL OF CAPT. JOHN ROADANNOUR'S MOUNTED COMPANY.
(From Gallia County.)
Served from August 1, to September 4, 1813.

Capt. John Roadannour	Lieut Luther Shepherd	Ensign Nathan Nuson
Ensign John Kerr	Ensign John Ellison	Sergt. Anthony R. Magnet
Sergt. Alvan Rathburn	Sergt. Frederick Kerns	Corp. William T. Graves
Corp John Vandenbender	Corp William Chandler	Musician, Jonah Powell
Privates.	**Privates.**	**Privates.**
Aleshire, John	Arthur, Benjamin	Aleshire, Peter
Aleshire, Abraham	Arthur, Amos	Arthur, Nimrod
Aleshire, David	Archer, Earl P.	Brown, James Ellison
Bucher, John	Bailey, David	Bailey, John
Blagg, Samuel W.	Byers, George	Burris, George
Benedick, E. H.	Cating, John	Calhoun, Robert V.
Cooper, Charles	Durst, Daniel	Denham, Daniel
Ewings, William	Enstminger, John	Fletcher, Joseph
Farr, George	Fuller, Alfred T.	Gaston, Jonah
Glasburn, George	Gillaspie, Moses	Holcomb, Samuel P.
Hubbel, Abijah	Hale, John	Hackett, Jeremiah
Highley, Cyrus	Holcomb, Stephen	Hank, Isaac, Jr.
Hughes, Silas	Hughes, Jonothan	Hysel, Frances
Humphrey, William	Hill, Jacob	Howell, William
Huston, Joseph	Heeten, David	Hawk, Isaac, Sr.
Hysell, Leonard	Hubbell, Jesse	Hoppis, George
Jones, Phillip	Jones, Thomas	Keeten, George
Kelley, Isom	Keeten, William	Lyman, Samuel
Lotz, Abraham	Lawless, Pressley	Long, Elisha
Long, Benjamin	Maples, Fanny	Mathews, James
Miller, Joseph	Miller, Isaac	Mosbarger, Joseph
Moore, Elijah	Mennehan, Edward	Moler, John
Miller, Charles	Moler, Daniel	Montgomery, David
McCoy, Joseph	McCarty, David	Pinkerton, John
Putnam, William	Parsons, Horris	Reese, Patrick
Rhay, Martin	Russell, William	Stone, Erastus
Shasteen, John	Smith, William	Scott, Charles
Saxton, John	Sharp, John	Swim, John
Shaw, Cushing	Scurloch, Hugh	Simonne, Francis
Thomas, Jason	VanShultz, Alexander	Wooten, Thomas
Wooten, Samuel	Wells, Zimri	Williams, Jonothan

Pages 239-240. Vol. I.

ROLL OF CAPT. DAVID SHELBY'S MOUNTED COMPANY.
(Probably from Ross County.)

Served from September 4, until October 14, 1812.

Rank and Name of Soldier.	Rank and Name of Soldier.	Rank and Name of Soldier.
Capt. David Shelby	Lieut. John Barnes	Ensign Jonothan Clark
Sergt. Samuel Jones	Sergt. Joseph Martin	Sergt. James Delay
Sergt. Moses Coleston	Corp. Elias Reed	Corp. Arthur Chenewith
Corp. James Ruckman	Corp. Henry Morris	
Privates.	**Privates.**	**Privates.**
Brown, William	Chenewith, Isaac	Chenewith, Thomas
Carter, Henry	Chenewith, John	Chenewith, Jacob
C———, Thomas	C———, Abner	Davies, William H.
Evans, John	Evans, Lewis	Frazier, David
Frazier, James	Gutheny, John, Jr.	Groves, Lewis
Glass, Joseph	Guthery, Joseph	Guthery, John, Sr.
Guthrie, William	Hamilton, William	Hopkins, William
Huston, James	Hotsenbiller, Jacob	Hatton, William
Howard, Joseph	Justice, John	Jenkins, James
Jenkins, Baldwin	Heaverlo, James	King, David
Kerr, Thomas	Krug, John	Manary, Hugh
Myers, Samuel	Perrell, John	Rawlings, Nathan
Rodgers, Hezekiah	Rodgers, Lewis	Stalcup, John
Shelby, Joseph	Stipp, Abraham	Swan, Thomas
Smith, Edward H.	Verden, William	Williams, Joseph
	Williams, Nathan	

Pages 272-273.

ROLL OF CAPT. JOHN LOGAN'S MOUNTED COMPANY.
(Probably from Ross County.)

Served from September 14, until December 9, 1814.

Capt. John Logan	Lieut. Francis Thompson	Ensign James Wells
Sergt. William Tangber	Sergt. James Gutherie	Sergt. Donty Utter
Sergt. Samuel Bennett	Sergt. Richard Johnson	Corp. Joseph Gossett
Privates.	**Privates.**	**Privates.**
Arthur, James	Barber, James	Calvin, Luther
Calvin, James	Corathers, Irwin	Cochran, John
Downing, Timothy	Emerson, John	Florer, James
Frazier, John	Henderson, James	Hizer, Andrew
Hedges, William	Justice, Jesse	Jenkins, Zepheniah
Latimore, Samuel	Latimore, John	Minor, Ephraim
Meranda, Samuel	Mathews, Nehemiah	McClure, Jonothan
McClean, Richard	Moore, Moses	Norris, James
Osburn, Benjamin	Parker, Jacob	Plicard, Henry
Perry, Joseph	Ross, Thomas	Prewin, Robert
Riley, Elexious	Shaw, Hugh	Swearingen, Van B.
Slider, Elijah	South, David	Smith, Johab
Suran, David	Sampson, Isaac	Sargent, Rezin
Taylor, Aaron	Wall, James	Williams, Eli
Watson, Jacob	West, Hugh	West, George

Page 274.

ROLL OF LIEUT. ANDREW GUTTERY'S MOUNTED COMPANY.
(Probably from Warren County.)

Served from September 20, to November 19, 1814.

Lieut. Andrew Guttery	Sergt. Benjamin Baldwin	Sergt. John Ulrey
Privates.	**Privates.**	**Privates.**
Coburn, Francis	Crosson, Barnwell	Cox, Richard
Cru, Robert	Feaster, Richard	Hale, Stephen
Leggett, Henry	Little, David	Miller, John
Nutt, Moses	Paxton, Samuel	Parker, George
Robertson, John	Sutton, Eli	Sibbit, Richard
Stout, Edward	Sergeant, David	Varner, Jacob

Page 310.

ROLL OF CAPT. ROBERT HAINES' MOUNTED COMPANY.
(Probably from Hamilton County.)

Served from July 29, until August 13, 1813.

Capt. Robert Haines	Lieut. Hugh Ferguson	Ensign Jonathan Donahm
Sergt. James Robb	Sergt. Hezekiah Lindsay	Sergt. Isaac Ferguson
Sergt. James Arthur	Corp. Thomas Littleton	Corp. Nathan Sutton
Corp. William Donham	Corp. Thomas Welsh	

Vol. I.
ROLL OF CAPT. ROBERT HAINES' MOUNTED COMPANY (Continued.)

Rank and Name of Soldier.   Rank and Name of Soldier.   Rank and Name of Soldier.

Privates
- Apple, Daniel
- Bollinger, Peter
- Chapman, Earnest
- Dillman, John
- Fitzpatrick, James
- Kinsey, Jacob
- Long, Samuel
- Miller, Hamilton
- Mattox, John
- Nichols, Philip
- Roberts, Edward
- Renker, Levi
- Whitaker, John

Privates
- Bell, William
- Cuppy, Henry
- Clift, Horatio
- Frura, Michael
- Hymer, Levi B.
- Lewis, George
- Lacock, Nathan
- Mourning, John
- McCone, Aquila
- Pricket, Isaiah
- Rardin, David
- Short, Jacob
- White, David

Privates
- Bittle, Josiah
- Chapman, Robert
- Dial, John C.
- Ferguson, Francis
- Hyrner, John B.
- Loyd, Reuben
- Mourning, Benjamin
- Mattox, Elijah
- Nichols, William
- Pricket, Nicholas
- Rhymor, Martin
- Snyder, Daniel

Page 366
ROLL OF CAPT. THOMAS HINKSON'S MOUNTED SPIES.
(County Unknown.)
Served from February 14, 1812, until May 5, 1813.

- Capt. Thomas Hinkson
- Sergt. William King

- Lieut. Archibald Dowden
- Sergt. Joseph Baker

- Lieut. Hugh Young

Privates
- Bradshaw, Robert
- Carter, Samuel
- Devne, William
- Hayes, Jacob
- Jenkins, John
- McGrew, John
- Spencer, William
- Spencer, James
- Thornton, James
- Walverton, Daniel

Privates
- Baker, Jacob
- Davis, Ezekial
- Good, Isham
- Hinkson, John
- Moore, William
- Redmon, Elijah
- Scroufe, John
- Taylor, Pierce
- Venard, William
- Workman, Daniel M.

Privates
- Carter, John
- Davis, Benjamin
- Graham, David
- Inman, John
- Mosher, Philip
- Robb, Andrew
- Steele, Jacob
- Tipton, William
- Venard, Francis

ROLL OF CAPT. DANIEL WOMELDORF'S MOUNTED COMPANY.
(From Gallia County.)
Page 376-377   Served from August 1, until August 18, 1813.

- Capt. Daniel Womeldorf
- Corp. John Cocomore
- Cornet, John Graham
- Sergt. Jacob Moler
- Saddler, Peter Chapdu

- Lieut. Nathaniel Gates
- Sergt. Tousaint Schouman
- Corp. Isaac Butler
- Corp. Amos Chitwood
- Farrier, John Campbell

- Lieut. James Bing
- Sergt. James Wilson
- Corp. John B. Noland
- Trumpeter James Van Sent

Privates
- Adkins, Philip
- Bing, William
- Collison, William
- Donally, Andrew
- Beck, John
- Hickle, George
- Martindits, John
- McCarley, John
- Rickabough, John
- Reed, William K.
- Symnes, Butler

Privates
- Brown, Jeremiah
- Boggs, Ezekial
- Donally, William
- Donally, John
- Fletcher, Joseph, Jr.
- Irvin, David
- Marvin, Calvin
- Nox, Nehemiah
- Rickabough, Adam
- Ridgeway, David
- Tyler, George
- Wilkes, James

Privates
- Buck, William
- Cushing, Henry
- Dowel, Robert
- Ewing, Andrew
- Forgey, Hugh
- Lasby, Jonothan
- Mathews, Thomas
- Potter, Pelig
- Rickabough, John, Jr.
- Robinson, James
- Tharp, James

Pages 387-388. Vol. 2.
ROLL OF CAPT. JAMES WILSON'S MOUNTED COMPANY.
(Probably from Ross County.)
Served from September 28, until October 5, 1812.

- Capt. James Wilson
- Ensign Joseph McClain
- Sergt. William Head

- Capt. Allen Trimble
- Lieut. Joseph McClain
- Sergt. Samuel Keys
- Sergt. Joseph Davidson

- Lieut. James Wilson
- Ensign James Odell
- Sergt. David Mitchell

Privates.
- Blunt, Eli
- Bryam, Edward
- Chapman, Isaac
- Combs, Job
- Evans, Isaac
- Hulet, William
- Hinton, William
- Keys, John
- Mushow, Solomon
- McConnel, David
- Odell, Thomas
- Rockhold, John
- Stafford, James
- Shelts, Peter
- Smith, Jeremiah
- White, William

Privates.
- Blunt, Solomon
- Boatman, George
- Chenney, Nathan
- Dunham, Samuel
- Greenfield, John
- Hindman, John
- Hare, William
- King, William
- Moyes, Littleberry
- Nichols, George
- Parmer, John
- Swearingen, Duke
- Swadley, Jacob
- Strain, Samuel B.
- Trop, Jacob
- Wilson, James

Privates.
- Boyd, Samuel
- Crawford, Alexander
- Chaney, Benjamin
- Davidson, John
- Grady, James
- Hinton, Benjamin
- Hougham, Isaac
- Lantz, Henry
- May, James
- Odell, James
- Patton, William
- Sharp, Andrew
- Stutts, Jacob
- Smallic, Isaac
- West, Hiram
- Wilson, Thomas

Pages 400, 401, 402 Vol. 2.

ROLL OF CAPT. GEORGE SANDERSON'S COMPANY.
27th United States Infantry.
(From Fairfield, Franklin, and Delaware Counties, and part of Western Reserve.)

Served in 1813 and 1814.

Rank and Name of Soldier.	Rank and Name of Soldier.	Rank and Name of Soldier.
Capt. George Sanderson	Lieut. Abner P. Risney or Pinney	Lieut. John H. Mifford
Lieut. Arora or Andory Butler	Lieut. Andrew Bushnell	Ensign William Hall
Lieut. Abraham Fisk	Lieut. Ira Morse	Sergt. Chaney Case
Sergt. Maj. Linus Williams	Sergt. John Vanmeter	Sergt. John Neibling
Sergt. Chauncey Miller	Sergt. Robert Sanderson	Corp. Peter Cary or Gary
Sergt. Joshua Pierce	Sergt. Luther Edson	Corp. Smith Headley
Corp. John Dugan	Corp. John Collings	
Corp. Daniel T. Bartholomew	Drummer John C. Sharp or Jonathan C. Shupe	
	Fifer Adam Leeds or Abraham Deeds	

Privates

Privates	Privates	Privates
Anderson, William	Anderson, Joseph	Atkins, John
Alloways, Joseph	Boyl, Thomas	Bartholomew, John
Berryman, John	Bixler, Henry	Bartholomew, Abraham
Bartholomew, Samuel	Braden, James	Beebee, Sheldon
Brown, James	Beaty, John	Brady, Eli
Burdinoo, Charles	Battiese, John	Baker, Daniel
Busley or Bussey, John	Billings, Thomas	Benjamin, Daniel
Case, Henry	Clark, Joseph	Cassy, Archibald
Clay, Joseph	Collins, Holden R.	Cremens, Blades
Cady, William	Case, Nathan	Cabe or Cole, Chester P.
Clark, Chaney	Cady, Samuel	Carlton, Almon
Cook, Stephen	Crosby, David	Canely, Peter
Canway, Lewis	Canway, Jacob	Davis, Jesse
Draper, Asa	Dunham, Walter	Daugherty, George
Devore, Enos	Daily, Benjamin	Evans, John
Ellinger, Joseph	Fulk, Peter	Forsythe, John
Filkall, Daniel	Faid, John	Grimes, Ephraim
Gregory, Elenathan	Gibson, Joseph	Gates, William L.
Gause, Samuel	Hunt, John	Haggarty, James
Hinkley, Josiah	Hall, John	Hartman, Frederick
Hughes, David	Holcomb, Perlin	Harter, John
Headley, Jacob	Harberson, John	Icas, John
Jee, John	Jackson, James	Jones, James
Johnson, John	Joice, Ambrose	Johnson, John L.
Kisler, John	Kissinger, George	Kincaid, James or Jonas
Kitzmiller, Jonothan	Kinisman, Samuel	Larimore, or Larimon, Joseph
Lief, Henry	Leonard, Amos	Leathers or Lathere, Fred'k
Miller, Peter	Merrill, Hosea	Mullen or Mellow, Joshua
Leonard or Loveland, Merinas W.	Lanther, or Luther, William	Mains, Henry
Moore, or Mose, James	Mapes, Thomas	McGarvey, Maurice
Miller, Andrew	McElwayne, John	McConkey or McCarkey, John
McClung, Joseph	McClung, John	McClair, or McClain, William
McCloud, Frances	McBride, John	Nickerson, Isacher
McConnell, John	McCord, Alexander	Pratt, Lemuel or Samuel
Naper, William	Osborn, George	Palmer, Luther
Parks, George	Paine, Powell or Roswell	Parkhurst or Burkhardt, Ben
Pierce, Arzell	Ray, John	Raphy, George
Ridenour, David	Reed, William	Shadley, Henry
Rogers, Elijah	Rose, Asa	Straller or Stratler, Joseph
Spry, Perry	Severs, David	Shypower, or Shyhawk, Christian
Severs, John	Smith, Christian B.	Summers, Ephraim
Sunderland, John	Shears, Mynder	Shoup, or Shroup, Jacob
Smith, Charles	Strait, Hendy C.	Skolls or Skills, Henry
Smith, John	Senor, or Siner Adam	Sheanar, Solomon
Serdan, Jonothan	Sharp, Thomas	Trevinger, Jacob
Shadwick, George	Taylor, David S.	Tucker, Frederick
Tesler, Frederick	Thorp, Benjamin	Tyler, Seymoor
Thorp, John I.	Twadle, Joseph	Vanney, L.
Vanney, I.	Vancleaf, P.	Weaver, James
White, Ansel	Walker, Alexander	Walters, David
Wright, Joseph	Wheatley, Thomas	Wolffly, Coonrod
Wheeler, Jacob	Welshaus, John	Wilson, Archibald
Williams, Flavel	Wallace, William	Wilson, Joseph
Woodsworth, D.	Watson, William	Zeigler or Zipler, Daniel
Young, J.	Zimmerman, Henry	

Pages 419-420. Vol. I.
ROLL OF CAPT. GROVE CASE'S COMPANY 27th U. S. INFANTRY.
(Probably from Licking County.)
Served from May 5, until May 18, 1813.

Rank and Name of Soldier.	Rank and Name of Soldier.	Rank and Name of Soldier.
Capt. Grove Case	Lieut. Alexander Holmes	Ensign William Stedman
Sergt. Silas Winchel	Sergt. William Holmes	Corp. Lester Case
	Corp. James White	
Privates.	**Privates.**	**Privates.**
Bancroft, Ethan	Case, Frederick	Case, Timothy
Critton, Gabriel	Critchet, Mathew H.	Comwell, Archibold
Carpenter, Benjamin	Colman, Julius	Every, Simeon
Elliott, Cornelius	Gillman, Elisha S.	Graves, Josiah
Holmes, Joseph	Knox, Titus	Kandol, Caleb
Messenger, Campbell	Mays, John	Munson, Jesse
Phelps, Levi	Pratt, Worthy	Phillips, John H.
Parker, John	Rose, Hilon	Rose, Samuel, Jr.
Stephen, Justice	Sennel, John	Wells, John
West, Joseph	Wilson, Amos	

Page 421.
ROLL OF CAPT. SAMUEL SWEARINGEN (26th U. S. INFANTRY NOT GIVEN.)
(Probably from Ross County.)
Served from January 1, until April 8, 1814.

Capt. Samuel Swearingen

Page 422.
ROLL OF CAPT. RICHARD GRAHAM (19th U. S. INFANTRY NOT GIVEN.)
(County Unknown.)
Served from April 1, until May 15, 1813.

Capt. Richard Graham   Lieut. John D. Reeves

Page 423.
ROLL OF CAPT. COLLINS (19th U. S. INFANTRY NOT GIVEN.)
(Probably from Ross County.)
Served from March 16, 1814, until March 6, 1816.

Capt. Collins   Private Levin Fisher

www.ingramcontent.com/pod-product-compliance
Lightning Source LLC
Chambersburg PA
CBHW030553080526
44585CB00012B/367